UNITED STATES-IRAQ
BILATERAL RELATIONS

To my parents
Frieda and Joseph Rosenstock Whiteson

United States-Iraq Bilateral Relations

Confusion and Misperception
from 1967 to 1979

SHULAMIT BINAH

VALLENTINE MITCHELL
LONDON • PORTLAND, OR

First published in 2018 by Vallentine Mitchell

Catalyst House,
720 Centennial Court,
Centennial Park, Elstree WD6 3SY, UK

920 NE 58th Avenue, Suite 300
Portland, Oregon
97213-3786 USA

www.vmbooks.com

British Library Cataloguing in Publication Data:
An entry can be found on request

ISBN 978 1 910383 72 8 (Cloth)
ISBN 978 1 910383 73 5 (Ebook)

Library of Congress Cataloging in Publication Data:
An entry can be found on request

Printed by Clays Ltd, Bungay, Suffolk

Contents

Acknowledgements

This book is the culmination of years of research and writing, spreading from Tel Aviv, to Chicago, Haifa, Washington DC, London and Copenhagen. Many people have helped and guided me along the way. First, I want to thank Professors Amatzia Baram and Zach Levey of the University of Haifa, for being my mentors in pursuing my long-time vision of writing a history of modern Iraq. They were professional and relentless as well as supportive and have always encouraged me to look for answers outside-of-the-box. I especially thank Professor Baram who had encouraged me to take on this demanding task in the first place.

I am in debt of many people who assisted me in the gathering and collection process. I would like to mention especially the late Haim Gal of the Arab Press Archive at Tel Aviv University. I was also greatly helped by Charlotte R. Bonnelli, Director of the American Jewish Committee (AJC) Archive in New York, by Amir Shaviv and the late Ralph Goldman of the Joint Distribution Committee (JDC), by Dr. Mary Elizabeth Currie of the National Security Archives at the George Washington University, and by Fella Sterzer, the librarian of the Israel Intelligence Heritage and Commemoration Center (IICC). I also thank Eliezer Tsafrir for his astute remarks regarding the Kurdish Revolt, Maurice Shohet of the Washington Institute for sharing his vast experience and knowledge of the fate of Iraqi Jews, Leslie H. Gelb of the Council of Foreign Relations in New York and Stuart E. Eizenstat in Washington, DC, for educating me with regards to the relevant Administration's discourse and context. My thanks and gratitude are also sent to psychologist Dalia Rubinstein of Haifa, to Professor Reeva Simon of Yeshiva University and Professor Miriam Joyce of Purdue University for their professional insights and remarks, as well as for their steadfast encouragement and friendship.

Thanks also to Vallentine Mitchell Publishers for taking upon themselves to bring out this corner of Mideast history. My heartfelt gratitude goes to all of the above-mentioned and to everyone else who have helped and supported me in this long journey. Any mistake or error in this book is of course entirely and solely my own.

Finally, I thank my husband, Ambassador Barukh (Bouby) Binah, and my daughters Nurit and Ronni Dror, whom I cherish above and beyond all else.

Copenhagen, October 2017

Foreword

In her conclusion Shulamit Binah writes: 'When observed through the prism of diplomatic relations, the US courted Iraq, assuming that for an emerging economy the very idea of active trade and relations with the US should be rewarding enough for a relatively small economy with an emerging oil production.' Until this book appeared, the period of the late 1960s and the 1970s in American-Iraqi relations was seriously under-researched. Using a wealth of sources, Binah's book corrects this research imbalance. It enables us to understand the roots of what later became a roaring confrontation. The book suggests that the US did not comprehend the depth of the Iraqi ideological commitment to the traditional Ba'thi anti-'imperialist' and anti-'Zionist' tenets of faith. These two negative principles that usually were expressed through the positive-sounding term of '*al-huriyya*' (Liberty, or Freedom from foreign occupation) represented a very central part of the regime's public legitimacy. In itself 'Liberty' is, of course, positive in every way, but by 1968 Iraq and the rest of the Arabs, except for the Palestinian Arabs, were already fully independent. And yet, following the Arab (including the Iraqi) defeat at the 1967 June war with Israel hostility toward American 'imperialism' was popular domestically. This was doubly so because the Ba'th were unpopular (their rule in 1963 left a very bitter legacy), and the US became a useful and reliable hate object. There were also some central positive components in Ba'th ideology, like 'socialism' (or more accurately a welfare state), Arab unity or pan-Arabism and secularism.

However, by the 1980s all three were vanishing. In 1968-70 the Ba'th regime in Baghdad accused Gamal Abd al-Nasser's regime in Egypt of the 1967 defeat. This left no room for Iraqi-Egyptian unification. In 1978-79 Saddam Hussein ended a rapprochement with Hafiz al-Assad's Ba'thist Syria, and pan-Arabism became an empty slogan. With Khomeini's rise to power in Tehran Saddam hoped that more Islam will secure for him more support from the Shi'i population that was, traditionally, more religious. This was when the erosion of secularism began. Finally, by 1982-83, as a result of the Iraq-Iran War, the financial reserve disappeared, the economy went into recession and there was very little left for the social safety net. The regime then was left with hate alone, concentrating on three enemies, one real, two imaginary: Khomeini, American 'imperialism' and Zionism. Saddam mentioned sometimes the danger of an American and Israeli attack on Iraq.

Yet, in his *modus operandi* (and in his July 1990 conversation with Ambassador April Glaspie) he seemed convinced that the US will always somehow tolerate his policies. The American intelligence support from late 1984 in the war against Iran, then the placing of a highly-competent US Army colonel in Baghdad to help with the use of that intelligence, then the American EXIM Bank credit for purchasing grains, all helped create this impression.

Binah shows clearly that the Ba'th regime never factored-in properly 'soft' American sensitivities, from human rights to WMDs. She indicates that they were convinced that the US is interested only in oil and profit, and therefore it will tolerate anything as long as the oil is gushing at a reasonable price. Even as early as 1972, the continued American courtship of Baghdad despite the latter's porcupine-style love affair with the USSR, and the American 1975 easy abandonment of the Kurds created and then supported this impression of Iraqi impunity. The Ba'th regime also did not understand the American decision-making system and therefore underestimated the approach of Congress and the media which, sometimes, was different from that of the White House and the Department of State. Congress sensitivity to the fate of the Iraqi Jews in 1969-72 took the Ba'th regime by surprise. Then, Congress and the US media indifference toward the Kurdish suffering convinced them that the Jews, including the case of US support for Israel, were a special case, but that otherwise human rights were not a serious American concern.

American indifference to the French-designed nuclear reactor in the second half of the 1970s convinced the Ba'th regime also that the US allows the development of WMDs. The weak American response to the Iraqi use of chemical weapons against Iranian troops since the early 1980s, too, created the same impression and probably led to the regime's feeling that it could use poison gas against the Kurds in March 1988 with impunity. This book shows convincingly all these points and many others. The book also demonstrates that the absence of clear and consistent American policy toward Iraq since the Ba'th takeover stemmed from Iraq's marginality in the global map of American interests. The Ba'th regime, for its part, drew the wrong conclusions from this American benevolent neglect. The result was a profound mutual misunderstanding which eventually led to repeated confrontations.

Professor Amatzia Baram,
Director, The Center for Iraq Studies
University of Haifa

Introduction

I had always been interested in Iraq, especially the demise of its 2,500-year-old Jewish community that began with the Babylonian exile from Jerusalem. Iraq's Jewish community was decimated first in the pogrom called *Farhud* of 1941, and later in many smaller attacks, until the vast majority of Iraq's Jews found refuge in the State of Israel. Still, many members of this exiled community maintain emotional links to their country of origin, and even today the number of fiction and non-fiction writings regarding the Iraqi past written by Israeli writers and poets of Iraqi descent is very impressive.

Iraq was a more modern and inclusive society. In the 1930s, Iraq could be seen as advancing towards modernity, with an active and lively discussion between nationalists, communists, Ba'thists, Sunnis, Shi'ites, Kurds, Christians and many Jews – all wanting to take part in the emergence of modern Iraq. However, another track was chosen, even if by default, for revolutionary Iraq, and this track has been followed since the overthrow of the monarchy in 1958. When the Ba'th party came to power in 1968, there were hopes in the West that Iraq would begin to look inward and concentrate on nation building, rather than turning to external adventures.

My early research dealt with the 1941 pogrom against the Babylonian Jewish community, known as the *Farhud*,[1] and had nothing to do with Iraq's diplomatic history or its relations with the US. But I was always curious about what went wrong in Iraq. A good place to begin that inquiry was in understanding the deterioration of Iraq-US relations. The years I have selected for this research encompass the first decade of Ba'th rule.

On a personal note, I began this research many years ago with the intention of studying the diplomatic history of two countries I had become interested in. I soon found out that old demonsdie hard. This period was the first time that an Arab country had been governed by a party based on a secular ideology devised by an Arab nationalist who was a Christian (Syrian) thinker, Michel Aflaq. He envisaged a unified Arab political entity in which all three monotheistic religions could be regarded as expressions of the genius of the Arab nation. Still, even in this idealistic regime, Jews (and Israel) were regarded in sinister, almost mythical terms. There were other factors in the Ba'th world view which will be dealt with in the course of this book, but the vehemence with which Israel (and the Jews) was regarded a quarter of a century after the *Farhud* was striking.

On the time-axis, my research encompasses two formative events in US-Iraqi relations: Iraq's breaking of diplomatic ties with the US in June 1967 in the wake of the Six Day War between Israel and several Arab states, and the partial and gradual thaw in US-Iraqi relations in 1979 during Iran's Islamic Revolution. The latter produced a joint US-Iraqi interest against a common adversary: Iran. In this twelve year period, Ba'thi Iraq was busy building and shaping a centralised regime and consolidating Saddam Hussein's rule, while the United States dealt with its regional repositioning and enhancing its involvement in the Middle East. Consequently, both countries did not consider bilateral relations central to their interests.

The premise guiding this book is that, during this period from 1967 to 1979, there developed erroneous mutual concepts that later led to crucial decisions that brought about an escalation of tensions between Baghdad and Washington, two rounds of war, and the US occupation of Iraq. This book analyses the mutual perceptions of Iraq and the United States, focusing on a portion of their relationship that scholars have not devoted much attention to.

Though it is beyond the scope of this study, it should be noted that, despite the two countries' resumption of relations in 1984 and the valuable intelligence provided by the United States to Iraq during the latter's war with Iran, American expectations for better relations with Iraq after the Iraq-Iran war ended were largely frustrated. Likewise, a series of mishaps demonstrate that President Saddam Hussein's Iraq had also misjudged the United States; for example, Baghdad did not anticipate the manner in which Washington responded to the Iraqi use of chemical weapons against the civilian Kurdish population in 1988 or to Iraq's threats against Kuwait.

Definitions

The Oxford Dictionary of English defines 'perception' as 'the ability to see, hear or become aware of something through the senses'. Perception could be based on facts, on beliefs or on a volume of data, either full or incomplete. Perception could be held in the eye of the beholder. It does not have to be permanent and it can be illusive and unstable. In general it is impossible to measure perception quantitatively. Perception could be individual or shared by a group of people or even an entire administration or nation. 'Misperception' is even harder to define, but though it is not the exact opposite or antonym of 'perception'; it could be defined as *the inability, or the failure to see, hear or become aware of something*. It could be affected by all the stipulations above.

As a professional term, 'perception' is derived from the field of cognitive psychology. Nevertheless, this book will use the not-entirely-defined term and contextual world of 'perception' and 'misperception' to examine and analyse more than a decade which was formative in shaping US-Iraqi relations. This is a known method in research intodecision-making processes in international relations, particularly in cases of military escalations. For example, Robert Jervis referred, as early as 1976, to misperceptions in the decision-making process of leaders as a key factor in erroneous decision-making; in later writings he went on to analyse misperceptions that led to wars.[2] In his 1988 article, 'War and Misperception', Jervis offered three interpretations on the subject. Firstly, he asserted that misperception is endemic and that errors in assessing an adversary's capabilities and intentions, or the inability to correctly process information, contribute to misperceptions. The second interpretation is that statesmen often fall 'into the trap of incorrectly believing that other statesmen are just like themselves'. In failing to empathise with the adversary's decision makers 'they pay insufficient attention to constraints and pressure faced by their opponent, including those generated by the decision maker's own state'. Finally, Jervis argues that analysis of the international system must account for misperception, especially when it comes to war. Given the nature of regimes such as Saddam's, careful historical work often provides the only viable way of examining misperceptions. However, while the historian's approach of relying heavily on 'reconstructing the world as the statesmen saw it' helps to account for the failures of theory, it falls short of accounting for how 'people perceive information'. Kevin Woods used Jervis' model and, based on the released collection of Saddam Hussein's recordings of his cabinet sessions, Woods examines Saddam Hussein's misperception that led to the two military confrontations with the US.[3]

Be that as it may, I do not intend to discuss the development of Iraqi and American mutual perceptions and misperceptions *per se*, or to examine their relations as a case study of misperception. This is not a study in cognitive psychology but rather a study in diplomatic history, in which the issue to be examined is the relations between the two nations, utilizing various aspects of social science in order to draw a picture of the way Iraq and the US viewed each other and to suggest a perceptive explanation of their relationship and offer 'mutual misperception' as a factor in the twenty-five-year-long US-Iraqi crisis.

This study takes into account the built-in asymmetric relationship between a super-power and a developing country. Exploring the perceptions of decision-makers, either of individuals or of groups, would necessitate frequent reference to cultural and psychological aspects as well as to specific personalities. However, the research method employed in this study is that of history writing rather than that of social science. It does not focus on the contents of each specific perception, but rather on their expressions in the unfolding events and developments that led to the formation of bilateral relations. At the same time, this study attempts to integrate cultural and cognitive aspects to make the most of the mutual perceptions of these two countries within a whole picture. This includes an attempt to propose a conceptual explanation for the development of Iraqi-US relations, and to retrospectively place the misconceptions that led to the crisis.

The study comprises two principal sections. The first part consists of three chronological chapters reviewing the historical events and highlighting the main aspects of the bilateral relationship. The second section is analytical, consisting of three subjects over which Iraq and the US had, or should have had, meeting points. These issues serve as prisms for the examination of bilateral relations and mutual perceptions throughout the period covered. The three prisms are the Kurdish problem, the Arab-Israeli conflict and the Persian Gulf.

In examining these prisms, this book takes into consideration the ever-present perspective that affected the whole situation – the Cold War and the pattern of relations between the two countries. It also includes a look, in hindsight, at two issues that were not in Washington's focus until the 1990s: the early stages of Iraq's programs to develop weapons of mass destruction (WMD) and the impact of Saddam Hussein's personality on the process of Iraqi decision-making and his perception of the United States.

The hypothesis is that both Iraq and the United States greatly misperceived each other. The United States focused on Iran and Saudi Arabia as barricades for American interests in the area (known as the twin-pillar policy), and later gradually turned her attention towards Israel and the Arab-Israeli conflict. Iraq was hardly referred to outside these parameters. On the other hand, Iraq did not understand the complexity of the American system and the political motivation of a superpower. It viewed the United States through one-dimensional spectacles – driven primarily by its energy needs and its greed.

The United States consulted regularly with the British because of the latter's expertise and long experience in the area – particularly in Iraq. Despite the British colonialist past, the Ba'th regime resumed diplomatic relations with Britain but not with the United States, which became extremely unpopular in Ba'thi-expressed public opinion. The United States was attacked constantly in the media and by government spokesmen. Throughout most of the period, though, references to bilateral relations – even at the low level of mutual interest – were minimised.

Like its predecessors, the Ba'th party criticised the US position over three main topics: US support of Israel, its dominance in the global oil market and its sympathy for the Kurds. American global dominance had been evident since the end of the Second World War; its sympathetic approach towards the Kurds could be seen in the framework of regional alliances (with Iran), but no such explanation could be offered for the US approach towards Israel as this country was embroiled in a mortal conflict with regional allies of the

US. The Ba'th regime had not understood, or stopped to ponder over, the role of the American Jewish organisations and their commitment to Israel. Likewise, Israel's military might and victories could be seen as unnatural. Hence, perhaps, the demonic view which the Ba'th regime held of Israel, the entire Jewish-Israeli relationship and what seemed to Iraq as the US succumbing to the mysterious power of the Jews.

At the same time, the Ba'th regime, like its predecessors and despite its resentment of the US policy, admired American technology and medical and scientific research, and was interested in their procurement, particularly that of military technology. But the Ba'th's self-image was that of an ideological regime that aspired to legitimacy as the genuine representative of Arab nationalism (especially vis-à-vis its rival, the Syrian Ba'th party), while coping with the military prowess of a US ally, Israel, and confronting internal strife from opposition groups.

The United States saw Iraq, especially in the first half of the period under study, as a weak, unstable and radical Third World country, linked with the Soviet Union and the Eastern Bloc, but not as a real threat to the Persian Gulf or as a factor to reckon with globally.

Two major factors, present throughout the period under review, will not be dealt with independently in the analytical chapters: the Soviet Union and oil. Despite their magnitude, these factors had a relatively small influence on the development of Iraqi and US perceptions – more accurately, misperceptions – of one another.

Sources of Information

American-Iraqi asymmetry is naturally evident in the type and scope of material sources, particularly primary sources. The American government's materials are voluminous, and almost entirely accessible. I have explored US attitudes towards Iraq through official documents, both by administrations and Congress and opinion-makers. Some documents, mostly on the Kurdish issue, were obtained under the Freedom of Information Act (FOIA). Another source is memoirs, books, articles and previous interviews given by decision-makers. The Library of Congress's oral-history project and the Association for Diplomatic Studies and Training (ADST) provided valuable informal on, and personal insights of, retired American diplomats on their service in Iraq.

British diplomatic correspondence also offered valuable insights into US-Iraqi relations, since the United Kingdom and the United States regularly consulted regarding Iraq; some British documents provided insights, absent from American reports. (The British maintained a fully functioning embassy in Baghdad during most of the period studied.)

Iraq's views on its relations with the United States were derived from personal statements, made by Iraqi leaders and officials, publications of the

Ba'th party and a close tracking of the Iraqi daily press and magazines. Some of these views were later corroborated by statements made by Saddam himself to FBI interrogators after his capture by US forces in 2003, as well as by recordings of his secret meetings with his staff – recordings seized by the US Army.

Sources on the rescue of Iraqi Jews, which occurred from 1969 to 1974, were available in the Jewish archives in New York. The Israeli perspective was researched in the Israel State Archives and in the Central Zionist Archives.

Since the topic of the study deals with perceptions, important background information was revealed through personal interviews with former American diplomats, leaders of American-Jewish organisations and Iraqi Jews who had left their homeland.

Technical Notes

Transliteration from Arabic to Roman alphabets follows the conventional rules, except regarding the names of people and geographical locations that have already became common in English: for example, Hussein for Husayn, Assad for Asad, the title mulla for mala, Beirut for Bayrut.

Hebrew transliteration to English follows the guidelines of Israel's Academy of the Hebrew Language.

References to State Department telegrams in the period 1973–8 that do not mention the location or the database come from the US National Archives and Records Administration's – Access to Archival Databases – Wars/International Relations: Diplomatic Records (https://aad.archives.gov/aad/).

All other documents' references are mentioned by name: Israel State Archive (ISA), Central Zionist Archive (CZA), the National Archives (TNA) of the United Kingdom, the Ford Presidential Library, etc.

Notes

1   S. Binah, *The Anti-Jewish Farhud in Baghdad, 1941 – Jewish and Arab Perspectives* (unpublished Master's Thesis, CUNY, New York, 1989).
2   R.Jervis, *Perception and Misperception in International Affairs* (Princeton NJ: Princeton University Press, 1976);R. Jervis 'War and Misperception', *Journal of Interdisciplinary History*, 18, No.4 (1988) pp. 675–700; R. Jervis, 'The Compulsive Empire', *Foreign Policy*, 137(July – August 2003) pp. 82–7.
3   K.M. Woods & M.E. Stout, 'Saddam's Perceptions and Misperceptions: The Case of "Desert Storm"', *Journal of Strategic Studies* (2010), 33:1, pp.5–41, DOI: 10.1080/01402391003603433.

List of Acronyms

ABST	Arab Ba'th Socialist Party, Iraq
ACDA	Arms Control and Disarmament Agency, USA
ADST	The Association for Diplomatic Studies and Training, Library of Congress
AJC	American Jewish Committee – Global Jewish Advocacy, USA
ALF	Arab Liberation Front – Palestinian organisation based in Lebanon, sponsored by the Iraqi Ba'th
APP	The American Presidency Project, USA
BPC	Basra Petroleum Company, Iraq
CDC	Centers for Disease Control and Prevention, USA
CZA	Central Zionist Archive, Jerusalem, Israel
CRS	Congressional Record Service, USA
DNSA	Digital National Security Archive, George Washington University, USA
DoD	Department of Defense, USA
FRUS	Foreign Relations USA, Department of State
HIAS	Hebrew Immigrant Aid Society, USA
HEU	High Enriched Uranium
IAEA	International Atomic Energy Agency, Vienna
ICP	Iraqi Communist Party, Iraq
ICRC	International Committee of the Red Cross, Geneva
INA	Iraqi News Agency, Iraq
INFCIRC	Information Circular, IAEA, Vienna
INR	Bureau of Intelligence and Research, Department of State, USA
IPC	Iraqi Petroleum Company, Iraq

ISA	Israel State Archives, Jerusalem, Israel
JDC	Joint Distribution Committee – Jewish humanitarian assistance organisation, USA
JIC	Joint Intelligence Committee, UK
DCI	Director of Central Intelligence, USA
JCS	Joint Chief of Staff, US Department of Defense
DFLP	The Democratic Front for the Liberation of Palestine – Palestinian organisation: radical left
FAO	Food and Agriculture Organization, United Nations, Rome
FCO	Foreign and Commonwealth Office, UK
KDP	Kurdish Democratic Party – Kurdish leading faction led by Barzani, Iraq
LAT	Los Angeles Times, USA
MEES	Middle East Economic Survey, Newsletter, Cyprus (formerly Lebanon)
MFA	Ministry of Foreign Affairs, Israel, Iraq
MOC	Memorandum of Conversation
NAM	Non-Allied Movement, UN
NARA	National Archives, USA
NIE	National Intelligence Estimate, USA
NPT	Non Proliferation Treaty, IAEA
NSG	Nuclear Suppliers Group, IAEA
NSSM	National Security Study Memorandum, USA
NTIS	National Technical Information Service, USA
NYT	The New York Times, USA
PFLP	The Popular Front for the Liberation of Palestine
PFLP– GC	The Popular Front for the Liberation of Palestine – General Command, Ahmad Jibril Faction
PNC	Palestinian National Council, PLO
PPSF	The Palestinian Popular Struggle Front – A small Palestinian radical faction led by Samir Ghosha
PRC	People's Republic of China
PUK	Patriotic Union of Kurdistan – Kurdish Faction led by Talabani, Iraq

RCC	Revolutionary Command Council, Ba'th Iraq
SAVAK	Domestic security and intelligence service, Iran
SI	Socialist International, Europe
SNIE	Special National Intelligence Estimate, USA
SRG	Special Review Group – White House group headed by the President, USA
SSM	Surface to Surface Missile
SWB	Summary of World Broadcast – BBC transcript service, UK
TNA	The National Archives, UK
UNHCR	United Nations High Commissioner for Refugees, Geneva
UNSC	United Nations Security Council, United Nations, New York
UNMOVIC	United Nations Monitoring, Verification and Inspection Commission, Iraq (1999–2003)
UNSCOM	United Nation Commission, Iraq (1991–8)
USTR	United States Trade Representative – Agency responsible for foreign trade policy, USA
WASG	Washington Special Actions Group, The White House, USA
WHO	World Health Organization, United Nations
WIPO	World International Property Organization, United Nations
WMD	Weapon of Mass Destruction (nuclear, biological, chemical and WMD capable missiles)
WP	The Washington Post, USA

1

1967–72

Man can be both a soldier and an individual. That is our strength – if we are smart enough to use it. It can be our weakness if we aren't ... American success or failure in Iraq may well depend on whether the Iraqis like American soldiers or not ... by getting along with the Iraqis and making them your friends. And the best way to get along with people is to understand them.[1]

US Army, *Instructions for American Servicemen*
in Iraq during World War II (1943)

The Six-Day War broke out on 6 June 1967. At 02:15 on 7 June, Baghdad time, the deputy foreign minister of Iraq, Nuri Jamil, notified the American *chargé d'affaires*, Enoch Duncan, that Iraq was severing relations with the United States and Great Britain for assisting Israel in the war. On the very same day, Iraqi President Abd al-Rahman Aref ordered a complete halt of oil production and transit from Basra.[2]

Belgium assumed the role of protecting power, mostly for the personal acquaintance between Ambassador Marcel Dupret of Belgium and US Ambassador Robert Strong. India became the protecting power for Iraq in Washington, DC. The State Department assessment was that the move was a typical decision by the unstable Iraqi regime, and anticipated that relations would resume shortly.[3]

Aref, who wanted to express his commitment to the Arab states, sent a full army division to the Syrian front with Israel, and two Iraqi Hawker-Hunter squadrons, and Tupolev bombers were assigned to the Iraqi air force and were instructed to scramble. This decision was costly, since Aref had thereby transferred elite units, deployed near the Kurdish area, that were preparing for that summer's campaign against the Kurdish rebels.[4] Only one brigade arrived in Jordan on time to participate in the fighting on the Golan Heights. However, the war ended in less than a week, and Iraq, along with Syria, Egypt and Jordan, had to face a bitter military defeat.[5]

To calm the furious public, the Iraqi leadership toned down measures against the opposition, for example, by allowing some prominent Ba'thi leaders in exile, Ali Sa'di, Mundher al-Windawi and Hardan al-Takriti to return to Baghdad. The invigorated Ba'th used the sense of economic despair and humiliation over the war to stir the masses against the Aref regime. In this explosive atmosphere, hostility was directed at the West, primarily Israel, Britain and the United States. France was the only Western country granted special status, as a payoff for her pro-Arab position and her arms embargo against Israel.

The Ba'th Takeover and the Lost New Beginning

The next summer saw a new crisis. On 17–30 July 1968, the Ba'th, together with the commander of the Republican Guard, Ibrahim al-Da'ud, and the commander of military intelligence, Abd al-Razzaq al-Na'if, carried out a military coup. It was the fourth coup d'état in the country in a decade, following the Aref regime's failure to deal with the political and economic crisis, and the humiliating defeat to Israel. Ahmad Hasan al-Bakr was declared president, and a Revolutionary Command Council (RCC) was formed. The officers al-Na'if and al-Da'ud, who played essential roles in the coup, were granted senior positions, as members of the RCC, but were dismissed thirteen days later, when the Ba'th completed the 'July Revolution'.[6]

Washington reacted at first with relief, since the Ba'th was perceived as nationalistic and right-wing, and definitely anti-communist, just as the first Ba'th coup, in February 1963, which overthrew Abd al-Karim Qasim, was welcomed by the United States. Washington was hoping to develop a close relationship with the Ba'th, which it considered a pro-Western regime.[7] This optimism held for a few months. The Central Intelligence Agency's approach was more realistic, evaluating the new regime as more difficult to deal with.[8]

Indeed, the regime's first mission was to establish its authority, by using aggressive, anti-Western language in expressing hostility in particular towards the United States. Early in its rule, the Ba'th detected and disrupted no less than thirteen plots to overthrow the government. It considered foreign intervention to be responsible: United States, Great Britain, Israel and Iran.

The Ba'ths thus purged Iraqi figures with connections to the United States. One who was murdered was Dr Nasir al-Hani, known in the United States as a moderate, pro-American diplomat, who served in Washington under three Iraqi regimes, including as an ambassador to the UN under Qasim and to Washington DC from 1964 until 1967. His liquidation substantiated the Ba'th's image as brutal, ruthless and obviously anti-

American.[9] Others eliminated were political figures representing a wide spectrum: communists, pro-Nasserists, pro-Syrians, and former government officials, agents of foreign companies and Jews who were not involved in politics. Most were charged with conspiracy and espionage for Israel, NATO, Iran and the United States.[10] The anti-America campaign was directed at individuals and institutions as well: teachers and faculty members of Al-Hikma College and its girls' school, established and administered for decades by the Jesuit Order of New England, were expelled. Also evicted were aid workers in northern Iraq and Americans employed in the oil industry, some of whom were accused of espionage.[11] In January 1969, following a show trial, the first group was hanged in Baghdad central plaza, while the incited and agitated mob harassed the families of the accused and later abused the bodies of those executed. There were nine Jewish men among those executed, an event which had a shocking impact on the international media as a human rights issue and there was great concern about the fate of the Iraqi Jewish community.[12] The second group included three former Aref ministers: Rashid Muslih, Abd al-'Aziz 'Uqayli and Shukri Zaki, all accused of being recruited by the CIA by Lutfi 'Ubaydi, an Iraqi businessman living in exile in Beirut. Ubaydi had business dealings with American businessman Robert B. Anderson, who was promoting investments in Iraq.[13] Others executed included political figures in the Aref regime, such as the former mayor of Baghdad Midhat Siri, accused of having relations with United States, and Zaki Abd-al-Wahab, who represented Coca Cola and confessed to having been a British agent since 1956. [14]

How Iraqi Jews were Continuously Penalised

Persecution of Jews intensified following the Six-Day War. The president of Iraq's Jewish community, Meir Basri, was arrested and interrogated regarding a meeting he had held with an American researcher upon the request of the Ministry of Education a year earlier. The deterioration of law and order in Baghdad following the humiliating 1967 defeat, that brought about mass demonstrations, coincided with growing anti-Jewish incitement and name calling of Jews as a fifth column and as agents of imperialism and Zionism. This situation was initiated and encouraged by the government. Jews were dismissed from public offices and private businesses. Financial restrictions on Jews impaired Jewish businesses. The Jewish community became impoverished as well as victimised.[15]

The charges of an alleged 'spy network' operated by Israel, and the public executions of Jews, were intended to appease the incited masses. Most Jewish victims were neither communist nor connected to any political activity. The government's motive in persecuting these specific individuals was, apparently, greed; although the small community of Iraqi Jews in the late 1960s, which at the time numbered about 3,500, was not as wealthy as it used to be in the 1940s, the victims were relatively well to do, and had their property confiscated.[16] Only one historian in the West, Iraqi expatriate Majid Khadduri, seemed to accept the Iraqi accusation against Jews. He cited the official Iraqi argument that the indicted Jews were Iraqi citizens who were executed alongside Iraqi Muslims and Christians. He also quoted the statement of the Grand Rabbi of Iraq's Jewish community Sasson Khadduri in support of the government, accusing 'the overreaction of the Jews in the West' and stating that the trial was fair and that the Jewish community enjoys freedom and security.[17] Future Deputy Prime Minister Tariq Aziz would later admit that the public execution of Jews had been planned and was aimed at deterring any doubters at home regarding the regime's capability to detect and destroy 'espionage networks and other traitors'.[18]

The public executions raised criticism in the West, as well as in some Arab states, against Iraq for staining the image of the Arabs. Columnists in the Lebanese weekly *Al-Hawadess* and the Egyptian daily *Al-Ahram* claimed that the public executions took place at the wrong time and under inappropriate circumstances. These criticisms were most disappointing for the regime, with Baghdad official radio complaining of 'the unnatural' Arab silence regarding the protest.[19]

Extending a helping hand to Jews facing difficulties wherever they are is a fundamental ethos of the State of Israel. The shock expressed by Prime Minister Levi Eshkol at the Israeli parliament, as well as by various other Israeli politicians with regard to the executions of Iraqi Jews, raised concern in the American embassy in Tel Aviv. In a dispatch to his superiors at the State Department, US ambassador Walworth Barbour stated that Israel might respond by force, and suggested that the department issue an immediate statement denouncing Iraq.[20] Barbour was not alone in his concern for Israeli retaliation. A report by the department's Bureau of Intelligence and Research (INR) asserted that, though the Jewish victims were innocent of the espionage charge, their executions could have been a reaction to Israeli Air Force raids on Iraqi artillery batteries in the Jordanian cities of Mafraq and Irbid in December 1969.[21] The United States asked Israel to show restraint and avoid any retaliation.[22]

The administration reacted promptly on another front. Secretary of State William P. Rogers appealed to the United Nations Security Council to take action based on the UN charter's humanitarian articles.[23] The UN Secretary General U Thant sent a message through Iraqi diplomat Ismet Kittani to President al-Bakr.[24] The State Department initiated practical steps with Iran on a possible rescue corridor for Iraqi Jews via Iran.[25] Israel preferred to act discreetly, while Jewish organisations in the United States and in Europe pressured Iraq to avoid further persecutions of Jews and allow them to leave Iraq.[26]

Leading the campaign for Iraqi Jews were major, New York based philanthropic organisations, which flexed their muscles in terms of experience and connections, such as the American Jewish Committee (AJC) and the Joint Distribution Committee (JDC). Prominent American-Jewish figures weighed in, including Senator Jacob K. Javits and Arthur J. Goldberg, the American ambassador to the UN and a former associate justice on the Supreme Court.

Iraq Foreign Policy, 1968–70: Regrouping

From the moment the Ba'th regime assumed power, it became aware of the importance of foreign policy and of its international image. Like under its predecessors, the Ba'th was politically active at the UN General Assembly and the Security Council within the Arab League states and the Non-aligned Movement (NAM) states, receiving assistance in grain from the Food and Agricultural Organization (FAO) and medical assistance from the World Health Organization (WHO).[27] A special effort was made towards the countries constituting the (NAM), the largest group in the UN.[28] As a revolutionary regime the Ba'th welcomed relations with the Eastern bloc. It hailed the Soviet Union's invasion of Czechoslovakia in August 1968, and on 1 May 1968, it was the first Arab state to recognise East Germany. In return, Iraq was granted technological and military assistance from East European states. It also selected a company in Poland to supply Iraq with machinery and equipment for sulphur production, rejecting the American entrepreneur Anderson, who was expecting to win the concession[29].

The Ba'th devoted significant resources and effort in the Arab arena – firstly as a revolutionary party striving for Arab unity, but mostly as a means to monitor subversive elements outside the country that were hostile to the Iraqi leadership. Early on, the Ba'th used revolutionary rhetoric, with Marxist nuances, describing itself as being at the vanguard of the 'Permanent Revolution' (*al-thawra al-da'ima*).[30] It criticised the conservative monarchies of Jordan and Saudi Arabia as 'reactionaries' for their willingness to accept Secretary Rogers' peace plan to resolve the Arab-Israeli conflict. The Ba'th called Nasser a 'defeatist' and accused Syria of not representing the 'authentic Ba'th'.[31] Clinging to 'revolutionary' principles and supporting Marxist movements led to rigid hardline foreign policy isolating Iraq in the Arab and international arena.

The Ba'th neighbors, in Baghdad and Damascus, were bitter rivals competing for legitimacy, and they indulged in mutual suspicion for subversive activity. The Iraqi Ba'th was mainly concerned with conspiracies it alleged were supported by Syria and Egypt. It arrested and executed Iraqis suspected of having contacts in Syria. Abd al-Karim Mustafa Nasrat, an Iraqi who was close to the Syrian Internal Security Chief Abd al-Karim al-Jundi, was assassinated in his home on 27 January 1969.[32] The mutual hostility, consistent throughout the period of this research, was an aggressive struggle, expressed in propaganda in the media; it became violent at times and turned into a personal power struggle between the Syrian President Hafez al-Assad and, on the Iraqi side, primarily Saddam Hussein. In parallel, Syria and Iraq maintained practical contacts on essential issues, such as water management of the Euphrates River, which flowed from Syria and stood as a vital life stream for Iraq. Trade relations grew, including the transit of Iraqi oil from a pipeline in the Iraqi city of Kirkuk and through Syria to the Mediterranean.[33]

During this period, the historical conflict endured between Persians and Iraqi Arabs, over the maritime boundary in the Persian Gulf, known by the Arabs as the Arabian Gulf. Meanwhile, the Iranian monarchy was the antithesis of revolutionary, socialist, anti-imperialist Iraq, as well as being a major ally of the United States, while Ba'thi Iraq was an ally of the USSR and the Soviet Block. Major territorial controversies between Iraq and Iran have dealt with the demarcation of the strategic maritime border of Shatt al-Arab, at the confluence of the Tigris and Euphrates rivers, and the Iranians' taking over three islands in the Straits of Hurmuz (Greater Tunb, Lesser Tunb and Abu Musa). The Ba'th has also accused Iran of being behind the failed attempt of Abd al-Ghani al-Rawi to overthrow the regime in 1970, following which Iraq arrested and executed thirty-seven people and expelled the new Iranian ambassador in Baghdad.[34] As a close ally of Iran, the United States was blamed in an Iraqi official broadcast as being 'interested in eliminating [*qada 'ala*] the Iraqi regime.'[35] Iraq's main concern was that Britain's withdrawal from the Gulf would be replaced by Western dominance. Iraq perceived US support of Iran, Saudi Arabia and the Gulf states on 'Gulf security' as a strategic threat to its narrow access to the Gulf.[36]

Crisis in Jordan

During the Black September crisis in Jordan in 1970, the United States and Iraq stood on opposite sides: the Iraqi expedition force in Jordan was expected to join the Palestine Liberation Organization's fight against the monarchy, while King Hussein was an important ally of the United States and a potential partner for peace with Israel. Moreover, the radical Popular Front for the Liberation of Palestine hijacked three Western civilian aircraft and landed them in Jordan. PFLP founder George Habash called the act a protest against the Egyptian-Israeli ceasefire agreement at the Suez Canal front in August. Apparently, the choice of Jordan as the landing spot was intended to escalate the ongoing, heated conflict between the King and the PLO.[37]

For the Ba'th, the crisis in Jordan was a challenge. The Salah al-Din Force, based in Jordan since spring 1967, had reached 50,000–60,000 men – almost half of the Iraqi army.[38] Al-Bakr stated that the presence of the expedition force in Jordan underscored Iraq's commitment to the Palestinians, and added that, if necessary, it would have been placed under Palestinian command.[39] On 1 September, Iraq issued an ultimatum to Amman, warning the King that the force would step in if the Jordanian army would not cease shelling the Palestinian.[40] The Jordanian attack continued, killing hundreds of Palestinians and injuring thousands. On 17 September, when Jordanian tanks attacked Palestinian positions in Amman, the Iraqi leadership instructed its forces to refrain from any involvement in the fighting and to make preparations to retreat eastward.[41] Simultaneously, Iraqi leaders and the media continued to express support for what they called the heroic struggle of the Palestinians, including by orchestrating mass demonstrations in Iraq and harshly criticising King Hussein.[42]

American Response and Crisis Management

Black September was among the first challenges to the Nixon Doctrine of July 1969.[43] September 1970 had been an eventful month for the administration, compelled as it was to deal with several evolving crises, all of which could have deteriorated and led to Soviet military involvement in Cuba, Chile or Vietnam. Nixon's then national security advisor, Henry Kissinger, manoeuvered to manage these hotspots simultaneously. His biographer, Walter Isaacson, described this conduct as 'the art of crisis juggling'.[44] American mistrust of the Soviet Union's intentions in the Middle East had increased since early August following the Soviets' deployment of SAM 3 missiles along the Suez Canal, which the United States perceived as a violation of the 7 August 1970 ceasefire agreement between Egypt and Israel.[45]

The White House team known as WSAG (Washington Special Actions Group), headed by Kissinger, feared that Iraqi military involvement in supporting the Palestinians might undermine the moderate, pro-Western King. Furthermore, it could spark a regional war.[46] The King appealed urgently for assistance from Great Britain, whose cabinet debated in closed session and decided to avoid military involvement in Jordan. One argument raised against interceding was that the King had only a slim chance of surviving the crisis. Britain forwarded Jordan's request to the United States, and assisted Washington in its communication with the King via the MI6 station in Amman. Otherwise, London remained behind the scenes.[47] The Nixon administration's strategy was to act diplomatically vis-à-vis the Soviets, assuming that any Iraqi military activity would require Soviet supply. The Americans requested of the Kremlin that it restrain Iraq.[48] Kissinger was not satisfied with the Soviets' mild response; in particular Ambassador Anatoly Dobrynin's not cutting short his vacation in Moscow to return to Washington to deal with the crisis. To Kissinger, it was clear that the Soviets had no interest in calming the situation. On 15 September, the King notified Washington that he had decided on a showdown with the PLO and said he might ask for American support if Iraq or Syria intervened.[49] Kissinger decided that the most effective way to support the King was to increase the American military presence in the Mediterranean to deter such intervention and to overwhelm the Soviets. Two of the US Sixth Fleet's aircraft carriers, the *Independence* and the *Saratoga*, had already been deployed southeast of Crete, facing Lebanese and Israeli shores, and the carriers *John F. Kennedy* and the helicopter carrier *Guam* were ordered to move towards the Mediterranean. Other North Atlantic Treaty Organization air bases in Germany and Turkey were put on alert.[50] Kissinger sent directives to US agencies to make plans for contingencies, such as militarily supplying Jordan, evacuation of American civilians and US airstrikes or ground assaults in support of the King.[51] Mohammad Reza Pahlavi, the Shah of Iran, was asked to be prepared to engage Iraqi forces deployed in the Kurdish area in case of Iraqi involvement in Jordan.[52] Israel was an important source of tactical intelligence on Syrian and Iraqi forces, as well as an active partner in creating deterrence. 'I want them to know we're moving,' Nixon told Kissinger. 'I want everything that can be done to be done in the open. The wear and tear on the nerves between the Syrians and Iraqis is very important'.[53]

Indeed, the Salah al-Din Force, based in Zarqa, Jordan, was not instructed – despite the Ba'thists' previous statements – to interfere when the Jordanian army was striking the PLO nearby, or when the Syrian tanks were crossing the Jordanian border and heading towards Irbid. Israeli intelligence reported, on 17 September, that the Iraqi force was ready to move, yet it turned east, back towards the Iraqi border.[54] The crisis was over, and on 27-8 September, Nixon celebrated the diplomatic success by visiting the Sixth Fleet in the Mediterranean.[55]

During those hectic events, controversy emerged between the White House and the Department of State. Rogers was criticised for taking a diffident approach since early September: instead of expressing full support for the King, as per the latter's urgent appeal, he recommended avoiding military intervention by appealing to the UN Security Council.[56] As a result, the crisis in Jordan was managed directly by the White House, with Kissinger taking the lead in both interagency decision-making groups: the Washington Special Actions Group (WSAG) and the Special Review Group (SRG). Nixon did not hide his disregard for the State Department, telling the newly appointed ambassador to Amman L. Dean Brown, 'Keep me informed. Remember what I need. I don't want the State Department garbage. Keep me informed.'[57]

The United States did not attribute much attention to Iraq's restraint, though it was a major element that might have called for Israeli or American military intervention. Mentions of Iraq during WSAG discussions came only regarding the military or technical aspect of the conflict. Chairman of the Joint Chiefs of Staff Admiral Thomas Moorer, mentioned that the Iraqi position was ambivalent, and Assistant Secretary Joseph Sisco admitted that the Iraqi issue 'was treated in a very fuzzy fashion'.[58] No serious questions were raised regarding the Ba'th regime or its conduct and direction. Israeli assessments that Ba'thi Iraq posed a threat to the King and the region as a whole were not taken seriously, probably because they were considered biased. King Hussein confirmed the Israeli assessment in November, during his visit to Washington, maintaining that the Iraqi threat was more serious than anticipated, since the Salah al-Din Force planned to attack and isolate Amman.[59]

In addition to the success of American diplomacy and of Soviet pressure on Damascus and Baghdad, unrelated circumstances facilitated the crisis' end. Paradoxically, rival elements joined hands to keep the Hashemite throne intact. Iraq was concerned that Palestinian control of Jordan would be under the auspices of its own rival, Syria. Syria then was locked in a domestic dispute between General Sallah Jedid the strongman of Syria, and Assad, Minister of Defense and former Air Force commander, who refrained from providing air cover to the Syrian units on the ground. All this was against the backdrop of the controversy mentioned earlier within the Iraqi Ba'th leadership that ended in the dramatic decision to avoid fighting against the King. Meanwhile Egyptian President Gamal 'Abd al-Nasser, who had owed a debt of honour to the King since June 1967, when he convinced him to join the Arab military campaign against Israel, played an important role in supporting Hussein discreetly but effectively. When Hardan al-Takriti expressed concern that low-ranking Iraqi officers might disobey the Ba'thi order to avoid fighting with the PLO, Nasser gave his word that it would not happen since they were his 'people', meaning Iraqi pro-Nasser nationalists.[60]

The British deputy chief of mission in Baghdad, Sir Donald Hawley, considered the Iraqi RCC decision of non-intervention to be an ideological change. 'The Ba'thists of Iraq are Iraqi first and Ba'thist ideologues a long way second,' he said, correctly assessing that the Ba'th was not a provisional regime, but was there to last.[61]

The Iraqi Perspective

The nonintervention decision took its toll by raising harsh criticism in the Arab world, as well as inside Iraq – including within the RCC. Scholars of Iraq Marion and Peter Sluglett adopted the Palestinian view claiming that the Ba'th's vocal support of the PLO was merely lip service, in spite of the continuous Iraqi financial and military support of the Palestinians.[62] Israeli scholar Amatzia Baram asserted that the dramatic decision was an outcome of a tempestuous debate within the leadership of the Ba'th: the party's radical faction, led by Michel Aflaq and his supporters within the Pan-Arab Command of the Ba'th Party (*Qiyyada Qawmiyya*), and 'Abd al-Khaleq al-Samra'i of the Regional Command of the Party (*Qiyyada Wataniyya*). The so-called pragmatist faction, led by Al-Bakr, Saddam Hussein, Hardan al-Takriti, and several senior army officers, tipped the scale on 17 September as the RCC decided to refrain from fighting alongside the Palestinians against the Jordanian King.[63] The latter faction included officers who recognised the weakness of the Iraqi army should it face the well-trained and equipped Royal Jordanian Legion, as well as coping with the Israel Defense Forces, in a clash likely to follow.[64] The Salah al-Din force experienced several Israeli Air Force raids in 1969, and the military presence in the Kurdish provinces was still essential, regardless of the agreement in March with the Kurds. A failed confrontation in Jordan could have threatened the survival of the Ba'th. Simultaneously, Iraqi media covered, on the front pages, the massive show of force by the Sixth Fleet in the Mediterranean and the British Royal Navy in the Persian Gulf, which clearly had an effect on Iraq as well. The threat of an attack on Basra and the southern region from the sea was viable. An RCC statement issued on 27 September explained the party's policy and how the Iraqi decision actually 'saved' the Palestinians.[65]

Iraq did not sever relations with Jordan following Black September. Even as it launched media attacks on King Hussein and praised what it called the heroic fight of the PLO, Iraq turned over a new page by granting financial assistance to Jordan and maintaining cooperation based on joint interests.[66]

The decision to avoid intervention in Jordan was finally accepted by the Iraqi leadership, but raised questions and criticism amongst the Iraqi public. Ba'thi veteran and admired army officer General Hardan al-Takriti, who opposed military interference in Jordan, was made the scapegoat, with blame cast on him personally. Hardan was dismissed, refused to accept a diplomatic post and, during an official visit to Kuwait, was shot, gangster-style, as the US embassy in Kuwait City termed it in its report.[67] The Ba'th didn't relate his dismissal to his opposition to military involvement in Jordan that both al-Bakr and Saddam adhered to, and were reluctant to commit to carrying out full military involvement in the Palestinian fight against the King of Jordan.[68] Rather, rumours against Hardan were spread, with one suggesting that he reached a separate agreement with the King. The Ba'th issued a gallant denial of these accusations, and took the position that Iraq was not strong enough to fight Israel.[69]

Consolidation of Ba'th Rule, 1970–2

The regime created political and legal institutions based on Ba'th ideology. The first priority was to establish its authority and gain legitimacy. However, since Iraqi society consists of ethnic, religiously and ideologically diverse groups, the regime sought to form a cohesive coalition, which it called the National Progressive Front (*Al-Jabha al-Wataniyya al-Mutaqaddima*), to encourage major groups to join and participate in the government and other state institutions. The Front was established in 1973 following long negotiations with the Iraqi Communist Party, which accepted the dominance of the Ba'th. The Kurds signed a framework agreement with the Ba'th in March 1970, and were expected to join as well. An interim constitution came into being in July 1970, and a national charter in November 1971. The Agrarian Reform Law was promulgated in May 1970.[70] Some political prisoners were set free, and Interior Minister Salih Mahdi Ammash announced the annulment of all restrictions imposed on Jews under the Aref regime. As a result of the bitter experience of the short lived Ba'thi rule in 1963, the RCC assumed full, unlimited control of the economy and development as well as of all government agencies and the military.[71]

Veteran, popular Ba'thi members were dismissed from key positions. Ammash was sent into 'diplomatic exile', Hardan al-Takriti refused to leave Iraq and was murdered. Minister of Culture Sallum al-Samra'i, Shafiq al-Kamali and Abd al-Karim al-Shaikhli were replaced by other party members, who pledged allegiance to the existing leadership. Similar reshuffling took place in the army and civil services.[72]

The Agreements with the Kurds and the Communists

The agreement with the Kurds on 11 March 1970, following long negotiations between Deputy President Saddam Hussein and the Chairman of the Kurdish Democratic Party (KDP) Mulla Mustafa Barzani, ended a military battle that was initiated by the Kurds in summer 1968. It was actually a framework agreement on principles, to be used as the basis for further negotiations to be completed within four years between Mulla Barzani and the regime on establishing Kurdish autonomy within Iraq. Simultaneously, the Ba'th approached the Iraqi Communist Party (ICP), which, like the Kurds, experienced clashes with the central government.[73] During the short-lived Ba'th reign in 1963, the Communists suffered ruthless persecution as revenge for their support of the Qasim regime. The Ba'th renewed persecution of Communists right after their return to power at the July 1968 coup.[74] A rift within the ICP and secession of radical factions, headed by 'Aziz al-Hajj, facilitated the Ba'th initiative to have the Communist central body, under Aziz Muhammad, join the National Front. On 14 May 1972, after long negotiations, the ICP joined the Front with the blessing of the Soviet Union. Two members of the ICP Central Committee were appointed ministers, and the party was legally allowed to publish the daily *Tariq al-Sha'b*, and the monthly magazine *Al-Thaqafa al-Jedida*.[75]

The regime took harsh measures against the Communists' radical faction ICP-Central Leadership that opposed any dialogue with the Ba'th. 'Aziz al-Hajj, who led the split with the mother party, ICP-Central Committee was arrested and tortured, and was forced to appear in a TV broadcast to tell his people to stop activities against the regime.[76] During the winter of 1970–1, the regime ran a violent anti-Communist campaign in southern Iraq that included assassinating leading Communists.[77] The major Communist faction, ICP-Central Committee, emphasised the principles shared with the Ba'th, such as close relations with the Soviet Union and the Eastern bloc, reaching agreement with the Kurds, agrarian reform, and nationalisation and improving the conditions of workers and peasants. ICP's position regarding Israel was left ambiguous, since the USSR recognised Israel and supported a solution to the conflict.[78]

The Shi'a Community: The Everlasting Suspicion

The regime suspected the Shi'i community of disloyalty. In this, there was an ideological dichotomy between the religiously conservative Shi'a and the secular, revolutionary socialist Ba'th.[79] The regime's suspicion lay mostly, however, in the power and authority the Shi'a religious leadership wielded over its community in the agrarian south. It could oppose the agrarian reform that was the Ba'th's flagship program, such as by arranging mass demonstrations.[80] Moreover, the Iraqi Shi'i community had close relations with the Iranian and Lebanese religious leaderships, so it was suspected of collaborating in anti-Ba'th activity supported, mostly, by Iran. Each conflict between Iran and Iraq resulted in punitive measures against Shi'a students or permanent residents of Iranian or foreign descent. In April 1969, about 20,000 students were expelled in retaliation for Iran's terminating the 1937 agreement on the Shatt al-'Arab, and similar steps were taken in 1970 after Al-Rawi's abortive plot to overthrow the Ba'th – a plot attributed to Iran.[81]

Nonetheless the major threat to the Ba'th in the southern provinces was the emergence of political Islam throughout the 1970s. The Da'wa Party (*Hizb al-Da'wa al-Islamiyya*) emerged under the leadership of Muhammad Baqr al-Sadr. Since 1966, it promulgated the theory of unanimity of religious and political authority, thus challenging the Ba'th's secular authority.[82] At the *Madrasat Sheikh Muhammad* seminary in the holy city of Najaf in early 1970, Iranian cleric Ayatollah Rohallah Khomeini delivered a series of lectures, entitled *Wilayat al-Faqih* (Guardian of the Islamic Law) that by decade's end had become the basic theory of the Islamic revolution in Iran.[83] Despite his religious posture, Khomeini had no impact on the growth of the Da'wa, self-defined as an Iraqi party that promoted the concept of Muslims sharing common ground.[84]

All this while, the evolution of political Islam and the persecution of the Shi'a didn't draw much attention in Washington.

The Ba'th and the Soviet Union: Blowing Hot and Cold

The US commitment to supporting Iran with state-of-the-art weaponry on the one hand, and Iraq's isolation in the international and Arab arenas on the other, enhanced Iraqi-Soviet relations. The USSR was openly pro-Arab, severed relations with Israel following the Six-Day War and supported the PLO. Furthermore, the Soviets were willing to supply Iraq with military equipment and technology, as well as building infrastructure for oil production and transportation under generous financial terms. The Soviets then interfered and encouraged the Ba'th to embrace the ICP and fair share in the National Front allegedly as a partner in the Iraqi leadership.[85] The Iraqis needed technical and financial support to develop and operate oilfields. In Baghdad on 9 April 1972, Al-Bakr and Soviet Premier Alexei Kosygin signed a fifteen-year, bilateral treaty on friendship and cooperation.[86] The Ba'th portrayed the treaty as an Iraqi achievement, though some Ba'thi members expressed concern that the treaty and its affiliated agreements might create a dependency on the Soviets for supplies for its military and oil industries. Others complained that the treaty introduced Soviet interference in domestic affairs through Soviet promotion of agreements with the Communists and the Kurds.[87]

The Nixon administration was neither surprised by the treaty, nor did it consider it a Soviet gain at America's expense. Instead, it was viewed as similar to the treaties the Soviet Union had already signed with Egypt and Syria. The State Department had already reported in 1971 that the Soviets promised to supply Iraq with $750 million in military assistance.[88] The American assessment was that the assistance was needed domestically to counter opposition groups and the Kurds, and would not pose a threat to Iran or to the Persian Gulf.[89] Nevertheless, US allies, like Iran and the Gulf states, did not share this assessment and warned Washington that the Soviets sought access to the Persian Gulf, and that a strong Iraqi army would constitute a regional threat.[90] The USSR, which was then establishing closer relations with Iran, may have calmed Teheran's view of Moscow's treaty with Iraq. The Soviets also turned down Iraq's request to denounce the Iranian seizure of the strait's islands, and refrained from supporting Iraq over border disputes with Kuwait and Iran. Furthermore, the treaty with Iraq did not include any Soviet obligation to assist Iraq, were Iran to attack it.[91]

The CIA did not share the Department of State's optimistic view, and noted that the Soviets might request docking services in Iraqi ports. Additionally, it was concerned by the Iraqi obligation to annually sell up to two million tons of oil to the Soviets at a low price until 1980.[92] This relaxed attitude of the administration towards the treaty, that Iraqi-Soviet alliance may not turn Iraq into a regional threat, was based on the perception that the Iraqi regime was weak and its army was incompetent and unprofessional due to inappropriate political promotions – and, therefore, that it would not be able to utilise sophisticated weapons systems, such as the SA-3 missile. The paper handed to Nixon concluded: 'Generally, the Iraqis suffer from weaknesses common to all Arabs.'[93]

As opposed to the relaxed evaluation of the strategic and political implications of the Iraqi-Soviet treaty, Nixon and Kissinger adopted a more cautious approach. They viewed the pact as being 'not only weapon supply, but synchronization of foreign policy,' and therefore one that should be contained by increasing US support to Iran; that would be accomplished by responding favorably to the Shah's repeated requests for the most sophisticated military supplies, and directly supporting the Kurdish rebellion.[94] Nixon's decision on the matter was unexpected, and came without prior consultation.[95]

Subsequently, on 30 May 1972, Nixon and Kissinger arrived in Teheran directly from Moscow, following six intensive days of deliberations with the Soviets, culminating in the signing of two landmark arms-control agreements, namely the Anti-Ballistic Missile (ABM) Treaty and the first Strategic Arms Limitation Talks (SALT I).

Iraq Oil Resources Nationalised

American companies held 23.75 percent of the shares of the IPC (Iraqi Petroleum Company) with British, Dutch and French companies holding the rest. Nationalising Iraq's oil industry was a preliminary goal of the Ba'th, yet only on 1 June 1972 did Al-Bakr pronounce Public Law 69 to nationalise the IPC.[96] The announcement ended a long dispute between the foreign oil companies forming the IPC and the government of Iraq, initiated by Qasim. The Ba'th was reluctant to nationalise the domestic petroleum industry earlier, since Iraq's economy was wholly dependent on the IPC's technological resources for production, shipment and marketing, while oil revenues were vital at 95 percent of all Iraqi exports in 1971.[97] However, following numerous agreements – mostly with the USSR and the Eastern bloc, guaranteeing technical and economic support, including marketing – the time was deemed right for the move to nationalise.

The regime seemed well aware of the risk it was taking, especially in a possible decline of its main revenue source, due to the difficulties of selling nationalised oil. Most consumers were in the West, and would be expected to show solidarity with IPC. Indeed, Saddam Hussein told his biographer, Fuad Matar, that he himself had surveyed the consequences of the nationalisation, consulting energy and finance experts including considering loans[98] In November, Al-Bakr reported to the Ba'th National Command that the regime was prepared for a decline in oil revenues, including by declaring martial law, if necessary.[99] Indeed the full scale marketing resumed following the compensation settlement which was reached on 28 February 1973, and as the decline in revenues was short-lived.[100]

However, the nationalisation move was a great public success, portrayed in the media and in party publications as a proper national Arab response to Western imperialism, akin in magnitude to Nasser's nationalising of the Suez Canal in 1956. The decision became ingrained in the Ba'th ethos as a great achievement and was celebrated every year as '*Id al-Ta'mim*.[101]

Nationalisation of the IPC seemed to defy the United States, since IPC was a major player in the global oil market and the move had a major effect on American companies holding key stakes in the IPC, such as Exxon and

Mobil. As it turned out, there was no significant economic or political impact on the United States, which had not been importing Iraqi oil, and there was no oil shortage worldwide.[102] Still, the administration was disappointed that the French government accepted Iraq's nationalisation and signed a separate oil contract, which tightened their bilateral, prosperous friendship in the years to come.

Iraq granted the French company CFP (Compagnie Française des Pétroles) most-favoured status for Paris's 'positive attitude towards the Arabs', by which it meant, ostensibly the French arms embargo of Israel in 1967. This typified Iraq's approach: rewarding Western states for assuming pro-Arab positions with attractive oil deals, hoping to diminish the diplomatic influence of Britain and the United States.[103]

Against the balanced and relatively relaxed response of the administration, the American IPC representatives protested in Congress and the media that the administration was too supportive of Israel, and called for more positive policy towards the Arabs.[104]

Expropriation of the US Embassy Building

There was no American diplomatic presence in Baghdad until November 1972, yet relations reached their lowest ebb in May 1971, when the regime seized the US embassy building following two years of failed negotiations with the protecting power, Belgium.[105]

The legal basis for the expropriation was that the building was in a military area and that the Iraqi seizure was legal, according to their interpretation of the Vienna Convention on Diplomatic Relations. Baghdad then transferred $28,000 to the embassy of Belgium as compensation. The Belgian embassy had urged the US previously to respond to the Iraqi request to evacuate the building, since it had not functioned as a diplomatic mission since 1967, and to reach a compensation settlement, but the State Department refused. Therefore, following the enforced seizure of the premises[106] and in the absence of American diplomats in Baghdad, the State Department considered freezing Iraqi assets in the United States and expelling the two Iraqi diplomats serving in Washington at the embassy of India.[107] The outraged Belgian Ambassador Marcel Van De Kerckhove responded harshly that such American retaliation would risk the Belgian embassy. The Belgian ambassador complained that Brussels was paying a diplomatic price for representing Washington, due to the American refusal to evacuate the building, in fact violating Iraqi law.[108]

The State Department instead issued a letter of protest, and even dispatched American diplomats to run the US Interest Section at Belgium's embassy. Doing so acknowledged Iraq's growing importance in the region and in the Organization of the Petroleum Exporting Countries (OPEC), as well as America's interest in forging closer relations with Arab states in general.[109] Previously, the Americans did not dispatch diplomats to Baghdad, because the Iraqis insisted on approving only one low-ranking diplomat. (The other employees in the American Interest Section were local Iraqis.)[110]

In January 1972, Washington, via Belgium, notified the Iraqi Ministry of Foreign Affairs that it intended to dispatch three diplomats, with the head of mission holding the rank of first secretary. The State Department implied that Iraq's rejection of the move would result in the expulsion of Iraqi diplomats from Washington.[111] The Ba'th then was also interested in establishing low-level relations, and it created a pattern that lasted for twelve years: attacking US policy and using anti-American slurs openly, while evincing interest in procuring Western, including American technology.[112] Baghdad might have seen the Americans' opening of an Interest Section as accepting that Iraq was not a Soviet satellite in spite of the treaty. In any case, it was clear that the Ba'th tried to keep America's diplomatic presence below the radar, most likely because some elements in the public (including the Communists and Ba'th elements) opposed any relations with Washington. When the State Department issued a press release with the names of its diplomats appointed to serve in Baghdad, the Iraqi Ministry of Foreign Affairs issued a statement that there was no change in its policy towards the United States due to America's hostility to the Arabs through its support of Israel.[113]

The diplomat appointed as Head of Mission was Arthur L. Lowrie, who had joined the Foreign Service in 1956. He spoke Arabic fluently and had served previously in Aleppo, Syria, from 1957–9; in Khartoum, Sudan, from 1962–4; and in Tunisia from 1964–7. Since 1972, he had served in Washington as INR Algerian desk officer, dealing with energy companies. He had applied to be head of the Interest Section in Baghdad as for him it would be a wise step, creating a likely promotion that he might not otherwise get at that point in his career.[114]

In many ways, Lowrie had the typical features of an Arabist in the Foreign Service.[115] The term 'Arabist' originally referred to government Middle East specialists, most with Arabic-language training. Yet, some foreign service officials who had spent extensive time in the Middle East and joined the foreign service after the Second World War, inclined to identify with the Arab cause or generally became 'pro-Arab' criticising the American support of the Iranian Shah, and Israel.

As a First Secretary, Lowrie's relations with the Iraqi MFA consisted mostly of administrative and protocol matters. Most of his contacts were with other foreign diplomats who related to him as they would with any Head of Mission.[116]As a result, his reports were based on secondary sources, like the Iraqi media and other diplomats. Still, as an Arabic reader, his reports shed light on the domestic situation in Baghdad. He described a police state, arbitrary arrests, and a suspicion of foreigners that kept the American diplomats isolated.[117] The bilateral situation looked grim. An NEA (Bureau of Near Eastern and South Asian Affairs, Department of State) report noted in December 1972 that, 'The Ba'th government sees no particular benefit in significantly improving relations with the US. American "imperialism" particularly in terms of US support for Israel and the activities of the US oil companies, remains the regime's favorite whipping boy and scapegoat.' The report concluded by stating that distrust of Washington ran so deep in Iraq that no internal faction would risk rowing against the tide.[118]

Notes

1. United States Army. *Instructions for American Servicemen in Iraq during World War II*: 'pocket guide' prepared by the Special Service Division of the Army Service Forces, 1943 (Reprinted Chicago IL: University of Chicago Press, 2007), pp. 1–2.
2. Baghdad (Duncan), 6 June 1967, 23:15Z, *FRUS XXI* #194; London (Kaiser), 6 June 1967, *DNSA*.
3. State Circular airgram CA-8354 to Brussels, 29 May 1968. *FRUS 1964-68 XXI* #198.
4. S. Shay, *The Iraqi-Israeli Conflict – 1948–2000* (Tel Aviv: Maarachot, 2002), pp. 57-9.
5. *Ibid.*, pp. 61–3; P. Malovany, *The Wars of Modern Babylon* (Tel Aviv: Maarachot, 2009), pp. 65–7.
6. For further description of the preparations for the coup and chronology see: M. Khadduri, *Socialist Iraq, A Study in Iraqi Politics since 1969* (Washington: Middle East Institute 1978) pp. 21–8; H. Batatu, *The Old Social Classes, and the Revolutionary Movements of Iraq* (Princeton NJ: Princeton University Press, 1978) pp.1073–9; P. Marr, *The Modern History of Iraq* (Boulder CO: Westview Press, 1985), pp. 211–15; Sluglett & Sluglett, *Iraq since 1958, From Revolution to Dictatorship* (New York: Palgrave Macmillan, 1987), pp.107–23; M. Mufti, *Sovereign Creations Pan-Arabism and Political Order in Syria and Iraq* (Ithaca NY: Cornell University Press, 1996), pp. 197–201; A. Dawisha, *Iraq – A political History* (Princeton, Princeton University Press 2006), pp. 209–51.
7. Memorandum from JCS to Secretary McNamara, 9 March 1963, *FRUS XVIII* #184; Memorandum from State (Brubeck), to NSC, 13 February, 1963, *FRUS XVIII* # 157; State to Baghdad, 18 April, 1963, *FRUS XVIII* #216; Memorandum from State (Rusk), to the President, *FRUS XVIII* #161.
8. Memorandum from NSC (Foster) to Rostow, 17 July 1968, *FRUS XXI* #199; Intelligence note from INR (Hughes) 6 August 1968, *NARA*, RG 59, POL 15, Iraq.
9. Marr, *The Modern History of Iraq*, p. 213; Beirut (Porter) 14 November 1968, *NARA*, POL 6, Iraq.
    The American ambassador in Beirut, who was in touch with the Iraqi exile community, suggested sending a formal letter of condolence to Hani's widow.
10. Among the senior detainees: former PM Abdal-Rahman al-Bazzaz and Khayr al-Din al-Khasib, Sluglett & Sluglett *Iraq since 1958, From Revolution to Dictatorship*, p.118.

11. Research Memorandum from INR (Hughes), 14 February 1969, *FRUS* E-4 # 251; American Christian Institutions in Iraq, Department of State, The Office of the Special Assistant of the Secretary for the Coordination of International Educational and Cultural relations, *International, Cultural and related activities for Iraq* (January 1961), pp. 16–18; American Protestants established elementary schools in Basra, Kirkuk and Erbil by Mrs Van-Ess in 1910–13.

12. *Baghdad Observer*, 18 December 1968.

13. Robert Anderson, a former Treasury secretary under President Eisenhower, was a businessman and investor. According to Aburish, before the 1968 coup, he mediated between Ba'thi leaders and American companies regarding sulphur and oil concessions, to be granted when the Ba'th assumed power. Following the coup, the Ba'th turned against Anderson and persecuted Iraqis involved, and granted production and development concessions to a French and Soviet firms; *WP*,18 June 1969, 28 November 1969; MOC: 'How to Buy a Revolution: Talk with an Iraqi Plotter', Talcott Seelye, Loutfi Obeidi, Washington, 19 October 1969, *FRUS* E-4#262; Said K. Aburish: 'The Survival of Saddam: Secrets of his Life and Leadership': Interview for *Frontline*, PBS, 25 January 2000, transcript, http://www.pbs.org/wgbh/pages/frontline/shows/saddam/interviews/aburish.html.

14. Sluglett & Sluglett, *Iraq since 1958, From Revolution to Dictatorship*, pp. 121–2; *WP*, 28 November 1969.

15. Further details on persecution of Iraqi Jews in 1967 see: Memoirs of M. Sawadayee, *All Waiting to be Hanged: Iraq Post-Six-day War Diary*)Tel Aviv: Naharayim, 1994); I. Levin, *Locked Doors: The Seizures of Jewish Property in Arab Countries* (Tel Aviv: Maarachot, 2001), pp. 117–38; I. Bezalel, *Alone in the Final Stronghold: The Disappearance of Iraqi Jewry* (Tel Aviv, Maariv, 1976); C. Basri, *The Jews of Iraq: a forgotten case of ethnic cleansing*, Policy Study No. 26,World Jewish Congress 2003.

16. S. Binah, 'The anti-Jewish Farhud in Baghdad, 1941 – Jewish and Arab perspectives' (MA Thesis, CUNY: New York, 1989).

17. Khadduri, *Socialist Iraq*, p. 51.

18. Al-Thwara, 17 July 1972; Tariq Aziz, *The Revolution of the New Way: Arab Ba'ath Socialist Party* (Baghdad, 1974), pp. 25–6.

19. N. Qazzaz, *Sofa shel Gola Hayehudim be-Iraq 1951–2000 (The End of the Iraqi Jewish Diaspora 1951–2000)* (Or Yehuda: Babylonian Jewish Heritage Center, 2011), p. 41; Iraqi Government Announcements: 31 January1969 in *Nida al-Watan*, Lebanon ; *Time Magazine*, 7 February 1969.

20. Tel Aviv 321 (Barbour), 27 January 1968, *NARA* RG 59, 1967–1969, POL 29 Iraq.

21. IDF raids on Iraqi Expedition Force in Jordan in December 1968 retaliating for Iraqi shelling on civilian settlements in the Beit Shean Valley. Shay (2002), pp. 66–8.
    22 *WP*, 29 January 1969; Lee Hamilton, House of Representatives, *Congressional Record*, 8 May 1973, 119: 69.

23. State (Rogers) to New York UN Mission, 29 January 1968, *FRUS* E-4, Iraq #246.

24. Washington (Ben Ahron) to MFA Jerusalem, 2 January 1970. ZCA (Zionist Central Archive) S-610813.

25. Memorandum from Sisco, 1 January 1969; Memorandum from Rogers, 1 February 1969, *FRUS*, E-4 #249. Arthur Goldberg joined the AJC after he finished his term as US Ambassador to the UN in 1968.

26. In August 1969, as a result of a fire in Al-Aqsa Mosque by a foreign tourist. Israeli diplomats suggested keeping a low profile on the efforts to save the Iraqi community.

Washington Telegram 1731 A. Naim to S. Hillel, 27 August 1969; J. Ben-Ahron Washington to S. Hillel, 7 November, 1969. CZA Jerusalem, 6557/20.

27. *Iraq Observer*, 15 January 1970.
28. For example, Iraq signed friendship treaties with India and Indonesia. *Al-Nur* (Iraq), 13 January 1970; Reuters, 18 January 1970.
29. PAP (Polish News Agency), 23 January 1970. In *Sijel al-Araa*, February–March 1970.
30. A.Baram, 'Qawmiyya and Wataniyya in Ba'athi Iraq: The Search for a New Balance', *Middle Eastern Studies*, 19(2) (April 1983).
31. A. Baram, *National Integration and Exclusiveness in Political Thought and Practice in Iraq under the Ba'th 1968–1982*. PhD dissertation, (The Hebrew University of Jerusalem, 1986), pp. 110–13.
32. A. Baram, *Syria*, unpublished work, 1990 p. 69; BBC, 10 February 1969, quoting Damascus Radio, in E. Kienle *Ba'ath v. Ba'ath The Conflict between Syria and Iraq 1968–1989* (London: I.B. Tauris, 1991), p. 41.
33. The Euphrates River in Iraqi territory is 1,200km long, and an essential life line for agriculture. Syria and Iraq were discussing coordination on water distribution and dam construction. INA, 4 May, 1971, in *Sijel al-Araa* April–June 1971; Joint Committees for economic and trade cooperation had been established to deal with the growing Syria Iraqi trade. INA 1 April, 4 May 1971, in *Sijel al-Araa* April–June 1971.
34. Marr, *The Modern History of Iraq*, p. 214.
35. Baghdad Radio, 24 January1970. In Sijel al-Araa, January 1970.
36. Tim Niblock, *Iraq: The Contemporary State* (London: Croom Helm, 1982), pp. 126–7.
37. Further reading on the 'Black September' crisis: A. Douty, *Middle East Crisis: U.S. Decision-Making in 1958, 1970, 1973* (Berkley, University of California Press, 1984); H. Kissinger, *White House Years* (Boston: Little Brown & Co., 1979); A. Baram, 'Baathi Iraq and Hashimite Jordan: From Hostility to Alignment', *Middle East Journal*, 45(1) (1991) pp. 51–70; N. l. Ashton, *King Hussein of Jordan – A political life* (New Haven, Yale University Press, 2008), pp. 148–9; R. Mobley, 'U.S. Joint Military Contribution to Countering Syria's Invasion of Jordan', *Joint Force Quarterly*, 55(4) (2009), pp. 160–7.
38. The Iraqi army in 1970 consisted of six divisions (15,000 men in each division according to the Soviet model). Interview with Pesach Malovany, 25 March 2010; according to the London Institute for Strategic Studies the Iraqi military force numbered 101,800 men. IISS, *The Military Balance 1972–1973* (London, 1972), p. 31.
39. *Al-Jumhuriyya*, 27 September 1970; Al-Bakr in *Al-Jumhuriyya*, 18 July 1971.
40. *Al-Jumhuriyya*, 2 September 1970; Kissinger, *White House Years* (Boston: Little Brown & Co., 1979), pp. 598–9.
41. Baram, 'Baathi Iraq and Hashimite Jordan: From Hostility to Alignment', p. 53; RCC Announcement (*bayyan*) *Al-Jumhuriyya*, 27 September 1970.
42. *Al-Jumhuriyya* published, 2 September 1970, two letters signed by President Al-Bakr supporting the Palestinians, one of which addressed and was read by the Iraqi delegation to the Arab-American Students Conference.
43. Based on Vietnam lessons, according to the doctrine, the United States would support allies facing military threats with economic and military aid rather than with ground troops. President Richard Nixon, Second Annual Report to Congress on US Foreign Policy, 25 February 1971, *The American Presidency Project* (APP).
44. W. Isaacson, *Kissinger – A Biography* (New York, Simon and Schuster, 2005), pp. 285–315.
45. W. Quandt, 'The Middle East conflict in U.S. strategy 1970–1971', *Journal of Palestine Studies*, 1(1) (1971), p. 45.

46. Minutes of Combined WSAG and Review Group Meeting, 9 September 1970, *FRUS XXIV* #214.
47. N. Ashton, 'A "Special Relationship" Sometimes In Spite of Ourselves: Britain and Jordan, 1957–73', *The Journal of Imperial and Commonwealth History*, 33:2 (May 2005), p. 234; N. Ashton (2008), pp. 148–9; State (Rogers) to Amman, 20 September 1970; London 7568 to State, 20 September 1970, *FRUS XXIV* #279.
48. Kissinger, *White House Years*, p. 599; WSAG Meeting,10 September 1970, White House Situation Room, *DNSA*.
49. Kissinger, *White House Years*, pp. 605–6; Isaacson, *Kissinger – A Biography*, p. 291.
50. Memorandum from CIA/DDO (Miller), 9 September 1970, *FRUS XXIV* #212.
51. Kissinger, *White House Years*, p. 611.
52. Ambassador MacArthur appeal to the Shah: Tehran, 17 September 1970, FRUS XXIV#259.
53. Nixon-Kissinger Telcons, 17 September 1970, 9:00AM, (partially sanitised copy) *DNSA*.
54. WSAG Meeting, 17 September 1970, NSC Files, *Nixon Presidential Library*, H-77, OCI-0099/70.
55. Quandt, 'The Middle East conflict in U.S. strategy 1970–1971', p. 48.
56. R. Dallek, *Nixon and Kissinger – Partners in Power* (New York, Harper Collins, 2007), pp. 225–6.
57. L. Dean Brown Interview, 17 May 1989, *ADST*.
58. NSC Meeting, 21 September 1970, *FRUS XXIV* # 299; NSC Meeting 22 September 1970, FRUS XXIV#313.
59. Philip Stoddard INR quoted in Ben Ahron (Washington) to Jerusalem, 2 December 1970, *ISA* (Israel State Archive) 4548/14.
60. Dr Tariq al-Tel (Grandson of Wasfi al-Tel-PM of Jordan, assassinated by 'Black September') in an interview with Baram, Oxford, December 1989.
61. British Embassy Baghdad (D.F. Hawley): Iraq Annual Report for 1970, 4 January 1971, FCO 17/1532, *TNA*.
62. Sluglett & Sluglett, *Iraq since 1958, From Revolution to Dictatorship*, pp.133–4.
63. Baram, 'Baathi Iraq and Hashimite Jordan: From Hostility to Alignment'; Baram, *National Integration and Exclusiveness in Political Thought and Practice in Iraq under the Ba'th 1968–1982*, pp. 119–21; mass demonstrations in Iraq in support of the Palestinians in *Al-Jumhuriyya* 19, 29 September 1970.
64. Iraqi Salah al-Din Force experienced Jordanian shelling in early September, following the PFLP hijacking *Al-Jumhuriyya*, 9 September 1970.
65. *Al-Jumhuriyya*, 22 September 1970.
66. Baram, 'Baathi Iraq and Hashimite Jordan: From Hostility to Alignment'.
67. Kuwait (Walsh), 31 March 1971, *NARA*.
68. Baram, *Syria* (unpublished work, 1990?), pp. 241–2; Beirut (Buffum), 16 October 1970, *NARA* RG 59.
69. On the Ba'thi secret plan to incriminate Hardan: Hardan al-Tikriti, Ahmad Ra'if, *kunna 'Isaba min al-lussus wa al-qarala khalfa milishiyyat Saddam lil-i'dam: mudhkirat siyyasi Iraqi* (Cairo: al-Zahra, 1990).
70. The Interim Constitution was amended later. The official version of 1974 in English in Khadduri (1978), Appendix A, pp. 183–98,The National Charter of 15 November 1971, Appendix B, pp. 199–229.
71. Marr, *The Modern History of Iraq*, p. 215.

72. *Ibid.*, p. 216; Sluglett & Sluglett, *Iraq since 1958, From Revolution to Dictatorship*, pp. 134–5.
73. The Iraqi Communist Party (ICP) was founded in 1934. For further details: Tareq Y. Ismael, *The Rise and Fall of the Communist Party of Iraq* (New York: Cambridge University Press, 2008).
74. Batatu, *The Old Social Classes, and the Revolutionary Movements of Iraq*, pp. 988–90, 1099–191;Sluglett & Sluglett, *Iraq since 1958, From Revolution to Dictatorship*, p.140.
75. Mokram Talabani appointed as Irrigation Minister, Omar Abdallah as State Minister, Moscow 5798 (Beam), 16 June 1972, *FRUS* E-4 #317; Khadduri, *Socialist Iraq*, pp.98–100; Batatu, *The Old Social Classes, and the Revolutionary Movements of Iraq*, pp. 1108–9.
76. Batatu, *The Old Social Classes, and the Revolutionary Movements of Iraq*, pp. 1100–102. While Aziz Muhammad of the ICP-Central Committee, was negotiating with the Ba'th, the cessassionists faction ICP-Central Leadership led by Aziz al-Hajj tried to disrupt the negotiations violently, March–April 1969.
77. Batatu, *The Old Social Classes, and the Revolutionary Movements of Iraq*, p.1102. Based on Communist publications issued by exiles.
78. *MER* 1969–1970, pp. 723–4.
79. Ideological contradiction had an impact on daily life. Any 'progressive' legislation initiated by the Ba'th in particular on family issues, the status of women, banking and finance was in conflict with the Shari'a. Chibli Mallat, 'Shiism and Sunnism in Iraq: Revising the Codes', *Arab Law Quarterly*, 8(2) (1993), pp. 141–59.
80. *MER*, 1969–1970, p. 728.
81. C. Tripp, *A History of Iraq* (Cambridge UK: Cambridge University Press, 2001), p, 203; Ofra Bengio,'Shi'is and Politics in Ba'thi Iraq', *Middle Eastern Studies*, 21(1) (1985), pp. 1–14.
82. Baram, 'The Radical Shi'ite Opposition Movement in Iraq' in E. Sivan & M. Friedman (eds), *Religious Radicalism and Politics in the Middle East* (New York: SUNY University Press 1990), pp. 112–13.
84. Batatu, 'Shi'i organizations in Iraq: Al-Da'wa al-Islamiyyah wal- Mujahidin' in J.R.I Cole & N.R. Keddie (eds), *Shi'ism and Social Protest* (New Haven: Yale University Press, 1986), p. 180; C. Mallat, 'Religious militancy in contemporary Iraq: Muhammad Baqer as-Sadr and the Sunni-Shia paradigm', *Third World Quarterly*, 1(2) (1988), pp. 699–729; Baram, 'The Radical Shi'ite Opposition Movement in Iraq', p. 124.
85. *FBIS SOV* 23, 27 March 1969.
86. Marr, *The Modern History of Iraq*, p. 225.
87. Opposing the treaty were mostly the 'Radical faction' of the Ba'thi leadership, against the 'pragmatic faction' of Al-Bakr and Saddam Hussein.
88. State 12737 to Tehran, London and Moscow, 22 January 1972, *FRUS* E-4 #29.
89. P. Kiely, 'Through distorted lenses – Iraq and balance of power politics 1969–1979', Ryan and Kiely (eds) *America and Iraq: Policy-Making Intervention and Regional Politics since 1958* (New York: Routledge, 2008), pp. 44–5.
90. For example, statement of the Iranian F.M. Ardeshir Zahedi at Meeting of the CENTO Ministers with President Nixon, 14 May 1970, *FRUS XXIV* #66.
91. Memorandum from State (Eliot), 13 April 1972, RG 59, Central Files 1970–73, IRAQ-USSR, *NARA*.
92. CIA Information cable, TDCS DB315/02084-72, 10 March 1972, FRUS E-4 #300; CIA Intelligence Memorandum 0865/72, 12 May 1972. FRUS E-4 #307.
93. Briefing Paper for the President: 'Iraqi Politics in Perspective', 18 May 1972, FRUS E-4 #308.

94. Kissinger (1979), pp. 1262–3; Kissinger, *Years of Upheaval* (Boston, Little Brown & Company, 1982), p. 524.
95. Isaacson, *Kissinger – A Biography*, p.564.
96. INA, 1 June 1972.
97. Penrose & Penrose, *Iraq: International Relations and National Development* (Boulder CO: Westview Press, 1978), p. 433; Marr, *The Modern History of Iraq*, p. 223; M. Brown, 'the Nationalization of the IPC', *IJMES* 10:1 (February 1979), pp.107–24.
98. F. Matar, *Saddam Hussein – The Man, the Cause and the Future* (London: Third World Center, 1981), p. 233.
99. Arab Ba'th Socialist Party, *How the Revolution confronts the Imperialist – Conspiracy and the Counter Revolution* (Baghdad, 1972), p.38.
100. Marr, *The Modern History of Iraq*, pp.223–4; American companies (Exxon Mobile) maintained that the settlement was tilted and more favorable to the European partners.
101. *Al-Jumhuriyya*, 1 June 1972; Interview with Michel Aflaq Chairman of the Ba'th National Command and his deputy Shibli Aysami 1974,1975; M. Khadduri, *Socialist Iraq*, p. 125.
102. Memorandum from State, Bureau of Economic Affairs: 'Iraq's 1 June decision to nationalize the IPC', 2 June 1972, *NARA Nixon Library* ; CIA Intelligence Memorandum, ER IM 72-92, June 1972, *FRUS* E 4#311.
103. Jonathan C. Randall, 'Iraq and France reach accord after seizure of oil firm', *WP*, 19 June 1972; Saddam Hussein, 'The National and International Politics', Statement to the Iraqi ambassadors in Western Europe and Japan, 12 June 1975, in Saddam Hussein, *Social and Foreign Affairs in Iraq* (London, 1977).
104. Dusko Doder, 'Oil Companies Assail U.S. Support of Israel', *WP*, 8 June 1972.
105. Former Ambassador of Belgium Dupret served US interests dedicatedly since June 1967. He advised Washington not to ignore the Iraqi request to evacuate the building, out of concern for the safety of American citizens in Baghdad. Dupret had been known for his courage. The British ambassador Balfour-Paul wrote that he gave shelter to one of the leaders of the opposition, wanted by Iraqi security, and then smuggled him personally in the trunk of his car to Kuwait. Dupret was transferred to Morocco, and in July 1971, was gunned down in a party of King Hassan by armoured assailants. G. Balfour Paul, *Bagpipes in Babylon* (London: I.B. Tauris, 2006), p. 216; MOC Marcel Dupret, George Moffitt, Brussels, 20 March 1969, *FRUS*, E-4 #256; *Time Magazine*, 21July 1971.
106. Dusko Doder, 'Oil Companies Assail U.S. Support of Israel', *WP*, 25 May 1971; Jonathan C. Randal, 'Paris Dilemma: Iraq's Offer or Western Ties', *WP*, 14 June 1972.
107. Memorandum from State (Eliot) 25 May 1971, *NARA* (7107779), *Nixon Library*, NSC Files.
108. The message of the Ambassador of Belgium was transferred by the British Embassy to State Department: State 92470 to the Embassy in Brussels, 26 May 1971, *FRUS* E-4 # 291.
109. Interview with Arthur L. Lowrie, 23 December 1989, *ADST*.
110. Memorandum from State (Sisco), 25 May 1972, *FRUS* E-4 #309.
111. State 16061 to Brussels, 28 January 1972, *NARA* RG 59 POL 17 US-Iraq.
112. Ba'th, *How the Revolution confronts the Imperialist*, 17, 20, 22; *Al-Thawra*, 14 January 1972.
113. Belgium 2879, 3 August 1972, *FRUS* E-4#323. The rumours about closer bilateral relations had been denied in the *Alif Ba* magazine, 2 August 1971.

114. Lowrie was at a crossroad in his career, following his expulsion from Khartum as PNG. He was not admitted to the Tunisian desk, due to the objection of the Ambassador to Tunisia Russel. FSO ranks 3-4 had been considered a bottleneck for career diplomats that could have led to his compulsory early retirement. Head of Interest Section, was an opportunity for future promotion: interview with Arthur L. Lowrie, 23 December 1989, *ADST*; D.P. Warwick, *A Theory of Public Bureaucracy: Politics, Personality and Organization in the State Department* (Cambridge, MA: Harvard, 1975).

115. Lowrie's background was typical of the generalised definition of an 'Arabist'. Growing up in a small town in Pennsylvania, he encountered places far abroad as a young recruit to the air force stationed in Libya. With an army veteran scholarship he graduated Allegheny College in Pennsylvania. As a foreign service officer he acquired Arabic in Lebanon. After retirement he protested the label 'Arabist' attributed to him, and some of his colleagues that became a liable/derogatory. Yet, pretty much like the stereotype, he adhered to anti-Israeli criticism, attacking the 'Zionist Lobby' in the US for disrupting relations between the US and the Arabs.
Interview with Arthur L. Lowrie, 23 December 1989, *ADST*; Joseph Kraft, 'Those Arabists in the State Department', *NYT Magazine*, 7 November, 1971.

116. Letter from Baghdad (Lowrie) to NEA, 18 December 1972, *FRUS* E-4 #328.

117. Baghdad (Lowrie), A-6, 1 December 1972, *FRUS* E 4 #328.

118. NIE 36.2-72, 21 December 1972, *FRUS* E-4 #330.

2

Confronting Major Challenges, 1973–5

The consolidation of the ideological platform of the Ba'th, as reflected in the 1974 National Committee Conference, indicated a more pragmatic and proactive approach towards the West, alongside the intensifying of relations with the USSR. In October 1973, Iraq dispatched significant forces to the Syrian front with Israel, a move that improved Iraq's poor image among the Arabs resulting from the September 1970 events. The armed conflict with the Kurds reached a new peak, when Mulla Mustafa Barzani, supported by Iran, Israel and the United States, led a full-scale rebellion in April 1974. Saddam, seeing a dangerous risk to the regime, agreed to most of Iran's territorial demands in the Algiers Agreement in 1975, which instantly ended the Kurdish rebellion. Bilateral relations with the United States following 1973 showed some improvement, mostly in increased trade. Iraq did not comply with the Arab oil boycott of 1973, putting first financial considerations and benefitting from the sky-rising oil rates. It became an attractive destination for foreign investment. The richer and stronger Iraq became, the more of an anti-American radicalised position was taken by the Ba'th, in particular towards any initiatives to find a political solution to the conflict with Israel.

The exposure of an abortive plot against the regime, planned from within by Nazim Kzar, the head of the Iraqi Intelligence Service (IIS), known as the *Mukhabarat*, traumatised the leadership; as a result, even harsher oppressive measures were taken to deter and suppress any opposition or disloyalty. The coup attempt, on 30 June 1973, created a shock not just because Kzar was a trusted member of the leadership, but because of how close it came to succeeding. Kzar was affiliated with the hardline faction of the Ba'th leadership, and had voiced opposition to the March agreements with the Kurds and the partnership with the Communists. He called for more active support of the Palestinians and an Iraqi confrontation with Israel, rather than shelving the Palestinian issue. As head of *Mukhabarat*, he was known for his extreme brutality toward detainees.[1]

By 2004, Saddam had taken a lenient view of Kzar. While under arrest, he told the FBI that Kzar had 'old-fashioned' principles and an obsessive suspicion of communist presence among army officers and Ba'th youth and, therefore, 'became a burden on the party'.[2] In any case Al-Bakr and Saddam became more obsessive in their control, watching even the closest circles in the party and conducting purges in the leadership. Loyal confidants were appointed to the Regional Command, and ministers were reshuffled.[3] The United States' Interest Section reported on atmosphere of fear and anxiety in the streets, following the purges, oppressive measures against civilians and arbitrary arrests. Baghdad neighbourhoods became unsafe, due to rumours of gruesome violence, including rape and murders, occurring even in middle-class areas. Lowrie seemed to accept the official version that the crimes were perpetrated by criminals, and the regime established stability and public order. He concluded his report with a personal comment that, in spite of the internal power struggle within the Ba'th, Saddam was successful in promoting foreign and economic policies to expand economic relations with the West.[4]

October 1973: Once Again at War with Israel

Egypt and Syria did not include Iraq in their secret plans to attack Israel. As mentioned earlier, the Ba'th position opposed confronting Israel before gaining enough strength to tip the military balance.[5] Moreover, substantial army forces had still been deployed in the Kurdish area.[6] Nevertheless, as soon as war broke out, Al-Bakr announced that Iraqi forces would join the battle against Israel, and he dispatched a significant part of the Iraqi forces to the Golan Heights. Iraq also resumed diplomatic relations with Iran to calm the Kurdish-Iranian front and to make available the forces to 'confront the Zionist enemy'.[7]

The Iraqi leadership intended to dispatch three divisions to the Israeli front, approximately 60,000 men – half of the Iraqi infantry – two thirds of the armoured corps, and two thirds of the air force. After the war, the Iraqis claimed with pride that they succeeded in containing Israeli forces that were advancing towards Damascus. That occurred when the well-trained and equipped *Ibn-al-Walid* armoured brigade, arriving in the Golan front on 10–11 October, surprised an Israeli Defense Force (IDF) armoured division under the command of Major General Dan Lanner and delayed the Israeli counter-offensive towards Damascus.[8] Further Iraqi-Israeli military engagements occurred from 15–22 October when the UN ceasefire was declared. Other Iraqi units that reached the Golan before the ceasefire included two armoured divisions, two infantry brigades (including the Mountaineers Brigade), and two special-forces battalions (commando and paratrooper).[9]

In general, Iraqi forces did not demonstrate their full military capability. That could have been attributed to a lack of earlier, joint planning and coordination, since the Syrians had kept Iraq in the dark. Yet, major fundamental failures were intrinsic, especially in logistics, such as a shortage of tank transporters, and a lack of proper communication with the Syrian units.[10] The Ba'th presented the fight against Israel as a heroic victory, despite the high losses of about 1,000 dead and injured, 111 tanks destroyed and 26 airplanes shot down. Nevertheless, the Iraqi army gained practical experience, and lessons were drawn and applied later, when Iraq made a strategic decision to significantly increase the size of its army and its technological capabilities.[11]

During the war, the Iraqi regime had consistently opposed any ceasefire with Israel, including UN resolutions. On 29 October, the RCC announced the withdrawal of the expedition force from Syria in protest against the ceasefire. Immediately after, Iraq resumed propaganda attacks against Syria.[12]

American Involvement in the War

The 6 October outbreak of war took the United States by surprise, just as it did Israel. Nixon viewed the surprise Arab attack as Israel's Pearl Harbor. He was determined to get involved, and stated: 'The Israelis must not be allowed to lose.'[13] According to Kissinger, the United States could not tolerate a defeat of Israel's American-made weaponry to the Arabs' Soviet-made weaponry, for that could tip the political and strategic balance in the region to the disadvantage of American interests. Therefore, it was an American strategic interest to prevent an Israeli defeat, and deal with rapprochement with the Arabs later.[14] As with Black September, Kissinger used a direct, diplomatic channel with Moscow to prevent the Soviets' direct involvement through its Arab allies, and thereby reach a ceasefire. Kissinger considered that the United States, which enjoyed relations with both the Arabs and Israel, had leverage on all the parties in order to end the conflict.[15] Early in the war, Washington assumed that Israel could easily beat the attacking Syrian and Egyptian forces, and White House officials even raised their concern that an overwhelming Arab defeat by Israel would harm American relations with Arab states, thus reducing the incentives for Israel to reach a political solution to end the conflict.[16] As Kissinger told Defense Secretary James Schlesinger during the second week of the war: 'The best result would be if Israel comes out a little ahead but got bloodied in the process, and if the U.S. stays clean.'[17]

Consequently the IDF turned from defense to counterattack on both the Syrian and Egyptian fronts and, despite suffering heavy losses, it regained territory. The White House was reluctant to demonstrate open military support, mindful of its relations with oil-producing allies in the Gulf.[18] That concern proved to be a self-fulfilling prophecy. Perhaps, that was the reason for Kissinger's hesitant attitude regarding an airlift to Israel even on 10 October, when the Soviets' airlift to Syria, Egypt and Iraq was openly known. [19]Only on 14 October did America commence an airlift to Israel, sending a Hercules C-130 and a Starlifter C.[20] America's European allies – including Great Britain, its closest ally – did not share Washington's support for Israel. After a ceasefire was reached in December 1973, Kissinger even told his British counterpart, Sir Alec Douglas-Home, that the United States had not wanted an Israeli victory. Kissinger complained that he had been totally misled by Israel over its acceptance of the ceasefire, referring to the IDF's siege of the Egyptian Third Division west of the Suez Canal. He explained that tension intensified when intelligence revealed that, on 22 October, a Soviet vessel, carrying nuclear weapons, crossed the Dardanelles straits on its way from the Black Sea to the Mediterranean and returned a week later.[21] This argument intended to clarify the motive behind the American declaration of nuclear alert 24–5 October, as a strong response to the Soviet idea to dispatch forces to the Sinai to observe the ceasefire alongside the Americans.[22]

The United States was not surprised by the Iraqi decision to join the 1967 war. It did not consider Iraq's military to be a serious factor that might have made a significant impact on the battlefield.[23] Still, Iraq was a major landing point for the Soviet airlift. Between 11 and 15 October 1973, sixty-six Soviet cargo planes landed in Iraq, and from there carried supplies to the Syrian front, supplementing the 130 Soviet planes sent to Syria and 93 to Egypt.[24] Just before the war, fourteen Soviet TU-22 aircraft arrived in Iraq, manned by Iraqi pilots who had been trained in the USSR.[25] The Pentagon determined that this fourteen Tupolev shipment was a pre-planned procurement to offset the increased Iranian procurement of American aircraft, so it was not considered a risk to the regional balance.[26] Iraq was not mentioned in the ceasefire deliberations between Israel, Syria and Egypt. The United States had focused its diplomatic efforts on the Arab states that maintained regular diplomatic communication with Washington, namely, Jordan, Saudi Arabia, Kuwait, Morocco and Algeria.[27]

Domestically, the White House was handling the crisis in the Middle East under the shadow of dramatic developments in the Watergate scandal. On 10 October, the fourth day of the war, Vice President Spiro Agnew resigned. Nixon fired Watergate Special Prosecutor Archibald Cox, which prompted Attorney General Elliot Richardson to resign. The same day, Kissinger was in Moscow discussing a ceasefire.[28] While Nixon was involved in all diplomatic and military moves, in practice he gave Kissinger a free hand to manage the crisis. It was essential for the administration to demonstrate to Middle Eastern countries and to the Soviet Union that the

Watergate scandal and the deterioration domestically of trust in Nixon had no effect on the United States' conduct of foreign affairs and national security. Both the White House and Congress maintained bipartisan support for Israel and approved dispatching to Israel $2.9 billion in military supplies.[29]

On 9 October, Lowrie was summoned to the Ministry of Foreign Affairs to receive a demarche, demanding that Washington take all measures against the recruiting of 'mercenaries' to fight for Israel.[30] The State Department responded that it was illegal for American citizens to enlist themselves or others in the US for a foreign army, but there was 'no impediment to an American volunteering abroad to serve in armed forces of another country.'[31] From 14 October, news emerged about the American airlift to Israel. That infuriated all the Arab states. Iraqi newspapers attacked US-Israeli collaboration against the Arabs. Moreover, the Israeli attack that paralysed the Iraqi Petroleum Company's Banyas oil terminal in Syria was portrayed by Iraqi media as a 'special service by Israel to her American masters', avenging the American companies' nationalisation.[32]

Following the ceasefire and the return of the Iraqi expedition force, US citizens in Baghdad felt safe again. Lowrie's concern that American support for Israel in the war would harm the still-evolving economic relations proved false. In mid-November, Lowrie reported to Washington with great relief that the Iraqi government had resumed diplomatic contacts with him as before the war: back to procurement plans based on competition and business considerations, and expressing commercial interests in American technologies.[33]

'Iraq First': Evading the Arab Oil Embargo

The Ba'th held a hard-line position, rejecting all ceasefire agreements and, on oil policy, adopting a position independent of the Arab consensus.

Iraq's open rhetoric encouraged the use of oil as a weapon of political protest against the United States and other countries that had supported Israel. Iraq called on Arab states to nationalise all oil facilities, as Iraq had done. It encouraged oil consumer states to take anti-Israeli positions, and reciprocated with favourable oil-supply contracts.[34]

In practice, Iraq acted upon its economic interests and market conditions, avoiding any activity that might have harmed its oil revenues,[35] while preaching to other oil-producing states to boycott the United States in retaliation for its supporting Israel.[36]

Iraq did not join the Arab oil embargo on Western states that supported Israel (Canada, Japan, the Netherlands, the UK and the US), and had been criticised by other Arab oil suppliers. As soon as the war ended, Iraq initiated negotiations for compensation with the BPC (Basra Petroleum Company), which it had nationalised earlier, to resume oil production immediately.[37] Iraq continued to conduct an independent oil policy: it did not attend the Algiers Summit of 26–8 November 1973 that extended the oil boycott.[38] On 17 March 1974, Arab oil ministers lifted the oil embargo, yet, all oil producers, including Iraq, benefitted from the steep rise in prices that resulted from an oil shortage as well as from OPEC policies, following the market conditions rather than OPEC policy. For example, Iraq took advantage of the oil shortage and increased production ignoring the OPEC resolution, and exported Iraqi oil, at times below OPEC rates to compete with other suppliers.[39] When criticised by other OPEC members, Iraq denied all allegations.[40] But Saddam himself stated, on 21 December 1973, that reducing oil production would harm Western Europe and Japan, but not the United States.[41] A similarly surprising statement reached the White House from president al-Bakr. In a 23 January 1974 letter to Nixon that was submitted through Lowrie, the head of the Baghdad US legation Al-Bakr stressed an independent and responsible position on oil policy, and pointed out how Iraq in that way differed from other OPEC members. The long, detailed letter in Arabic, made public in the Iraqi media, rejected Nixon's invitation for cooperation, and mentioned that poor nations are 'victims of imperialism'. Lowrie, excited by receiving this unusual letter, said he viewed it as a positive signal Iraq was sending the United States.[42]

In Washington, however, the letter was received differently. Nixon had actually written to the heads of oil-producing countries, calling for close cooperation between supplier and consumer countries. Baghdad had been sent a copy by mistake. Al-Bakr's detailed response seemed, then, to reveal an eagerness of an ambitious Iraq for the very reference by the American superpower, and used it as an opportunity for further public defiance. From a Ba'th prospective, the United States marginalised Iraq and did not acknowledge that its independent oil policy was driven by 'capitalistic considerations'.[43] In fact, the United States had faced a serious energy crisis as a result of the shortage of oil and skyrocketing prices. The US State and Energy departments were aware, of course, of Iraqi oil policy, yet the main Arab suppliers were Saudi Arabia and Kuwait both of which followed OPEC price policy.[44] Iraq's emergence as the holder of the Middle East's second-largest oil reserves had been known but the US kept relying on her allies in the Gulf.

Iraq's Foreign Policy

On 15 July 1973, both the *N.Y. Times* and *Washington Post* stated that Saddam was interested in improving relations with Kuwait, Iran, and Great

Britain – and with the United States, conditioned on a 'change of attitude' in Washington regarding its pro-Israel bent. Saddam added that, in spite of enjoying close relations with the USSR, Iraq was not a satellite state, and that major markets for Iraqi oil were in the West. [45]When the Iraqi Interest Section in Washington was approached by the State Department, asking for clarification of this statement, the official answer was that Saddam meant improving economic, not political, relations with the United States, alluding to the suggestion that American companies would not be discriminated against. [46]

The Ba'th did choose a new and more sophisticated and nuanced orientation in foreign policy. According to the Eighth Congress of the Regional Command Report, the most important executive body of the Iraqi Ba'th, not all Western countries are 'enemies and capitalists' of Arabs; some disagree with the American position and have 'moderate views' toward the Arabs. The term for this trend is known in Ba'th ideological terminology as *istiqlaliyya* (independence)[47] which meant, in this case, keeping Iraq from dependence on any superpower, or from being held hostage to the East-West confrontation. This new orientation was guided by the principle of flexibility (*muruna*) or pragmatism in international relations. As defined in a Ba'thi publication: 'The principle of *istiqlaliyya* on the theoretical level, the decision-making level and the executive level, means rejection of all affiliation or alliance with any of the international blocs. The same principle applies for the Iraqi national (*watani*) level, and the Arab national (*qawmi*) level. This principle is fundamental to our right as a nation to choose our independent way to fulfill our eternal mission.' [48]

Iraq's Ambiguous Relations with the Soviet Union

During the period of 1972–5, cooperation between Iraq and the USSR reached new heights. The Soviets welcomed the nationalisation of the oil industry and the ICP's joining the governing coalition. Technological, economic and military cooperation between the two countries was legally binding in long-term contracts. The Soviets used Iraqi facilities to transport supplies, bound mostly for the Syrian-Israeli front and for the Iraqi expedition force. [49]

Nevertheless, from 1973 onward, Ba'thi Iraq expressed disagreements with certain Soviet positions, as well as disappointment with Soviet assistance and cooperation. But an exponential rise in oil revenues enabled the Ba'th to conduct a somewhat independent policy – for example, by objecting fiercely to all ceasefire negotiations with Israel, which went against the Soviet position, and by complaining about the efficiency of Soviet supplies during the fighting and about the price charged for spare parts.[50]

Other financial frustrations centered on the 1972 agreement for the Soviets to purchase Iraqi oil until 1980 at a low rate, with the right to resell it to a third party. The agreement was signed when Iraq intended to nationalise IPC and expected to have serious difficulties exporting oil. But even after oil prices soared to $18 a barrel, the Soviets were still paying $3, then reselling it at high profits to West Germany, Denmark, Switzerland and even the United States and the Netherlands that had been under the OPEC oil embargo. Detailed reports from Iraq's Interest Section actually served Baghdad's deliberate policy of ambiguity regarding its alleged intention to move away from the Soviet bloc.

These controversies had no effect on Iraq's intensifying relations with the USSR and Soviet allies. Indeed, Iraq closed down the cultural centres of Czechoslovakia, Bulgaria and East Germany as retaliation for those countries' not allowing the opening of similar Iraqi centres in their capitals. The trio were surprised by this demand for reciprocity, coming as it was from a Third World state. More damaging was Iraq's decision to stop the bartering of oil and instead demanding payment in hard currency.[51] Countries dependent on Iraqi oil had to swallow their pride and pay the higher rate demanded.[52] Lowrie also perceived Iraq's interest in Western technology as a blow to the USSR, particularly Iraq's preference for Boeing civilian aircraft over the Soviet Tupolev.[53]

Another signal of defiance was the Ba'th warming of relations with China. The Soviet-Sino split had been going on since the early 1960s, but relations became even more strained following the visit of President Nixon to China in 1972. The Chinese deputy minister for foreign trade was officially received by both al-Bakr and Saddam in a visit widely covered by the Iraqi press.[54] Diplomatic correspondence that reached Washington from Moscow and Baghdad reported on controversies with the Soviets but was apparently overstated, perhaps biased or wishful thinking.[55] In June 1975, Iraq was accepted to the Soviet-led Council for Mutual Economic Assistance (COMECON) as an observer.[56] Iraqi linkage with the USSR had been essential for the Iraqi army, whose doctrine, weaponry and logistics remained totally dependent on an ongoing Soviet supply.

The USSR and Iraq were aware of American and Iranian concerns regarding Soviet access to the Persian Gulf, as part of the American ambition to establish a naval presence in the Indian Ocean and the Horn of Africa[57]. Iraq issued an outright denial of US President Gerald Ford's statement alleging that 'active Soviet bases' existed in Iraq, including at the port of *Um Qasr* that was inaugurated that year, which happened to be a modern, deep-water harbour, constructed by the Soviets.[58] Yet Ba'th statements rejected all foreign presence in the Persian Gulf as inconsistent with its *istiqlaliyya* foreign policy, yet what they feared most was an American encroachment in response to Soviet presence. Tension increased when the United States and the British Royal Navy held a large naval manoeuvre, dubbed 'Midlink 74', in the Indian Ocean together with Central Treaty Organization (CENTO) states Iran and Pakistan. Consequently, Um Qasr did not turn into a Soviet naval base.[59] *Washington Post* columnists Rowland Evans and Robert Novak were invited by the Ba'th to visit and see for themselves that the port and naval base were Soviet free, staffed solely by Iraqis.[60]

Iraqi Diplomatic Activism vis-à-vis the Non-aligned Countries

In addition to enjoying close relations with the European member-states of the Socialist International, Iraq invested diplomatic efforts in the developing countries of Africa and Asia including India, China and North Korea. The Non-Aligned Movement (NAM) states had become the largest group in the UN, and had been growing ever since as newly independent states joined the world body.[61] Saddam visited India and Yugoslavia; in January 1975, he declared that Iraq considered non-alliance to be at the core of its foreign policy and intended to play an active role in the movement. Consequently, Iraq officially offered to host the NAM Summit in Baghdad in 1980.[62] Diplomatic exchanges with socialist and underdeveloped states served another purpose: gaining diplomatic support for low-cost financial assistance, even modest assistance was significant to some impoverished states. The missions from these states had been given generous hospitality, including media coverage. To Eastern Block and NAM states, Iraq dispatched Ba'thi delegates, Kurds, and Communists, all of which was meant to demonstrate the diversity of the Iraqi leadership.[63] In return, these states voted for Iraqi candidates in the international organisations and supported Iraqi-sponsored resolutions. India attracted special attention in Iraq. Beyond being a leading NAM state, India featured technological institutions and modern industry. During his visit to India in late March 1974, Saddam initiated a military-technology deal to purchase parts and components to service his country's Soviet-made MiG aircrafts, and thus reduce Iraqi dependence on the Soviet Union.[64] No sooner had this information leaked to the *Washington Post* than India denied it, aware of American sensitivity and a possible reaction.[65] The joint Iraq-India statement used moderate language, without the usual denunciation of the United States.[66]

Evolving relations with NAM states introduced some diplomatic contradictions and conflicts, For example, the Ba'th mass expulsion of Shi'i foreigners was aimed mostly at Shi'i students of Iranian descent, but included such friendly non-Sunni NAM states' citizens as India, Pakistan and Afghanistan. Iraq was the third state (after India and the USSR) to recognise the Da'ud regime that overthrew the Afghani monarchy, doing so in return for Afghanistan's support for Iraq against Iran. It should be noted, though, that Da'ud dispatched an envoy to Baghdad to protect the 28,000 Afghani citizens in Iraq.[67]

The efforts and resources the Ba'th invested in developing a proactive foreign policy even in remote or underdeveloped states, coupled with Iraqi declarations of *istiqlaliyyah*, sustained Iraq's international image as a pragmatic state and the illusion that closer relations with the United States was a matter of time.

The Ba'th's Seditious Policy

According to State Department reports, Iraq was financially supporting Ba'thi, pro-Iraqi organisations in Arab states, as well as assisting 'progressive' opposition organisations fighting such 'reactionary' regimes as Oman and Iran. Iraq was also directly recruiting supporters in Jordan and Saudi Arabia. It did so by operating radio stations, like *Sawt al-Jazeera* Broadcasting, targeting the Gulf States in various frequencies to counter Saudi jamming.[68] In early February 1974, about fifty organisations based outside Iraq participated in a conference in Baghdad, convened to support Iraq's fight against the Kurds and Iran. The list of participants reveals organisations outside Iraq presumably receiving Iraqi financial support.[69] The United States was aware of this activity, which was meant to destabilise conservative, pro-American regimes by supporting pro-Soviet groups.[70] In February 1973, Pakistan declared the Iraqi ambassador to Islamabad *persona non grata*, following detection of Soviet arms in an Iraqi diplomatic pouch. Pakistani-Iraqi relations improved only after al-Bakr's apology and Iraq's clarification that the weapons' destination had not been Pakistan, but the Baluchis in Iran, presumably for anti-Shah activity.[71] This incident indicated that the Ba'th's activity reached into Arab lands as well.

Bilateral Relations

Iraqi Mistrust of America

Despite Iraqi statements welcoming American business in Iraq, suspicion and mistrust of foreigners continued. The Iraqis introduced difficulties for American citizens applying for a visa, and those carrying diplomatic passports encountered suspicious attitudes that seemed like paranoia of American espionage. Even Lowrie, who had been eager to develop trade relations, advised businesspeople and other Americans to limit their visits to Iraq to essential trips, and instructed visitors to avoid any mention of having visited Israel.[72] Iraq refused to allow private aeroplanes to proceed through Iraqi airspace, and it denied visa applications from archaeologists from New York's Metropolitan Museum of Art, who had participated in excavations of *Al-Hiba*, in southern Iraq, for seventeen years; meanwhile, the archaeologists' colleagues from Belgium, France and Germany were allowed to return to Iraq.[73]

Another example demonstrates more explicitly that Iraqi mistrust was deeply rooted in a basic misperception of the United States, which produced distorted interpretations of American diplomacy. The US State Department had arranged a regional Chiefs of Missions Conference (COM) in Teheran, 23–4 April 1973. It was a regular forum the department convened worldwide for mutual updates and consultation of American diplomats on regional issues, as well as exchanges with officials from the State's Bureau of Near East Affairs who flew in from Washington.[74] This time, however, Iraq considered the gathering a direct threat. At least six editorials in Iraqi newspapers referred to the conference as a 'Zionist conspiracy' against Iraq. Iraqi Deputy Foreign Minister Taqa submitted a formal demarche to the Belgian ambassador in Baghdad, saying: 'We know it was directed against Iraq.'[75]

The NEA Chiefs of Mission conference, followed by CENTO Council of Ministers' Meeting from 9–11 June 1973 in Teheran as well, amplified Iraq's perception of an Iranian-Western conspiracy. Washington's appointment of CIA Director Richard Helms as ambassador to Teheran verified this perception in Iraqi eyes.

An editorial published in the *Alif Ba'* weekly magazine argued that the very fact that the United States appointed a senior intelligence official, who was an expert in contriving conspiracies, indicated that the Americans intended to increase their influence in the Gulf through Iran.[76]

Nixon's near-impeachment had been so foreign to Iraqi thinking that the country's newspapers attributed the Watergate scandal to an alleged Zionist conspiracy.[77] Similar assertions about the United States were repeated in Iraq over the years in public, by senior Iraqi officials during face to face meetings with American visitors.

US Export Control of Military Technology to Iraq

The United States closely followed the progress of the Soviet Union's military exports to Iraq. While encouraging civilian trade with Iraq, Washington under both the Ford and Carter administrations applied export controls on

American military exports. Boeing's contracts with the Iraqi government to supply civilian aircrafts reached $220 million by the end of 1975. Other civilian contracts had been signed, such as with the Houston Texas based Brown & Root for constructing an oil terminal.[78] The American Interest Section in Baghdad was promoting trade relations and facilitating contacts between the Iraqi government and potential investors.[79] The Ba'th party designed the ideological base for this trend to expand trade with the West, following the decision to build up the Iraqi army as capable and modern, equipped with the best Western technology. Diversifying sources of supplies, alongside the ongoing flow from the Soviet Union, served the Ba'th's ambition to enlarge the volume of the military and to adopt modern technology. This included establishing manufacturing plants for the self-production of spare parts and military components. Deputy Prime Minister Taha Yasin Ramadan, explained in 1981 that the decision to approach Western suppliers and to set up an Iraqi military industry came about from the lessons learned from the confrontation with Iran during the Kurdish revolt,[80] when the USSR slowed its delivery of supplies to protest Iraq's harsh measures against the Kurds.

In 1973, Spain requested a State Department permit to sell Iraq 200 recoilless 106 mm guns that had been produced in the United States during the Second World War. Production rights had been sold to Spain, but required US licensing to sell to a third country. In March 1974, Spain agreed to a five-year oil contract with Iraq. Most likely, the guns had been discussed beforehand. The State Department rejected the Spanish request outright, citing the absence of diplomatic relations and Iraq's close alliance with the USSR and its subversive activity against moderate states.[81] Spain unsuccessfully appealed the decision, then shipped the guns to Iraq without American approval.[82] Enforcing export controls on a third party proved problematic, and it agitated the United States' European allies as Iraq approached other states with similar requests. Italy requested and was refused permission to export 200 M-113 American-made armoured personal carriers (APC). Italy also signed an oil-for-goods contract with Iraq.[83] In April 1974, the State Department rejected a Belgian request to export APC transformer parts.[84] Nevertheless, American policy was different regarding the sale to Iraq of equipment used by police to maintain public order, with the State Department approving the export of Smith & Wesson .38 Specials, the same handguns that had been sold to the Egyptian police.[85]

Iraq expressed interest in purchasing American-made cargo planes. Lockheed Martin was asked by Iraq to supply 12 L-100 aircrafts (the civilian version of the Hercules C-130 military transport plane) as a precondition to purchasing older-generation civilian aircraft. The State Department rejected the request and instructed both Lockheed and Boeing to refuse to sell cargo aircraft that could be used for military purposes. Lowrie asked for a reconsideration of the ban that was issued in 1967, maintaining that rejection of this request would send Iraq and its business to other, non-American competitors.[86] Iraq did not give up on obtaining American-made aircraft and negotiated with Boeing, Lockheed Martin and McDonnell Douglas.[87] Nevertheless, from unhindered by export-control restrictions in 1974 France became a leading exporter of anti-Aircraft and anti-Tank Missiles, mortars, helicopters and light arms ($181.9 million), augmenting Spain's recoilless guns deal mentioned above ($6.2 million).[88]

US-Iraqi Cooperation in Science, Education and Nuclear Technology

Despite the limits imposed on the American Interest Section in Iraq, and the American export controls, Lowrie launched, in March 1973, scholarship programs for Iraqi students in the United States, financed by the State Department, that were aimed at improving relations.[89] The idea was not new. Iraqi students had received American scholarships since the 1950s, especially for graduate studies. In the 1970s some graduates from American universities held senior positions in Iraq – for example, Sa'dun Hammadi, the oil minister and later Foreign Minister. Most of the Iraqi applicants applied to study in American faculties of science and technology (including nuclear energy) and agriculture.[90] In 1973, the number of Iraqi students sent to American universities on full US government scholarships was 250, while 200 more students enrolled with partial scholarships or paid their own way. (By comparison, 4,000 Iraqis were studying then at British universities.) Iraq, apparently, was interested in increasing this number, so Baghdad University's Dr Tariq Rashad al-Rawi, who had returned to Iraq in 1971 after seven years at the University of Oklahoma, was selected to oversee the effort.[91]

Since Iraq was a 1968 signatory to the Treaty on the Non-proliferation of Nuclear Weapons (NPT), there was no legal barrier for the American Society of Nuclear Medicine (SNM) to supply Iraq with 16 grams of plutonium (one Curie source Pu/Be neutron). The NPT encouraged member states' nuclear-technical cooperation for civilian use.[92] The United States had assisted numerous countries on nuclear-related issues for medical and scientific uses within the framework of the International Atomic Energy Agency (IAEA), so cooperation with Iraq seemed benign.

Status of the Americans' Baghdad Interest Section

The diplomatic status of the interest section was such that US diplomats could have contacts with only low-ranking officials in the Iraqi government. Lowrie had not been invited to ambassador-rank briefings and events. He was not present even when congressional delegations visited Iraq and met ministers or Ba'thi leaders. The Americans had been more generous towards the Iraqi Interest Section, whose officials were invited to diplomatic and formal events in Washington, DC.

Since the scope of American economic activity in Baghdad had increased, and he thus had to deal with a growing number of American visitors, Lowrie asked for additional diplomatic staff. Only one official (dealing with economic affairs) was sent to Baghdad, making it three Americans in Baghdad, compared to eight Iraqi diplomats accredited to Washington.[93]

The Baghdad legation received a limited number of cables, probably due to the low-ranking status of the head of mission, but perhaps also due to security restrictions, and his residing in a foreign embassy rather than in an American facility. A limited number of classified cables had been sent through the diplomatic pouch and reached Baghdad late. Classified reports did not reach Baghdad at all – a frustrating obstacle for any head of mission. When Lowrie visited Beirut, he asked US embassy colleagues to prepare classified material for him to read.[94] This situation was typical in the first years of the Interest Section. As the diplomatic staff and the economic activity were growing, the head of mission had more access to the Ministry of Foreign Affairs, although the legation was operating officially under the Belgian flag. William L. Eagleton, who served in Baghdad in the early 1980s, described the Interest Section as functioning as a full embassy and treated by Iraqi accordingly.[95]

According to Lowrie, the Arab-Israeli conflict did not top the Ba'th agenda. He considered Iraq a secondary player in the conflict, and the country's statements committing Iraq to the Palestinian cause a necessity to attain Arab leadership. Lowrie mentioned in his reports several times the high 'price' the United States was paying for her special relationship with Israel.[96] Regarding the Kurdish issue, Lowrie accepted the Iraqi position unquestioningly. He repeatedly stressed that Iraqi Kurds' future lay under the Arab regime in Baghdad and that the Ba'th, by incorporating the Communists in the National Front, sincerely intended to create a genuine national front.[97] Lowrie was not aware of the secret CIA operation assisting Barzani, yet he adamantly objected to all American expressions of sympathy for the Kurds, which he believed might obstruct the improving US relations with Baghdad. Being proactive, Lowrie even suggested that the United States should discreetly encourage dialogue between Iran and Iraq to solve the Kurdish problem and end that conflict.[98] Yet when he repeated this suggestion during the Heads of Missions conference in Tehran, Helms warned against such an approach, since the Iraqi regime is 'radical and hostile to American interests' and would harm relations with the Shah. Helms was not only senior to Lowrie, but, of course, was well aware of the secret operation to assist Barzani that he'd authored as director of the CIA.[99] The State Department instructed Lowrie to refrain from any discussion of this kind with the Iraqis.[100] Lowrie did not give up. In December 1974, when the Iranian air defense hit two Iraqi fighter jets, he repeated the idea to approach the Shah and suggest that he appease Iraq. He also reiterated that the Ba'th regime had proved stable and that the collapse of the regime would not serve American interests.[101]

Empathy for the country in which one serves is common among diplomats, who are tasked with promoting relations with the host country. In the case of Iraq, it was a challenge to raise the diplomatic level and improve relations with a radical Arab state that signaled a pragmatic approach and an independent foreign policy. Lowrie occasionally included analytical comments in his diplomatic reports. The comments were optimistic and understanding, not critical. He was aware of the oppressive measures taken by the security forces against civilians – things that had not been published and were based on rumours. He expressed his personal involvement and protest only when his driver, Abbas Musa, was arrested by Iraqi security authorities. Lowrie asked the Belgian ambassador to act on behalf of the detained driver, and even requested that the State Department file an official complaint. Musa was released after three weeks of violent interrogations.[102] Apparently, the case had a deep impact on Lowrie, since he repeated the story years later in an interview for a Library of Congress oral history project.[103]

Iraq's Ambiguous Courtship of the US

In late May 1974, with the morale of the Iraqi forces particularly grim due to successful Peshmerga attacks, the country's Ministry of Foreign Affairs sent some friendly signals to Washington. The Interest Section reported on rumours of back-channel negotiations outside Iraq on resuming full diplomatic relations between Baghdad and Washington. The rumours were actually a trial balloon floated by a local employee of the Belgian embassy legation that the Iraqi regime may have sent directed at American ears.

In May 1974, Lowrie received an unusual request from his MFA contact in the protocol department to arrange for Saddam's wife to visit the United States for medical consultations. Moreover, the Iraqis stressed that the visit should be completely confidential. Mrs Hussein indeed travelled carrying a diplomatic passport under an assumed name and was treated by Dr Frank Furstenberg, allergy specialist at Johns Hopkins Medical Center.[104]

In June 1974, the US embassy in London reported to the British Foreign Office that the Iraqis had sent a feeler about the possibility of renewing relations with the United States in return for Iran ending its support for the Kurds.[105] It must be noted that these feelers were sent discreetly, so the Iraqi press continued attacking the United States for supporting Israel in what was apparently part of the ambiguous Iraqi courtship of the United States. The feelers sent by Iraq to the US through various channels generated expectations of Iraq's veering away from Soviet influence and resuming relations with Washington, in the wake of Egypt's example. The hope was even expressed in State Department correspondence that Iraq would soften its position towards moderate nations and perhaps even towards the Arab-Israeli conflict.[106]

The State Department welcomed Iraq's friendly signals, hoping to start negotiations on the embassy property eviction in return for the $2 million in frozen accounts held in American banks since 1967.[107] This scenario did not materialise. What did occur was a minor upgrade in 1974 in the level of communication with the Interest Section, replacing the Protocol Department that had been essentially a functional and technical department. The new Iraq-based point of contact for relations with the United States was Mun'em al-Zubaydi, a special assistant to the foreign minister.[108]

Another opportunity to start a dialogue occurred when Kissinger was seated next to the Iraqi ambassador to the UN Talib Shabib at an official UN event. Shabib was forthcoming and friendly, and the State Department assumed that the two men's discussion could be used as a vehicle to start a dialogue by sending a message to him at his new posting as ambassador to East Germany. But the effort was unsuccessful.[109] Kissinger persisted in sending similar messages – directly to Deputy Foreign Minister Taqa through Lowrie,[110] Egyptian President Anwar Sadat, and even through Syrian President Hafez Assad – stating that his relations with Baghdad had been very limited. All these efforts failed.[111]Lowrie himself responded to a State Department Office of the Inspector General report that criticised the interest section for a lack of progress in improving relations saying that every American approach or gesture to the Iraqi government had been repeatedly rebuffed.[112]

The Kurdish Revolt

The most intense military confrontation between the Iraqi army and the Kurds started in April 1974 and lasted almost a year. The Kurdish Peshmerga military force proved to have the fighting capabilities of almost a regular army, in addition to its guerilla capabilities. It was assisted by Iran, which supplied most of the weapons and financial backing, as well as the supply line for Israeli supplies via Iranian soil.[113] It was a confrontation between modern Soviet arms and the state-of-the-art American weaponry possessed by the Shah. From August 1974 to March 1975, Iraqi battles against the Kurds expanded into a full-fledged campaign between the Iranian and Iraqi armies that included air raids, anti-aircraft missiles and artillery. Both Iran and Iraq appealed to the UN Security Council, and the war ended abruptly with the Algiers Agreement on 6 March 1975.[114]

The Algiers Agreement that was announced on 6 March 1975 abruptly ended the fighting on the Kurdish front. It came as a surprise to the states involved – in particular for the immediate nature of its implementation. Saddam's readiness to make significant territorial concessions led the Shah to cut off instantly without prior warning transfer of all supplies from Iran to the Kurds – the lifeline of the Kurdish Revolt.[115]

Efforts to mediate between Iraq and Iran started in March 1974, with UN Secretary General Kurt Waldheim appointing Luis Weckmann Muñoz to investigate the border dispute at the Shatt al-Arab. Direct discussions were then held in Istanbul beginning in August of that year, but reaching a dead end in January 1975. Saddam had decided to end the military confrontation with Iran and the Kurdish rebellion even at the cost of giving up his previous demands, but he was looking for another channel of mediation, preferably an Arab one. He had been reluctant to travel outside Iraq, but visited Algiers in late July 1974; Algerian President Houari Boumediene reciprocated and visited Baghdad in January 1975, in the heat of the confrontation with Iran. The two leaders developed a good rapport, with Boumediene impressing Saddam as a leader who, like himself, combined revolutionary ideology with pragmatic practice.[116] The Algerian mediation was kept secret, and an agreement on principles was announced on 6 March 1975 during the OPEC meeting in Algiers, followed by immediate implementation by both Iran and Iraq. The formal, detailed agreement, that included the demarcation of the border, was signed on 13 June 1975.[117]

The agreement defined the land border according to the Constantinople Protocol of 1913. The nautical border at the Shatt al-Arab was left under Iranian sovereignty and validated the unilateral annulment of the 1937 agreement by Iran. Both sides committed to cease subversive activity. While the territorial principles were Iranian achievements, Iran agreed to cease supporting the Kurds and this was the most essential principle for Iraq, since it meant an immediate cutoff of all Iranian assistance to the Kurds, as well as blocking access to American and Israeli supplies to the Peshmerga. It practically meant the end of the rebellion. Additional concessions in the agreement seemed marginal but were perceived by Saddam as most humiliating: Iraq was obliged to stop criticising Iran for taking over the islands in the straits that Iraq considered to be infringing on Arab sovereignty. He saw it, too, as diminishing an old Iraqi claim on the Arabistan province in West Iran (called Khuzistan in Farsi) that was populated by non-Iranian Arabs.

The last phase of negotiations had been kept secret, a decision taken solely by Saddam and the Shah and known by Boumediene. The Shah did not consult with the United States, and the Iraqis did not share information with the Soviets, as obligated to by the Iraqi-Soviet agreement of 1972. The Soviets did welcome the Iran-Iraq agreement as corresponding with their own policy, although it was likely that Saddam had to explain the circumstances to the Soviets during his Moscow visit in April 1975.[118]

The US administration, meanwhile, expressed concern in classified sessions over the impact of the escalation on the Kurdish front, which it feared could harm its détente process with the Soviet Union. It also welcomed the optimistic evaluation, raised by Arab leaders, that ending the Iran-Iraq conflict would facilitate the resuming of American-Iraqi relations. The question of whether the US administration, and particularly Kissinger who maintained close relations with the Shah, had been involved in or were aware of the negotiations, or even could anticipate the abrupt cutoff of Iranian support to Barzani, will be discussed in Chapter 4: The Kurdish Prism. Some Arab states that were involved in diplomatic mediation efforts – Egypt, Jordan and Algeria – welcomed the agreement, while the Gulf Emirs told their American counterparts of their anxiety that a strong Iraq might issue territorial demands on Kuwait. Concerned about the threat of an Iraqi free of Kurdish and Iranian engagement, Syria criticised Iraq for giving away Arab territory to Iran.[119]

The Ba'th had the obligation to explain to the Iraqi public how the Algiers agreement contained significant concessions. During the first two weeks, the Ba'th kept a low profile. Then the Iraqi army seized all the Kurdish regions, and the regime initiated celebrations to mark the military victory over the Kurds. On 7 April, al-Bakr made a public speech in which he stated that containing the Kurds had been a great national achievement for both Iraqi nationalism (*wataniyya*) and for the Pan-Arab Nationalism (*qawmiyya*). Barzani was portrayed as a traitor who did not represent the

Kurdish people, due to his alleged cooperation with the enemies of Iraq: Iran, the United States and Israel.[120] Egyptian journalist Safi Naz Kazim visited Baghdad in September 1975 and described the euphoric atmosphere of ongoing celebrations that praised and glorified the victory of the Algiers agreement.[121]

The picture, however, was different within Ba'th institutions, with Saddam having to provide a detailed explanation for giving up his territorial demands. In a speech before the committees of the National and Progressive Front on 7 June 1975, Saddam rejected the argument raised that the regime abused the emergency situation declared during the fighting. He also refuted rumours that the party intended to change and redraw the Ba'th spiritual fighting doctrine (*hamasatha al-jabhawiyya*), presenting the agreement with Iran as a great victory against imperialism. A year later, speaking before the same forum, Saddam took pride in the army's significant military gains that led to the agreement from a position of strength.[122] Only in the 1980s did Saddam admit that, in 1975, the army had faced a serious shortage of ammunition due to the Soviets' delayed shipments.[123]

Notes

1. M. Khadduri, *Socialist Iraq – A Study in Iraqi Politics since 1969* (Washington, Middle East Institute, 1978), pp. 63–7; Samir al-Khalil (Kanan Makiya), *Republic of Fear – The Politics of Modern Iraq* (Berkley and London, University of California Press, 1989), pp. 6–7.

2. US Department of Justice, Federal Bureau of Investigation, Baghdad Operation Center, Interview session no. 6 conducted by George L. Piro, 16 February 2004, www.gwu.edu/~nsarchiv/NSAEBB279/07.pdf (accessed 28 August 217).

3. ABSP, *The 1968 Revolution in Iraq, Experience and Prospects – The political report of the Eighth Congress of the Ba'ath Socialist Party in Iraq*, January 1974 (London, 1979); A. Baram, 'The Ruling Political Elite in Ba'thi Iraq, 1968–1986: the changing features of a collective profile', *IJMES*, 21(1989), pp. 452–3; P. Marr *The Modern History of Iraq* (Boulder CO: Westview Press, 1985), p. 217; Sluglett & Sluglett, *Iraq since 1958: From Revolution to Dictatorship* (New York: Palgrave Macmillan, 1987), pp. 162–3.

4. Baghdad 492, 508, (Lowrie) 16, 22 September 1973.

5. A. Baram, *National Integration and Exclusiveness in Political Thought and Practice in Iraq under the Ba'th, 1968–1982*, Ph.D dissertation (Hebrew University Jerusalem,1986), p. 128; Iraqi editorials mocked at the unreasonable option that Egypt and Syria would turn to saber-rattling. *Al-Thawra*, 11–26 February 1973.

6. Iraq deployed a significant force against the Kurds: ~90,000 men, 1,200 tanks and armoured vehicles, and 200 aircrafts. P. Malovany, *The Wars of Modern Babylon* (Tel Aviv: Maarachot, 2009), p. 87.

7. ABSP, *About the 1973 October-War* (1977), pp. 16–19; M. Khadduri, *Socialist Iraq – A Study in Iraqi Politics since 1969*, p. 69.

8. *dawr al-jaysh al-Iraqi fi harb tishreen 1973* (Beirut, 1975), pp. 76–7; P. Malovany, *The Wars of Modern Babylon*, pp. 72–5.

9. E. Oren, 'IDF confrontation with the Iraqi Expedition Force in the Syrian Front at the Yom Kippur War' in S. Shay (ed.) *The Iraqi Israeli Conflict 1948–2000* (Tel Aviv: Maarachot, 2002), pp. 4–87.

10. Dawr al-Jaysh al-Iraqi (1975), pp. 221–2.

11. Malovany, *The Wars of Modern Babylon*, pp. 82–3; a Soviet diplomat in Baghdad told his Indian colleague that some of the Iraqi aircrafts had been hit by Syrian friendly fire. He added that Moscow considered the Arab military defeat in the October war as more severe than in 1967. Baghdad 579 (Lowrie), 27 October 1973.

12. Iraq Annual Review for 1974, 168/74, 7 February 1974, TNA, FCO 51/359; M. Khadduri, *Socialist Iraq – A Study in Iraqi Politics since 1969*, pp. 169–70; ABSP, *About the 1973 October War*, pp. 24–6.

13. MOC, the White House, 9 October 1973, 4:45p.m. *Ford Presidential Library*. Nixon suggested upgrading Israeli armour; Kissinger preferred to wait for two days.

14. Kissinger, *Crisis: The Anatomy of Two Major Foreign Policy Crises* (New York: Simon and Schuster, 2003) (Hebrew edition: Jerusalem, Shalem Center, 2004), p. 122.

15. Kissinger, *Years of Upheaval* (Boston: Little Brown & Company, 1982), p. 467; Department of State, MOC: 'Arab – Israeli Conflict', 17 October 1973, *DNSA*.

16. Memorandum from NSC (Quandt) to Secretary Kissinger, WSAG Meeting, 6 October 1973, 3:00 PM, *NARA, Nixon Presidential Library* NSC Files; Nixon to Kissinger, 8 October 1973, in Kissinger, *Years of Upheaval*, p. 490.

17. Isaacson, *Kissinger – A Biography* (New York: Simon and Schuster, 2005), p. 514.

18. For example: Nixon to Kissinger 7–8 October; Kissinger to Schlesinger 13 October. Kissinger, *Crisis*, pp.72, 116, 207.

19. Richard Perl, then Assistant to Senator Henry (Scoop) Jackson, criticised Kissinger for opposing direct air-lift flights, against the opinion of Defense secretary Schlesinger. An opposite assessment spread mostly in Israel, argued that it was the Department of Defense that caused the delays in activating the airlift. Isaacson, *Kissinger*, p. 523;

20. Zach Levey, 'Anatomy of an airlift: United States military assistance to Israel during the 1973 war', Cold War History, 8(4) (April 2008), pp. 481–501.

21. Draft Record of Conversation, US Secretary Kissinger and UK Foreign & Commonwealth Secretary Home, 12 December 1973, FCO/82/309, *TNA*.

22. Kissinger, *Years of Renewal* (New York: Simon and Schuster, 2000), pp. 575–99.

23. Memorandum from NSC (Saunders), 17 May 1973, FRUS XXV #61.

24. Soviet supplied Arab states, between 10–22 October, about 10,250 tons by air and sea, while US airlift to Israel between 14–22 October reached only 8,833 tons. Memorandum from NSC (Saunders): 'Comparative Soviet and US Resupply Efforts', 23 October 1973, *NARA* Nixon NSC/WSAG.

25. State 197541 (Rush) to Tehran, 4 October, 1973.

26. Michael Getler, 'Russia Sends Iraq a Dozen Supersonic Jet Bombers', *WP*, 2 October 1973.

27. For example Nixon and Kissinger meeting with Arab Foreign Ministers, 17 October 1973. MOC, Nixon, Kissinger, Sisco, Quandt, Saqqaf (Saudi Arabia), Benhima (Morocco), Al-Sabah (Kuwait), Bouteflika (Algeria), Washington, 17 October 1973, *FRUS XXV* #195.

28. Isaacson *Kissinger*, p. 514; Kissinger, *Years of Upheaval*, p. 470.

29. Telcon: Kissinger and Deputy Secretary of Defense Clements, 17 October 1973 in Kissinger, *Crisis*, p.233.

30. Baghdad 548,551 (Lowrie), 10, 12 October 1973.

31. State 207738 (Kissinger) to Baghdad, 15 October 2016.
32. Baghdad 561 (Lowrie), 15 October 1973.
33. Baghdad 620 (Lowrie), 18 November 1973.
34. Sa'adun Hammadi interview with *Al-Anwar* (Lebanon), 18 December 1973, *MEES 21* December 1973; Penrose & Penrose *Iraq: International Relations and National Development* (Boulder CO: Westview Press, 1978), p. 509.
35. Kissinger, *Years of Upheaval*, p. 873; RCC Announcement on nationalisation of Gulbenkian share in BPC (Basra Petrolium Company) at Baghdad Home Service, 20 December 1973, *SWB*, Part 4, 22 December, 1973.
36. Baghdad Radio, 16 October 1973, in M.S. Daoudi & M.S. Dajani, *Economic Diplomacy-Embargo Leverage and World Politics* (Westview Boulder CO, 1985), p. 137.
37. Baghdad 620 (Lowrie), 18 November 1973.
38. Daoudi & Dajani, *Economic Diplomacy-Embargo Leverage and World Politics*, pp. 161–3; Penrose & Penrose, *Iraq: International Relations and National Development*, pp. 506–11.
39. Aburish, *Saddam Hussein* (Hebrew), p. 93.
40. Paul Stevens, 'Iraqi Oil Policy: 1961–1976' in Tim Niblock (ed.), *Iraq: The Contemporary State* (1982), p. 177, quoting *MEES*, XVIII, no. 30.
41. Baghdad 690 (Lowrie), 'Iraq toughens its Oil Policy', 23 December 1973; *Baghdad Observer*, 7 December 1973.
42. The letter written in Arabic with the printed signature of Al-Bakr was handed to Lowrie by Deputy Foreign Minister Shazli Taqa, 23 January 1973, RG 59 NESA- Iraq 1973-1975, *NARA*; *Al-Jumhuriyya*, 16 February 1974.
43. Al-Bakr's response to Nixon's letter was presented in the Iraqi press as an appropriate Iraqi response to the US and as evidence of Nixon's failure to create discussion between oil suppliers and consumer states. *Al-Jumhuriyya* 24, 28 January 1974.
44. Baghdad 596 (Lowrie), 4 November 1973.
45. Thierry Desjardins, *Le Figaro*, 20 July 1973, in Eric Rouleau, *Le Monde*, 21 July 1973; Paris 197541 (Irwin), 21 July 1973; State (Rush) to Baghdad, 17 July 1973; *NYT*, *WP*, 15 July 1973; Saddam reiterated the new forthcoming approach to the West in a later speech before Iraqi Ambassadors to Western Europe and Japan on 12 June 1975. Saddam Hussein, 'Nidalna wal-Siyyasa al-Dawliyya' in Saddam Hussein *Al-Mukhtarat*, vol. 5, Chapter One.
46. State 167159 to London, 22 August 1973.
47. Arab Ba'th Socialist Party (ABSP), *About the 1973 October War* Report adopted by the Eighth Regional Congress, January 1974 (Firenze, 1977), pp. 223–6; Mahmud Salim al-Samra'i, *Istiqlaliyyat alSiyyasa al-Kharijiyya al-Iraqiyya* (Baghdad, 1985), pp. 20–1.
48. The term 'eternal mission' is part of the Ba'th original credo, as an all-Arab party. Jamal Abd al-Razzaq al-Badri, *Al-Thawra ... Wal-Siyyassa al-Dawliyyah* (Baghdad, 1980), p. 63.
49. Iraq Annual Review for 1974, 168/74, 7 February 1974, p.4, FCO 51/359, *TNA*; Fukuyama, *The Soviet Union*, pp. 35–7.
50. Baghdad 451 (Lowrie), 26 August 1973; Lowrie's source for the report, British Military Attaché.
51. Baghdad 340 (Lowrie), 17 June 1973.
52. Baghdad 351 (Lowrie), 22 June 1973.
53. Baghdad 037 (Lowrie), 29 January 1974.
54. Baghdad 604 (Lowrie), 14 September 1974.

55. Baghdad 153 (Lowrie), 27 March 1973.

56. Arab Report and Record, 1975, p. 386, quoted in Smolansky & Smolansky, *The USSR and IRAQ, The Soviet Quest for Influence* (Durham NC: Duke University Press, 1991), p. 22.

57. State 77826 to Islamabad, 'American News and Comments', 25 April 1973; R. Ramazani, 'The Persian Gulf and the Straits of Hormuz', in Gerard J. Mangone (ed.), *International Straits of the World*, vol. III (Alphen on the Rhine, Netherland: Sijthoff & Noordhoff, 1979), p. 48.

58. President Ford News Conference, 28 August 1974, *APP*; Baghdad 575 (Lowrie), 4 September 1974.

59. During the manoeuvre it had been planned that super carrier *USS Constellation* would enter the Saudi port of Dahran, accompanied by a flotilla. Smolansky & Smolansky, *The USSR and IRAQ*, pp. 177–8.

60. Rowland Evans and Robert Novak, 'The "Soviet Naval Base" in Um Qasr', *WP*, 12 February 1975.

61. Peter Mansfield, 'Saddam Husain's Political Thinking: The Comparison with Nasser' in T. Niblock (ed.) *Iraq: The Contemporary State* (London: Croom Helm, 1982), p. 63.

62. Baghdad 155, 13 February 1975.

63. For example: Aziz Sharif, State Minister, represented Iraq in a conference in Dacca, 28 May 1973; President of Chad visited Baghdad 26–9 April 1973; Baghdad 236 (Lowrie), 1 May 1973.

64. Baghdad 223 (Lowrie), 20 April 1974.

65. New Delhi 7418 (Schnieder), 25 June 1973; New Delhi 8086 (Moynihan), 11 July 1973.

66. Baghdad 191 (Lowrie), 29 March 1974.

67. Kabul 1840 (Eliot), 27 March 1974; Kabul 273, 14 January 1975. On 17 July 171973, Mohammad Daud Khan led a coup that overthrew Zahir Shah. Once in power, Da'ud Khan sought to suppress the left and lessen the country's dependence on the Soviet Union. On 27 April 1978, he was killed in a coup that brought to power a communist government.

68. Amman 2280 (Brubeck), 28 April 1973.

69. The list of participants published in the Iraqi media named left-wing opposition groups: the Ahwaz Liberation Front, the Omani Liberation Front, the Iranian National Front, the Popular Front for Liberation of Western Baluchistan as well as left wing Palestinian radical organisations. State 29446, 8 February 1975.

70. For example, assassination attempt of President of Yemen Aryani, and his emissary Muhammad Ahmad Nu'man in June 1974, were attributed to the Iraqi Ba'th. Sanaa 1142, 1147, 1168 (Crowford), 10, 11, 13 June, 1974; Sanaa 1945 (Newton), 17 September 1974.

71. Islamabad 3249 (Sanderhoff), 23 April 1973; Islamabad 3479 (Sober), 28 April 1973; Baghdad 462 (Lowrie), 2 August 1973.

72. Baghdad 198 (Lowrie), 9 April 1973.

73. State 237331, 29 October 1973. The final destination of the private plane that was not allowed to fly over Iraq was Tehran. The regional Conference of Chiefs of Missions was a routine professional Foreign Service forum, except the head of the US European Command (EUCOM) who had been invited. Perhaps the Iraqis mistakenly assumed that the participation of the USIA (The US Information Agency) Joseph Keogh was the CIA Director.

74. State 70221 to Tehran, 14 April 1973.
75. Samir Frangie, *Le'Orient Le Jour*, commenting on the Kazzar plot in: Beirut 7925 (Houton), 5 July 1973.
76. 'Helms and US Policy in the Gulf', *Alif Ba'* December 1973–January 1974.
77. *Al-Jumhuriyya*, 16 August 1974; *Al-Thwara*, 12 August 1974.
78. Brown & Root, Major American engineering, procurement and construction company, that received many contracts with the Pentagon and the Energy Sector for decades. Currently under the name KBR Inc. (Kellogg Brown & Root).
79. Baghdad 235 (Lowrie), 30 April 1973.
80. M.S. al-Samra'i, *istiqlaliyyat al-siyyasa al-kharijiyya al-Iraqiyya* (Iraqi Independent Foreign Policy, Baghdad, 1985), pp. 81–2.
81. Madrid 1846 (Rivero), 22 March 1974; State 124394 to Madrid, 26 June 1973.
82. State to Madrid, 22 January, 7 February, 19 June, 13 August, 19 September,1974; Madrid to State,16 January, 6 February, 22 March 1974.
83. State 240302 to Rome, 1 November 1974; Rome 4866, 8 April 1974.
84. State 76086 to Brussels, 15 April 1974.
85. State 257723 to Algiers, 22 November 1974.
86. Baghdad 053 (Lowrie), 18 January 1973.
87. Baghdad 1568 (Lowrie), 24 January 1975.
88. State 123568 to Baghdad, 19 June 1975.
89. Baghdad 0145 (Lowrie), 26 March 1973; State 076364 to Baghdad, 23 April 1973.
90. Department of State, The Office of the Special Assistant of the Secretary for the Coordination of International Educational and Cultural Relations, *International, Cultural and related activities for Iraq* (Washington DC, January 1961), p. 10.
91. Baghdad 505 (Lowrie), 21 September 1973.
92. US Mission to IAEA Vienna 6645 (Labowitz), 13 August 1973; State 169392 to Vienna, 24 August 1973.
93. Baghdad 665 (Lowrie), 28 September 1974.
94. Baghdad 641 (Lowrie), 21 September 1974.
95. W.L. Eagleton Jr., 'Evolutions of U.S. Interests Sections in Algiers and Baghdad' in David D. Newsom *(ed.)*, *Diplomacy under Foreign Flag* When Nations Break Relations (Washington DC, Georgetown University Press, 1990), pp. 90–8.
96. Baghdad 596 (Lowrie), 4 November 1973.
97. Baghdad 379 (Lowrie), 1 July 1973.
98. *Al-Fikr al-Jadid* (Communist) in Bagdad 363 (Lowrie), 24 June 1973; Baghdad 373 (Lowrie), 1 July 1973; Beirut 7351 (Houghton), 21 June 1973.
99. Tehran 2250 (Helms), 10 April 1973; State 60585 to Baghdad and other posts, 3 April 1973.
100. State 134384 (Rogers) to Baghdad, 10 July 1973.
101. Baghdad 898 (Lowrie), 23 December 1974.
102. Baghdad 470 (Lowrie), 9 September 1973; Baghdad 767, 4 November 1974.
103. Interview with Arthur L. Lowrie, 23 December 1989, *ADST*.
104. The specialist that treated Mrs Hussein, Dr Frank Furstenberg, was an active member in the local Jewish Federation.
105. FCO/MED (Wright), 19 June 1974, FCO 8/2314, *TNA*.
106. State 110858 (Ingersoll), 13 May 1975.
107. State 121823 to Baghdad, 10 June 1974.
108. Baghdad 457 (Lowrie), 2 August 1974.

109. MOC, Sadat, Fahmi, Abdul Ghafar, Marwan, Kissinger, Sisco, Eilts, Rodman, Cairo, 10 October 1974, *DNSA*.

110. State 45028 (Kissinger), 24 August 1974; Baghdad 543 (Lowrie), 27 August 1974; Baghdad 664 (Lowrie), 29 August 1974; *NARA*, Washington DC, RG 59.

111. MOC, Sadat – Kissinger, Cairo, 10 October 1974; *NARA* Washington DC, RG 59, Henry Kissinger Records. MOC, Assad, Khaddam, Kissinger, Murphy, Saunders, Rodman, Damascus, 11 October 1974; *NARA*, Washington DC, RG 59.

112. 'U.S. Government policies and programs in Persian Gulf States', September 1974, quoted in Baghdad 776 (Lowrie), 9 November 1974.

113. NSC MOC, 17 September 1974; *Ford Presidential Library*, Kissinger/Scowcroft West Wing Office Files.

114. O. Bengio, *The Kurdish Rebellion in Iraq* (Tel Aviv: Dayan Center, Tel Aviv University, 1989), pp. 88–90; Malovany, *The Wars of Modern Babylon* (Tel Aviv: Maarachot, 2009), pp. 145–7.

115. Joint Communiqué between Iran and Iraq, 'The Algiers Declaration', 6 March 1975, in J.M. Abdulghani, *Iraq & Iran, the Years of Crisis* (New York: Routledge, 1984), Appendix B.

116. Algiers 14343 (Simpson), 2 July 1974; British Embassy Moscow (R.B. Bone), 22 April 1975, FCO 8/2546 *TNA*; Smolansky & Smolansky, *The USSR and IRAQ*, p. 187.

117. 'Iran-Iraq Treaty on International Borders and Good Neighborly Relations' was signed in Baghdad, 13 June 1975, reproduced from the Baghdad Observer, 23, 24 June 1975, in Khadduri, *Socialist Iraq*, Appendix E, pp. 245–60; Abdulghani, *Iraq & Iran*, Appendix C.

118. Moscow 4330 (Stoessel), 29 March 1975.

119. E. Kienle, *Ba'ath vs. Ba'ath – The Conflict between Syria and Iraq 1968–1989* (London: I.B. Tauris, 1991), pp. 88, 96.

120. *Al-Thawra*, 7 April 1975 in Bengio, *The Kurdish Rebellion, in Iraq* (Tel Aviv: Dayan Center, Tel Aviv University, 1989) p. 171.

121. Safi Naz Kazem, *Yawmiyyat Baghdad 1975–1980* (London: Open Press, 1984), p. 11.

122. Saddam Hussein, *One Common Trench? Or Two Opposite Ones?* Meeting of the Committees of the Progressive Patriotic and Nationalist Front (Milano, 21 August 1976), p. 32.

123. Saddam confirmed to the Egyptian journalist that Iraq ran out of ammunition withheld by the Soviets. Muhamed Heikal, *llusions of Triumph – An Arab View of the Gulf War* (London, Harper Collins Publishers, 1992), p.85.

3

A Major Buildup, 1975–9

The Algiers agreement ushered in a period of Iraq's building up and setting out on the road to becoming a regional power. Free of the Kurdish threat, the regime adopted increasing totalitarian measures, and demonstrated even less tolerance for non-Ba'thi elements, like the Communists and the Shi'a. The regime carried out social and economic reforms, initiated cultural and educational programs and invested its oil revenues in a major buildup of the army and security apparatus and in infrastructure projects. The Ba'th Party established roots in all social institutions from tribal and traditional to the new roots in urban and rural areas – and, of course, in the army and security services.

The most dramatic event – the one with major implications for the focus of this research – was the Israeli-Egyptian peace treaty, shepherded by the Carter Administration. Following this first treaty between an Arab state and Israel, Iraq convened an Arab summit in Baghdad to lead the rejectionist front against any political settlement with Israel. The conference helped to fulfil an Iraqi Ba'th goal since 1968 to assume leadership status. Bilateral relations with the United States continued as before. Trade and congressional delegations visited Iraq. They heard from party leaders about Iraq's continued interest in expanding trade relations, without any hint of pursuing a diplomatic breakthrough to raise the level of diplomatic relations. This attitude towards the United States, defined by the Ba'th leadership, became a static pattern, indicating Baghdad's reluctance to resume full diplomatic relations with Washington, yet maintaining and expanding trade relations.

Reinforcing Cohesiveness of National Identity

In this period of economic growth and implementation of reforms, the regime integrated the Ba'th ideology as a platform of educational and cultural reforms, bolstering its vision of national identity for all Iraqis. A clear example of this trend is reflected in a new approach to the history of Iraq. Ba'thi revisionist history related to the great, pre-Islamic empires of Mesopotamia, Assyria and Babylon as the ancient roots of modern-day Iraq. Therefore, the regime encouraged archeological excavations and research. It built national museums, supported local folklore festivals, scientific conferences, literature, poetry, art and music. An educational project had been launched to increase literacy among adults throughout the state, simultaneous with infrastructure projects connecting remote rural areas to electricity, television and modern roads. These initiatives were aimed at enforcing patriotism at the local level, and creating a cohesive identity for all ethnic and religious groups under the authority of the Ba'th regime. This initiative had been planned in the early 1970s, but was accelerated after 1975 as part of the development plans and social reforms.[1]

Iraqi Obsession with the US: Kurdish Alliance

Following the Algiers Agreement, the Kurds were left on their own to cope with a suspicious, vengeful regime. The Ba'th regime that refused to allow any foreigners to deliver humanitarian aid inside Iraq had a motive for demonstrating good will towards the Kurdish population and the government's efforts to rebuild and reconstruct the war-stricken area. Government-guided tours for representatives of international organisations produced positive reports and led Waldheim to conclude that Iraq was very keen to ensure Kurdish rights.[2] Iraq published large advertisements in Western media, claiming that the large share of its development and infrastructure budget was invested in the Kurdish regions.[3] As in other peripheral provinces in Iraq, most of the development projects had been in transportation, and were dedicated not just to the rural population but also to easing security forces' movement in the harsh terrain of Kurdistan's mountains. Likewise, constructing modern communications enabled the broadcast of Ba'thi messages and enforced control even in remote areas.

The Ba'th regime continued to suspect the United States of supporting the Kurds. That suspicion increased in 1976, when the CIA's operation to assist Barzani was leaked to the American press. Iraqi officials repeatedly raised the issue with American visitors and diplomats, arguing that Washington's special relations with the Kurds were the main obstacle to closer relations with Iraq.[4] This view remained entrenched even after the administration cut off all contact with the Kurds. It could have been an angry Iraqi response to American media reports on oppression of the Kurds by the regime. The US was hosting ailing Barzani in Virginia, and allowing him to receive sympathetic politicians and journalists.[5] It could also have been a genuine anxiety over American intervention, an argument that was widely expressed by Ba'thi leaders and media that nourished an atmosphere of fear of an external threat. (Saddam's own anxiety and personality features are discussed in Chapter 8.) Another plausible explanation is tactical: the Iraqis used the Kurdish issue as an excuse to postpone resuming relations to an indefinite date, bearing unclear preconditions. The Ba'th saw its rejection of the American courtship to upgrade diplomatic relations as a most valuable card, one that brought the party public support and prestige domestically and among other Arab states – in particular, since there was no price to be paid for this attitude. The Interest Section was acting as a whole embassy, providing consular services to the numerous American businesspeople and encouraging trade, just as Baghdad dictated.

The fact that the US administration was avoiding any contact with the Kurds was an embarrassing reminder of the failed operation that was leaked to the press, and it appeased Baghdad. The Americans' complete separation from the Kurds included the intelligence community as well. In 1979, following the fall of the Shah and the rise of Khomeini, CIA director Stansfield Turner complained to national security advisor Zbigniew Brzezinski that most intelligence on the Kurds came from signal intelligence (known as SIGINT), while human intelligence (HUMINT) was very feeble.[6] This was an astonishingly changed reality, since the United States had held continuous, discrete intelligence relations with the Kurds since the 1950s.

The Rift with the Iraqi Communist Party

Following the Algiers Agreement, the regime gained confidence, and the Ba'th cooperation with the ICP became less essential for the consolidation of the Ba'th. The National Front continued for some time, but the ICP did not expand or increase its membership, while the Ba'th had grown significantly in all walks of life. According to the Iraqi-American scholar Majid Khadduri, ICP failed as an ideology that had to compete with Arab nationalism and socialism. In May 1976, the Communists reached their political apex in Iraq, with the Third National Congress of the ICP held publicly in the presence of their Ba'thi coalition partners. The ICP's Secretary General Aziz Muhammad praised the ruling Ba'th, and stressed the common interests for both parties: denouncing the disengagement agreement between Egypt and Israel, and resolving the Kurdish rebellion.[7]

No sooner had the Congress ended, though, than the regime started taking measures to limit the activity of the ICP, which had become too independent for the Ba'th. The Ba'th was also sending a message to the Soviets on behalf of the Iraqi Communists, wishing to avoid further interference in Iraqi affairs by using Iraqi dependence on military supplies as leverage.[8] In May 1977, several Communist activists were executed by the regime, ignoring an appeal by USSR premier Leonid Brezhnev to spare their lives. Months later, all political activity, except Ba'th's, was banned within the armed forces.[9] Purges of Communists continued in the public services, accompanied by arrests and dozens of executions.[10]

In July 1978, Saddam stated in a press conference that he would not allow anybody in the National Front to attempt to impose conditions on the Ba'th or to undermine the stability of Iraq.[11] In April 1979, the Communist daily *Tariq al-Sha'b* was shut down, and the two Communist ministers in the government were dismissed. Politburo members fled to Moscow, others went into hiding in Kurdistan, and some even joined the Talabani resistance forces in Iraqi Kurdistan.[12] The persecution of Communists, though they did not threaten Ba'th dominance, indicated deep Ba'thi mistrust and suspicion of a party with a tradition of underground activity, ideological commitment and fighting spirit. The Communists had also been historically close to the Kurds, and maintained a network of external relations with similar movements and the USSR.[13]

Pragmatically, the Soviets accepted the persecution of the Communists, and military and technical cooperation with Iraq continued to expand.[14]

Confrontation with the Shi'i Community

The Shi'i community had been a major concern for the B'ath, an attitude reflected in the few Shi'i members working in party institutions in the first decade of Ba'th rule. This contrasted with the higher Shi'i high representation through the mid-1960s, while some of the prominent party activists had been affiliated with the founders of the Iraqi Ba'th.[15] Moreover, while the regional leadership of the Ba'th was dealing with the Communists and the Kurds regarding joining in the National Front, the Shi'i community had not been mentioned.[16] The regime feared, above all, the forming of a Shi'i opposition group, inspired by a religious call. Anti-Ba'th pamphlets were circulated, signed by allegedly secret associations, such as the Iraqi National Association (*Al-Tajamu' al-Watani al-'Iraqi*) and the National Islamic Front (*Al-Jabha al-Wataniyya al-Islamiyya*).

Shi'i riots broke out in February 1977 during the 'Ashuara ceremonies at Najaf and Karbala, sparking a mass demonstration against the regime that followed the execution of Shi'i political prisoners in al-Gharib prison in Baghdad. The regime established a special court, headed by prominent Ba'th members, to try the demonstration's instigators, many of them clerics. The court sentenced eight of them to death and fifteen to life in prison; it released others. A few weeks later, the Ba'th dismissed the special court's two judges: Dr Izzat Mustafa, a Sunni physician, who had been an RCC member since 1969, a member of the Ba'th regional leadership and Minister of Labour and Social Affairs; and Fulayh Hasan al-Jasim, a Shi'i state minister to Kurdish autonomy.[17] The press insinuated that the judges were expelled for being too lenient. Other rumours suggested that the RCC was divided regarding the way to deal with the Shi'a community.[18]

Following those events, Shi'i party members were promoted in the Ba'th hierarchy. Hasan Amiri, Hikmat Ibrahim 'Azzawi and 'Adnan Hussein Hamdani joined the RCC and the Regional Command of the Ba'th. Shi'i ministers received more important portfolios, such as trade, industry and planning. The American-educated, soft-spoken Sa'dun Hammadi, who served the Ba'th as a foreign minister and an oil minister, joined the party leadership only in 1986.[19] Yet, these Shi'a members were secular and adhered to the Ba'th socialist ideology, while the Shi'i community in Southern Iraq was conservative and religious. Saddam perceived the Islamisation trend in Iraq as a threat to the Ba'th and to the national unity of Iraq, opposing introduction of Shari'a principles into the Justice system, by both Sunna and Shi'a. The newly begun secular offensive, however, was directed mainly at the Shi'a. He initiated legal reform to replace all Shari'a elements in the legal system with Ba'thi secular legal context.[20] The Ba'th did not consider Ayatollah Khomeini, who was preaching in Najaf, Iraq, as a threat, but they expelled him from Iraq at the request of the Shah in 1978.

The Shi'a crisis in Iraq did not draw much attention in Washington, although the Interest Section in Baghdad reported the facts. Marshall Wiley, who succeeded Lowrie as the Head of the American Interest Section in October 1975, remarked that the Shi'a posed a greater threat to the Ba'th than was recognised, yet he also concluded that 'the authorities appear to have stuffed the genie of Shi'a unrest back into the bottle'.[21] The violence was viewed as a domestic religious issue, without any implications for the United States or even for Iran, since both Iran and Iraq adhered to the Algiers Agreement. Retrospectively, these events signified the emergence of political Islam, particularly among the Shi'a, as a growing factor threatening the regimes of two allies of the United States in the area, Iran and Saudi Arabia.

The Consolidation of One-man Rule

During this period, Saddam, though formally second in command to Al-Bakr, as his deputy, consolidated his power, appearing to be not just the strongman of the Ba'th, but increasingly dominating the decision-making process. Saddam patiently paved the way for assuming the full power of the presidency from Al-Bakr, whom he addressed as *Al-Aab al-Qa'id*, The Leading Father, earning his trust. Saddam initiated a public relations campaign to build his image as the great man of Iraq, creating a Stalin-style personality, since Stalin was his role model for leadership.[22] There are some indications that Al-Bakr had granted Saddam significant authorities as early as 1974.[23] So, after Saddam had to elaborate to both the party and the masses the painful circumstances of the Algiers Agreement, and initiated a major buildup and development program, on 16 July 1979, Al-Baker announced that, for health reasons, he was resigning from all public offices. He was immediately succeeded by Saddam.[24] The civilian faction of the Ba'th took over the party's leadership, government institutions, and the military and state bureaucracy. Saddam became an absolute ruler, using purges and eliminating potential rivals or any members suspected of disloyalty. Those removed were replaced by Saddam confidantes – usually, members of his family. He appointed his cousin Adnan Khirallah Talafah as defense minister, encouraged young Sunnis from his hometown of Tikrit to join the army and the party and quickly promoted them to buy their total loyalty. He also used the tribal loyalties of his clan, Al-Bou-Nasir, to fill sensitive positions and to maintain his personal security.[25]

The Ba'th Party became the major instrument of the regime to recruit support as well as maintain control over all sectors and walks of life. Since the state owned and ran most economic sectors and was the largest employer, membership in the ruling party gave priority in employment, promotion and other perks. The party hierarchy from the bottom up was as follows: *halqa* (cell), *firqa* (division), *shu'ba* (section) and *far'* (branch). These divisions enabled the national leadership to transfer messages and guidelines, and control and monitor all members. The Ba'th expanded its base dramatically in the second half of the 1970s. By 1980, some 10,000 full members and 500,000 supporters (*ansar*) – constituting a pre-membership status – were on the rolls, according to the party's records. Those numbers reached the millions in the following years.[26]

The road to full membership was long, with candidates for Party membership having to undergo Ba'th indoctrination and prove their loyalty. The Ba'th Regional Command (*al-Qiyada al-Wataniyya*) became a ruling body, second to the RCC. Its authority superceded the official bureaucracy. The Ba'th Pan-Arab National Command (*al-Qiyada al-Qawmiyya*), under the Ba'th founder Michel Aflaq, filled mostly protocol functions for the party, like external relations, and was basically marginalised. The Pan-Arab National Command was allegedly in charge of inter-Arab affairs, including Palestinian affairs. In practice this pan-Arab body of the Party followed the guidelines of Saddam. To secure his control, Saddam appointed his confidant, Na'im Haddad, as head of the Bureau for Palestinian and Armed Struggle Affairs.[27]

American diplomatic dispatches from Baghdad, sent to the State Department, stressed the consolidation of the civilian faction of the party and portrayed Saddam when he assumed the presidency as a strong, pragmatic leader and, therefore, potentially a partner for dialogue with the United States.[28] However, a closer look at the Ba'th under Saddam reveals that the regime often defined by the West as 'civilian' is highly inaccurate. The party's hierarchy and discipline were strict and relied on the military and the internal-security apparatus.[29] Al-Bakr was an admired general, and while Saddam had no significant military record, he recognised the impact of an army record on his and his party's image. Thus, from 1969 on, he used to visit army units regularly, accompanied by the press, and was photographed observing military manoeuvres. On Army Day of 1976, he assumed the rank of *Fariq Awwal* (equivalent to a four-star general) and, on special occasions, appeared publicly in uniform.[30]

Iraq's Major Military Buildup

Lessons were drawn from the Iraqi military's 1973 confrontation with Israel, and its fighting against the Kurds and Iranian forces in 1974–5. The Ba'th initiated a major buildup of the military, both in volume and quality. In 1978, the Iraqi forces numbered 222,000 men in four armoured divisions, two mechanised divisions and four infantry divisions. In addition, there were two Special Forces brigades, one independent armoured brigade and one mechanised brigade of the National Guard.[31] In comparison, by 1980, the army had twelve divisions. Most of the efforts to modernise the forces indicated that the Ba'th was planning to build a large force with offensive capability and high mobility for long-distance operations. The regime also strengthened its armoured units, logistics and air force.

At the same time, the regime invested in constructing communication and transportation infrastructure, and in establishing modern industry, encouraging technological education, and procuring production plants, mostly from the West. Iraq seemed to be pining to become a regional power with the largest Arab army in the Persian Gulf.[32] Washington did not consider the massive military buildup as a threat to American interests, but, rather, as a sensible tactic to deter such strong rivals as Iran and Syria, as well as to discourage domestic challenges from the Kurds (PUK) led by Talabani. Moreover, the administration and the US business community watched with frustration Iraq's multi-billion procurement of civilian and military equipment in France, Italy and West Germany, and were eager to join the competitive bids as soon as US-Iraqi relations resumed and restrictions were removed.

In early March 1975, on his way to the OPEC conference in Algiers, Saddam stopped in Paris and submitted to Prime Minister Jacques Chirac a list of military items he sought to buy immediately.[33] It was exceptionally huge and included Mirage F-1 aircraft, only recently introduced into the French air force; also, gunship helicopters, missiles, armoured vehicles and radar systems. Iraq was also interested in constructing, with French aid, a plant to produce Mirage engines, a clear indication of Saddam's ambition for self-reliance. Other civilian projects proposed to France were the construction of oil refineries, an airport, communications infrastructure, and plants to produce pesticides and electronics and much more.[34] US allies, Iran and Israel, alerted Washington that the purpose of the civilian contracts was not just modernisation of the army and building scientific infrastructure, but to develop military capabilities, including secret programs of Weapons of Mass Destruction (WMD). A French source also admitted that Paris was facing difficulties in supplying Iraq with the most advanced military equipment, on the same level as American supplies to Iran.[35]

Foreign Policy

Iraqi Soviet Relations 1975–9

The year 1975, according to Francis Fukuyama, marked the peak of Iraqi-Soviet relations, with both states standing shoulder to shoulder against American involvement in the Middle East. Yet gradually, as the Ba'th gained confidence, Iraq's more independent policy revealed deviation from the Soviet line.[36] For example, on 1 October 1977, the Soviet Union joined President Carter's initiative and published a joint statement regarding the Middle East peace process. The Iraqi Ba'th viewed the Soviet position as opposite to Iraq's fundamentalist, rejectionist principles.[37] Another difference of opinion related to the Horn of Africa: the Soviets supported Ethiopia, while Iraq supported Somali and the Eritrean Liberation Front. Saddam even alerted the Soviets that Iraq would not allow Soviet aircraft to fly over Iraq on their way to Ethiopia.[38] In the spring of 1978, the regime demanded the immediate evacuation of the Soviet embassy compound in Baghdad, suspecting eavesdropping on the presidential palace nearby. Like the United States earlier, the Soviet Union rejected the demand, so the regime disconnected the water and power supplies.[39]

The regime's attitude, especially considering Baghdad's ruthless persecution of domestic Communists, reflected a self-confidence that reached the level of defying the superpower that had been a strategic ally – one that Iraq was dependent upon. Still, neither Iraq nor the USSR publicly admitted any rift or dispute. In fact, their cooperation continued and even expanded.[40] A billion-dollar agreement on economic and military cooperation was signed in May 1976, placing Iraq atop the list of Third World countries receiving Soviet assistance.[41] By the end of the decade, France was the second-leading supplier for the growing Iraqi military, in particular for advanced technologies. Most Iraqi army units, including those newly formed, were equipped by the Soviets, including with tanks, artillery, armoured vehicles, missiles and most aircraft.[42] Moreover, American intelligence reported that, as of 1979, 1,100 Soviet military advisers were present in Iraq.[43]

The Carter Era: A Novice Administration

The Carter Administration fundamentally changed some basic concepts in American foreign policy. The most pronounced one was the shift from the political-rational realism of Kissinger, which resulted in American pragmatic-activist foreign policy, to the moral principles based on utopian values espoused by Jimmy Carter. Unlike Kissinger's acting to keep the Soviet Union away from active involvement in a peace process in the Middle East, Carter, at least in the first year of his presidency, considered the USSR a legitimate partner in the mediation between Israel and the Arab states.[44]

Carter was determined to make a change in the Middle East. He assumed that the Arab regimes, the traditional and the radical, were disappointed with the Soviet role and would follow Egypt and allow American involvement in the Middle East because of its relationship with Israel. As Secretary of State Cyrus R. Vance said, the moderate Arab states realised that the American commitment to Israel's security could not be changed, yet the flip side of that commitment was that the United States was the only player with leverage over Israel.[45] Vance's first tour of the Middle East, during the transition period prior to Carter's inauguration, did include Damascus, but not Baghdad, a fact that raised great suspicion in Iraq. Media commentators maintained that Vance was no different to Kissinger and that he was mocking Arab regimes anticipating and hoping for a new American policy.[46]

The strategic goals of this policy had been clearly defined in *The Brookings Report* of 1975. Three of its authors were appointed to senior positions at the administration: Vance, Brzezinski and William B. Quandt.[47] According to their approach, Kissinger's step-by-step shuttle diplomacy had been exhausted, and President Carter was now hoping for an overall solution. They saw the first step as working towards an international conference.[48] Carter's lacking foreign policy experience was evident in some of his steps and statements that were perceived as tilting towards the Arab position and as eroding America's traditional commitment to Israel. On 16 March 1977, Carter said that the Palestinians deserved their own homeland and should have been compensated for their suffering. His remarks surprised the State Department and were criticised in both Israel and Jordan.[49] Undaunted,

Carter repeated his position when he met with Arab leaders in Geneva in May 1977.[50] The statements raised concern in Iraq as well, with *Al-Jumhuriyya* casting doubt on the credibility of the statement, and conveying mistrust in the American administration.[51]

The administration worked on a strategy to persuade Israel and American Jews, who were sceptical of the new president, to cooperate with the plan articulated by the Brookings Report authors regarding a political solution to the Arab-Israeli conflict. Carter had little experience in foreign policy and no previous acquaintance with American Jewish active involvement in Washington in the White House and on Capitol Hill.

A document handed to the President by Chief of Staff Hamilton Jordan for Carter's eyes only, was aimed at gaining American Jews' support for the plan by convincing them that Israel would benefit. The unsigned document referred to some of the mistakes inherent in the president's statements, as being novice in foreign affairs in the early months of his term. The document sought to educate the president, someone who, being from the southern state of Georgia, had little interaction with the state's small Jewish community and, of course, had no experience in the workings of lobbying Congress. The document provided such basics as a definition of Zionism and an explanation of American Jews' ties to Israel. Jordan's paper described what he called a 'Jewish American paranoia', something he considered justified, especially following the Holocaust. The document's map of Jewish political organisations, national and regional, gave a sense of Jewish political power that the president and the Democratic Party were committed to.[52] The very fact that Carter needed such basic information indicated that he had neither previous awareness of the Middle East nor, possibly, of foreign policy issues generally. One can assume that he had limited knowledge of Iraq, and could marginalise Iraq in his peace plan.

The Arab-Israeli Peace Process: An Evolving American Misperception

On foreign policy matters, the first months of 1977 had the administration focused on convening a summit in Geneva. Iraq, which was vehemently against it, feared most of all that the PLO might join a Carter-convened peace process due to the president's statements, and, with the Arab states bordering Israel, would form a separate peace treaty, based on UN Security Council resolutions 242 and 338, namely, a Palestinian state on part of Palestine that would recognise Israel – totally unacceptable to the Ba'th ideologically and, even worse, leaving Iraq out of the picture. Iraq called the peace process a conspiracy meant to drag the Arabs into an American plan that would advance the Zionist entity and remove the Palestinian problem.[53] Syria felt similarly, yet in discreet talks with American officials insinuated the option of concessions in return for proper compensation.[54]

The US was aware of the Iraqi position. A State Department report to the president described Iraq as strongly opposed to any negotiations with Israel and in support of radical Palestinian terrorist organisations. The administration was optimistic regarding another rejectionist regime, Syria, following Carter's meeting with Assad in Geneva in May 1977. Iraq and Libya in immediately denouncing the Israeli-Egyptian negotiations but, rather, maintaining a cautious silence, struck Washington as a good sign.[55] This optimism regarding Syria joined the optimist evaluation from the Baghdad Interest Section. It also correlated with Carter's optimistic, utopian world view that even radical states would not be able to resist the achievement of peace and would end up welcoming the United States as a fair and balanced mediator who cared for the Palestinians and was the only player capable of inducing Israel to withdraw from the occupied territories. Until 17 September 1978, when Begin and Sadat reached an agreement in Camp David (the formal peace treaty between Israel and Egypt was signed in Washington on 26 March 1979) the Americans assumed that Iraq would stick to its rejectionist position, but would not disrupt a comprehensive peace process, particularly if the Arab states bordering Israel (Jordan, Lebanon and Syria) agreed to it.

The realisation that the Peace Treaty between Israel and Egypt would be rejected by most Arabs dawned on the American and Egyptian negotiators in late August 1978, just before the final negotiations at the presidential retreat at Camp David, when King Hussein of Jordan expressed his disappointment and reluctance to join the peace process, due to Israeli refusal to withdraw from Palestinian territories.[56] But Sadat, eager for the first stage (and largest) of Israel's multi-stage withdrawal from the Sinai peninsula under the Camp David Treaty, did not insist that the regional clauses of the pact, including the Palestinian issue, would be a precondition for the treaty's implementation.[57] The Americans were certain that Sadat would successfully convince Iraq and Syria to support his position, and they did not foresee a scenario under which radical Iraq, unpopular if not resented by most Arab leaders, would drag all Arab League states, including the moderate states, into a hardline, rejectionist front against Egypt and the United States. Likewise, the administration did not anticipate the response of Arab Americans, many of them third-generation citizens who, in a White House meeting with NSC officials Gary Sick and William Quandt, protested America's support of Sadat in the early stages of the peace negotiations.[58]

The agreement reached between Begin and Sadat in Camp David in September 1978 that led to the Egypt-Israel Peace Treaty signed by Sadat, Begin and Carter in Washington in March 1979, helped Israel to break out from diplomatic isolation, something Iraq and others feared. A Ba'th statement called for the establishment in Baghdad of a united Arab front against the separate treaty with Israel. The move, the statement said, would 'protect the honor and the historical rights of the Arabs'. As a practical measure, the Ba'th called for establishing a financial foundation to assist the states confronting Israel and dissuading other countries from forging similar agreements.[59]

In fact, Saddam started planning a conference in Baghdad on Arab rejection of the negotiations as soon as Sadat famously visited Jerusalem in 19 November 1977.[60] The Baghdad summit opened on 2 November 1978 and was a major success, in particular in beating Libya and Algeria to relinquish their attempts to convene the conference in Tripoli and Algiers. This Iraqi diplomatic achievement showcased Saddam as a strong leader with politically pragmatic skills in the Arab arena. He seized the opportunity of the vacuum created by Egypt's expulsion, and the fact that Arab leaders were shocked and overwhelmed, to rehabilitate Iraq's status and reputation, even at the price of appeasing Iraq's rivals. To ensure the participation of Arab states that had endured Iraqi subversion and violence, Saddam initiated an 'appeasement tour' of Saudi Arabia, Kuwait and Jordan. Iraq provided Jordan with a \$30 million grant. Iraq promised to cease its subversive activities in Syria and Yemen, and to expel anti-PLO terrorists based in Baghdad, conditioned by Arafat. The most blatant step was Saddam's appeasement of his arch-rival, Syria, by decreasing Iraqi support for anti-Assad Palestinian organisations in Lebanon.[61]

The Israeli-Egyptian treaty, especially as it involved the leading Arab country, was also a feather in the cap of US foreign policymaking – and perhaps a first step towards a comprehensive regional Pax-Americana. For rejectionist Iraq, though, Washington was the epitome of an imperialist enemy that had succeeded in seducing Egypt and breaking Arab consensus and solidarity. Saddam appeared to Arabs as a leader who had formed a rejectionist front against the process, in clear defiance of the United States – all the while continuing to expand trade relations with America.

The End of an Era

On 28 July 1979, shortly after Al-Bakr announced his resignation as president and Saddam took over, Saddam told his party's leadership that he had discovered a conspiracy to topple him. In a horror scene recorded and photographed, he conducted an immediate, comprehensive purge, executing twenty-two party members, including five RCC figures. The purge continued into early 1980 and included close confidants of Saddam and prominent figures the United States knew of, such as former foreign ministers 'Abd al-Karim al-Shaikhli, who served as ambassador to the UN, and Murtada al-Hadithi, an ambassador to Moscow.[62]

That was the beginning of a new era, of Saddam as a totalitarian ruler, surrounded by a small group, mostly from his hometown of Tikrit, and relying on tribal loyalty, commitment and fear.[63]

The geo-political arena underwent a major change, with the emergence of the Islamic Republic of Iran in February 1979, following the overthrow of the Shah. Khomeini was well known in Iraq from his exile there in 1965–78 in Najaf. The Iraqi Ba'th had to cope with a charismatic leader with admirers in Iraq's Shi'a community, someone who preached the export of the Islamic revolution throughout the Muslim world and, therefore, stood as a threat to the secular Sunni Ba'th.

Iraq was concerned mainly with the collapse of the Algiers agreement that had kept the long Iraq-Iran border calm since 1975, even with the potential of Iran's support for opposition groups in Iraq. Moreover, the Iranians dominated the Straits of Hormuz and could easily block Iraqi access to the Persian Gulf – the main oil-export route. Seen from America's perspective, the fall of the Shah was a disaster, the loss of a major ally who had protected American interests in the Gulf and in the Middle East, a pillar of American foreign policy. The new balance of power required new strategic thinking and the design of new plans for military intervention to protect the oilfields of Persian Gulf states and the maritime navigation route in the straits. It seemed that the evolving crisis between the United States and Iran created an opportunity to reexamine American relations with Iraq.

Notes

1. A. Baram, 'Qawmiyya and Wataniyya in Ba'athi Iraq: The Search for a New Balance', *Middle Eastern Studies*, 19:2 (April 1983), pp. 188–200; A. Sousa, 'The Eradication of Illiteracy in Iraq' in T. Niblock (ed.) *Iraq, the Contemporary State* (London: Croom Helm, 1982), pp. 100–8; E. Davis, *Memories of State: Politics, History, and Collective Identity in Modern Iraq* (Berkley: University of California Press, 2005), Chapter 6, pp.148–75; A. Rohde, *State-Society Relations in Ba'thist Iraq* (London and New York: Routledge, 2010).
2. Denis Payot SG, International Federation of Human Rights, 17 June 1977, Geneva, FCO 8/3025, *TNA*.
3. Reuters, 9 June 1978; Record Development Budget to the Kurdish Autonomous Region, Press Release, Iraqi Interest Section, Washington, 24 January 1977; 13 June 1977, FCO 8/3025 *TNA*; according to an official Iraqi statement: the development budget for the Kurdish people reached 690 million IQD (Iraqi Dinar) in 1978; CIA National

Foreign Assessment Center, 'The Kurdish Problem in Perspective', August 1979, www.foia.cia.gov.Last accessed 13 August 2017.

4. Hammadi-Kissinger meeting December 1975; Senator Abourezk visit January 1974, and Senator Stevenson in November 1976; report by Senator Adlai E. Stevenson on his trip to the Middle East, 10–25 February 1976, Committee on Banking, Housing & Urban Affairs, *GPO*, April 1976; Baghdad 1692 (Wiley), 13 November 1976.

5. *WP*, 15 January, 4 April, 26 December 1977; *WP*, 12 June, 8 August 1978.

6. 'Intelligence on the Kurds', Memorandum from DCI (Turner) to Brzezinski, 16 May 1979, *DDRS*.

7. M. Khadduri, *Socialist Iraq – A Study in Iraqi Politics since 1969* (Washington, Middle East Institute, 1978), pp. 90–1.

8. T. Ismael, *The Rise and Fall of the Communist Party* (New York, Cambridge University Press, 2008), pp. 181–203, 236–7; Al-Rasid, 4 May 1978; *Al-Thawra*, 28–9 May 1978 in: *MECS* 2 (1977–8), pp. 519–20.

9. In May 1978, at least thirty-one ICP members and supporters had been executed following a hasty trial, *Ibid.*

10. Jammal al-Din Nuri, *Mudhakirat Baha' al-Din Nuri* (London: Dar-al-Hikma, 2001), pp. 466–76.

11. Saddam Hussein in a press conference, 18 July 1978. In S. Hussein, *Al-Iraq Wa al- Siyyasa al-Dawliyya*, Vol. 5 p. 165.

12. C. Moss Helms, *Iraq: The Eastern Flank of the Arab World* (Washington: Brookings Institution Press, 1984), p. 79; P. Marr, *The Modern History of Iraq* (Boulder CO: Westview Press, 1985), p. 239; *MECS* 2 (1977–8), pp. 519–20.

13. T. Ismael, *The Rise and Fall of the Communist Party*, p. 181.

14. 'The Soviet Union and the Third World: A Watershed in Great Power Policy?', *CRS Report*, 8 May 1977; 'Soviet Scientific and Technical cooperation with the Countries other than the United States', *CRS Report* to the House Committee on Science and Technology, February 1979.

15. Data on Ba'th members representation in the Party institutions by ethnic, social and religious features, since 1952: H. Batatu, *The Old Social Classes, and the Revolutionary Movements of Iraq* (Princeton: Princeton University Press, 1978), pp. 1080–8; A. Baram, *National Integration and Exclusiveness in Political Thought and Practice in Iraq under the Ba'th, 1968–1982*, Ph.D dissertation (Jerusalem Hebrew University, 1986), pp. 52–87.

16. O. Bengio, 'Shi'is' Politics in Ba'athi Iraq', *Middle Eastern Studies*, 21:1 (January 1985), p. 3.

17. U. Dann & O. Bengio, 'Iraq', *MECS* Vol. 1(1976–7), pp. 405, 408; A. Baram, *Saddam Husayn and Islam, 1968–2003 Ba'thi Iraq from Secularism to Faith* (Washington DC: Woodrow Wilson Center, John Hopkins Press, 2014), pp. 124–8.

18. Al-Hawadess (London), 1 April 1977 in Bengio, 'Shi'is Politics...' p. 4; Sluglett & Sluglett, *Iraq since 1958, From Revolution to Dictatorship* (New York: Palgrave Macmillan, 1987), p.199;

19. A. Baram, 'The Ruling Political Elite in Ba'thi Iraq, 1968–1986: The changing features of a collective profile', *International Journal of Middle East Studies*, 21(1989), pp. 447–93.

20. A. Baram, *Saddam Husayn and Islam*, pp. 129, 132; Bengio, 'Shi'is politics', p. 4.

21. Baghdad 520, 824 (Wiley), 26 March, 1 April 1977.

22. A. Dawisha, *Iraq – A Political History* (Princeton NJ: Princeton University Press, 2006), p. 211. Dawisha is quoting Iyad 'Alawi who heard from Saddam, in 1970, how he admired

Stalin and his control over the masses, adding that Saddam considered Stalinism was the most appropriate model for Iraq.

23. *Ibid.*, p. 212. Based on the memoires of Taleb Shabib.
24. On the soaring political power of Saddam 1975–1977 see: A. Baram, 'Saddam Hussein - A Political Profile', *The Jerusalem Quarterly*, 17(1980), pp. 128–32.
25. A. Baram, 'Saddam's Power Structure: The Tikrities before, during and after the war' in T. Dodge & S. Simon (eds), *Iraq at the Crossroads: State and Society in the Shadow of Regime Change* (IISS Adelphi Paper 354:59, 2003), pp. 93–113.
26. Batatu, *The Old Social Classes*, p. 1078; Sluglett & Sluglett, *Iraq since 1958, From Revolution to Dictatorship*, pp. 184–5.
27. For the Ba'th hierarchy and the process of recruitment see J. Sassoon, *Saddam Hussein's Ba'ath Party: Inside an Authoritarian Regime* (Cambridge and New York: Cambridge University Press, 2012), Chapter II.
28. For 'civilian' description of the regime as reported to Washington from Baghdad: Baghdad 167, 380, 31 March, 1 July 1973; Baghdad 280, 1 May 1974; Baghdad 506, 1 May 1975.
29. P. Malovany, *The Wars of Modern Babylon* (Tel Aviv: Maarachot, 2009), pp. 50–3; Marr, *The Modern History of Iraq*, pp. 215–16.
30. Malovany, *The Wars of Modern Babylon*, pp. 54–5.
31. 'The Military Balance 1979-1980' (IISS London) in *MECS* III (1978–9), p. 527.
32. Malovany, *The Wars of Modern Babylon*.
33. Saddam insisted that a French technical team would come to Baghdad within a week of his Paris visit. *Al-Jumhuriyya*, 4 March 1975: K. Timmerman, *The Death Lobby – How the West armed Iraq* (New York: Bantam Books, 1991), p. 24.
34. Memorandum from Brzezinski to the President, 21 November 1977 (Top Secret-Sensitive), Carter Presidential Library, NSA-Brzezinski material, President's Daily Report File.
35. NSC Memorandum for Brzezinski, Middle East, 28 November 1977, *DDRS*.
36. F. Fukuyama, *The Soviet Union and Iraq since 1968* (The Rand Corporation, Santa Monica, 1980), p. 42; O. Smolansky & B. Smolansky, *The USSR and IRAQ – The Soviet Quest for Influence* (Durham NC: Duke University Press, 1991), pp. 25–6.
37. K. Stein, *Heroic Diplomacy: Sadat, Kissinger, Carter, Begin and the quest for Arab-Israeli peace* (New York, 1999; Tel Aviv, Maarachot, 2003), pp. 255–6; W. Quandt, 'The Middle East conflict in U.S. strategy 1970–1971', *Journal of Palestine Studies*, 1:1: 1971, pp. 39–52.
38. *MECS* II (1977–8), p. 527.
39. C. Moss-Helms, *Iraq: The Eastern Flank of the Arab World*, pp. 78–9; Smolansky & Smolansky, *The USSR and IRAQ*, p. 27.
40. Smolensky & Smolensky, *The USSR and IRAQ*.
41. U.S. ACDA 1980, 180 in Smolansky & Smolansky, *The USSR and IRAQ*, p. 29.
42. 'The Military Balance 1979-1980' (IISS London), in *MECS* III (1978-9), pp. 582–3.
43. CIA memorandum (Turner) to Brzezinski, 'Communist Intervention Comparison', 15 August 1979, Carter Presidential Library, NSA-Staff Material, North/South.
44. A. Ben-Zvi, *From Truman to Obama: The Rise and the Early Decline of American-Israeli Relations* (Tel Aviv: Yedi'ot Ahronoth, 2011), pp. 142–4.
45. C. Vance, *Hard Choices: Four Critical Years in Managing America's Foreign Policy* (New York: Simon and Schuster, 1983), pp. 160–1.
46. *Al-Jumhuriyya* 17, 21 February 1977.

47. Diary, 7 March 1977, in J. Carter, *Keeping Faith – Memoirs of a President* (New York, Bantam Books, 1982), p. 273.
48. Stein, *Heroic Diplomacy*, pp. 227–9.
49. Nicholas Veliotis, Deputy Assistant Secretary of State for Near Eastern and South Asian Affairs, criticised the President's statement saying that it did not make sense to promise the Palestinians US public support without any Palestinian concession in return. Stein, *Heroic Diplomacy*, p. 243.
50. Brzezinski interview with Stein, 30 October 1992, in Stein, *Heroic Diplomacy*.
51. *Al-Jumhuriyya*, 20, 30 June 1977.
52. Memorandum from Hamilton Jordan to President Carter, Confidential/Eyes Only, June 1977, *Carter Presidential Library*, Chief of Staff Jordan Files, Foreign Policy Issues Work Plans, 34 A.
53. *Al-Jumhuriyya*, 14, 23 September, 1977.
54. In addition to the rivalry between the Syrian and Iraqi Ba'th over legitimacy, Syria considered Lebanon, as a natural Syrian sphere of influence. E. Kienle, *Ba'ath v. Ba'ath – The Conflict between Syria and Iraq 1968–1989*. (London: I.B. Tauris, 1991), p. 93.
55. C. Vance, *Hard Choices*, p. 176.
56. Message for President Carter from King Hussein, 28 August 1978, *FRUS* IX #17.
57. Carter, *Keeping Faith*, p. 384; W. Quandt (ed.), *The Middle East: Ten Years after Camp David* (Washington DC: The Brookings Institution, 1988), p. 255.
58. Memorandum from Quandt & Sick to Brzezinski, 11 August 1977; Letter from The Association of Arab American University Graduates to the White House, 11 July 1977, *Carter Presidential Library*, WHCF Brzezinski.
59. INA, 1 October 1978.
60. Sluglett & Sluglett, *Iraq since 1958, From Revolution to Dictatorship*, p. 230. Based on Correspondent David Hurst reporting how Head of the Iraqi delegation to the Arab League Taha Yasin Ramadan was obviously active in disrupting the possibility of convening the summit in Algiers.
61. Bengio, 'Iraq', *MECS*, Vol. III (1978–9), pp. 572–3.
62. Both individuals had been Ba'th veterans. In 1978, Al-Shaikhly was sentenced to six years' imprisonment, and was murdered in prison in April 1980. Murtada al-Hadithi was called from his post in Moscow and was executed in June 1980. Bengio, 'Iraq', *MECS*, Vol. IV (1979–80), pp. 504–5.
63. On Saddam's buildup of power and support based on traditional loyalties: A. Baram, 'Saddam's Power Structure: The Tikrities before, during and after the war' in Toby Dodge and Steven Simon (eds) *Iraq at the Crossroads: State and Society in the Shadow of Regime Change* (London: Routledge, 2003), pp. 93–114.

4

The Prism of the Kurdish Revolt

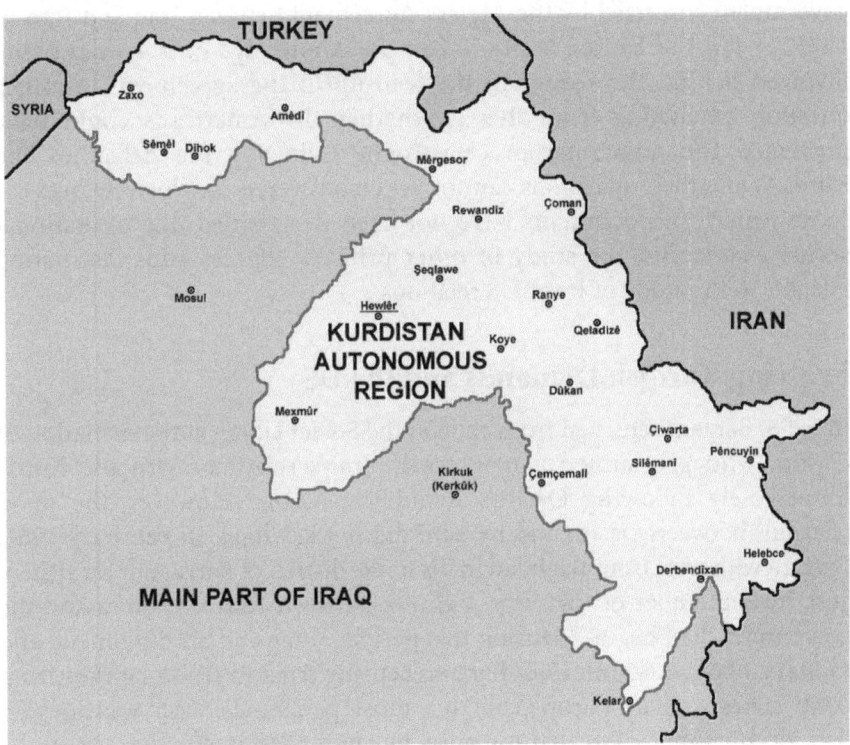

Kurdistan Autonomous Region in Iraq (in 1975)

The Kurdish issue provides an interesting prism for the examination of Iraqi-US relations. The question of Kurdish self-determination, which would apply to one-fifth of Iraq's population, while Iraqi Kurdistan comprises less than 10 per cent of Iraq's area, troubled the central government from the time the country gained independence in 1932. The Kurdish uprising led by Barzani in 1961 continued intermittently until its collapse in 1975 (though it was re-ignited following the Gulf War). The United States was involved in two opposite aspects of the uprising: granting financial and strategic support (even though not officially admitted) to the Kurds, while attempting to draw closer to the Ba'th-run government. The support Barzani received from two American allies, Iran and Israel, together with America's ongoing concerns regarding the possibility of Soviet involvement, was an important regional combination in and of itself. This combination turned the Kurdish issue into an opportunity for a comprehensive examination of regional and global factors influencing foreign policy in both Washington and Baghdad, and their bilateral relations.

One of the key questions asked in this chapter is: Was the United States government surprised by the Algiers Agreement between Iraq and Iran in 1975, or did the United States have prior knowledge of it – even being involved behind the scenes in the lead-up to the agreement? Another question emanating from this is whether the Americans could have prevented the humanitarian catastrophe following the defeat of the Kurds.While these questions cannot yet be answered conclusively because some American documents have not been declassified due to 'national security concerns', the study of other primary sources adds fascinating insights to the study of Iraqi-US relations.

Evolving Kurdish Demands and the US

In 1958, Barzani returned from exile in the Soviet Union at the invitation of Qasim, who proclaimed a new era in Iraq's relations with the Kurds immediately following Qasim's Republican coup.[1] However, the good relations between Qasim and Barzani did not last long. In February 1961, Barzani withdrew from Baghdad to his home district of Barzan, in Kurdistan, and, by September of that year, fighting between Kurdish forces and the government had begun.[2] During this period, alongside his diplomatic and military struggle within Iraq, Barzani actively tried to enlist support from Arab states and in Europe, but his most passionate wish was to gain American support. For that purpose, he conducted major changes in the Kurdistan Democratic Party's (KDP) institutions and political orientation. The party shed its revolutionary nature and redefined its goals as aspiring toward Kurdish autonomy within the Iraqi state – rather than independence from it – with moderate social policies.

This fundamentally distinguished the KDP from the ICP and the Soviet Union.[3] Subsequently, the Kurds entered negotiations with the regimes that succeeded Qasim over the recognition and implementation of Kurdish rights, alongside alternate military battles with government forces. In September 1965, the Iraqi Provisional Constitution that had been introduced in May 1964, was amended to include a general recognition of Kurdish ethnic identity within the framework of the Republic of Iraq.[4] In May 1966, the Kurdish forces, the Peshmerga, defeated the Iraqi forces in Mount Hendrin, which led Prime Minister Abd-al-Rahman al-Bazzaz to issue a twelve point program that grantedunprecedentedrecognition and rights to the Kurds as an ethnic group.[5] The Kurds' military victory may have played a part in inspiring the 1974 uprising.

Barzani consolidated his policy towards the government by demonstrating his willingness to negotiate, even after incidents of violence and the severe harassment of his men. Barzani was also careful to distinguish between relations with the government and with the Iraqi people. When his forces captured non-Kurdish Iraqi soldiers, he released them, merely availing himself of their weapons. This was a humanitarian gesture, but it was related to his inability to feed and hold prisoners. When an Israeli military adviser, Zuri Sagie, suggested that Barzani seize an opportunity to encircle a complete Iraqi division at Hendrin, Barzani refused, not wanting to humiliate the Iraqis.[6] David Karon, a Mossad liaison officer to the KDP, confirmed that Barzani repeatedly refrained from increasing military pressure on the Iraqi army, because he argued that one day he would need his connections with Baghdad to sign a peace treaty.[7] The defeat of Iraqi forces (alongside other Arab armies) in the Six-Day War elevated Kurdish morale and self-esteem as well as their confidence in the military option and Israel's offered support. His close ties with Israel, a US ally, further increased Barzani's motivation to strengthen his own direct ties with the United States.

In 1962, Barzani first requested military aid from the United States through an interview he did with a *New York Times* correspondent, Dana Adams Schmidt. Barzani claimed that the Iraqi Kurds could be of great assistance to the United States, more so than the Iranians and Turks could.[8] Further pursuit by Barzani's representatives to US embassies in Arab capitals and in Iran and Washington, requesting closer relations and financial assistance were given cautious rejections. Contact with Barzani – a nationalist tribal leader leaning toward separatism, who was violently confronting Baghdad – was considered by the Americans to be a thorn in the side of US-Iraqi relations, and his repeated appeals were perceived as a nuisance.

Moreover, the Americans suspected Barzani, who had strong contacts with the ICP and had been exiled to the Soviet Union for many years, of being a 'red Mulla' connected to the Soviets.[9] On the other hand, the Kurds were an important source of intelligence on Iraq. Though the Kurds emphasisedthat the goal of their struggle was Kurdish autonomy within the political framework of Iraq, the US reacted cautiously and continued to declare that the Kurdish struggle was an Iraqi affair.[10] America's policy of avoiding involvement in the Iraqi-Kurdish conflict remained in place, reduced to voicing support for an agreement to be reached between the government and the Kurds. According to State Department 1963 analysis, 'Failure to find a political solution soon would benefit only the Soviets and the Iraqi Communists…The United States should continue to regard the problem as strictly an internal Iraqi matter.'[11]

Washington's reports of repeated Kurdish requests for support reflect a patronising and often arrogant attitude that portrayed the Kurds as belligerent and unwilling to compromise. They also viewed Kurdish national aspirations as unrealistic.[12] Prior to Iraq cutting off relations with the US in 1967, Strong, the US ambassador in Baghdad since 1963, would regularly visit Kurdish areas and meet with members of the Kurdish establishment and administration, as well as with Kurds in Baghdad – all with the knowledge of the Iraqi authorities.[13] In May 1965, Strong was asked by Foreign Minister Naji Talib to expel Ismet Sheriff Vanly, Barzani's confidante in Europe, who was visiting the United States at that time. Talib claimed that Vanly was 'trying to establish a US headquarters of Kurdish rebels'. Vanly also requested that the United States persuade Iran to stop aiding the Kurds.[14] Washington agreed to approach the Shah on the Kurdish topic, but to tone down the language of the request.[15]

When Vanly came to Washington, he was met with across-the-board refusals from officials he had hoped to meet. The White House refused to accept letters from Mulla Barzani to President Lyndon Johnson and Secretary of State Dean Rusk. Israel's embassy in Washington, on the other hand, organised meetings for Vanly with Leonard Farbstein, a Jewish congressman (D. New York), with congressional staffers and supporters of Israel, as well as press briefings and lectures in academic forums.[16] The meetings were in accordance with clear direction from Jerusalem to assist the Kurds with their public relations in the United States.[17]

In February 1967, Barzani's representative Zaid Uthman succeeded in delivering a letter to Secretary Rusk, requesting humanitarian aid. The State Department responded by saying that such aid would be provided only by normal channels, meaning, through Baghdad.[18] Uthman had been a good source for US second secretary at the Baghdad embassy, Thomas Scotes, delivering information and assessments on the internal situation regarding the unstable government of Bazzaz and Talib.[19] After the Iraqis broke off relations with the United States in 1967, Barzani hoped for a change in attitude, and continued approaching the United States by dispatching his representatives to various American embassies.[20] But this effort failed.

The State Department assumed that the break in diplomatic relations would be temporary and that Iraq would reinstate them soon. Moreover, the State Department clung to the derogatory perception of the Kurds. An INR document of September 1967 portrayed Barzani as an aggressive leader, exploiting the weakness of the government. It also included general descriptions of the militancy of his forces. 'Kurds feel that they must be militant. The Arab defeat [to Israel] encourages Kurdish militants', it stated. 'Younger Kurdish militants must want to seize the opportunity to pounce on the defeated Arab armies and Mustafa may be concerned to hold their loyalty.'[21]

In summary, during the 1960s, Barzani adopted policy principles that, in his opinion, would allow for American support for the Kurdish demand for autonomy in Iraqi Kurdistan. Firstly, distancing the KDP from the Soviet Union and the ICP, and emphasising its social-democratic ideological platform; secondly, defining and limiting the demand for Kurdish autonomy to being within the borders of the Iraqi state. He also proclaimed maintaining a dialogue with Baghdad to encourage its recognition of Kurdish self-rule, while building a Kurdish military force that would allow for control of the Kurdish territory. Lastly, he promoted extensive diplomatic activity outside Iraq, mainly in the West, to achieve recognition and support.

American diplomats' meetings with Kurdish representatives continued discreetly in various embassies, usually at the level of low-ranking US officials. Kurds were considered a valuable source of information on the domestic situation in Iraq and on the stability of the regime, as well as on military matters such as the delivery of Soviet supplies. While regarded as biased to their own interests, the Kurdish sources sometimes delivered strategically valuable military information.[22] They received no commitments of support for their struggle in return, but embassy staff did listen, sometimes sympathetically, to descriptions of the plight of the Kurds and occasionally provided US immigration visas, as was done for the Assyrian Christian community.

With the Ba'th regime holding public, unabashed and brutal executions, Kurdish representatives in Western capitals found it easier to raise sympathy for their plight. Still, they were unable to mobilise political support. The State Department adhered to a policy of non-intervention in domestic affairs, and it blocked all of the Kurds' diplomatic initiatives. Through Barzani's representative, Prince Kumran Ali Bedir Khan appealed at the UN for a stop to what he called the 'genocide' against his people. That effort fell on deaf ears, too. The KDP continued appealing to the US for direct humanitarian aid, but wasconsistently denied.

In June 1969, the State Department had agreed to discuss the Kurdish problem at higher levels and to receive Barzani's letters, even with the actual policy unchanged. In May, Deputy Assistant Secretary of State Rodger Davies received William Younan, an American citizen serving as the president of the Assyrian American National Federation (AANF). Younan had met with Barzani in Kurdistan. Younan sought American help in the name of the Kurds and the Assyrians fighting for autonomy. He attended a second meeting at the State Department in June, this time accompanied by a KDP representative who was a US resident, Shafiq al-Qazzaz. They were received by Talcott W. Seelye, the country director for Syria, Lebanon, Jordan and Iraq. Qazzaz apparently felt the need to explain the motives behind the Kurdish attack on Iraqi oil installations in early March, because of the involvement of US companies in the IPC facility in Kirkuk. He admitted that the Kurds' aim was to overthrow the Ba'th and replace it with a more sympathetic regime that would grant them autonomy. Seelye was noticeably angered by the direct nature of the Kurdish request and firmly rejected the idea of American aid, overt or covert, to a Kurdish-Assyrian insurgency. He warned Younan that Assyrian participation in the Kurdish uprising threatened the Assyrian community in Iraq.[23] This was the only meeting that appeared in any records regarding the US-based Assyrians, a well-established community that attempted to support the Kurdish uprising.

Despite the lack of access to documents about the secret US-Kurdish contacts, it is clear that, even before 1972, covert contacts handled by CIA as opposed to open meetings did not exact a political 'price' from the United States and weren't reported to the State Department.[24]

Whether the United States had official relations with the Kurds before April 1972 is unclear, due to the lack of reliable information. However, there are claims that the United States provided financial aid to the Kurds in the 1960s. *Al-Ahd*, a pro-Iraqi Lebanese newspaper, reported that Barzani met with two American officials who flew in a specially commissioned plane from Baghdad to visit the Mulla in August 1969, signing a secret agreement and promising $14 million in assistance to the Kurds. In return, the Kurds committed to distancing themselves from the Communists and to severing their ties with the Soviet Union. Edmund Ghareeb, a researcher who quoted this source, said that a State Department official, whom he didn't name, denied the existence of such an agreement.[25]

US Allies Assisting the Kurds

Iranian-Kurdish lifeline

The Iranians had their own agenda. They were willing to support the Kurds, including providing them with military equipment, but they were strongly opposed to a negotiated agreement between the Kurds and the Baghdad government. Iran even threatened to cut aid to the Kurds due to the negotiations, which they considered to be not in their interest.[26] In retrospect, this could have been a premonition for the future. Iranian support for the Kurds was solely intended to serve Iranian interests, and Teheran would not hesitate to sacrifice the Kurds once they had served their purpose. Indeed, this is exactly what the Iranians did in 1975.

During talks between the Kurds and the Ba'th party in 1970, which culminated in the March agreement, Iran used the approach of persuasion and temptation. On 4 March, a week before publication of the statement on the 11 March agreement, Iran summoned the Mulla's son, Idris Barzani, to Tehran for a meeting with Israeli representatives, who tried to persuade him to resume military operations against the Iraqi army and promised to provide him with anti-aircraft missiles and light artillery.[27] Days later, the Iranians promised additional aid to the Kurds, wanting to convince them to reject or to avoid implementing the agreement with the Ba'th party and instead to continue the military struggle. In March 1970, Iran and Israel combined to provide $3.36 million in aid to the Kurds.[28]

Israeli Assistance

Contacts between Israel and the Kurdish national movement began before Israel became a state, in the 1940s, when the Jewish Agency's representative in Paris, Maurice Fisher, had close ties with Kumran Ali Bedir Khan.[29] Israel's direct aid to the Kurdish uprising started in April 1965, when David Kimche, stationed at the Israeli embassy in Tehran, operated as a liaison officer to the Mulla. Israel had sought to strengthen ties with the non-Arab Muslim, pro-Western states in the region, as allies against her front-line enemy states. Israel thus agreed to Iran's request to cooperate with the Kurds. Both countries wished to see Iraq weakened.[30] In practice, Israel supplied weapons, other military equipment and provided training by experienced commanders in the IDF, along with medical assistance such as a military field hospital and training of Peshmerga paramedics.[31] US intelligence agencies were aware of the Israeli-Kurdish relationship and how it evolved, but were not updated on details of Israeli military involvement in Peshmerga operations on the ground – what the American diplomats knew tended to arrive via rumours, much to the chagrin of US ambassadors. For example,the US Ambassador to Israel complained in May 1968 about not being notified of Barzani's visit to Israel and asked Washington for details of the visit.[32]

Israel's victory over Arab countries in June 1967 was celebrated by Barzani's with the Israeli mission at *Hajj Umran*,with a special greeting from Barzani, saluting the Israeli forces for gaining control of Jerusalem's Temple

Mount. In the Kurdish villages 'People were dancing in the streets, rejoicing the defeat of the Iraqi air force that was bombing daily the area with NAPLAM bombs.'[33]

Not surprisingly, the results of the war reinforced the Kurds' confidence in the military assistance provided by Israel.

The Six-Day War was over quickly, without a real Israeli need for mobilisingthe Kurds. However, Barzani was reluctant to engage with the Iraqi army at this time, and kept his front quiet during the Arab war with Israel. Kurdish-Israeli cooperation was actually at its peak when the Six-Day War broke out, following the important Kurdish achievements during the Mt Handren campaign. The Mulla's son Mas'ud (Massoud)Barzani, in his 2002 book, recalls that, on 5 June 1967, a military delegation headed by the Iraqi Chief of Staff, Hammudi Mehdi, was sent to the Mulla, asking the Kurds to desist from military operations while the Iraqi army was deployed on the front against Israel. The delegation had also asked the Kurds to send fighters on their behalf to the front.

Barzani refused, and the delegation rushed away after receiving news of the outbreak of war.[34] Later, the Mulla stressed that his contribution to Israel had been essentially expressed by his refusal to participate in the war. In April 1968, Barzani visited Israel and met the top government and security officials, including President Zalman Shazar, Prime Minister Levi Eshkol, Foreign Minister Abba Eban, Defense Minister Moshe Dayan, IDF Chief of Staff Chaim Bar-Lev and intelligence chiefs. The Mulla reiterated to the Israelis that he was interested in the support of the Americans for the Kurdish struggle and asked the Israelis, whom he thought had a decisive influence in Washington, to act on his behalf.[35]

Talks with the Ba'th Party and the Agreement of 11 March 1970

One lesson the Ba'th leadership learned from its failure to maintain the reins of power in 1963 was that silencing the Kurdish front was an essential precondition for stabilising the regime. Ba'th's concerns over Kurdish insurgency were not limited to military aspects, but included a fear that the Kurds could open an inroad for foreign influence. Therefore, as a first step, as early as August 1968, Al-Bakr announced his willingness to hold talks with the Kurds. He intended to declare an amnesty for KDP fighters, yet insisted that Jallal Talabani, the leader of Barzani's rival Kurdish faction, attend the talks. Employing the tactic of 'divide and rule', he sought to take advantage of the Kurds' internal dissension. The Iraqi army then surprised KDP forces with an air offensive in January 1969. The Ba'th support allowed Talabani forces loyal to the government to regain territory controlled by

Barzani, including Penjwen and Qal'atDiza.[36] In early March 1969, the Kurds launched a counteroffensive, in which Barzani's forces – the Peshmerga, numbering about 20,000 well-armed men – struck Talabani fighters, supported by the Ba'th party but with half the men of Peshmerga. Barzani, exploiting the weakness of the new regime, attacked an Iraqi soft belly, namely IPC oil facilities in Kirkuk.[37] The regime responded harshly with artillery and air attacks against the main Kurdish strongholds in Zakho, Rawanduz, Raniya and Qala't Dizah, inflicting civilian casualties, with extreme brutality. For example, the Kurds alleged that the government forces found a group of civilians hiding in a cave near Dukan Dam and started a fire, burning alive almost seventy people. In October, according to the Kurds, the Iraqi troops massacred the entire population of two villages. Kurdish deserters who joined the Iraqi forces and took part in the battle were mocked with the nickname *jahsh*, for donkey.[38]

The agreement between Baghdad and the Kurds, reached on 11 March 1970, marked the beginning of a hiatus in the war-battered region. From Barzani's perspective, the negotiations with Iraq had brought about the latter's recognition of his leadership – an endorsement that was well received by the other Kurdish factions. A secret clause in the agreement stated that military forces would withdraw from the region of Kurdistan; that the military forces of the faction opposing Barzani, led by Talabani, would be disbanded; and that the Peshmerga would remain in the area 'to protect its borders'.[39] The Ba'th presented the agreement as a gesture to the Kurds. After all, it included the term 'self-rule' (*hukmdhati*), recognised the Kurdish language and culture as having a place amidst the Iraqi people and included a clause obligating the inclusion of Kurdish representatives in government institutions in Baghdad.

Indeed, the Iraqi Declaration of the March agreement was the first time that any Iraqi government had recognised Kurds' right to territorial autonomy. This had great significance in the agreement's being made with a radical, pan-Arab party.[40]

From the point of view of the Ba'thists – especially Saddam –the driving force behind the agreement was that the deal was essential for the continued consolidation of Ba'th rule, particularly since the Iraqi Communist Party supported it.[41] The agreement reduced the burden on the Iraqi army, more than half of which had been engaged in combat in that area. It also prevented, or at least deferred, the escalation of Iraq's conflict with Iran, allowing the regime to concentrate on other concurrent concerns and direct its energies towards implementing agrarian reform and development programs, in order to increase the revenues of Iraq and gain popular local support for the regime. This agreement underscored the pragmatic nature of the Iraqi Ba'th

Party, which gave priority to domestic issues.[42] Negotiations with the Kurds were controversial among Ba'th leadership. Members of the civilian wing of the party, who were more pragmatic, concurred with the need to reach an agreement with the Kurds, even at the cost of making a concession and recognising the national rights of this ethnic minority. This pragmatic wing, headed by al-Bakr and Saddam Hussein, showed a novel approach to Pan-Arab ideology.[43] The very recognition of the national rights of a non-Arab minority, going so far as to openly express its opposition to Arab unity, was a highly significant change in the ideology of the two-year-old Ba'th regime. Saddam repeatedly claimed that the Kurdish problem was the most difficult challenge facing the party, and that its resolution would strengthen Iraq against its enemies, notably Iran, which had exploited the Kurdish problem.[44] The agreement was reiterated both in the interim constitution and in the National Covenant, which was published in November 1971 and promoted 'the historical alliance between the Kurdish the Arab peoples'.[45] In the eighth national conference of the Ba'th Party, the agreement was defined as a turning point for Iraq, which could now focus on the struggle against Zionism.[46] Indeed, the truce with the Kurds allowed the Iraqis to deploy more troops against Israel in the 1973 war. After Saddam was captured in 2004, he told his American interrogators that the 11 March agreement with the Kurds was one of his major achievements.[47]

For Barzani, the very idea of autonomy, within the framework of the Iraqi state, had been a declared goal. Suspicions remained, though, regarding the Ba'th party's seriousness over the implementation of the agreement. At the beginning of negotiations with the Ba'th regime, Barzani's envoy, Dara Tawfiq, met in Beirut with Michel Aflaq, the Syrian ideological founding father of the Ba'th Party. He did this at the prompting of Baghdad, to dispel Barzani's suspicions. Aflaq enthusiastically supported the reconciliation between the Ba'th and the Kurds and helped to convince Barzani to agree to the negotiations.[48] Some KDP leaders opposed Barzani's claims that the regime had exerted extraordinary pressures to encourage him to agree to the treaty, while, in practice, he could not actually reject the offer of autonomy for which he had fought over so many years.[49]

Meanwhile, the Kurds' covert cooperation with Israel continued. It included a modest Israeli presence in Iraqi Kurdistan, in anticipation of events.[50] Israeli officials, however, relayed to the United States their grave concerns regarding the possible consequences of the agreement.[51] At the end of September 1971, the director of the Mossad, Zvi Zamir, and the head of the agency's foreign liaisons department, Nahum Admoni, visited Kurdistan. A failed assassination attempt on Mulla Barzani occurred during their visit, with strong indications that Baghdad was behind it. It was clear to the guests that a deterioration in the Kurds' relations with Baghdad, and the renewal of the armed conflict, were inevitable[52]

The lull in the fighting following the 11 March agreement allowed Israel to harness the Kurds to help with the escape of Iraqi Jews through Iran. At first, the Kurdish leadership was afraid to take part in the operation, for fear of sabotaging the agreement with the Ba'th party. Jews who escaped did so independently, with the help of local smugglers, dealing with severe difficulties and hardships on the way. When it became apparent that the Ba'thists were turning a blind eye to the escape of Jews, KDP members helped the Jews' escape, with Barzani's blessing and the knowledge of a limited number of his confidants. The Israeli government gratefully acknowledged the Kurds' assistance and Barzani's patronage of the operation.[53] Because it represented the United States in Iraq, the Belgian embassy responded to requests for information from American Jewish philanthropic organisations and reported Barzani's part in the operation that helped Jews to leave Iraq for Iran through Kurdistan.[54]

The Iranians were strongly opposed to the 11 March agreement and tried to dissuade the Kurdish leadership from signing it until the last minute. However, Barzani, who saw the Ba'th proposals as unprecedented, decided to accept the offer in spite of his suspicions. On 8 March, Barzani informed Iran's Prime Minister Abbas Hoveyda that, in view of the Ba'th party's consent to grant autonomy to the Kurds, and agreeing to other demands of the KDP, he would suspend his military struggle against the regime. The Shah, incensed, threatened to withdraw his support of the Kurds, which had reached record levels. In a message to Washington, the Shah noted that he regarded the agreement as evidence of increasing Soviet influence in Iraq, and warned that the agreement would release some 20,000 soldiers from the Kurdish front who could pose a threat to the Gulf. He maintained that the Soviets strove to make the Kurds' autonomous region into an independent state under Moscow's auspices. Following this bleak forecast, the Shah demanded that Washington extend credit and aid to Iran, to enable it to deal with the new situation.[55] Despite its criticism of Barzani, Tehran maintained its ties with the Kurdish leadership in the event of the agreement's collapse – a scenario that did not seem unlikely.[56]

The Soviet Union had been one of the sides encouraging the agreement, so, of course, it welcomed it, as did the Iraqi Communist Party. Moscow regarded Iranian aid to the Kurds as an imperialist plot and encouraged the two sides to reach an agreement. One of the Iraqis involved in the negotiations was the Minister of Justice, Aziz Sharif, a former communist who was encouraged by Moscow.[57]

The US, like Britain, did not publicly address the March agreement, regarding it as an internal Iraqi matter. The State Department, contrary to the opinion of Iran and Israel, did not consider it as an indication of an increased Soviet influence in the region. Its assessment was that the agreement was more serious than any prior arrangement reached, but that its terms were vague regarding the autonomous area and its borders, and that its postponement for four years raised doubts as to its eventual implementation as a permanent settlement of the conflict between the Iraqi government and the Kurds. Furthermore, the State Department considered that even after calming the Kurdish front, the government would not rush to withdraw its forces from that area and redeploy them in the Persian Gulf. If, indeed, a decision to deploy these troops was taken, it would be more likely that they would be transferred to the Israeli front, rather than to the Gulf.[58]

In line with this evaluation, there was no change in declared US policy toward the Kurds. The Americans continued to monitor the implementation of the agreement, Iraq's internal stability, its relations with the Soviet Union and all relevant developments.

From March 1970 to May 1972: Dialogue and Suspicion

During the first year of the agreement, there were encouraging signs regarding its future implementation. Iraq invested large sums that reached, in March 1974, about 315 million British pounds in developing the area and rehabilitated buildings destroyed in the fighting.[59] Kurds were appointed to positions in Erbil, Dahuk and Sulaymaniya, and many Peshmerga fighters were enlisted in the Border Police. Educational and cultural institutions, together with communications centres– all operating in the Kurdish language – were established. The KDP openly held its convention in July 1970, with the participation of Kurdish colleagues from Syria and Iran, as well as communists. There was a relaxed sense of well-being ahead and of economic prosperity under the undisputed leadership of the Mulla.

However, disputes arose over problematic clauses in the agreement: the lack of territorial definition, the balance of powers, and the status of the KDP both in Baghdad and in the autonomous areas and the demand of Baghdad to delay full implementation of the agreement for four years in opposition to Barzani's position.[60] During the first year of implementation, Barzani attempted to unify the Kurds, and he sent emissaries to London to persuade Ibrahim Ahmad and other members of the rival Talabani faction to join him.[61] The scholar Ofra Bengio described the relations between the parties from June 1970 until September 1971 as being conducted on two different levels. Publicly, both Baghdad and Barzani expressed their desire to continue and negotiate the implementation of the agreement, while on the practical level, there was a process of deterioration and mistrust underway, emanating from both internal controversies within the Ba'th leadership and from a mutual lack of trust between the two sides about the sincerity of the other side's intentions to observe the agreement.[62] Such was the territorial problem which was focused on the oil-rich Kirkuk province; Barzani was given control of the province, but not over the city of Kirkuk, which had a mixed population. Furthermore, the government had been taking steps to settle non-Kurds in the city to weaken Kurdish claims that these strategic areas should be incorporated in the autonomous region.

The issue of representation in Baghdad also fell short of Kurdish expectations. While five Kurds were appointed as ministers with minor portfolios, the function of the vice president, who was supposed to be a Kurd, was weakened by the appointment of several additional vice presidents. The Ba'thists ruled out the candidacies of two central Kurdish figures: Ibrahim Ahmad, due to a communist past, and Habib Muhammad Karim, because of his Fayli (Kurdish Iranian Shi'i) origins. No Kurdish candidates were nominated for the higher Council of Ministers. Friction also developed over disarming the Peshmerga.

Until the end of 1971, external appearances were maintained, with negotiations seemingly progressing towards the implementation of the agreement. Even after the attempted assassination of Idris Barzani on the night of 6 December 1970, Barzani announced that he would continue abiding by the agreement. A further assassination attempt on Mulla Barzani himself, on 29 September 1971, finally signaled the true intentions of Saddam Hussein towards the Kurds. This marked a turning point, with the parties becoming more entrenched in their demands. Prospects for reconciliation deteriorated.[63]

In July and November 1971, Barzani sent his personal envoys to the US embassy in Beirut to request American direct assistance, indicating that the Ba'th regime was on the verge of collapse due to widespread anti-Ba'th opposition. The US official with whom the envoys met explained that Washington's policy of non-intervention had not changed, and added a personal observation that repeated meetings with Barzani's representatives 'engender false hopes and future misunderstandings'.[64]

Though his representatives, Barzani claimed that, as the relationship between the Ba'th and the Soviet Union grew closer, the US would be convinced to support the Kurdish struggle. He found the CIA to be more understanding of his appeals.

Kurdish sources reported regularly to the CIA about Kurdish-Iraqi tension and their anticipated confrontation with Baghdad.[65] In March 1972, a CIA source confirmed that the Soviets were putting pressure directly on the Mulla to give in to the Ba'th demand to join the National Front alongside the Iraqi Communist Party, whose members had also been recruited to persuade Barzani to join the Ba'th-ICP coalition. The pressure increased after the ICP joined the coalition. Barzani conveyed a message to the US that the Kurds would not sign any agreement with the Ba'thists if the United States were to change its position.[66] The Iranian intelligence service *Savak* warned the Americans that the National Front with the Communists and Nasserite parties would be hostile to both Iran and the United States and would turn Iraq into a Soviet satellite state.[67] According to American intelligence documents, though, most of the sources who volunteered information about Kurdistan were the Kurds themselves. In some of the reports, the metaphorical fingerprints of *Savak* are discernible, while others may have originated from *Savak*. That raises the possibility that these reports were biased towards the Iranians and the Kurds, who were trying to involve the United States in the conflict.

In mid-March 1972, Barzani's envoy presented to the CIA his pretentious plan to establish a Kurdish-Arab opposition movement that would be open to exiles opposed to the Ba'thist party and whose main purpose would be to bring down the pro-Soviet Ba'thist regime under the slogan 'The Iraqi Revolution in the North'. The Kurdish envoy expressed a lack of trust in Iranian intentions and asked for a full and direct diplomatic communication network to be established between the Kurds and the United States. In that meeting with NSC, including Richard Helms, he also reported that the Soviets promised Saddam Hussein, during his February 1972 visit in Moscow, that it would further upgrade the Iraqi military with naval mines, torpedo boats, tanks and MiG 23s and other aircraft. He added that Soviet advisers were already working on the establishment of surface-to-air missile defense systems, and that Saddam Hussein had already confided to the Soviets his plan to nationalise the Iraqi oil facilities.[68] After his son's assassination attempt, Barzani apparently approached other factors including Iraqi exiles and others hostile to the Ba'th regime in Syria, Egypt and Jordan, but without success.[69] In an attempt to keep up the appearance of continuing negotiations with Baghdad, Kurdish negotiators Salih al-Ysusfi, Dara Tawfiq and Muhammad 'Sammy' Abd al-Rahman were instructed to maintain a rigid position and assume that the Ba'th party would defer the Kurdish demands.[70]

On 3 April 1972, just before the signing of the Iraqi-Soviet agreement, Barzani's envoy, Zaid Uthman, was sent to Washington. In a meeting with his State Department acquaintance, Thomas Scotes, he noted the pressures being exerted on the Kurds, including by the Soviets, to join the National Front, and requested urgent assistance, without which they would be forced to join the Front. Uthman's request was for money to pay the salaries of some 24,000 Peshmerga fighters, and to double their number.[71] The State Department rejected the Kurdish requests, casting doubt on the Mulla's intentions of setting up an Arab-Kurd coalition party; however, the Kurdish request was forwarded to the CIA for a second opinion.[72] News of a ceremony marking the signing of the Soviet-Iraqi pact on 9 April, one week after the Uthman-Scotes meeting, validated Kurdish claims of an intensification of Soviet influence.

Change in US Policy towards the Kurds

Why did the Americans refuse to acquiesce to the requests from Barzani, Iran and Israel, and why did they eventually agree to it in 1972? Although most critics of the administration saw the policy change as coming on a spur-of-the-moment and as an ill-considered decision taken by Nixon and Kissinger, it is more likely that the shift was preceded by a re-assessment of the Iraqi Ba'th regime.

Washington's ignoring or rejecting the Kurds' requests for direct and indirect aid had been motivated by a commitment to non-interference in Iraq's internal affairs. This approach is the modus operandi of diplomacy generally. Supporting any subversive activity against the Iraqi government would have violated the political fabric of bilateral diplomacy and even jeopardised the possibility of the resumption of full diplomatic relations between Baghdad and Washington.

Moreover, from the American point of view, no radical change in policy was needed. The administration felt that it was sufficient to watch from the sidelines and express silent agreement with the support given by America's allies without becoming openly involved. Throughout this decade of conflict, the United States monitored events involving its allies and friends in the region, including the Kurdish assets, and through an ongoing dialogue with Britain, Iran and Israel. Kissinger, who described the process of change in policy, cited the US ambassador to Iran, Joseph F. Farland, who warned that, 'once launched, a Kurdish covert operation would risk becoming open-ended and if stopped, would be vulnerable to "unfortunate misinterpretations."' In this, he predicted the outcome without realising it.[73]

Until 1971, three key perceptions dominated Washington's approach to Iraq. The first perception, which was held from 1969 to 1971, was that Iraq was a weak fragmented country and did not constitute a real threat to those around it or to American interests.

Accordingly, the US viewed the regime's brutality towards its opponents and its aggression against the Kurds as due to 'aggressiveness of the weak', which indicated insecurity and instability. US intelligence stressed the inferiority of the Iraqi army. According to a September 1970 report 'The Iraqis, despite their nearly 10 years of warfare against Kurdish guerrillas, do not seem to have developed much spirit and dash. Their senior officer corps has been decimated several times by political purges'.[74] Furthermore, officials regarded the Iraqis as 'slow to implement modern weaponry. The subordination of the military under the Ba'th Party control, also left the army in poor condition'.[75] They undervalued the Iraqi army's professionalism and technological skills even following the flow of Soviet equipment and training. INR's detailed analysis of Iranian and Iraqi military forces concluded that 'the Iraqi air force suffers from a generally low level of education, training, morale, and discipline' as well as poor effectiveness of the ground forces, naval and logistical capabilities.[76] US intelligence predicted that the regime wouldn't last, in view of the attempted coups. All of these attempts were made with the blessing and assistance of Iran. However, the regime's ability to withstand these challenges, and its strengthened position subsequently, contributed to a reassessment of the situation in 1971 in both the US and the UK. The reassessment held that the Ba'th regime was actually becoming stronger and more stabilised, with no indications of its imminent disappearance.[77]

The second perception was that the closer relations between Iraq and the USSR, which stemmed from Iraq's weakness, did not present a real risk to regional stability, nor were they a catalyst in advancing a significant Soviet presence in Iraq[78] Those opposed to granting assistance to the Kurds argued that direct American aid to an insurgent faction, in opposition to a country supported by the Soviet Union, would accelerate the supply of Soviet arms to Iraq and the arms race in general – and could lead the Soviets to oppose the Kurds.[79]

The third perception relates to the professional and cultural backgrounds, and possibly the mindset, of many decision makers in Washington. Many followed a classical diplomatic approach and were reluctant to be in contact with a dissident, non-Arab faction, hoping to improve relations with the Arab countries. This approach was supported by a romantic concept of the State Department's so called Arabists who, even if not necessarily anti-Kurdish, were generally sympathetic to the Arabs, and criticised the close relations with the Shah of Iran. This approach was based on the perception that a friendlier attitude towards Iraq, including even toning down the American support to Iran, would benefit the United States. They opposed American support for the Kurds and criticised the close relationships with Iran and particularly with Israel, both of which they perceived as the main obstacles to a rapprochement with the Arabs.[80]

In almost a mirror image of the initial refraining from granting aid to the Kurds, the main reasons for Washington's policy change vis-à-vis Iraq related to global considerations, regional developments and the very nature of determining foreign policy in the Nixon-Kissinger administration.

Firstly, there was the matter of deepening Soviet influence. The main development causing concern among the countries in the region and in the US administration was the strengthening of ties between the Ba'th regime and the Soviet Union. It included an expansion of cooperation on an unprecedented scale, including the Soviets' supply of advanced weapons and the highly publicised signing by Premier Alexei Kosygin of a treaty of friendship and cooperation in Baghdad on 9 April 1972.[81] The signing did not cause immediate concern in Washington. However, with time, especially in the light of the diminished status of Egypt and President Anwar Sadat's expulsion of Soviet technical advisors on 18 July 1972, there was an accumulation of signs of the Soviets' intention to make Iraq their central ally in the Middle East. American intelligence analysts continued to express concern should the USSR have access to airports built for Iraq and to the port of Umm Qasr on an estuary of the Shatt al-Arab leading to the Persian Gulf.[82]

Israel and several Gulf states expressed their concerns over a more militant Iraq that might develop through increased Soviet assistance. The State Department regarded these fears as exaggerated or biased. The Iranians repeatedly appealed to the United States to upgrade military aid, in accordance with Nixon's doctrine of the Twin Pillar Policy that viewed Iran and Saudi Arabia as blocking the advance of Soviet interests in the region.[83] The Shah, who supported the Kurdish rebellion against its adversary Baghdad, had twice asked President Nixon to join in assisting the Kurds, in November 1971 and March 1972. In late March 1972, King Hussein relayed to Nixon a direct request on this issue, with Israel indirectly doing the same.[84] In a letter to Barzani on 31 March 1972, a senior Israeli figure (presumably the Mossad Director Zvi Zamir) stated that the Israeli government would work to deepen American awareness of the Kurdish issue. The thinking behind the letter was that the anticipated Soviet courtship of Barzani, following the Soviets' formalised and strengthened ties with Iraq, might convince Washington to support the Kurds. That, of course, had long been Barzani's ambition, one that had not been achieved.[85]

Despite the Kurds' repeated requests to the United States to give aid directly to Barzani, the National Security Council recommended that the administration continue its existing policy, which was supported by both the

State Department and the CIA. The report, written by then NSC analyst Harold Saunders, determined that Barzani could get all the assistance he needed from Iran and Israel.[86] While the requests were still rejected, this time the subject was discussed at the highest level by the White House.

Was the policy change a whim of Nixon's? On the eve of Nixon's visit to Moscow on 22–30 May 1972 to sign the historic Strategic Arms Limitation Talks agreement (known as SALT I), Iraq had already become a real threat to American interests in the Gulf, one that Kissinger defined as a 'geopolitical challenge'. Iraq was on its way to becoming a key regional ally of the Soviet Union following the treaty's signing about a month earlier and the far-reaching Soviet commitment to sending Iraq military supplies.[87]

The decision to help the Kurdish uprising was made during President Nixon's visit to Tehran on 30–31 May 1972. No discussions at the White House preceded this decision – the landmark policy change was taken by the president himself – and the subject was not included in the agenda of the visit, although it was included in background papers on Iraq and the Kurds. Kissinger had, until that point, opposed direct American involvement in the Kurdish-Iraqi conflict.

Nixon and Kissinger arrived in Tehran from Moscow, physically and mentally exhausted from a highly charged summit with the leader of the USSR Leonid Brezhnev that included the signing of the groundbreaking Anti-Ballistic Missile (ABM) and the first Strategic Arms Limitation Treaty (SALT 1) under intense media coverage. Nixon, a hardline Republican, found it difficult to digest the fact that he was the first American president in the history of the Cold War to sign an arms-limitation agreement with the Soviet Union. It was important for him to reassure the Shah that nothing had changed in Washington's attitude towards its important ally, Iran – and that the US could be counted on, even after signing the two critical agreements with the Soviet Union, not to allow Arab radicalism or Soviet weapons to serve the goals of the Arabs in the Middle East.[88] On the afternoon of 30 May, the Shah received Nixon and Kissinger in the Sa'dabad palace in Tehran. He expressed his concerns about the developments in the region, and Nixon replied that he saw no reason for euphoria following the agreement with the Soviet Union. The Soviets, he said, clung to their long-term goals of increasing leverage in the Middle East. He explained that the purpose of his visit to Iran was to reassure America's allies. The Shah reiterated the need for Iran to have the most modern weaponry to cope with Iraq and other regional allies of the Soviet Union, and expressed his concern about the possibility that the Kurds, under Soviet pressure, would be compelled to join the coalition with the Ba'th. When Kissinger sought suggestions on what could be done, the Shah replied that Iran could help the Kurds.[89]

There is no official record confirming that Nixon promised to help. However, Kissinger fills in some gaps in his book, *Years of Renewal*, noting that, during this visit, Nixon made two decisions following his conversation with the Shah. The first was to provide Iran with the F-14 or F-15 aircraft, that had been requested and ordered by the Shah but were withheld due to opposition in the Pentagon; the second was to provide direct aid to the Kurds. According to Kissinger, Nixon concluded that 'without US aid, the Kurdish uprising against the government in Baghdad may collapse'.[90] Kissinger stressed that the aid was a tribute to American allies Iran and Jordan, and was intended to maintain a regional balance. Until this point, Kissinger had also objected to the transfer of direct aid to the Kurds, and he felt that Nixon's promise was made to appease the Shah. It was important to Nixon, especially after his visit to Moscow, to bolster the Iranians and to curb the advance of Soviet interests in the Middle East.[91]

In the public debate that followed the 1976 leak (two years after Nixon's resignation) of America's aid to the Kurds, it was argued that Nixon's decision in Tehran was a sudden, even impulsive whim on Nixon's part – a hasty, irresponsible decision that had not been properly considered and approved in Washington.

However, a study of the reports and background material from April and May 1972 indicates that American perceptions of Iraq were changing in that period, with developments in Iraq and Kurdistan becoming matters of concern to US interests. The administration was no longer viewing Iraq as a weak country with domestic challenges, but, rather, as a threat to the moderate states and the Persian Gulf, including Iran. The State Department, whose officials were the main opponents to granting aid to the Kurds, had been continually pushed to the margins of decision-making in Nixon's centralised government. The perception shift may explain Nixon's decision to help the Kurds, while allowing him to satisfy the Shah's requests and allow the Iranians to procure advanced weapons systems that it couldn't obtain from Washington previously.

By May 1972, the State Department had finally come to acknowledge Barzani as the undisputed leader of the Kurds and his main rival Talabani's accepting his leadership of the struggle. The US diplomats also understood that the Kurds were convinced that the Ba'th had no intention of implementing the agreement, and therefore did not wish to join the National Front alongside the communists and nationalists. At least one of their assessments predicted that, if an uprising were to break out, the Soviets would support Baghdad. The authors of this State Department INR assessment estimated that, if the Kurds were to succumb to the demands of the Ba'th, Iraq would pose an increased threat to Iran, with the former's troops currently fighting against the Kurds being directed towards Tehran. This assessment seemed realistic in view of the deteriorating relations between Iraq and Iran following Tehran's takeover of the Gulf islands in November 1971 and the attempted coup in Iraq of Abd al-Ghani al-Rawi in January 1970 carried out with Iranian support. The State Department's assessment of the situation concluded that a takeover of the area by either a complaisant (Kurdish) pro-Ba'th faction or pro-Soviet control of Iraqi Kurdistan would increase the pressure on Iran and create a nuisance in eastern Turkey.[92]

The NSC's briefing of Nixon prior to his trip to Iran used even stronger language. It portrayed Iraq as being politically unstable, with an extreme nationalist ideology, building closer relations with the Soviet Union and being capable of threatening the Gulf States. A document from the briefing stated: 'Chronic instability and extremist nationalism bordering on the xenophobic have led Iraq to be regarded as the most unreliable and least realistic of Mideast states ... Iraq has some scare power over its weaker neighbors such as Kuwait, causing the latter to waffle on issues important to the Shah.' The document depicted the Kurds as 'the most serious threat to the stability of the regime'. The briefing notes criticised the opinion of US officials who advocated investing efforts in expanding American commercial ties with Iraq, stating that the chances of improving relations seemed nonexistent.[93] The prevailing assessment in the administration was, therefore, that the Soviet threat to the Gulf was mounting. Indeed, in Kissinger's meeting with the Chinese Premier, Zhou Enlai, on 22 June 1972, he described the Soviet Union as trying to encircle Iran through the Pakistani province of Balochistan. In that scenario, the Kurds of Iran would be encouraged to rebel against the Shah.[94]

Activating a US Covert Kurdish Operation

At the beginning of June 1972, the Shah requested that Kissinger meet two representatives of the Mulla, Idris Barzani and Mahmud Uthman, in Washington, to discuss American assistance to the Kurds. CIA Director Richard Helms advised Kissinger not to meet them. He believed that the aid should be managed as a covert operation, without publicly changing the policy of non-involvement, and noted that State Department officials of lower rank had already met Kurdish representatives.[95] Before reaching Washington, Idris Barzani and Uthman had stopped in Israel for consultations.[96]

The Kurdish representatives met on 30 June 1972 with Helms himself and an NSC official, Colonel Richard T. Kennedy. The Kurds were carrying a tiger hide from Kurdistan as a gift from the Mulla for President Nixon. The next day, the Kurdish delegates presented the CIA officials with an update on the Soviet threat and on the volatile situation within Iraq, and gave details of their military needs. Barzani requested political, financial and military support as well as assistance with intelligence. His wish list included regular, direct contacts with US government representatives.

Helms stipulated several pre-conditions. Firstly, he said, the very existence of the relations with the US must be kept under cover as a *sine qua non*, and the United States would not publicly support the Kurdish pursuit of autonomy. Secondly, there would be no American direct communications with the Mulla, but messages would be transmitted through Tehran. Thirdly, the US would not transfer military equipment directly, so as not to expose its involvement; it would do so indirectly, probably via Iran.[97]

Nixon assigned his former Treasury Secretary, John B. Connally, to carry out the new policy. He focused mainly on the military procurement package, but also had to reaffirm to the Shah the US's willingness to help the Kurds. Kissinger's cable with instructions to Connally was shared on a need-to-know basis, and the State Department was not informed of its contents.[98]

CIA officials would later testify before the House Permanent Select Committee on Intelligence on the clashing views within the agency, and stated that the CIA was not consulted on 'whether the project should be done'.[99] Helms formulated a proposal for the aid package to the Kurds, in response to the requests from Idris Barzani and Uthman. Alexander M. Haig, Kissinger's deputy, noted in his own handwriting on the proposal that the importance and urgency of the program had increased in the light of Egypt's expulsion of Soviet advisers on 18 July 1972 and the assumption that the Soviets would invest additional efforts to pressure the Kurds in Iraq.[100] In the document, Helms recommended denying both the Kurdish request for $60 million a year in assistance, as well as the request to turn the Peshmerga from being a defensive guerilla force into a larger force capable of taking the offensive. Helms believed that it was not in America's interests to encourage the Kurds to undertake any major military operations that could prompt a Soviet intervention. The CIA proposed $18 million in aid over three years, with the Iranians expressing a willingness to provide $9 million of that. Helms also recommended granting the Kurds' request for $2 million annual aid in weapons and ammunition, on the condition that the items' American origins would not be identified.[101]

The aid operation was planned under high secrecy. Information remained strictly compartmentalised, with only a few White House officials aware of the covert operation. Some details, including technical activities, were conveyed orally only, at Nixon's order.[102] To maintain secrecy throughout the process of authorisation of the operation, Helms wanted to bypass regular procedures through the Forty Committee, an executive-branch oversight body that reviewed and approved covert operations, and to inform only four senior members of the panel – Helms included. The NSC document stated that the United States supported limited military action to bolster the Kurds' defense capabilities against Iraqi military attacks. The Kurds were permitted only to initiate small-scale guerrilla attacks, 'at which traditionally they excel'.[103] The author of the document did not mince words in warning against escalating the situation to draw direct Soviet involvement, and also mentioned Turkish sensitivities. The assistance had to be kept secret because of the State Department's desire to raise the level and scope of diplomatic relations in Baghdad.[104] The plan went into action as a covert operation with the approval of President Nixon. The US allocated $250,000 a month in direct support for FY 1973, plus $2 million for ammunition, at the total of $5 million a year; the Shah contributed a larger sum. Total aid to the Kurds including from Iran, Israel and Britain amounted to $1 million a month.[105]

The Pike Committee, named after Rep. Otis Pike, the chairman of the House Select Intelligence Committee, was charged in June 1975 with investigating the processes of approval and control of covert operations, especially in the CIA. The panel selected the US's covert operation in the Kurdish uprising from 1972 to 1975 as one of the test cases. Parts of the committee's report were leaked to New York's *The Village Voice* weekly newspaper, and revealed that US aid totaled $16 million and proceded without the deliberation and approval of the Forty Committee. Members of the committee received a single paraphrase regarding the nature of the operation and were asked only to acknowledge its receipt, due to the secrecy and compartmentalisation surrounding the matter.[106] Kissinger later stated that the Pike Committee had blown up the claim that no discussions had been held regarding approval of the plan. He retorted that the committee's chairman and vice chairman, who were exposed to the plan, could have expressed objections, but, according to the Intelligence Committee tradition of consensual non-partisanship, chose not to do so.[107] It is clear, however, that the aid operation to the Kurds was carried out covertly to allow deniability where necessary. The contacts with the Kurds were carried out verbally or through the Iranian channel, with no written or signed agreements. In the opinion of the American journalist Jonathan Randal, who addressed the matter in the late 1990s, Kissinger did not meet the Mulla and his representatives, and avoided making any written commitment to Barzani, though it is doubtful whether even that would have prevented the Shah from withdrawing his commitment to the Kurds, as he did in 1975.[108]

The Americans received regular reports on the situation from Iranian and Israeli sources.[109] In fact, the US ran a dual policy toward Iraq. On the political level, open attempts were made, led by the State Department, to renew diplomatic relations with Iraq and expand economic cooperation. On the security level, steps were taken to undermine the radical, pro-Soviet Ba'th regime by supporting the Kurds.[110]

The Consolidation of the KDP

July 1972 through to April 1974

Riots broke out spontaneously in the Kurdish region in response to Iraq's nationalisation of oil facilities on 1 June 1972, since the move weakened the Kurds' demand for a share of the oil-production revenue from Kirkuk. Iraq suppressed the riots by police and army contingents supported by the air force.[111] In July 1972, the Kurds reported another assassination attempt on Barzani, this time by a person posing as a journalist. Meanwhile, the Kurds found Baghdad's process of appointing Kurds to government positions to be unsatisfactory.[112] Despite the lack of trust between the sides, the 1970 agreement endured until April 1974.

Thanks to the US aid, bolstered by assistance from Israel and Iran, the Kurds began a process of military buildup and establishing a political system. Barzani was able to impose his authority over almost the entire area of Kurdistan, although he was criticised by some of his own party. Those on the left were critical of Barzani for distancing himself from the communists, and accused him of aggressive centralist tribal activity and promoting a personality cult. This criticism culminated in the defection to the Iraqi side of key Kurdish figures in 1974.[113]

American aid began to arrive in the summer of 1972, transferred by the Iranians through CIA channels. The first shipment included 500 AK-47 rifles and ammunition. The CIA reported, in October, that the regime showed signs of distress at Barzani's reluctance to cooperate and deployed two-thirds of the army to the Kurdish region.[114] The National Intelligence Estimate (NIE) in December 1972 stated that, since Barzani was granted significant aid, he was less likely to succumb to Iraqi and Soviet pressure to assent to the Ba'th demands.[115] Consequently, Kissinger backed, in March 1973, the suggestion of the then-CIA Director James Schlesinger to increase American funding for the Kurds. In his memo to the president, Kissinger emphasised that the Kurds should be supplied with defensive weapons only, and that there was no intention of giving the Kurds the impression that there was any kind of long-term American commitment.[116] Retrospectively, it appears that there was no adequate follow-up and evaluation of the aid program, and Kissinger noted the lack as a lesson to be learnt from the episode.

October 1973: The Kurds Refrain from Assisting Israel

Kissinger apparently did not want to obstruct future negotiations with Iraq. In October 1973, the Israeli liaison officer in Tehran, identified only as 'B', asked Barzani to act militarily against Iraqi forces in Kurdistan, thereby reducing the expedition force moving towards Israel. Israel sent a similar message to the Shah and the US. Barzani was reluctant to act and forwarded the Israeli request to the US, under the pretext that such decisions were the Americans' to make. Helms, who was aware of the Shah's position against assisting Israel in its campaign with the Arabs, consulted with new CIA Director William Colby. Both recommended to Kissinger that the Kurds not be allowed to attack the Iraqi army for the sake of Israel.[117] It is possible that the Kurdish operations personnel on the ground were more concerned about the continuity of and consequences for the aid program, which had begun a year earlier. The CIA's opinion reached the White House for approval on 15 October. The Yom Kippur War had been launched against Israel a week earlier, and Kissinger convinced Nixon to object to Israeli requests that Barzani take the offensive against the Iraqi army.[118] Since the start of the American involvement, in a covert operation with the Kurds, Washington had become the dominant factor influencing Barzani's decision-making process, with Israel taking a minor role. The Kurds' refraining from assisting Israel at a critical time of the latter's war was a major disappointment to the Jewish state's leadership. Nahum Admoni, then head of Mossad's foreign liaisons department, was quoted as saying, 'We expected them to do the very least of the least. Stopping the Iraqi forces from heading to the front would have been significant, but they let us down.'[119]

The US position, which reflected Kissinger's personal view, seemed strange to the members of the Pike Committee. 'During the Arab-Israeli war, when the Kurds might be able to strike at a distracted Iraqi government, Kissinger, according to the (Pike) report, personally restrained the insurgents from an all-out offensive on the occasion when such an attack might have been successful',[120] the committee said in a report.

NY Times columnist William L. Safire attacked Nixon's decision in 1976, after reports were leaked to the press, claiming that the Kurds had prepared to initiate an offensive, but Kissinger had prevented them from taking action. This claim is partially substantiated. While Barzani was not eager to help

Israel in 1973, as he was unenthusiastic in 1967, it is reasonable to assume that he would have acceded to the Israeli requests had there been a United States' agreement. Only one source –Massoud Barzani's 2002 book, *Al-Barzani wal-Haraka a-Tahririyya al-Kurdiyya* (Barzani and the Kurdish Liberation Movement) – cites a promise made by Barzani to the Iraqis not to take advantage of future Arab-Israeli wars by engaging with the Iraqi army.[121] It is safe to assume that any such promise was not known to the United States. Kissinger's stance remained perplexing to the Pike Committee.[122] In a 1976 interview, the Mullah explained that it had been a Kurdish conviction not to engage with the Iraqi army during conflicts with Israel as he did in 1967. He denied receiving any instruction from Kissinger.[123] This Kurdish attitude is consistent with the Mullah's principle of keeping an open channel for future political arrangement with Baghdad, and with other Arab states.

In his 1979 book, *White House Years*, Kissinger responded to his critics, claiming that there was a consensus among American intelligence personnel that the Kurds would be defeated in such an attack. In his view, the Israelis were also party to this appraisal.[124] This explanation inferred Kurdish military inferiority. Kissinger may have been referring to earlier Israeli assessments regarding difficulties the Peshmerga had faced in acquiring the military tactics of regular armies. Some of those difficulties existed because of the traditions of tribal and small-scale guerilla warfare. Irrespective of these explanations, Kissinger's arguments were irrelevant to the Israeli request. In his *Years of Renewal*, published in 2000, Kissinger put forward another argument. He stated that the idea for the Kurds to attack using guerrilla warfare tactics had only been raised on 15 October, when the war had already turned in Israel's favour on the southern front; that obviated the need for such a Kurdish attack. Whatever his motives, Kissinger ultimately accepted Colby's view that a Kurdish offensive would endanger Barzani and his entire operation.[125]

Several factors were involved in the Kurds' decision not to mount an attack on the Iraqi army during the Arabs' war with Israel. Each side was protecting its own interests. Barzani wanted to maintain his good image in the eyes of the Iraqi people and other Arab countries. According to Massoud Barzani's book, the Mulla, through Sadat, had even given his word to Baghdad ahead of the war. The Shah wanted to continue his secret negotiations with Iraq on the Shatt al-Arab waterway dispute and to avoid an open confrontation with other Arab countries. And the Americans were concerned with exposure of their undercover aid to the Kurds.

Kissinger had no qualms, however, about enlisting the Kurds to promote his negotiations with Syria. In early 1974, the Shah was asked to apply military pressure on Iraq, through the Kurdish forces, to minimise Iraqi resistance to the military-disengagement agreements that ended the Yom Kippur War. Iraq opposed any ceasefire agreement or any negotiations with Israel, and accused Assad of treason. Kissinger would later boast to Israeli Prime Minister Golda Meir that this was the reason for the Iranian-Iraqi border clashes during February and March 1974. The well-known Egyptian journalist and writer Muhammad Hasnin Heikal confirmed the American request to the Shah.[126] In March 1974, Kissinger sent a request to the Shah to encourage the Kurds to continue engaging with the Iraqi army until a separation and disengagement of forces agreement was reached on the Golan Heights.[127] The Shah passed the American message, on 19 March, to Barzani, who, in turn, asked for political assistance; that included diplomatic support in the UN for the Kurds' request for autonomy and a significant increase in Washington's aid commitment, to $360 million a year. Helms reported that the Shah was reluctant to continue meeting the growing Kurdish financial demands, especially since he realised that the commitment would last as long as the Iraqi blockade on Kurdistan continued. Helms noted that the Shah was only prepared to assist the Kurds up to a limited degree, enabling them to subsist under the blockade; he was basically interested in preventing them from acceding to Baghdad's demands, but nothing further.[128] In Helms's assessment, it was already clear in March 1974 – one year before the Algiers Agreement – that the Shah set limitations on his support for the Kurds and made clear that the aid was aimed solely at weakening Baghdad and the Soviet influence.

The Great Rebellion: March 1974 to March 1975

Iraq's involvement on the front with Israel in October 1973 did not directly affect the regime's relationship with the Kurds. From the government's perspective, the process of implementing the autonomy agreement continued, while Barzani continued to rule over quite an extensive area, using an unrelenting, tribal style of dealing with any opponents. The monetary and military aid he received went to strengthen and enlarge the Peshmerga, with the fighting force reaching 50,000 to 60,000 men. The Iraqi military had also emerged with renewed confidence following its participation in the war in Israel, and the troops were welcomed in Baghdad as heroes.

In mid-April 1974, the Kurds captured a 435-mile-long strip of land along the Turkish and Iranian borders, enabling them to take control of vital supply routes.[129] The Iraqis started an assault on 15 April during the snow's thawing period, after the ultimatum delivered to Barzani to accept the Autonomy Act had expired. The Iraqi forces deployed against the Kurds numbered some 90,000 men, 1,200 tanks, armoured personnel carriers and 200 aircrafts.[130] From this point onwards, there was a gradual but growing deviation from the goals agreed with the Iranians and the Americans. The Kurds requested additional American military and financial aid, and Barzani announced his intention to make a unilateral declaration of autonomy, which was beyond the agreed scope of the covert American aid operation to the Kurds. The operation gradually began to change from a limited one, designed to weaken the Iraqis and to prevent the Kurds from joining in a coalition with the communists, and get their autonomous rights in Iraq, into a full-scale military engagement with Iranian active participation in providing aerial and artillery support.

The Mulla's proposal to make a unilateral declaration of autonomy could have advanced the prospect to be extended beyond the Iraqi borders, with possible ramifications for the Iranians and Turks, both allies of the United States with significant Kurdish populations. Kissinger rejected the Kurdish request to double the financial aid, and instructed Helms to reiterate to Barzani the agreed scope and aims of the operation: to allow the Kurds a better position in their negotiations on autonomy with the Baghdad government by keeping the Iraqi army occupied. There had been no intention to support any withdrawal of the Kurds from the Iraqi state boundaries and create a Kurdish independent state. In May, the Shah also warned Barzani against a public declaration of a de-facto autonomy, issuing an instruction that he stick by the agreed-upon plan, according to which the Kurds were conducting a defensive campaign against a tyrannical regime to gain freedom for all Iraqis.[131]

The Americans did offer a new aid package, increasing aid from $5 million to $8 million, in addition to the $1 million they allocated to assist Kurdish refugees who had to flee their homes in Kurdistan.[132] Kissinger suggested to Nixon that, in FY1975, American aid would remain at the newly increased 1974 level, and stressed that Iran was providing more than that in aid to the Kurds.[133]

Several misunderstandings and different interpretations persisted about US policy towards the operation. According to Kissinger, retrospectively, key parties involved – the Shah, Barzani and even the CIA – each had their own ideas about the situation. The CIA field agents who handled contacts with the Kurds complained that aid was being delayed. The Shah saw a stalemate in the fighting. Barzani predicted victory even without the resources he had asked for. The Americans also had problems in assessing and focusing on the Kurds' precise needs, although it was clear that the Kurdish requests had often been exaggerated. Kissinger alluded to failures in the operation, especially failures by the CIA which was in charge of handling the operation directly with Barzani via Iran. In his memoirs, he maintains that the Kurdish autonomy campaign needed to be waged through a long-term, low-intensity struggle, such as light engagements – a sort-of a war of attrition, instead of an elongated stalemate.[134]

Then there was the issue of the covert nature of the Americans' involvement. Unlike his predecessors, Helms and Schlesinger, CIA director Colby opposed the continued aid to the Kurds. He was concerned that it would lead to a confrontation with Congress, so he delayed the transfer of aid.[135] Under the military conditions that Kissinger preferred, it would have been difficult if not impossible for the Kurds to make gains while maintaining confidentiality over the US role. It is possible that, at the time he wrote his books, facing widespread public criticism, Kissinger felt obliged to share responsibility with others. In general, apart from a single apologetic reference in his 1999 book *Years of Renewal*,[136] and in his testimony before the House Intelligence Select Committee, chaired by Otis Pike and assigned to oversee intelligence operations (which has not been released so far to the public record), Kissinger had avoided discussing the matter. From his point of view, apparently, it was a covert operation of limited scope that achieved its goals for a limited period, but then, regrettably, despite efforts to prevent the spread of classified information, it was leaked to the press under public and political pressure.

Once they got into difficulties, the Kurds also asked Israel to exert its influence on the White House to increase aid. Indeed, PM Golda Meir, when she met with Kissinger on 7 May 1974, did just that. Israel's ambassador to the United States, Simcha Dinitz, submitted a written brief summarising the situation in Kurdistan, describing the massive Soviet military involvement in Iraq and suggesting that the United States provide the Kurds with what they needed most: anti-aircraft and anti-tank weapons.[137] In August 1974, Iraqi forces re-captured strategic strongholds from the Kurds. Dinitz and White House officials formulated a detailed plan to upgrade the Kurds' combat capabilities.[138] Under the plan, approved by Nixon's successor, Gerald Ford, on 26 August, Israel would transfer to the Kurds Soviet armaments it had captured in previous wars with Arab armies that would fit the Kurds' needs, up to $28 million in value.[139] That included 82 shoulder-fired anti-aircraft SA 7 Strela missiles, 705 anti-tank Sagger missiles and 22 launchers. In return, the Americans pledged to provide parallel amounts of upgraded US equipment to the IDF.

Colonel Kennedy described the arrangement as 'a private deal between Kissinger, the Iranians and Israelis'.[140] Kissinger allowed the Iranians, who also wanted to operate within Iraq, to enter these territories for limited amounts of time. The CIA opposed this move, but Kissinger seems to have been able to overrule Colby's reservations and obtain President Ford's consent.[141] The Kurds' October 1974 request list for US munitions indicates that they held 155mm Howitzer guns, Soviet-made mortars of various types, 106mm and 107mm recoilless guns, and rocket propelled anti-tank grenade launchers RPG-7s. (Israel later supplied 57mm anti-aircraft Doshka guns as well.) A letter from Barzani was attached to the list, urging that the ammunition be supplied urgently to avoid a Kurdish collapse in the face of Iraqi military superiority; his letter requested additional air defense and anti-tank missiles.[142] The Iranians acceded to Kurdish requests for additional arms, and raised their level of support. In addition to artillery cover with batteries of 130mm and 175mm guns, the Iranians set up batteries of Rapier anti-aircraft missiles purchased from the United Kingdom and used immediately by retired British army officers at the request of Iran.[143]

From August 1974, the Kurds' weapons were upgraded by Israel. Israel supplied captured Soviet weapons and ammunition, or compatible Israeli-made weaponry, and purchased other items, paying cash,[144] including from black-market arms dealers. In this way, Israel benefited from the US aid to the Kurds. The $28 million in weapons procurement was not included in the US budget for the covert operation, but was attached to the military aid for Israel in FY1976, over which there were no differences of opinion in Congress. The subject came up in February 1975, when Dinitz asked the United States to speed up the payment to Israel, which was included in the budget for the following fiscal year in 1976. Kissinger's Deputy Brent Scowcroft retorted, in a reprimand, that a request to advance the payment and its inclusion in the supplementary budget could attract Congress's attention and prompt demands for explanations. Regarding the cash purchases, Scowcroft suggested that Israel ought to approach the Shah,[145] insinuating American deniability of black market weapon deals.

August 1974–February 1975:
Signs of Diminishing American Support

The additional aid, meant to prevent the collapse of the rebellion, was not enough. In the coming months, Barzani continually turned to the Shah and to Kissinger to request significant increases in aid. However, the expanding scope of the war, the increasing Iranian involvement and the humanitarian problem of Iraqi-Kurdish refugees who fled to Iran, all these factors had begun to make the operation a burden for both Iran and for the US.

In September 1974, the US rejected Barzani's proposal to further escalate the fighting by attacking the oil facilities in Kirkuk. The US wanted to avoid an escalation in the fighting and a worse oil crisis.[146] Barzani's motive for escalation into a full-scale offensive was to disrupt the regional balance that perhaps would enable a declaration of an independent state. These ideas caused grave concern in both Washington and Tehran. In a letter to Kissinger on 22 January 1975, Barzani indicated that he'd not given up hope of gaining full US political backing. He highlighted the Peshmerga's achievements and requested further assistance for the spring offensive. Barzani described the Ba'th regime as weak, divided and on the verge of collapse. He suggested that, together, he and Kissinger should devise a scheme to replace the Ba'th regime.[147] Colby suggested holding a meeting with a representative of Barzani, even though the most Washington intended to offer was encouragement, while refusing his request for additional aid.[148] Kissinger's reply, dated 20 February 1975, invited Barzani's representative for talks.[149] It also indicates that, at that time – about two weeks before the Algiers Agreement – even if he was aware of the contacts between Iran and Iraq, Kissinger did not believe that they would culminate in an immediate agreement. Rather, he expected the fighting to continue.

At the same time, the State Department,which was kept out of the loop, maintained deniability. The American Interest Section in Baghdad continued reporting on the heated bickering between the Ba'th newspaper *Al-Thawra* and the Kurdish daily *Al-Ta'akhi* over the implementation of the March 1970 agreement. Articles included exchange of allegations that reflected the growing gap and mistrust between the negotiating Ba'th and the Kurds. However, the fighting itself was given scant coverage in the Iraqi press.[150] According to the Ba'th, the military offensive against the Kurds was as an internal Iraqi dispute. On 20 April 1974, the heads of the Arab diplomatic delegations in Baghdad were summoned to the foreign ministry for a briefing. Iraq's deputy foreign minister, Abd-al-Hussein al-Jammali, denounced foreign intervention in the dispute with the Kurds, mainly blaming Iran. He mentioned evidence of Saudi funding and American weapons being used by the Kurds. Head of US Mission Lowrie got the impression that al-Jammali's call for Arab solidarity in facing Iran on the Kurdish issue was made mainly by choice of language and intonation.[151]

American diplomats in Iraq and Iran who received requests for humanitarian aid – meant to assist the growing number of Kurdish and Assyrian refugees who fled into Iran – transferred those pleas to the Red Cross, emphasising America's policy of neutrality in this conflict.[152] The KDP representative in Washington, Shafiq al-Qazzaz, complained that the State Department not only refused to deliver humanitarian aid directly to the Kurds, but also would not encourage any of the KDP's fundraising activities, even in private, within the US.[153] State Department officials repeatedly reiterated that their policy remained unchanged, and that humanitarian relief should pass through the Iraqi government channels. The British Foreign Office held the same position. British ambassador J.A.N. Graham even described Saddam Hussein as a 'pragmatic leader', and, from January 1975 onward, reported to London that Iraq demonstrated flexibility and a willingness to reach an agreement with Iran.[154] This illustrated the more realistic viewpoint of the British in Baghdad regarding the Ba'th regime, as compared with the vision of the State Department.

The Kurds, who were experienced in recruiting support abroad, hoped to garner international support by highlighting Iraq's human rights violations against the Kurds. They did not have much success. In April 1974, their appeal to the UN Secretary General was rejected due to the near-unanimous support the countries forming the Non-Aligned Movement (NAM) provided for Iraq, and because many countries were reluctant to discuss an internal conflict within the borders of a fellow NAM country. In early January 1975, the Kurds asked to join the International Labor Organization and to be given observer status in the International Committee of the Red Cross (ICRC) in Geneva – both diplomatic initiatives geared toward their being recognised. Both requests were refused.[155] As the Kurdish humanitarian issue worsened, while one third of the million and a half Iraqi Kurds were displaced from their homes, many crossed the border to Iran, fearing Iraqi revenge. The United States urged Arab countries to work diplomatically to influence the Iraqis to stop the fighting. The American consul in Tabriz, Iran, Ronald Neumann, warned that, in spite of the non- intervention policy, the United States' image would be damaged by inaction during a calamitous humanitarian crisis.[156]

American and Iranian concerns that a military escalation on the Kurdish front would deepen Soviet involvement did not materialise. The Soviets did not approve of Iraq's launching of full-scale assaults against the Kurds, including the use of Soviet-made artillery, resulting in a larger confrontation between Iran and Iraq. As a consequence, the Soviets reduced or delayed munitions shipments to Iraq, to the dismay of the Ba'th leadership, though the Soviet supply chain did not come to a halt. The Iraqis continued to receive significant upgrades, including MiG-23 planes. The USSR also reassured Iraq that they would provide them with Scud missiles. In September 1974, the Soviets hinted to Iran that they were concerned about the latter's support for the Kurds, and, in November, directly asked the Shah, during his visit to Moscow, why he was arming the Kurds.

'You are doing the same thing in North Vietnam with this small difference: The Kurds are being killed by Iraqis who are using the most modern weapons and have every intention of annihilating them'. The Shah responded to Brezhnev, according to the Shah's secretary, AsadollaAlam, in his report to Helms. 'The Kurds do not have these modern weapons ... Iran is helping an oppressed people [the Kurds]; you are helping aggressors.'[157]

The Soviets feared an uncontrolled military flare-up, and were concerned about their future relations with Iran. They asked the Ba'th leadership to reduce the scale of their attacks on the Kurdish population and to give Barzani the opportunity to retract. This request was made after a Kurdish delegation arrived in Moscow, asking the Soviet Union to mediate between the Kurds and the Iraqi government.[158] Graham, the British ambassador in Baghdad, had stated, in November 1974, that the Soviets were interested in resolving the conflict and were capable of applying sanctions against Iraq, which was dependent on Soviet arms.[159] Graham demonstrated again that British diplomats understood the situation in Iraq better than their American counterparts.

The Kurds Abandoned

Despite Saddam's promise to the Shah in Algiers to cease hostilities, Iraqi forces renewed their attacks on the Kurds the following day, 7 March, and, indeed, kept up the onslaught until the ceasefire took effect on 13 March. The Shah, for his part, adhered to the agreement and stopped all aid to the Kurds on 13 March. Helms, who greeted the Shah on his arrival to Tehran, described how the Shah was so determined that while still at the airport he started handing out instructions to carry out the agreement to his surprised ministers.[160]

Conveying the news of the agreement to the sides on the battlefield wasn't so simple, though. The 155mm gun batteries which had provided the bulk of the artillery cover to the Peshmerga, together with the rest of the Iranian forces, were ordered to immediately withdraw. Neither the Kurdish fighters, nor the Israelis in Barzani's headquarters, at Hajj Umran were aware of the agreement. They had no advance warning of the Shah's intention to abandon the Kurds. The Israeli delegation was instructed only on 8 March to evacuate immediately. The Iranian commanders on the ground were hastily evacuated earlier, on 6–7 of March, with a forty-eight-hour warning.[161] In February, an advanced course had been held for forty Kurdish battalion and company commanders at Iran's Reza base under the command of Israeli instructors and, during the first week of March, the Mulla had gone with Dr Mahmud Uthman to a regularly scheduled meeting with senior Iranian leaders in Tehran. The head of the Iranian intelligence service Savak, Nematollah Nasiri, told Barzani about the accord and about the Shah's decision to stop supporting the uprising.[162] Barzani found the news difficult to believe until he heard it directly from the Shah himself on 11 March. The

Shah pledged to take in the Kurdish leadership and protect Kurdish refugees within Iranian territory.

The refugee flow included a mass exodus of Kurdish fighters crossing the Iraqi border to Iran, the only place of refuge, since the USSR, Syria and Turkey had closed their borders. On 21 March, Barzani announced an end to the uprising and ordered his fighters to lay down their weapons and flee to Iran. He would be criticised by political opponents for abandoning the uprising and leaving the fighters without leadership.[163] The Iraqis did not keep their promise to the Shah to enforce an immediate ceasefire, and continued attacking the defeated Kurds. The Iranian leader complained to the Algerian mediator, and Iranian newspapers completely ignored the Iraqi violations. The Shah had decided to meet his obligations to Iraq, and also expedited the withdrawal of his troops.[164]

It became clear early on that the Shah was unwilling to force Iraq to uphold the agreement. Instead, he left it to Arab 'observers' to monitor the Iraqi compliance with the agreement. This included a general amnesty with the Kurds and encouraging safe return to Iraq of the more than 200,000 Kurds in Iranian refugee camps. It was clear that the Kurds, who were at the mercy of the Ba'th forces, would face oppression and acts of revenge in addition to the physical hardship and poverty of displaced people. CIA agents in Tehran were the first to issue this warning, on 10 March 1975, regarding the human tragedy taking place following Iran's hasty withdrawal and abandoning of the Kurds.[165] Most of the information about the situation reached the State Department through the US Consul General in Tabriz, David Newman, and from the US embassy in Tehran. According to its policy to refrain from direct aid, the United States mainly channeled assistance through the International Red Cross and through the United Nations High Commissioner on Refugees.[166] The refugee problem grew progressively worse. The Shah and Barzani both asked the United States to take action in the international arena for the displaced refugees in northern Iraq and for the hundreds of thousands of people in camps in Iran. After the Algiers Accord, the number of refugees had increased significantly when the Peshmerga fighters fled the advancing Iraqi forces in fear of retaliation.[167] Nevertheless, after the signing, Iran and Iraq rejected offers of international assistance or intervention for the refugees, and declared that they were coping with the problem themselves.[168]

The IRC announced, on 3 April, that it was halting its aid to the Kurds because of the Iran-Iraq agreement and because of Iraq's opposition to the organisation's activities on its territory, especially the IRC's supervision on the resettlement of refugees.[169] Both the US and the United Nations High commissioner for refugees (UNHCR) could explain their lack of involvement on the technical and legal grounds that the refugees, citizens of Iraq, had been pardoned and allowed to return to their homeland, which made them ineligible to meet the criteria for refugees. Kissinger would express contrition regarding the Kurdish refugees and, in his memoirs, accused CIA chief Colby of culpability for not sending direct humanitarian aid to them before the Algiers' Agreement was applied.[170]

The ailing Barzani was left behind in Iran with his sons Massoud and Idris, and a handful of confidants, including Muhammad Mahmud Abd al-Rahman, aka Sammy, who later withdrew following disagreements with Idris.[171] George Meany, the veteran leader of the powerful labour union, the American Federation of Labor and Congress of Industrial Organizations, who followed the Kurdish struggle, appealed to President Ford on 21 March for American involvement in resolving the Kurdish refugee problem.[172] When Meany petitioned again, Ford reiterated his claim that the United States was involved in the international aid effort and was monitoring the situation – even though this was not the case.

The Iraqi regime continued to argue that it held 'no grudge against the Kurdish people, who had been misled by their leader Barzani'. It organised tours for diplomats in the Kurdish region, including meetings with residents and local government officials.[173] During the first few months, the Iraqis exercised restraint in order to encourage the Kurds to return *en masse* from Iran. Those who came back were questioned at length about their activities during the uprising and had to sign a confession that they had been forced to leave their homes by the KDP.[174] The Iraqis also warned the Kurds that continued political activity wouldn't be tolerated, and that the regime would take harsh measures against offenders. In May, the *Washington Post* reporter Jim Hoagland wrote an article about information he'd received from KDP leader Habib Karim, claiming that thirty-eight Kurdish prisoners had been executed, including a senior officer of the Peshmerga, called Fridun. The group had participated in attacks on Iraqi oil facilities and later returned from exile in Iran, not heeding the advice of Barzani. The Iraqis claimed that the prisoners were executed for criminal, not political offences.[175] In August, Idris Barzani submitted to officials from the American consulate in Tabriz a list of 233 Kurds who were executed by the Iraqis during the first two months of the ceasefire.[176] The regime, he charged, was persecuting Barzani's men abroad as well. According to Vanly, an October 1976 attempt on his life was made at his Lausanne, Switzerland, home by two men presenting themselves as diplomats from the Iraqi trade mission in Geneva.[177]

There are several estimates of the number of Kurdish refugees, especially regarding their rate of return to Iraq. According to the UNHCR data, some 50,000 refugees had returned by June 1975. In mid-November, 15,000 refugees remained in camps and 35,000 intended to settle in Iran. The extent of the Arabisation of Kurdistan was even more unclear and kept secret. A Dutch estimate stated that 200,000–500,000 Kurds – up to a third of the entire Kurdish population – were not allowed to return to their homes in Kurdistan. There were also reports about the evacuation of villages in the ethnically-mixed districts in the provinces of Kirkuk, Diyala and Nineveh, and the evacuation of Kurdish villages near the Iranian border in entirely Kurdish provinces entitled to be included in the Kurdish autonomous region. Those residents were resettled in southern Iraq, cut off from their communities.[178]

Iraq's public relations effort regarding the situation of the Kurds bore some fruits through the reports of some Baghdad-based diplomats. It also served the State Department in responding to questions referred to President Ford by members of Congress and by George Meany, who, as stated above, joined together with Senator Jackson in an effort to help the Kurds.[179] Similar activities aimed at helping the Kurds were conducted in the British Parliament, notably by Conservative MP Thomas King. Several governments addressed the problem of the Kurdish refugees by stating that it was being dealt with by the Iraqi government. Consequently, the UNHCR also called off its activities in Tehran in April 1975.[180]

Ismet Sheriff Vanly was aware of the Iraqi disinformation effort when he visited the Kurdistan region in August and September of 1975. His delegation met Hashem and Aziz Aqrawi, who had defected from the Peshmerga to Baghdad and were participating in the Ba'th PR campaign. Vanly, who met with Aziz Aqrawi alone, reported that he had found a broken man, eaten away by remorse. Vanly reported that, in addition to the regime's vast Arabisation policy, that is of changing the demography of the Kurdish and mixed regions, the government wiped out all signs of ethnic identity granted in 1970. The government replaced the Kurdish school curriculum with an Arabic one, appointed non-Kurdish teachers and even renamed villages. In September 1975, the regime created new maps for the provinces, especially in the Kirkuk region, combining artificial new, non-Kurdish districts.[181] This was intended to scatter and isolate the Kurds, more effectively supervise their activities and make the Kurds' territorial claims unviable.[182]

The Shah, who met with Helms on 8 March, presented the agreement with Iraq as a national achievement for Iran. He explained that the Kurdish revolt had been on the verge of a serious escalation that could have deteriorated into open warfare against Iraq, which would have escalated Barzani's requests for additional military aid and made more likely his intention to declare Kurdish independence following the example of Cyprus. On 2 March, the Shah had met with Ashraf Marwan, Sadat's envoy, who conveyed from Baghdad a message of Saddam's willingness to withdraw from the Soviet sphere of influence if the Iranians withdrew from the north. Helms confirmed to the Shah that this fact was known to him.[183] The Iraqis apparently had sought to disseminate this message through Arab sources whom both the Shah and the Americans considered to be reliable. Helms agreed that the Iraqi willingness to give up claims to the Shatt al-Arab was too good an offer to refuse, and expressed understanding for the concerns of the Shah. According to Helms's analysis, the Shah had to consider the Arab states' pressure to end the fighting. Iran was also aware of the need to improve relations with Arab states, especially considering its own history of supporting Israel, including by supplying oil.[184]

Immediately after the declaration of the agreement, the CIA Station Chief, who had been Barzani's main contact, warned of an imminent humanitarian catastrophe that would befall the Kurds once the Iranians abandoned them. The officials' primary concern, however, was that the Kurds, if they felt that the US has abandoned them, would expose the CIA operation.[185] Helms passed Barzani a letter to Washington, suggesting that Colby would send him a conciliatory letter – 'some kind of comforting message' – to assure him that US support would continue.[186] Kissinger did not respond himself to Barzani's desperate letter, and refused to meet with him when he came to the US for medical treatment. Years later, Kissinger explained that there was nothing he could have said to Barzani to comfort him since, without an agreement with Iran and in the light of the closure of the Iranian border, the US could not continue supporting the Kurds.[187]

Kissinger and Helms could have known that something was brewing between Iran and Iraq prior to the Algiers Accord. However, in their books, both noted that the agreement caught them by surprise. The Shah, after all, did not consult with the Americans prior to making his decision. Indeed, the agreement was an Iranian achievement, and the Shah described it as a done deal, though he was the one who urged the United States to help the Kurds three years earlier.[188] Still, Helms expressed satisfaction with the agreement and advised President Ford to extend congratulations.[189] Kissinger, who was then in Israel for meetings, sent the Shah a telegram on 10 March, hinting at a disagreement concerning the Kurdish question, while noting that the Shah was entitled to act in his country's best interest. Kissinger added that the US would continue to follow with interest Iraqi policies in the area, following the reconciliation with Iran – in particular Iraq's ties with the Soviet Union.[190] Kissinger also rejected similar advice from Lowrie to send formal greetings to Saddam, though he allowed him to convey a spoken message to that effect and to encourage improving relations.[191] The British, on the other hand, allowed their representatives in

Baghdad to congratulate Saddam on the agreement.[192] In an interview with American journalist Donald Neff, Helms noted that Kissinger received the news of the agreement not only with surprise but also with great concern, but knew he could not do anything to change it.[193]

Kissinger's message to the Shah was cool, but not hostile. American relations with Iran were too important, and the Shah was determined to carry out the agreement if the Iraqis kept their commitments to Iran, even if they didn't keep them with regard to the Kurds. Kissinger thanked the Shah for his work with OPEC that led to the body's blocking a draft resolution, sponsored by Libya, Iraq and Algeria, to condemn the US for its aggression against Arab oil fields.[194] A study of correspondence between the US embassy in Tehran and Washington indicates that there was no change in the close bilateral relationship, with economic and military cooperation continuing, including the planning of a much-publicised visit of the Shah and his wife to the US capital in May. In his later writings, Kissinger admitted that the Shah's decision was consistent with overall American interest, namely to prevent a deterioration of the military conflict into an all-out war. He concurred with the Shah's assessment that Iraq's superior military strength meant that it was inevitable that they would defeat the Kurds, and any realistic effort to save them would have required military intervention involving two full Iranian divisions and US financial support of at least $300 million, which Congress would not have approved. Kissinger stressed that the Shah had made a decision fully in line with his rights as a sovereign ruler.[195]

Was the US Involved in the Algiers Agreement?

The Kurds' main complaint was that the administration, following Kissinger's lead, had been involved in the processes that led to the Algiers Agreement or, at the very least, that Kissinger knew that the agreement was being prepared but did not warn Barzani. This claim cannot be confirmed, because some of the presumed evidence remains classified by the United States on national security grounds. The material that has been released paints a picture that reflects the administration's policy and the United States' basic conception about Iraq, rather than about the Kurds. While no evidence points to Kissinger's active involvement in mediation, a listing of chronological circumstances may suggest that the Americans could have predicted this move. The purpose of this retroactive analysis is to examine, even in the absence of all or some relevant evidence, whether the Americans could have inferred the progress toward such an agreement (see Appendix I).

Saddam and the Shah met at the OPEC convention in Algiers 4–6 March 1975. Their negotiations were mediated by Algerian President Houari Boumedienne, who also served as interpreter, with the Shah speaking in French and Saddam in Arabic. Saddam agreed to the Shah's demand that he recognise Iranian sovereignty over the eastern side of the River and to set the river's thalweg[196] as the demarcation line – meaning, to cancel the 1937 agreement – and to grant amnesty to Kurdish refugees returning to Iraq. Saddam also agreed to set up a joint commission to prevent the entrance of undesirable elements, such as communists, into the Kurdish region.[197]

According to Kurdish sources, on 5 March 1975, Naseri, the head of Savak, bluntly informed Barzani in Teheran that all aid to the Kurds was being immediately cut off, and that the borders would be closed. He urged him to reach an agreement with the Iraqis. The source stated that Barzani received the news with a frozen expression and could not believe what he heard. Uthman called the move a 'betrayal'. The Shah apologised for what he said was Naseri's rude behaviour, but did not retract his decision to cut off aid immediately. Barzani returned to Kurdistan.[198]

The Shah was an autocratic leader who made decisions without consulting even his closest advisers, as can be seen in the diary of his Royal Court Minister, Asadollah Alam. Nixon, Ford and Kissinger saw Iran as a principal, powerful ally, and the Shah as a valuable asset who should be kept happy. In Zurich in February 1975, the Shah told Kissinger of his intention to meet with Saddam. Kissinger, who was focused on obtaining the Shah's consent to increase oil sales to Israel in exchange for Israel's returning the Sinai oil fields to Egypt, missed the magnitude of this shift. Two weeks later, Iran agreed to purchase US goods and services totaling $15 billion over five years. (Unofficial estimates talked of a trade volume of up to $26 billion during that period.[199])

The chain of events from 6 March onwards indicates that the Americans were surprised by the timing and by the abrupt manner with which the Shah ordered his troops to be withdrawn. The US, apparently, had not prepared a contingency plan for this eventuality and abstained from intervening. From 5 to 12 March, the Iranian artillery was withdrawn and the Kurdish front was abandoned. The Iraqis did not keep their commitment to effectuate an immediate ceasefire and continued to bomb the Kurds until 13 March.

On 9 March, Kissinger, meeting with Rabin in Zurich in his shuttle diplomacy to promote a diplomatic solution to the Arab-Israeli conflict, admitted that the Shah had alerted him of his hypothetical intention to hold talks with the Iraqis at the OPEC summit in Algiers. Kissinger reiterated that he had expressed strong opposition to the idea.[200]

On 10 March, Barzani sent a desperate letter to Kissinger, begging for direct American aid.[201] Colby decided that Barzani's letter should be kept in Washington until Kissinger returned. Fearing that the Kurds would leak the information, Colby authorised continued aid through March.[202]

During a meeting with the Shah on 25 March, Helms came to understand that the latter had moved ahead as soon as he had got what he wanted out of the agreement. The Shah stated that he was not optimistic about Iraqi intentions and expressed concern regarding Soviet-inspired Iraqi pressure on the Gulf States.[203]

On 30 April, as the expiration date neared for the final amnesty and closure of the border, the White House grew increasingly concerned about the fate of the Kurds. Kissinger quotes King Hussein in saying that he believed that Iraq intended to fulfill its commitment on Kurdish autonomy. Assistant Secretary of State Alfred 'Roy' Atherton stated that Algerian, Iranian and Iraqi observers were invited to monitor the implementation of the agreement.[204] It was convenient for the State Department to believe this in justifying its lack of intervention.

The Shah and his wife arrived in May for a well-publicised visit to Washington that demonstrated the continued close relationship between the US and Iran. In meetings with Ford and Kissinger, according to available documents, the Kurdish issue was not brought up[205] so as not to upset the Shah, who was sensitive to the media criticism of his abandonment of the Kurds.

Examining available information may suggest that the US, as well as Israel and the Kurds themselves, had reasonable indications of the progress of mediation made by Jordan, Saudi Arabia, Egypt and Algeria in the months leading to the agreement, but none of the parties believed that the attempts would succeed and that Iraq would agree to far-reaching concessions and that the Shah might cease all aid to the Kurds overnight.

Kurdish sources maintain that Kissinger was actively involved in fashioning the agreement. Khorsan even called him the 'Engineer of the Agreement', and claims that Egypt and Jordan were involved in the initiative, too.[206] In his 2002 book, Massoud Barzani blames Israel, saying that the Israelis knew of the agreement and did not exercise their influence over the Shah or the US government or warn the Kurds.[207] Marshall Wiley, who was appointed head of mission in Baghdad shortly after the signing of the agreement, is the only American official who openly argued that Kissinger played a role as mediator in the agreement. In an interview in 1989, he stated that Kissinger had brokered the agreement. Wiley did not provide his sources and wasn't officially in touch with senior Iraqis, even while serving in Baghdad. It's hard to know whether his claim is credible. He could have been repeating a widespread rumour, which he may have considered sensible and believed to be true, or he may have invented it to harm Kissinger, who, he claimed, harassed Arabists in the State Department, especially those who criticised Kissinger's close relationship with the Shah.[208] On the basis of the material available, there is no reason not to accept Kissinger's version that he was surprised by the agreement and by the speed of its implementation.

However, the materials also indicate that the US saw signs foreshadowing an agreement, following King Hussein's report to the British ambassador that the Iraqis were ready to discuss the Shatt al-Arab.[209] Kissinger shared with Dinitz his view that the concerned Shah was inclined to reach an agreement with Saddam. He did not give Dinitz, during a 22 February meeting, a reason to believe, though, that the two could actually reach an agreement so quickly. Kissinger's 22 February letter to Barzani also supports the hypothesis that he did not know about the coming agreement. Kissinger appeared to have anticipated a drawn-out stalemate.[210] His cold-shoulder response to the Shah, albeit while continuing the close cooperation with Iran, could reflect his coming to terms with the abrupt decision by the Shah, yet there is no indication that he supported the turn of events.

Possible US Involvement through Egypt

Kissinger was in frequent contact with Sadat within his shuttle diplomacy, hoping to use the close relations to reach a disengagement settlement between Egypt and Israel over the Sinai. Although there is no published evidence regarding possible American involvement in the mediation, there is a possibility, although based only on circumstantial evidence, that Kissinger was also updated in real time about the Iraqi willingness to compromise, and perhaps even sent messages which encouraged the agreement to be reached via the Egyptians.

Most writers on the process that led to the Algiers Agreement relate mainly to Boumediene's role as an intermediary, even if they briefly mention Jordan, Saudi Arabia or Egypt. As mentioned, it was King Hussein who reported to the British about Iraq's willingness to compromise on the Shatt al-Arab and to make concessions to the Kurds.[211]

According to the theory that sees American involvement, through Egypt, in reaching the Algiers Accord, Sadat identified an opportunity in Iraq's weakness. He then persuaded Iraq to moderate its position towards the peace process, and to curb Syrian criticisms, in exchange for a settlement with Iran and an end to the Kurdish uprising. According to a *L'Express* reporter in March 1976, the idea was hatched at a summit in Rabat, Morocco, in October 1974 as part of a joint initiative of the Americans and Egyptians. The initiative proposed that Iraq persuade the Shah to stop supporting the Kurds in return for Iraq moderating its stance toward the Israeli-Egyptian agreement.[212] Sadat sent his confidant, Ashraf Marwan, whom he'd appointed in February 1974 as secretary for foreign relations, on intensive shuttle trips to update Arab leaders on Sadat's endeavours with the United States, the Soviet Union and Israel, and to deal with any resistance to the diplomatic process. The Egyptians reported regularly to the Americans on these contacts. (The Head of the American Interest Section in Baghdad received regular updates from the Egyptian embassy there, indicating to Lowrie that the Egyptian rapprochement was intended to restore Iraq to the bosom of the Arab consensus. However, he did not hint at any initiative.[213])

Because of its strong opposition to the entire process, and the competition with Syria to pioneer a diplomatic settlement with Israel, Iraq was a particular challenge for Marwan. He had been working since July 1974 to encourage a rapprochement between Egypt and Iraq ahead of the Geneva Conference. Reports from Lowrie and Helms to the State Department depicted Marwan as a 'moderating' influence whom they valued for his efforts to distance Iraq from Soviet influence.[214] There is some circumstantial evidence that Marwan mediated between Iran and Iraq. He visited Baghdad in December 1974 and in late February 1975, and Tehran on 2 March 1975. The Intelligence historian Uri Bar-Yosef described how Marwan's influence in Sadat's inner circle outweighed that of Fahmi and Kissinger. His entourage was amazed by his success in removing obstacles in Damascus, Algiers and Jeddah before signing the disengagement agreement between Israel and Syria in May, as Marwan was in close contact with Kissinger's staff and with CIA representatives in Cairo.

It is possible that messages from the US were transferred through this channel, promoting an end to the conflict between Iran and Iraq, as well as to the Kurdish uprising that had, in the eyes of the US government, become a burden. According to Bar-Yosef, Kissinger and Sadat believed that, in return for persuading the Shah to stop supporting the Kurds, 'Iraqi support would become available for an Egyptian interim agreement with Israel' and Iraq could be distanced from the Soviet Union.[215] However, no documents have been found to support this claim. Marwan's frequent journeys are public knowledge and indicate that Iraq wanted to be free of its dependency on the Soviet Union and to strengthen its ties with the West without relinquishing its rejectionist stance regarding Palestine or moderating its criticism of Syria.[216] Any involvement by the US through this channel remains speculative, probably connected to Kissinger's close relationship with Sadat while working to secure an Israeli withdrawal following the Yom Kippur War. Bar-Yosef's assessments of the situation to have been affected by Kurdish and

Syrian sources, thus substantiating his theory that the United States – and Kissinger in particular – could have been behind the Algiers Agreement, seem plausible. Iraqi concessions to Iran over the Shatt al-Arab made any American-Egyptian persuasion unnecessary, and the Shah was prepared to negotiate a quick end to the fighting, which had burdened him, too. The Iraqis, after all, had backed down and made both symbolic and substantial territorial concessions, combining for an Iranian success. In an additional clause of the agreement, Iran forced Iraq to give up its claim to Arabistan-Khuzestan, an area populated by Arabs within Iranian borders.

The Iraqis welcomed the Egyptian delegation to the July National Day celebrations in 1974, even though Sadat had met with Ford in Salzburg in June, and it was clear that Egypt was determined to make progress with Israel. This fitted with Iraq's policy of ambiguity that was designed to achieve immediate goals without compromising its principles on the Arab-Israeli conflict.

US Interest in Ending the Kurdish Operation: Rapprochement with Baghdad

Although the decisions on the ceasefire and its timing were made by the Shah, the hidden interests of the United States should not be ignored. The administration was increasingly determined to see an end to the war and to terminate the covert operation. (This is not meant to indicate America's active involvement in the Algiers Agreement.) Kissinger felt that the operation was getting out of control and that the Kurdish uprising faced certain defeat without the injection of extensive support from Iran. America also had other significant interests in the region to consider, including protecting its oil supplies and preserving Iran's as keeper of stability in the Gulf.[217]

In 1975, Ford was seen as increasingly vulnerable in a bid for election on his own merit in the following year. Kissinger's central role under Nixon didn't help Ford's standing. Kissinger was aware of the executive branch's long-standing reservations regarding Kurdish aid. He became persistent over the secrecy of the activities within the CIA, where he had better control than in the State Department.[218] Kissinger opposed increasing the Kurdish aid budget from $16 million, so he continued to channel military supplies through Israel, bypassing congressional approval. Kissinger knew that Barzani's request to increase aid more than twenty-fold, to $360 million annually, would be instantly rejected by Congress.[219]

The administration understood that the operation had reached its limits and that it no longer served US interests.[220] In retrospect, it could be said that the policy objectives that led to the administration's complying with the Shah's request to support the Kurds had been met. The Kurds had not joined a coalition with the Ba'th and the Communist Party. They had cooled relations with the Soviets and had occupied the Iraqi army during the critical period of Kissinger's shuttle diplomacy between Jerusalem, Damascus and Cairo – and that dissuaded the Soviets from over-involvement in the Gulf. However, in the end, the Kurds became a burden and a risk factor in US planning. Despite their initial successes, they could not seriously take on the Iraqi army.

At this point, Iraq began to tone down its criticism of the US. The regime signaled to the American Interest Section and to official American visitors that it desired improved relations with the United States, and that the main obstacle to that was Iran's continued support of the Kurds against Iraq. On various occasions, the Iraqis claimed that the Kurds were the most aggravating issue to the regime, while the US position towards Israel and the Arab states was secondary. Iraq was most effective when it conveyed to the United States, at the end of the Kurdish campaign, its wish to diminish its dependency on the Soviet Union.

The Iraqi press was laden with vitriolic attacks against the United States, including calling America Iraq's and the Arabs' deadly enemy. It also ran cartoons mocking Kissinger himself and the entire notion that Washington's policy was friendly toward the Arabs.[221]

The nuanced Iraqi approach did have an impact on the US optimism regarding forthcoming strengthening of relations with Iraq, but did not seem to affect the US approach to the Kurdish rebellion. The US administration had its own motives for putting an end to the Kurdish rebellion that seemed to have lost control, but there was no evidence found supporting Kissinger's active involvement in the mediation process that led to the Algiers Agreement.

The Kurdish Episode: The US Perspective

From time to time over the following years, Kissinger was asked about the Kurds, and promised to talk about it in due course. In his last public reference to the issue, in his 2000 book, he responded with a somewhat apologetic tone to the criticisms raised by the Pike Committee. He said he had supported the campaign for years and fought the CIA's objections, but that his hands were tied. Drawing on the tough lessons of the Kurdish operation Kissinger referred retrospectively to: 'a case study', when he wrote about the 'need to clarify the objectives at the outset, relating goals to available means and the need to review the operation periodically and coherence among allies'. Through this, he hinted at the unilateral Iranian decision to withdraw their support to the Kurds with the Algiers Agreement. While these factors were discussed at the time, their application was not decisive enough. Kissinger concluded that the operation had met US objectives because the Iraqis may have exerted pressure on the Persian Gulf as early as 1972 had they not been distracted by the Kurds and may have sabotaged diplomatic efforts in the aftermath of the 1973 war.[222] For the Kurds, of course, this was a small consolation.

The US aid operation to the Kurds was not supposed to be exposed for many years. The first bits of information about the US aid to become public occurred after the Algiers Agreement, that had so abruptly ended the Kurdish rebellion and the American covert operation, and then from the congressional investigation committee headed by Rep. Otis Pike (a Democrat from New York). The House Intelligence Select Committee created the panel as part of its commissions of inquiry to review the integrity and effectiveness of covert operations. The committee's report included details of the operation and aroused both moral criticism of the operation itself and of covert operations as a tool for carrying out foreign policy.[223] The publication of information on the secret US operation with the Kurds embarrassed the administration. The Kurds naturally saw the Algiers Accord as a betrayal by the Shah, the US and Israel and were utterly unprepared on the announcement of the agreement. The committee did lead to tighter control by Congress over the intelligence community.

The New York Times' influential foreign affairs correspondent Cyrus Sulzberger was on his way to meet with Barzani in Tehran when the Algiers Accord was announced. Barzani promptly cancelled the interview. Barzani then published an article in favour of the Kurds' fighting for the right to self-determination. He harshly criticised the US's desertion of the Kurds, and expressed concern for their future under Ba'th rule.[224] After details of the operation were leaked from the Pike Committee, Sulzberger was joined by columnists and leaders of public opinion, including William Safire and Seymour Hersh. This time the subject was presented as proof of the failure of covert operations, as well as criticism of Nixon's and Ford's administrations' foreign policy. Safire, the *NYT* columnist, called the Kurdish campaign 'Mr. Ford's Secret Sellout'[225] and criticised Kissinger's stating that 'covert action should not be confused with missionary work'.[226]

Kissinger's comment apparently came during his testimony in a closed session before the Pike Committee. It related to the moral aspect of the covert operation, a factor he considered irrelevant. Clandestine activity, he told the panel, is, by definition, limited to specific purposes and operates under a different moral code, which is why it is undercover in the first place. By all of its definitions, the aid to the Kurds still had 'deniability', so there had been no lingering compelling rationale for continuing the operation after its objectives had been attained. On the other hand, continuing the operation may have exposed the US to certain risks, especially after the Shah, the main ally of the US and the central axis of the operation, had withdrawn his support for the Kurds.

The scandal over the covert aid program occurred in an atmosphere of lingering public disgust over the Watergate scandal. But there was more to it than the Kurds – much more. The catalyst for the congressional investigation of CIA operations and intelligence community activities in the first place was Hersh's bombshell story in the *Times* in which he wrote that the CIA acted against American citizens who opposed the Vietnam War.[227]

That led to Congress establishing investigative committees to look into the integrity of clandestine activities and to ensure that the cover of secrecy was not being misused for undemocratic activities. The Pike Committee was designed to examine the benefits and detriments of covert operations.[228] The committee did not intend to test or criticise policy. Until then, Congress had approved, almost automatically, any clandestine activity. Afterwards, constant tension between the CIA and Congress was the norm regarding the approval of and appropriations for clandestine activities, with the demand for Congressional oversight in terms of both budgetary and ethical aspects of covert operations.[229] The ninety-fourth Congress (1975–7) had Democratic majority in both the House and the Senate, and public opinion had turned against the Republican Party of Nixon, the president behind the Watergate scandal, and Ford, who pardoned Nixon. Given the political context, the Kurdish operation and the intelligence community's central role were used by critics to attack Ford and Kissinger.

Even if the US was genuinely surprised by the Algiers Accord, the question remains as to whether Kissinger should have pressed the Shah to protect the Kurds and to cushion the harsh process of their repatriation. Kissinger and Helms argued that it was impossible to influence the Shah on the matter due to his decisive personality and his hypersensitivity to criticism. It is clear that the US did not wish to spoil the relationship with the Shah, and certainly not for the Kurds. Still, the Shah was completely dependent on the United States militarily and politically, so Kissinger could have pressed him on his disregard of Iraqi violations of the terms of the agreement regarding the Kurds. He also could have been pressured to improve conditions under which the Kurds withdrew from their territories and thus helped to prevent a humanitarian disaster. US and Western pressure only postponed the date of closure of the border for one month.

Barzani's Obsession with America

Barzani wanted the Kurds to attain 'special relations' status with the United States in the same way as Israel did: receiving open backing, open political support and military aid. From the US point of view, of course, aid to the Kurds would remain covert, designed to achieve specific strategic objectives within the framework of the Cold War and, in particular, to assist a major US ally, the Shah.

After the collapse of the Kurdish revolt, many writers accused Barzani of having relied entirely on the United States, which led him to reject the Iraqi and Soviet propositions of reconciliation. Even Massoud Barzani and other Kurdish leaders claimed in the press that, had it not been for the support of the United States, Barzani would not have rejected the approaches of the Ba'th, the Soviet Union and the Communist Party or alienated the left wing of the Iraqi Kurds. Barzani was aware of the meetings between foreign ministers Hammadi and Khalatbari (of Iran and Iraq, respectively) in Istanbul – and, according to Dr Mahmud Uthman, Barzani's physician and confidant, he also knew about the two countries' significant contacts at the Arab summit in Rabat in October 1974, mediated by Jordan's King Hussein and Egyptian President Sadat, but reckoned that nothing would come of them. An earlier Egyptian attempt to mediate between Iraq and the Kurdish rebels failed because of the Shah's angry reaction when Sadat sought to summon Sami Abd al-Rahman. There had been rumours about Jordanian and Algerian mediation between Iran and Iraq as well.[230]

Yet, Barzani saw the US as the only factor through which he could achieve the goals of the Kurdish national movement, a stance he had held and maintained from the early 1960s. After the Algiers Agreement was reached, Barzani's opponents and the Iraqi propaganda machine emphasised with glee the failure of Barzani's attempts to identify with the United States. Sallah Khorsan's book, on the political movements in Iraqi Kurdistan, included interviews with both Arab and Kurdish sources, even purported to quote a letter sent by Barzani to Kissinger on 16 January, with an outlandish request to become the 51st state of the United States.[231] No such letter was ever found, though, and it is doubtful that it was ever written. Even if it was fabricated to discredit Barzani, it demonstrates the criticisms directed at the leader due to his insistence on cozying up to the US.[232]

Barzani misread Kissinger's positive response to a request to meet his representative in early 1975, and it had never occurred to him that the operation could be abruptly terminated. None considered the possibility that

Iran and Iraq may even reach an agreement, let alone implement all of its clauses immediately. Even if Barzani did realisethe limited nature of his relationship with the US (and, therefore, sought to upgrade it), he definitely regarded the US as being a morally committed guarantor, according to the Pike Committee's report, and expected the Americans to prevent the Shah from blocking their aid supply routes. Indeed, the greater his expectations, the greater his disappointment. Ambassador James Akins, who served in Iraq during the 1960s, visited Barzani at his sick-bed in the US, and heard from him that, 'Yes, we were somewhat skeptical, but we'd been urging the United States for 20 years to give us support, and finally the United States was giving us support. How could I not believe [Kissinger]?'[233]

Barzani's Unrealistic Expectations

Barzani's personality and his obsession with America also played a part in the Kurdish rebellion. Beginning in the early 1960s, Barzani sought American backing, and his conduct over the years served to emphasise this, as he withdrew from socialist and communist circles. As a traditional tribal leader, Barzani was able to persuade his people of his view that the US would be key to the success of the uprising. Barzani hoped to gain sweeping American support for the Kurds, similar to US political and military support for Israel. He adopted the Israeli example of a small country, made up of a persecuted people, receiving massive support on the basis of common interests, strategic benefits and maintaining a special relationship with the United States. Barzani's Israeli contacts coached Kurdish officials heading to Washington, even offering public relations advice regarding Capitol Hill and the media. Mulla Barzani considered the Israeli-Kurdish connection as strong and unshakeable, and disregarded the fact that Israeli assistance was dependent on Iran.[234] Barzani was unable to understand, and presumably refused to believe, that the Americans were only committed to providing limited, covert support. He did not appreciate the US's insistence on carrying out its assistance indirectly through its declared allies, Iran and Israel, to preserve deniability.

Not only Barzani's opponents, led by Jallal Talabani, but even his supporters and his son Massoud saw this as a fatal mistake, even while they pointed an accusing finger at the United States for disappointing them. According to his supporters, the Mulla would not have refused proposals made by Iraq and the Soviets so utterly had he not thought that the United States was backing him. Even the American reluctance to allow the cancer-ridden Mulla to come to the United States for treatment was regarded by the Kurds as a shameful and probably intentional insult. When Kissinger was married in February 1976, Barzani sent him a pearl necklace and carpets,[235] innocently believing that he could make Kissinger feel guilty and thus convince him to meet.

American Ambivalence towards the Ailing Mulla

The US government hoped to keep the CIA-led relief operation to the Kurds out of the public eye. However, given the plight of the refugees – particularly Barzani's close men, whose return to Iraq endangered their very lives – the embassy in Tehran recommended that the US Immigration and Naturalization Service (INS) send a representative to consider granting refugee status to Kurds who met admission criteria.[236] Mohammad Dosky, the American citizen who represented Barzani in Washington, asked Kissinger to grant refugee status to hundreds of Kurdish students,[237] a move that infuriated the Iraqis.

The US Interest Section strongly opposed granting Barzani asylum in the US, since 'presence of Kurdish leaders in USA likely to be constant future irritant in bilateral relations.'[238] The US rejected Barzani's request for political asylum in March 1975 and even refused to allow him to visit Washington. He stayed in Tehran as the Shah's guest, under the watchful eye of the *Savak*. In July, he was diagnosed with cancer and asked to receive medical treatment in the US. The visit was approved under the CIA's restrictions that were meant to keep the Mulla's presence on US soil confidential. He was not allowed to meet journalists. Barzani arrived in the United States on 30 July 1975, accompanied by his sons and his personal physician, Dr Mahmoud Uthman. He hoped to meet with Kissinger, who refused and instead dispatched Undersecretary of State Joseph Cisco. Cisco had been kept out of the loop regarding the Kurdish operation mission back when he wasAssistant Secretary for Near East and South Asian Affairs. Now, he listened to Barzani's complaints and reproaches about the Kurdish leader's misplaced trust in the United States and the distress caused to him by the Shah's betrayal.[239] At the end of October, the Mulla was returned to Iran against his wishes; his doctors at the Mayo Clinic in Minnesota thought that he only had a few months left to live. Both the Americans and the Iranians wanted to keep their involvement in the Kurdish rebellion, and their later abandonment, out of the media, especially in light of the investigation conducted by the Pike Committee on the functioning of the CIA in the affair which was not known yet to the public.

Eventually, Dosky leaked the full story about Barzani to CBS broadcaster Daniel L. Schorr. Schorr's report then ran in other media, and was quoted in the Iraqi press.[240] In May 1976, Dosky gave an ultimatum to

US Deputy Assistant Secretary of State Sydney Sober: if Barzani did not get a US visa, he would leak further details about the US treatment of Barzani, their dying and defeated ally. The State Department gave in. Dosky agreed to the US's demand that Barzani refrain from giving interviews but asked that the Mulla be given freedom of movement and be allowed to meet with people at will.[241]

During his second stay in the USA, from June 1976 until his death on 6 March 1979, Barzani remained in the Washington area, aside from his treatment at the Mayo Clinic. Iraqi intelligence followed him in the US and Barzani received FBI protection because of assassination threats.[242] Visitors included Senators Henry Jackson and William Proxmire, Congressman Stephen J. Solarz and Meany. Barzani also met with influential journalists and human rights activists, including Roberta Cohen, William Safire, Jack Anderson and Dana Adams Schmidt. Others were happy to help because of the humanitarian aspect and because of the Kurds' help in smuggling Jews out of Iraq. The Israeli embassy handed Dosky a list of friendly journalists. Jewish activists for the Kurds included Maurice Amitay, Senator Ribikoff's assistant, as well as Richard Perl, Senator Jackson's assistant.[243] Sympathetic members of Congress, as mentioned above, supported hosting ailing Barzani in the USA as well as granting student visas to Kurdish former Peshmerga fighters who could not return to Iraq safely.[244]

Massoud Barzani, describing his father's final days, directed most of his criticism at the Shah, Israel and the US. He said that both Israel and Iran were interested in prolonging the fighting, with no conclusive outcome. He thought that Israel had prior information about the Algiers Accord and should have influenced the United States – or at least warned the Kurds that the agreement was being hatched.[245] This accusation seems unfounded, given Eliezer Tsafrir's descriptions of the Israelis' utter surprise in Kurdistan and their orders to hastily evacuate – which only arrived from Israel on 8 March, when Iraqi troops began to advance and to pose a real threat to the Israelis.[246]

Massoud, in his 2002 book, did not criticise the United States, which had by then helped to establish a Kurdish autonomous region following the first Gulf War. However, David Korn, a State Department official, who described in a 1994 article the Mulla's last years in the US, highlighted the administration's embarrassment during the Mulla's residence in the country and the efforts made by the CIA and the State Department to maintain secrecy while expressing support on humanitarian grounds alone. According to Korn, Barzani's indefatigable struggle on their behalf gave Kurds everywhere a sense of national pride, but he overestimated his own powers, and his fall led to the destruction of everything he had built over the span of four decades. Ironically, Barzani's death coincided with the Shah, the main cause of Barzani's fall, losing his throne and being cast away by Iran's Islamic Revolution.[247]

Richard Helms: A Central Figure in the Kurdish Relief Operation

The CIA station at the US embassy in Tehran coordinated activity with Savak and with the Shah, without the knowledge of Ambassador to Tehran Joseph Farland (1972–3) or other embassy officials. Helms, who began his tenure as ambassador in Tehran immediately after completing his term as director of the CIA, had helped in drawing up the aid program for the Kurds. As an ambassador, Helms did not share all his actions and correspondence with the State Department and consequently had strained relations with the rest of the staff at the embassy, and especially with his deputy chief of mission, Jack Miklos.

David C. McGaffey, who was appointed as the US consul in Tabriz in 1976, said that Helms was the only embassy official with access to the Shah and his ministers. McGaffey stated that Helms censored one of his reports from Tabriz about the public feelings against the Shah.[248] Helms, who requested Nixon to be posted in Tehran, was familiar with Iran and the Pahlavi dynasty. As a CIA agent involved in the CIA operation in 1953 that toppled Iranian Prime Mininster Mohammed Mossadegh, Helms knew Iran and the Shah's family well.[249] He was also involved in planning operations in Iraq, when, in 1960, the CIA had considered the assassination of Qasim, in his capacity as deputy director of operational planning.[250]

Helms enjoyed a special relationship with Kissinger that continued after he left the CIA. From his post in Tehran, he had direct communication with Kissinger and with Kissinger's deputy at the NSC, General Brent Scowcroft. Like Helms, Kissinger did not particularly appreciate Colby and continued to consult with Helms on various topics unrelated to Helms' role in Tehran.[251] During his four year term as ambassador in Tehran, Helms traveled to Washington sixteen times, an unusual frequency for that era. Several of those visits were to testify before a congressional intelligence committee, and to defend himself after being accused of failing to tell the truth before Congress about past intelligence activity.[252]

Helms enjoyed strong ties with Washington's elite, including the Rockefellers (Nelson Rockefeller served as Ford's vice president) and, while in the capital, probably let his opinion be heard on current affairs. Helms was considered to be a professional bureaucrat – a man of action who avoided politics and initiating policy. Kissinger stated that Helms never offered a political proposal, and always answered exactly what he was asked, providing his best professional opinion, even if it was opposed to his personal position or to that of the president.[253] Thomas Powers, who wrote a critical biography of Helms, concluded the opposite – that Helms was too attentive to the president's wishes.[254] His efficiency as an operative bureaucrat was evidenced in how quickly he drew up the Kurdish relief operation in the spring of 1972, despite the reservations of the professional staff.

Summary: US-Iraqi Relations through the Kurdish Prism

Examining US-Iraqi relations through the Kurdish prism from 1968 to 1975 provides a glimpse of the components affecting their bilateral relations: the Cold War, Iran, Israel, the Middle East peace process and the Arab world, the Persian Gulf, energy, human rights and domestic factors. From March 1975 to the end of the period under consideration, in 1979, the Kurdish issue had almost completely disappeared from the bilateral agenda, even though members of the Ba'th feared that the United States and Iran would once again support dissidents in Kurdistan.

The Iraqi regime kept on with this argumentation until the resumption of full relations with the United States in 1984. This, despite the US having severed support for the Kurdish uprising and maintaining that Barzani's medical treatment and the visas granted to Kurdish students were solely humanitarian gestures. For the Ba'th regime, the Kurdish uprising was entirely a domestic threat; its reference to foreign elements was primarily directed at Iran and Syria for being involved in attempts to overthrow the Ba'th regime. US involvement, which became public knowledge in late 1975, only intensified Saddam's obsessive fear of US power, which seemed capable of toppling him.

Throughout the Kurdish crisis, the Iraqis related to the US in a restrained, sophisticated manner characterised by obfuscation and double meaning. Suppression of the Kurdish uprising was regarded as an absolute necessity for the very survival of the regime. However, the Ba'th was not persistent in its direct criticism of the United States, and signaled that relations with the United States would improve after the fighting with the Kurds ended. That, Iraq hoped, would move the US to exert its influence on Iran. Iraq sent indirect messages to the US with greater frequency in the second half of 1974 by spreading rumours, visiting American politicians (including the banker and CEO of Chase Manhattan David Rockefeller and Senator Edward Kennedy) and by using such channels as the United Nations. Other options arose in early 1975 through Arab countries – especially Egypt, Jordan and Algeria – who had recently become closer with the US. The messages were mainly intended to please the United States and to encourage its support for an Iraqi agreement with Iran.

The messages were issued to convey Iraq's intent to strengthen its relations with the US after the war with the Kurds ended, with additional intimation that Iraq would also distance itself from the Soviet Union because it would not need to rely so heavily on Soviet supplies. Even if the Iraqis overestimated the US influence on the Shah, and even if Kissinger was not involved in the Algiers Agreement, they could consider their conduct a success, because the United States ceased its support for the Kurds and was reluctant to extend even direct humanitarian aid to them, anticipating resuming full relations with Iraq.

From the American point of view, the Kurdish issue was seen in the context of Iraq's domestic situation, while primarily a byproduct of Washington's special relationship with Iran and even Israel. In acquiescing to the Shah's original request to support the Kurds and to weaken Iraq, Nixon was motivated by Cold War considerations: he was concerned that a strong, pro-Soviet Iraq could threaten US interests in the region, especially Washington's ally, Iran. In March 1975, the Soviet threat through Iraq to Iran or to the Gulf States had somewhat dissipated and the United States saw Iraq more as an ascendant, oil-rich country.

While the Kurdish issue was critical for Iraq – an existential threat to the survival of the Ba'th regime – and for Iran, it was a marginal issue for the United States in comparison with other global concerns. This was so even in the context of US policies in the Middle East, which were then focused on efforts to reach a diplomatic solution to the Arab-Israeli conflict. The administration held a lenient attitude towards the Shah. The Shah viewed the Kurdish issue as resting within his sole jurisdiction. Given the decisive steps he took and his rigid personality, the Nixon administration decided to refrain from putting pressure on this sensitive issue. It preferred safeguarding the important Iran-US alliance.

Still, from the time of the Algiers Agreement onwards, the US modified its Kurdish policy. Though the administration cut off completely all relations with the Kurds, the Kurdish problem became a constant element in US relations with Iraq in the coming decades. The administration was criticised domestically for acquiescing to the Shah's abandoning of the Kurds at the same time the Iraqis – in violation of the terms of the agreement – continued to fight and abuse the Kurds. There was also strong criticism in the media regarding the administration's attitude towards the ailing and exiled Barzani, who was allowed to remain in the US only because of public pressure and was subject to strict conditions of residence. The subject returned in full force when the Ba'th used chemical weapons against the

Kurds in a massacre in Halabja in 1988. The Kurdish autonomous region became a stronghold for US-led coalition forces that defeated Saddam after he invaded Kuwait in 1990.

Notes

Map of Iraqi Kurdistan: https://commons.wikimedia.org/wiki/File:Kurdistan_1975.png#file, last accessed 25 February 2017.

1. Mulla Mustafa Barzani returned from his exile in the USSR to Bagdad on 7 October 1958 as a national hero. For further details on the process of Barzani's resettling in Iraq till the deterioration of his relations with the Qasim regime see: Sa'ad Jawad, *Iraq & the Kurdish Question 1958-1970* (London: Ithaca Press, 1981), pp. 36–95; A.H. Rubin, 'Abd al-Karim Qasim and the Kurds of Iraq: Centralization, resistance and revolt, 1958-1963', *Middle Eastern Studies*, 43(3), pp. 353–82.

2. Details of the military battles in P. Malovany, *The Wars of Modern Babylon* (Tel Aviv: Maarachot, 2009), pp. 83–6; E. O'Ballance, *The Kurdish Struggle 1920-1994* (New York: Palgrave-Macmillan,1996), pp. 47–64; G. Chaliand*The Kurdish Tragedy* (London: Zed Books, 1994), pp. 56–63.

3. Serge Gantner, 'Le mouvement national kurde', *Orient* (Paris) 9:32–3 (1964–5), pp. 28-120 ; I.S. Vanly, 'Kurdistan in Iraq' in G. Chaliand(ed.), *People Without A Country* (London: Zed Books, 1993), pp. 153–204.

4. Article 19: 'The Iraqi citizens are equal in general rights and duties without any discrimination on the grounds of race, origin, language, religion, or any other cause. This constitution confirms the national rights of the Kurds within the Iraqi people in fraternal national unity', Embassy of the Republic of Iraq, London, *Bulletin of the Republic of Iraq for the months November–December 1965*.

5. *Al-Jumhuriyya*, 30 June 1966, in O. Bengio*The Kurdish Rebellion in Iraq* (Tel Aviv: Dayan Center, Tel Aviv University, 1989), pp.199–201; E. Ghareeb, *The Kurdish Question in Iraq* (Syracuse NY: Syracuse University Press,1981), pp. 72–4.

6. Interview with Eliezer (Geizi) Tsafrir, 11 October 2012, Ramat Hasharon.

7. Interview with AmatziaBaram, 13 February 2010; Karon was a member of Baram's Kibbutz, and they used to discuss the Kurdish issue, as a topic of mutual interest.

8. D. A. Schmidt, 'The Kurdish Insurgency', *Strategic Review*, 2 (1974), p. 54; D. A. Schmidt, *Journey among Brave Men*(Boston: Little Brown, 1964), p. 203.

9. In 1959, when Israel considered strengthening ties with the Kurds, the Foreign Office requested the Ambassador in Washington to get details about Barzani from the US administration. The ambassador's report, which reflected the American attitude and that of the intelligence community, confirmed that he deserved the nickname 'The Red', i.e. that he had Soviet-Communist leanings. See: S. Nakdimon, *AHopeless Hope: The Rise and fall of the Israeli-Kurdish Alliance:1963–1975* (Tel Aviv: YediothAhronoth-Chemed Books, 1996), p. 54

10. Douglas Little, 'The United States and the Kurds: A Cold War Story', *Journal of Cold War Studies*, 12(4) (2010), p. 68.

11. Circular Telegram from State (Rusk), 2 March1963, *FRUS* XVIII #174.

12. State (Rusk) to Baghdad, 5 April 1963, *FRUS* XVIII #208.

13. In March 1967, Ambassador Strong went on an official visit to the north and met with the governor of Erbil – the *Mutasarrif*. American financial aid and supervision of development plans for the area were under discussion. The Ambassador invited the *Mutasarrif* for a 45 day visit to learn about the matter. See Baghdad (Strong) A682, 19 April 1967, NARA Pol 2 Iraq. Box 2220.

14. Baghdad 956 (Strong), 5 May 1965, *FRUS* XXI #174.

15. State to Tehran, 11 August 1965, *FRUS* XXI #175.

16. Nakdimon, *Hopeless Hope*, pp. 96–7.

17. During this time, the Israeli Foreign Ministry instructed embassies in Washington and Paris to assist the Kurds with public relations. The Ambassador in Paris, Walter Eytan, continued his long term contacts with Kumran Ali Bedir Khan, the European representative of the Kurdish national movement, and helped expand the Kurds' connections with African states. MFA (DG Levavi) to Paris (Eytan), 1 September 1965, *Israel State Archive*: 93.2, 966/10; Embassy in Washington activities in the media and in congress: Washington (Minister Gazit) to MFA, 9 January 1966, *Israel State Archive*: 93.8, 966/10.

18. Memorandum from State (Read) to Rostow, 16 February 1967, *FRUS* XXI #189.

19. Baghdad A-719 (Duncan), 3 May 1967, *NARA*, RG 59, POL 13-3.

20. In November 1967, he sent another letter to President Johnson through his representative in Tehran, Mufti Shams al-Din,Tehran A-290 (Meyer), 30 November 1967, *NARA*, RG 59 POL 13-3.

21. Intelligence Note from State (Hughes) to Secretary Rusk, 1 September 1967, *FRUS* XXI#197.

22. For example, in June 1974, the Kurds reported an expected delivery of Soviet SCUD missiles to Iraq, *CIA Helms Collection*, 26–7 June, 10 July 1974.

23. MOC, 13 June 1969, 'Kurdish/Assyrian Appeal for U.S. Assistance', Qazzaz met with Deputy Assistant Secretary Davies 29 May, and with Talcott W. Seelye, 13 June 1969, *FRUSE*-4 #259. Talcott Seelye was an 'Arabist' with typical background: he had grown up in Beirut, his father was a Professor at the American University in Beirut and his grandfather was a missionary priest. R.T.D. Kaplan, *The Arabists – The Romance of an American Elite* (New York: Free Press, 1993), pp. 78, 111, 161; and Joseph Kraft, 'Those Arabists in the State Department', *New York Times Magazine*, 7 November 1971.

24. CIA Information Cable TDCS DB-315/01044-70, 9 March 1970, *NARA*, Nixon Presidential Materials, NSC Files Box 601.

25. Ghareeb, *The Kurdish Question in Iraq*,pp. 138–9.

26. In June 1966, for example, after a ceasefire was agreed between the Kurds and Baghdad, the US embassy in Teheran reported that the Iranians had closed the border and stopped their aid to the Kurds, Letter from Ambassador Meyers, Tehran, 22 October 1966, *FRUS XXII* #178.

27. This promise was not carried out after consideration by the Security Forces in Tel Aviv, even though some Kurds had already undergone artillery training in Israel. Interview with Eliezer (Geizi) Tsafrir, Ramat HaSharon, November 2010.

28. CIA Information Cable, TDCS DB-315/01044-70, *FRUS* E-4 #267.

29. Nakdimon, *Hopeless Hope*, Chapter Two; Bedir Khan, a Kurdish leader exiled to France who had studied in the Sorbonne, initiated the contact with Israel. Bedir Khan had close connections with Maurice Fisher, the Jewish Agency representative in Paris and with senior members of the Foreign Office after that. After Fisher's death in 1965 the Foreign Minister, Golda Meir, ordered the Ambassador in Paris, Walter Eytan, to be Bedir Khan's

new contact, even though the Foreign Ministry had already established direct formal contacts with Barzani at this time. See Foreign Ministry (Levavy) to Paris Ambassador (W. Eytan), 1 September 1965.

30. D. Kimche, *The Last Option – After Nasser, Arafat & Saddam Hussein* (New York: Scribner, 1991), p. 190.

31. Detailed descriptions of the Israeli-Kurdish connections can be found in E.Tsafrir, *Ana Kurdi* (Or-Yehuda: Hed Artzi Publishers, 1999).

32. The American Ambassador to Israel, Barbour, complained about not being notified of Barzani's visit to Israel and asked Washington for details of the visit. See: Tel Aviv 3705 (Barbour), 14 May 1968, *NARA*, POL 7 Iraq.

33. Tsafrir, *Ana Kurdi*, pp.117–18; Nakdimon, *Hopeless Hope*,pp. 194–5.

34. M. Barzani, *Al- Barzaniwal-Haraka al-Tahririyya al-Kurdiyya* (Barzani and the Kurdish Liberation Movement 2002), Part III, pp. 193–4, www.koord.com/webbook/aras/aras1/Book/sbarzani, last accessed 8 April 2014.

35. Nakdimon, *Hopeless Hope*,pp. 192–4, 221–3, 205.

36. O'Ballance, *The Kurdish Struggle 1920–1994*,p.86.

37. *The Daily Telegraph* (London), 11 March 1969, indicated that Israel was behind the attack that caused about 1000 Iraqi injuries. The Iraqi army, in response, raided the Kurdish villages with napalm and phosphor bombs.

38. O'balance, *The Kurdish Struggle 1920–1994*, pp. 87–9.

39. The secret clauses were kept away from the public eye to take into consideration the sensitivities of those who opposed the agreement – the Iraqi army and the Kurdish forces following Talabani – this making it easier for the Ba'th leadership, some of whom were also opposed to the agreement, to represent it as a positive achievement to the Iraqi public. See Bengio, *The Kurdish Rebellion in Iraq*, pp. 50–1.

40. For a detailed description of the negotiations see Bengio, *The Kurdish Rebellion in Iraq*, pp. 25–52; Ghareeb, *The Kurdish Question in Iraq*,pp.80–91; N. Entessar, *Kurdish Ethnonationalism* (Boulder CO: Lynne Rienner Publishers, 1992), pp. 69–71;Text of the agreement: Bengio, *The Kurdish Rebellion in Iraq*, Appendix II, pp. 203–5; M. Khadduri*Socialist Iraq – A Study in Iraqi Politics since 1969* (Washington: Middle East Institute, 1978), Appendix C, pp. 231–40.

41. Ghareeb, *The Kurdish Question in Iraq*,pp. 77–9.

42. A Baram, *National Integration and Exclusiveness in Political Thought and Practice in Iraq under the Ba'th, 1968–1982*, PhD dissertation (Jerusalem: Hebrew University, 1986) pp. 116-118.

43. N. Entessar (1992) p. 70.

44. MENA (Egyptian News Agency) 18 March 1970, quoted in Bengio, *The Kurdish Rebellion in Iraq*, p. 52; Ghareeb, *The Kurdish Question in Iraq*,p. 82.

45. Ahmad Hasan al-Bakr, *Mithaq al-Amal al-Watani*.(The National Charter as announced by President Ahmad Hasan al-Bakr, 15 November 1971), p.25; Official text of the interim Constitution in M. Khadduri, *Socialist Iraq*,Appendix A, pp. 183–98.

46. ABSP *Revolutionary Iraq 1968–1973 –The political report adopted by the Eighth Regional Congress of the Ba'ath Socialist Party-Iraq* (English, Baghdad, 1974), p. 104.

47. FBI Baghdad Operations Center, Interview by SSA George L. Piro, 7 February 2004. http://nsarchive.gwu.edu/NSAEBB/NSAEBB279/02.pdf, last accessed 11 August 2017.

48. E. Tsafrir, *Ana Kurdi*, p. 136.

49. Ghareeb, *The Kurdish Question in Iraq*, p. 89.

50. The small Israeli delegation remained inside Iraq, without military advisers, and was, primarily, engaged in running hospitals, training medical staff and setting up a broadcasting station, Nakdimon, *Hopeless Hope*, pp.310–12; Tsafrir, *Ana Kurdi*, pp.139–41.

51. The Director General of the Israeli MFA Gideon Rafael, presented Secretary Rogers with a grim picture, interpreting the agreement as the first step towards Iraq interceding in the Persian Gulf, maintaining that the Soviets were behind the agreement, State 54598 to Tel Aviv, 14 April 1970, *FRUS* E-4 #69.

52. Nakdimon, *Hopeless Hope*, pp. 328–30.

53. Tsafrir, *Ana Kurdi*, pp.160–2.

54. Direct Israeli involvement was not mentioned at all in the report Brussels A-477 (Eisenhower), 16 October 1970, *FRUS* E-4 #277.

55. Tehran 928 (MacArthur), 12 March 1970, *FRUS* E-4 #53.

56. Special National Intelligence Estimate (SNIE) 34-70, 3 September 1970, *FRUS* E-4 #86.

57. Ghareeb, *The Kurdish Question in Iraq*,p.90; Bengio, *The Kurdish Rebellion in Iraq*, p. 43; Smolansky&Smolansky,*The USSR and IRAQ – The Soviet Quest for Influence* (Durham NC: Duke University Press, 1991), pp. 69–70.

58. Washington to Tehran, 14 March 1970, *FRUS* E-4 #268.

59. Hugo Anson, *The Daily Star*, 14 January 1975, FCO 8/2534, *TNA*.

60. CIA Information cable IN 243628, 10 August 1970, *FRUS* E-4 #273.

61. *Ibid.*

62. Bengio, *The Kurdish Rebellion in Iraq*, p. 59.

63. For details of the deteriorating relations between the Ba'th and the KDP see Bengio, *The Kurdish Rebellion in Iraq*,pp. 59–69; M. Gunter, *The Kurds of Iraq, Tragedy and Hope* (New York: Palgrave Macmillan, 1992), pp. 15–16; Ghareeb, *The Kurdish Question in Iraq*, pp.105–13. The latter focuses on the Iraqi domestic arena, and tends to be more critical of the Kurds.

64. Zaid Ahmad Uthman was a legal adviser by profession and Barzani's confidant. He approached the Beirut embassy in July, Habib Muhammad Karim in November; Beirut (Buffum) 222, 9689, 16 July, 3 November 1971, *FRUS* E-4 #292, #293.

65. CIA Information cable IN 243628, 10 August 1970, *FRUS* E-4 #273.

66. Memorandum from CIA/NESA (Waller) to State (Sisco), 9 March1972, *FRUS* E-4 #299.

67. Memorandum from NSC (Saundres) to Haig, 27 March 1972, *FRUS* E-4 #301.

68. Memoranda from CIA (Helms) to Kissinger, Rogers and Laird, 29 and 31 March 1972, *FRUS* E-4, #302, #303; Document 302 is partially sanitised and did not reveal the identity of the Kurdish emissary, yet I assume it was MassoudBarzani that was the liaison officer to the CIA.

69. Massoud Barzani, *Al- Barzaniwal-Haraka al-Tahririyya al-Kurdiyya*, pp. 273–4; Memorandum from State (Scotes), 3 April 1972, *NARA*, RG 59, POL 13-3 Iraq.

70. Muhammad 'Sammy' abd a-Rahman, born in 1932, graduated as an engineer from Manchester University, joined Barzani, and served as a minister in autonomy rule 1970–4. He remained loyal to Barzani after the collapse of the rebellion in 1975, but left the KDP in 1979 following a rift with Massoud Barzani. He was killed in a suicide bombing in Erbil in February 2004. *Sunday Times*, 26 February 2004; Memorandum from CIA (Helms) for Kissinger, Rogers and Laird, 31 March 1970, *FRUS.E-4 #303*.

71. Memorandum (Scotes) Department of State, 3 April 1972, *NARA* RG 59, POL 13-3 Iraq, Box 1.

72. Memorandum from State (Killgore), 5 April 1972, *NARA* RG 59, POL 13-3 Iraq.

73. Henry Kissinger, *Years of Renewal* (New York: Simon and Schuster, 2000), p. 581.
74. CIA, SNIE 34-70, 3 September 1970, *FRUS* E-4 #86.
75. US Department of State, Office of the Historian.Summary Foreign Relations, 1969–1972, *FRUS* E-4, Iran and Iraq.
76. State/INR, Research Study RNAS-2, 28 January 1972, *FRUS* E-4 #164.
77. Unofficial Summary of Foreign Relations, Iran and Iraq, *FRUS* E-4.
78. NIE 36/2-72, 'Iraq's Role in Middle Eastern Problems', 21 December 1972, *FRUS* E-4 #330.
79. NSC Memorandum (Saunders), 27 March 1972, *FRUS* E-4, #301.
80. Kaplan, *TheArabists*, pp. 246–52.
81. CIA Information cable TDCS DB315/02084-72, 10 March 1972, *FRUS* E-4 #300 (partially sanitised).
82. NIE 11-6-70, 5 March 1970, 'Soviet Policies in the Middle East and Mediterranean Area' https://www.cia.gov/library/readingroom/docs/DOC_0000273218.pdf; Memorandum, Meeting of the CENTO Ministers with the President, Washington, 14 May 1970, *FRUS XXIV* #66; Baghdad 150 (Lowrie), 27 March 1973.
83. President Richard Nixon, 'Second Annual Report to Congress on U.S. Foreign Policy', 25 February 1971,*APP*.
84. Kissinger, *Years of Renewal*, pp. 580–1.
85. Nakdimon, *Hopeless Hope*, pp. 333–4.
86. NSC Memorandum (Saunders) for Haig, 27 March 1972, *FRUS* E-4 #301.
87. Kissinger, *Years of Renewal*, p. 581.
88. *Ibid.*, p. 582.
89. MOC, Shah Mohammad Reza Pahlavi, President Nixon, National Security Assistant Kissinger, Saadabad Palace, Tehran, 30 May 1972; Kissinger Telcons, Geopolitical Files, Iran (Top Secret; Sensitive, Exclusively Eyes Only) *FRUS* E-4 #200.
90. Kissinger, *Years of Renewal*, p. 583.
91. Gunter, *The Kurds of Iraq, Tragedy and Hope*, pp.26–7.
92. 'The Kurds of Iraq: Renewed Insurgency?' Research Study RNAS-10, INR, 31 May 1972, *FRUS* E-4 #310.
93. 'Iraqi Politics in Perspective', NSC Briefing Paper Prepared for President Nixon, 18 May 1972, *FRUS* E-4 #308.
94. MOC, Kissinger, Cou En-lai, Beijing, 22 June 1972, *FRUS XVII* #233.
95. NSC Memorandum from Saunders for Kissinger, 7 June 1972,Nixon Presidential Library.
96. Nakdimon, *Hopeless Hope*, p. 338.
97. MOC, Washington Meetings with Kurdish Representatives, 5 July 1972, *FRUS*, E-4 #319.
98. Backchannel message from the President's Assistant for National Security (Kissinger) to the Embassy in Singapore for Former Secretary of the Treasury Connally, 29 June 1972, *FRUS* E-4 #209; Tehran 4274 (Farland), 15 July 1972, *FRUS* E-4#213.
99. The Pike Papers, The Select Committee's Investigative Record, *The Village Voice*, 16 February 1976.
100. Memorandum from Haig to Kissinger, 'Kurdish Problem', 28 July 1972, *Ford Presidential Library*, National Security Adviser, Kissinger/Scowcroft West Wing Office Files, Box 19.
101. CIA memorandum (Helms), 18 July 1972, 'Assistance to Iraqi Kurdish Leader, Mulla Mustafa Barzani', attachment B to Haig Memorandum.

102. 'Circumvent the 40 Committee and go directly by memorandum to the President and then deal solely with OMB and Helms, or – Inform 40 Committee principals only – Johnson, Rush, the Chairman JCS and Helms – but avoid any paper and tell them that the President wants this done. Memorandum from Haig to Kissinger, 'Kurdish Problem', 28 July 1972, *Ford Presidential Library*, National Security Adviser, Kissinger/Scowcroft West Wing Office Files, Box 19.

103. *Ibid.*

104. The four principals from the 40 committee who were to be informed of the covert operation were: Helms himself; Alexis Johnson, Under Secretary of State for political Affairs; Kenneth Rush, Deputy Secretary of Defense and Admiral Thomas Moorer, Chairman of Joint Chiefs of Staff. *Ibid.*

105. Kissinger, *Years of Renewal*, p. 584.

106. 'The Pike Papers, The Select Committee's Investigative Record', *The Village Voice*, 16 February1976.

107. Kissinger, *Years of Renewal*, p. 584.

108. J.C. Randal, *After such knowledge what forgiveness?* (Boulder CO: Westview Press, 1998), pp. 157–8.

109. Kimche, *The Last Option*, p. 194.

110. Memorandum from Haig to Kissinger: 'Support for Barzani: A preliminary estimate', 28 July 1972, *Ford Presidential Library*, National Security Adviser Kissinger/Scowcroft West Wing Office Files, Box 19.

111. Lebanon (Houghton) 7605, 13 July 1972, *FRUS* E-4 #320.

112. Nakdimon, *Hopeless Hope*, p. 339.

113. O'Ballance, *The Kurdish Struggle 1920–1994*, pp. 94–5; Khadduri, *Socialist Iraq*, p. 94.

114. Memorandum from Kissinger to President Nixon, 'Progress Report on the Kurdish Support Operations', 5 October 1972, *FRUS* E-4 #325. The document is partially sanitised. The unnamed supplier of Soviet weapons was most likely Israel, which had large stockpiles of Kalashnikov submachine guns (AK 47) seized during the 1967 Six-Day War.

115. NIE36/2-72, 'Iraq's Role in Middle Eastern Problems', 21 December 1972, *FRUS* E-4 #330.

116. Kissinger, *Years of Renewal*, p. 353.

117. William Colby started his tour of duty as CIA Director only a month earlier (4 September 1973) succeeding James Schlesinger who was a temporary director, following on from Richard Helms who was removed from office and sent as an Ambassador to Iran (April 1973).

118. Memorandum from the White House (Kissinger) to CIA Director (Colby), 16 October 1973, *Ford Presidential Library*, WH NSC, Kissinger/Scowcroft West Wing Office File, Box 19.

119. Nakdimon, *Hopeless Hope*, pp. 348–9.

120. The Pike Papers, *The Village Voice*, 16 February 1976, p. 71.

121. al-Barzani, *Al- Barzaniwal-Haraka al-Tahririyya al-Kurdiyya*,Part III, pp. 287–9.

122. William Safire, 'Mr. Ford's Secret Sellout', *NYT*, 5 February 1976; Barzani, *Al-Barzaniwal-Haraka al-Tahririyya al-Kurdiyya*, pp. 193–6.

123. Ghareeb, *The Kurdish Question in Iraq*,p. 144. Interview with Mustafa al-Barzani, 13 September 1976; Interview with DrUthman in Le MondDiplomatique, 14 April 1974, quoted in Nakdimon, *Hopeless Hope*, p. 350.

124. Kissinger, *White House Years* (Boston: Little Brown & Co., 1979), p. 1265.

125. Kissinger, *Years of Renewal*, pp. 586–7.

126. M.Heikal, *Iran: The Untold Story* (New York: Pantheon Books,1982), p. 103.
127. Tehran (Helms) to the White House (Scowcroft), 16 March 1974, *CIA Helms Collection*.
128. Tehran (Helms) to the White House (Scowcroft), 20 March 1974, *CIA The Helms Collection*.
129. Nakdimon, *Hopeless Hope*, p. 357.
130. P. Malovony, *The Wars of Modern Babylon* (Hebrew)(Tel Aviv: Maarachot, 2009), pp. 83, 87.
131. Tehran (Helms) to the White House (Scowcroft), 21 May 1974.
132. Memorandum from Kissinger to the President, 11 April 1974, 'Further Support for the Kurds in Iraq', *Ford Presidential Library*, Kissinger/Scowcroft West Wing Files, Box 19; Kissinger to Tehran (Helms), n.d. 1974, *CIA Helms Collection*;The document is partially sanitised, and has no mention of the exact sum, but suggests to re-consider the volume of the assistance for the Kurds.
133. Memorandum from Kissinger to the President, 24 June 1974, 'Fiscal Year 1975 "Support for the Kurds"', *CIA Helms Collection*.
134. Kissinger, *Years of Renewal*, pp. 589–92.
135. *Ibid.*, p. 590.
136. *Ibid.*
137. MOC, Jerusalem, Kissinger, Meir, Dayan, Dinitz, 7 May 1974, *DNSA.*
138. Cable from Jerusalem translated by Shalev and dictated to General Scowcroft, 24 August 1974, *Ford Presidential Library*, Kissinger/Scowcroft West Wing Files, Box 19; Tsafrir, *Ana Kurdi*, p. 203; Israel suggested providing the Kurds with TOW and LAW missiles, and encouraging the Iranians to assist the Kurds with 155mm artillery coverage.
139. Kissinger, *Years of Renewal*, p. 591.
140. NSC Memorandum (Col. Kennedy), 17 September 1974, *Ford Presidential Library*, Kissinger/Scowcroft West Wing Files, Box 19;according to the document Israel received in return 82 Red Eye Missiles and 507 anti-tank TOW missiles.
141. MOC, Ford, Kissinger, Scowcroft, 26 August 1974, *Ford Presidential Library*, Kissinger/Scowcroft West Wing Files, Box 19.
142. Mulla Mustafa Barzani to Kissinger, 22 October 1974, Attachment: List of military needs, *Ford Presidential Library*, Kissinger/Scowcroft West Wing Files, Box 19.
143. AsadallahAlam, *The Shah and I – The Confidential Diary of Iran's Royal Court* (London: I.B Tauris, 1991), pp. 392, 403.
144. Kissinger, *Years of Renewal*, p. 591; MOC, Kissinger, Scowcroft, Dinitz, Shalev, 5 February 1975, *Ford Presidential Library*, http://www.ford.utexas.edu/library/document/memcons/1552943.pdf, last accessed 18 June 2012.
145. Dinitz raised this request with Scowcroft after Kissinger left the room. *Ibid.*
146. Kissinger, *Years of Renewal*, p. 590.
147. Mulla Mustafa Barzani to The Secretary of State Kissinger, 22 January 1975, *Ford Presidential Library*, Kissinger/Scowcroft West Wing Files, Box 19.
148. 'A visit of this kind would serve no purpose except as a hand holder', Memorandum from Peter Rodman to Kissinger, 6 February 1975, re: Reply to letter from Barzani, *Ford Presidential Library*, Kissinger/Scowcroft West Wing Files, Box 19.
149. Letter from Henry A. Kissinger to Mulla Mustafa Barzani, 20 February 1975, *Ibid.*
150. Baghdad 373, 480 (Lowrie), 1 June, 13 September 1973.
151. Baghdad 252 (Lowrie), 27 April 197; the sources for this information were the Egyptian Ambassador in Baghdad and the French Consul, who represented the North African states.

152. State 95811, 9 May 1974.
153. Beirut (Houghton) 7351, 21 June 1973; Al-Qazzaz was a US resident, and the permanent KDP representative to Washington DC. Other representatives were sent from time to time to the UN Headquarters in New York.
154. British Embassy Baghdad, J.A.N. Graham to London, 23 January 1975, FCO 8/2541, 16, 22 January 1975, FCO 8/2547,*TNA*.
155. London Times, 8 January 1975, in Ghareeb, *The Kurdish Question in Iraq*, p. 169.
156. Tabriz 22 (Neumann), 17 September 1974; Eilts the US ambassador to Cairo agreed with this assessment .Cairo 7218 (Eilts), 17 September 1974.
157. Tehran 9935 (Helms), 25 November 1974; this quote of the Shah appears in Alam's memoirs as well, published in 1991. A. Alam, *The Shah and I*,p. 398. According to Helms' report it seems that the Soviets were more concerned by the American presence in the Indian Ocean than their possible involvement in the war in Kurdistan.
158. Ghareeb, *The Kurdish Question in Iraq*, p. 167.
159. British Embassy Baghdad (Graham), 27 November 1974, FCO 8/2309, *TNA*.
160. R. Helms and W. Hood, *A Look Over My Shoulder – A Life in the CIA* (New York: Random House, 2003), pp. 417–18.
161. Tsafrir, *Ana Kurdi*, p. 254; Kimche, *The Last Option*, pp. 194–5.
162. Tsafrir, *Ana Kurdi*, pp. 244.
163. O'Ballance, *The Kurdish Struggle 1920–1994*, p. 177.
164. *Ibid.*,pp. 99–100; Tehran 2272 (Helms), 11 March 1975, *Ford Presidential Library*, National Security Adviser/ Country Files Middle East, Box 14.
165. W. Safire, 'Son of "Secret Sellout"', *NYT*, 12 February 1976;Kissinger, *Years of Renewal*, pp.595–6.
166. Geneva 434 (Dale), 27 January 1975; Tehran 344 (Helms), 14 January 1975;Helms, reporting the Kurdish plight, mentioned private NGOs' aid from Britain and Scandinavia, since FCO insisted, like the US on avoiding official involvement in spite of the humanitarian disaster .
167. Kurdish sources estimated that, in early 1975, one third of 1.5 million Kurds in Iraq were either displaced or refugees. Following the Algiers Agreement the number of Kurdish refugees in Iran reached 210,000, Vanly, 'Kurdistan in Iraq', p.176; Guardian, 24 October 1975 in Ghareeb, *The Kurdish Question in Iraq*, p. 176; 'Defense and Humanitarian Support for General Barzani', 31 October 1974, *Ford Presidential Library*, Kissinger/Scowcroft West Wing Files, Box 1; British Embassy Baghdad (Graham), 5 April 1975; FCO/MED (Lucas), 15 April 1975, FCO 8/2536 *TNA*.
168. Memorandum from NSC (Oakley, Clift) to Kissinger, 7 May 1975, *Ford Presidential Library*, WH General Files.
169. International Committee of the Red Cross (ICRC), Press Release, 3 April 1975, 1226b Geneva, in FCO 8/2536, *TNA*.
170. Kissinger, *Years of Renewal*, pp. 595–6.
171. M. Gunter, *The Kurds of Iraq, Tragedy and Hope*, pp. 33–5.
172. George Meany to the President, 21 March 1975; President Ford response n.d., *Ford Presidential Library*,WHCF, Box 25; Memorandum from Kissinger to the President, 19 May 1975, re: George Meany; Memorandum from NSC (Oakley, Clift) to Kissinger, 7 May 1975, *Ford Presidential Library*, WH General Files Box 66.
173. Tabriz 17 (Neumann), 10 April 1975; Baghdad 410 (Lowrie), 12 April 1975.
174. *Guardian*, 1 May 1975.
175. Jim Hoagland, *WP*, 16 May 1975; Beirut 6381 (Godley), 19 May 1975.

176. Tabriz 43 (Neumann), 11 August 1975.
177. The British Ambassador Graham heard the information from his French colleague. The report most likely was forwarded to WashingtonBritish Embassy Baghdad 149 (Graham), 3 March 1977, FCO 8/3025, *TNA*.
178. British Embassy Baghdad (Graham), 19 January 1976, FCO 8/2802, *TNA*.
179. George Meany visited ailing Barzani in Virginia, as well as former senior officials such as Ray Cline, DDI of the CIA and other officials without publicity. Aaron Latham, 'What Kissinger was afraid of in the Pike Report', *New York Magazine*, 4 October 1976.
180. As reported by Ambassador Graham following a meeting with Deputy President TahaMuhi al-Din Ma'ruf: British Embassy Baghdad (Graham), 5 April 1975; FCO/MED (Lucas), 15 April 1975, FCO 8/2536 *TNA*.
181. The Vanly delegation included Bahir Boumaza, an Algerian observer and former FLN activist, Jean-Claude Luthi, a human rights activist from Geneva and the Chaldean Catholic Priest, Joseph Pari, a native of Sulaymaniyyah.Vanly, 'Kurdistan in Iraq', pp. 177–87.
182. The UN Mission was visiting Kurdistan 8 August,6September 1975. *Ibid.*, pp.177–87.
183. Tehran 2237 (Helms), 10 March 1975, 06:07.
184. Tehran 2254 (Helms), 10 March 1975, 09:59; Tehran (Helms), 25 March 1975; MOC, President Ford, Shah of Iran, Kissinger, Scowcroft, 15 May 11975, *Ford Presidential Library*, NSC Files, Box 1.
185. Kissinger, *Years of Renewal*, p. 596; W. Safire, 'Son of "Secret Sellout"', *NYT*, 12 February 1976.
186. Tehran (Helms) to the White House, 10 March 1975, Secret/Eyes Only, *Helms Collection*.
187. Kissinger, *Years of Renewal*, p. 596.
188. Helms & Hood, *A Look Over My Shoulder*, pp. 417–18.
189. Tehran 2254 (Helms), 10 March 1975, *Ford Presidential Library*,National Security Adviser, Country Files, Box 14; David A. Korn, 'The last years of Mustafa Barzani', *The Middle East Quarterly*, 1(2) (June 1994).
190. Kissinger (Jerusalem) to Helms (Sensitive/Eyes Only), 10 March 1975, *Ford Presidential Library*, Kissinger/Scowcroft West Wing Files, Box 19.
191. Jerusalem 397 (Kissinger), 10 March 1975.
192. FCO/MED (Williams) to Baghdad, 17 March 1975, FCO 8/2547, *TNA*.
193. D. Neff, 'The U.S., Iraq, Israel and Iran: Backdrop to War', *Journal of Palestinian Studies*, 20(4) (Summer 1991), p. 27.
194. Tehran 2216, 2403 (Helms), 13, 16 March 1975.
195. Kissinger, *White House Years*, p. 1265.
196. 'Iran-Iraq Treaty on International Borders and Good Neighbourly Relations' Baghdad, 13 June 1975, Reproduced from the Baghdad Observer, 23-4 June 1975, in Khadduri, *Socialist Iraq*, Appendix E, pp. 245-260; J. M. Abdulghani, *Iraq and Iran: The Years of Crisis* (New York: Routledge, 1984) Appendix C, pp.244-249.
197. Tehran 2237 (Helms), 10 March 1975; R. Helms, A Look over my shoulder - A Life in the CIA (New York: Random House, 2003) pp. 417-418.
198. Beirut (Godley) 3252, 15 March 1975; Sardar Aziz, Interview with Mahmud Othman, 'The American Kurdish (Kissinger-Barzani) Relationship: an Orientalist Reading', 27 March 2007, http://namoy.blogspot.com/2007/03/american -kurdish-barzani.html, last accessed 9 September 2011.

199. J.A. Bill, *The Eagle and the Lion: The Tragedy of American-Iranian Relations* (New Haven CT: Yale University Press, 1989), p. 204.
200. Kissinger, *Years of Renewal*, p. 593.
201. Tehran (Helms) to Scowcroft (Eyes Only), 10 March 1975, *Helms Collection*.
202. Kissinger, *Years of Renewal*, p. 595.
203. Tehran 9523 (Helms), 26 September 1975; Tehran 9808 (Helms), 6 October 1975, *Helms Collection*.
204. White House, MOC, 30 April 1975, *DNSA*.
205. MOC, President Ford, Shah Mohammed Reza Pahlavi, Kissinger, Scowcroft, 15, 16 May 1975, *Ford Presidential Library*, Digital.
206. *Al-Khabat*, Kurdish daily, 4 June 1996, quoted in Khorsan, pp. 224–5.
207. Barzani, *Al- Barzaniwal-Haraka al-Tahririyya al-Kurdiyya*, p, 381. When Massoud's book was published the Kurds practiced autonomy under American protection, therefore I assume he had no interest in repeating his criticism of the US.
208. Marshall W. Wiley, Interview, 18 April 1989, *ADST*.
209. The King reported in late January 1975 that Iraq was prepared for compromise even on the Shatt al-Arab. It is likely that this information was passed to the US, yet it seems that the US as well as Britain did not attribute much importance or credibility to this report. Amman (Balfour-Paul), 31 January, 1975, FCO 8/2547, *TNA*.
210. Letter from Henry A. Kissinger to Mulla Mustafa Barzani, 20 February 1975, *Ford Presidential Library*, Kissinger/Scowcroft West Wing Files, Box 19.
211. Amman (Balfour-Paul), 31 January 1975, FCO 8/2547, *TNA*.
212. Emile Guikovaty, 'Comment les Kurdesontetetrahis', *L'Express*, 8–14 March 1976, in Chaliand(1994), p. 170.
213. Baghdad 214 (Lowrie), 1 March 1975.
214. Baghdad 476 (Lowrie), 9 August 1974; Cairo 5597, 6551 (Eilts), 26 July, 26 August 1974; Tehran 2237 (Helms), 10 March 1975.
215. U. Bar-Joseph, *The Angel: Ashraf Marwan, the Mossad and the surprise of the Yom Kippur war* (Or Yehuda: KinneretZmora-Bitan Publishers, 2001), pp. 265–6.
216. Bar-Yosef might have relied upon interviews with people who refused to let their identities be made public. He relies openly on Vanly's interview in L'Express from 1976 citing the words of the Minister of the Royal Court, Asadollah al-Alam, that the US had been pushing for an agreement because of its own interests at the expense of the Kurds.
217. Tehran 2751 (Helms), 25 March 1975.
218. Following criticism, from November 1975 Kissinger was Secretary of State only.
219. Kissinger, *Years of Renewal*, p. 594.
220. *Ibid.*, p. 596.
221. *Al-Thawra*, Editorial, 17 January 1975.
222. Kissinger, *Years of Renewal*, p. 596.
223. Academics joined journalists and pundits in criticising the administration policy as taking advantage of the ethnic conflict to promote American interests. For example, Douglas Little suggests that the American support of the Kurds was along the same lines as in 1958 againstQasim, in 1972–5 against the Ba'th and in the 1990s to weaken Saddam Hussein. Little, 'The United States and the Kurds: A Cold War Story', *Journal of Cold War Studies*, 12(4) (2010).
224. C.L. Sultzberger, 'To Be Obscurely Hanged', *NYT*, 12 March 1975.
225. W. Safire: 'Mr. Ford's "Secret Sellout"', *NYT*, 5 February 1976; Safire, 'Son of "Secret Sellout"', *NYT*, 12 February 1976.

226. Aaron Latham, 'Introduction to the Pike Papers', *The Village Voice*, 16 February 1976.
227. Seymour Hersh, 'Huge C.I.A. Operation Reported in U.S. against Anti-War Forces', *NYT*, 22 December 1974.
228. The first Committee, led by the Vice President Nelson Rockefeller, examined the CIA activities on US soil. The main committee was appointed in February 1975 and led by Senator Frank Church (D-Idaho) to assess the overall activities of the intelligence community, in particular legal and ethical aspects (such as CIA activity to overthrow regimes and assassination of political leaders. Gerald K. Hanes, 'The Pike Committee Investigations and the CIA', 20 November 2007, *CIA Website*, www.cia.loc.gov, last accessed 11 August 2017.
229. For covert action, foreign policy and Congress see: Lock K. Johnson, 'Covert Action and Accountability: Decision making for America's secret foreign policy', *International Studies Quarterly*, 33(1) (March 1989), pp. 638–63.
230. Sluglett Farouk, M. Sluglett P., *Iraq since 1958: From Revolution to Dictatorship* (New York: Palgrave Macmillan, 1987), p. 170; Dr Mahmoud Uthman in an interview with FRONTLINE transmitted on PBS, http://www.pbs.org/wgbh/pages/frontline/shows/saddam/interviews/othman.html, last accessed 5 April 2014; S. al-Khorsan, *Al-Tayyarat al-Siyyasiya fi Kurdistan al-Iraq: Qira'a fi Mulaffat al-HarakatwalAhzab al-Kurdiyya fil 'Iraq 1946–2001* (Beirut: Mu'asasat al-Ballagh, 2001), p. 225.
231. Al-Khorsan points at Jordan and Egypt as partially responsible for the Algiers agreement. King Hussein refused to meet Barzani's representative Dizaii, while Sadat received Barzani's message by Ashraf Marwan and agreed to meet 'Sammy' Abf al-Rahman. Al-Khorsan, *Al-Tayyarat al-Siyyasiya fi Kurdistan al-Iraq: Qira'a fi Mulaffat al-HarakatwalAhzab al-Kurdiyya fil 'Iraq 1946–2001*, pp. 224–5.
232. Barzani to Kissinger, 22 January 1975 (13 pages), *Ford Presidential Library*,Kissinger/Scowcroft West Wing Files, Box 19.
233. Ambassador James Akins interview to *PBS*, January 2000, http://www.pbs.org/wgbh/pages/frontline/shows/saddam/interviews/akins.html, last accessed 10 April 2012.
234. Massoud Barzani told Amatzia Baram in 1999 that the Head of Mossad gave his word to his father to keep on supporting the Kurds. Baram interview 2010.
235. Kissinger presented and registered the gifts to the protocol as required by Federal regulations, but requested authorisation to use the Kurdish rug in his White House office. Iraqi newspapers mentioned the gifts to Kissinger and the American assistance to the Kurds in an anti-Barzani campaign, along with routine attacks on the US and Kissinger in particular. The Shah's role is not mentioned at all. Memorandum from Chief of Protocol to Kissinger, 12 February 1976, *Ford Presidential Library*, Kissinger/Scowcroft West Wing Files, Box 19; Baghdad 135 (Wiely), 3 February 1976.
236. Tehran 3772 (Miklos), 23 April 1975.
237. Mohammed S. Dosky to Secretary Kissinger, 12 May 1975. Israel State Archive: 1975 6701/8 -3.8.
238. Baghdad 303 (Graham), 24 March 1975.
239. Nakdimon, *Hopeless Hope*, pp. 403–4.
240. CBS News, Christian Science Monitor, 3 November 1975; *WP*, 4 November 1975; State 260094 (Kissinger), 3 November 1975; *Al-Thawra*, 1 February 1976, quoting the New York Times.
241. D.Korn, 'The last years of Mustafa Barzani', *The Middle East Quarterly*, 1(2) (June 1994.
242. Nakdimon, *Hopeless Hope*, pp. 410–12, quoting Dosky.
243. Some Israeli diplomatic correspondence from Washington has been declassified indicating a list of pro-Israeli contacts willing to assist the Kurds: on 12 March 1975,

Washington reported on the meeting of Dosky with Richard Perl, Senator Jackson's assistant D. Torgeman to Ephraim Halevi, Washington, 12 March 1975. I SA, Section 93.8: 6710/8.

244. House of Representatives, Committee on Foreign Affairs, Subcommittee on the Near East and South Asia, 'The Middle East 1974', 27 June 1974,*GPO* 1974.

245. Barzani, *Al- Barzaniwal-Haraka al-Tahririyya al-Kurdiyya*, pp. 380–2.

246. Tsafrir, *Ana Kurdi*, pp.253–5.

247. D. Korn, 'The last years of Mustafa Barzani'.

248. David C. McGaffey interview, 8 September 1995, *ADST*.

249. J. Bill, *The Eagle and the Lion*,pp. 67, 213.

250. T. Powers, *The Man Who Kept Secrets – Richard Helms and the CIA* (New York: Knopf Book Club Edition, 1979), pp. 161, 163, 184.

251. Helms openly criticised DCI Colby's dealing with Congress, and held him responsible for leaking information to Seymour Hersh, that resulted in congressional investigative committees of the Intelligence Community. IA/CSI, 'Reflections of DCI Colby and Helms on the CIA "Time of Troubles"', CSI Publications, *Oral History*, 51(3), https://www.cia.gov/library/center-for-the-study-of-intelligence/csi-publications/csi-studies/studies/vol51no3/reflections-of-dci-colby-and-helms-on-the-cia2019s-201ctime-of-troubles201d.html, last accessed 11 August 2017.

252. Helms claimed that he could not relate secret information in a public hearing, and was finally acquitted. *Ibid.*

253. Kissinger, *White House Years*, p. 37.

254. T. Powers, Interview, 'In Memoriam Richard Helms', *PBS* News Hour, 23 October 2002.

5

The Prism of the Arab-Israeli Conflict

Even as the United States and Iraq had held diametrically opposed views on the Arab-Israeli conflict, their diplomatic and trade relations remained open and vibrant. The Americans' effort in the Middle East was focused on reaching a politically sustainable solution to the conflict and avoiding another war. That solution, following the Six-Day War of June 1967, seemed straightforward: an Arab recognition of Israel in exchange for Israel's withdrawal from territories it occupied in the war, along with assurances for her security.

Iraq rejected any solution that even implied recognition of what the Arab world termed 'the Zionist entity' so as to avoid uttering the word 'Israel'. Saddam feared that a political settlement would diminish his stature as an Arab leader who claimed to represent authentic Ba'th values.

The Ba'th had viewed the Palestinian issue as central to its ideological and national beliefs, and as intertwined in the Ba'thi goal of Arab unity. Ba'th leaders proclaimed their commitment to the Palestinians and used the Arabs' defeat including that of the Iraqi army in June 1967 to blame the previous regime as a pretext for the 1968 coup.[1] Iraq, like other Arab states, manipulated the conflict with Israel to create popular consensus and support for the regime domestically and to distract the public's attention from economic and social problems.

Unlike Syria and Egypt, which shared borders with and lost territories to Israel, Iraq could afford to cling to its rejectionist views.[2] Sadat and Assad accepted US mediation to negotiate, with Israel, an IDF withdrawal from newly occupied territories in October 1973 in the Egyptian western side of the Suez Canal and in an enclave overlooking Damascus. This hardline image of the Iraqi Ba'th was wholly supported amongst the Iraqis and Arabs, in particular after the Pike Committee report exposed American and Israeli support for the Kurdish rebellion against the Iraqi government. The Ba'th had long wielded its uncompromising approach as an asset, rallying the masses to believe its charge that Israel, backed by the US, constituted a direct threat. Israel's air raid on Iraq's OSIRAK nuclear facility in 1981, and the Irangate scandal in Washington, only amplified this trend in the 1980s.[3]

The years 1967–75 were marked by America's increased involvement in the Middle East to protect its strategic and economic interests. That decade is notable for two wars and Palestinian terrorism, whose roots were in Sudan and Lebanon. American cooperation with Israel increased in scope and quality and would reach an unprecedented level of closeness in what came to be called 'special relations',[4] a pattern that has deepened and solidified through to today. Nonetheless, there were serious differences regarding the ways and means to approach the conflict, just as they exist now as well.

The US also sought closer relations with Arab states, including such radical states as Iraq, and encouraged them to move away from the Soviet Union. Iraq's radical, rejectionist attitude towards Israel, its lack of full diplomatic relations with the US and the fact that Iraq did not share a border with Israel made Iraq less relevant in promoting the peace process or some of America's other interests in the area, such as calming the situation in Lebanon or counter-terrorism. As a result, Iraq was further marginalised in various US administrations' consideration of the Middle East.

How the Iraqi Ba'th Regarded Israel

Even before Iraq declared independence in 1932, Iraqis, like other Arabs, expressed a fierce rejection of Zionism and of British colonialism.[5] The Ba'th won the hearts and minds of the Iraqi public and the military in July 1968, following the Arabs' defeat in 1967 and the clear incompetence of the Aref regime. The Iraqi Ba'th leadership adopted a more radical attitude than other revolutionary regimes in the region, such as Algeria, Libya and South Yemen, and other Iraqi opposition groups like Nationalists and the Nasseristes.[6]

Moreover, the Ba'th Party motto called for Arab unity and stated that Israel was a non-Arab foreign entity backed by imperialism and should be eradicated.[7] The fundamental contradiction between the Iraqi Ba'thi revolution and imperialism, Zionism and creationism appears in the first paragraph of the Iraqi Charter of National Action (*Mithaq al-'Amal al-Watani*), enacted in 1971. The Ba'th portrayed the 'Zionist entity' as a conspiracy created by Britain with the Balfour Declaration in 1917, and reignited in 1947 by other Western states that supported UN General Assembly resolution 181 to partition Palestine into Jewish and Arab states. The conspiracy held, too, that the West supported the creation of a Jewish state as compensation for Hitler's crimes against the Jews in Europe – and that this support was at the expense of the Arabs.[8]

Later in the 1970s, in a project to rewrite history, Iraqi Ba'th theorists linked the pre-Islamic era of Mesopotamia to Iraqi nationalism, and painted the Babylonian King Nebuchadnezzar as an ancient Iraqi-Arab hero connected to the Ba'thi idea of liberation of Palestine, since he occupied Judea and destroyed the Jewish temple in 587 BC. As Saddam told his biographer Fuad Matar: 'Nebuchadnezzar was the one who brought the bound Jewish slaves from Palestine ... I like to remind the Arabs, Iraqis in particular, of their historical responsibilities.' Another hero of Saddam was Sallah al-Din al-Ayubi, whom he called 'a Muslim Iraqi' who conquered Palestine against the Crusaders.[9] The ideological platform of the Ba'th included some anti-Semitic views that were an exact copy of the original Ba'th platform in the 1940s. It portrayed Jews as greedy in character and acquiring most of the world's wealth through their mythical power. From this standpoint, the Jews in Palestine were portrayed as aiming to destroy the Arab world's economy.[10]

Looking Inward – Iraq First

In spite of this ideological approach towards Israel, the Ba'th leadership focused on consolidating its authority in Iraq. In Ba'thi terminology, that meant prioritising *Wataniyya* (Iraqi nationalism, patriotism), and dealing with *Qawmiyya* (Arab nationalism) later.[11] The idea had been raised at the Eighth Conference of the Regional Command of the Iraqi Ba'th in January 1974, following the participation of Iraqi forces in the war against Israel. The Ba'th stressed the need to focus on Iraq first and solve the Kurdish problem, then reinforcing the revolution through economic and social reforms, by adopting modernisation and increasing technological capabilities. Only then would Iraq be able to confront Israel within a unified, all-Arab force.[12]

Iraqi pragmatism was demonstrated in refraining from the battle in Jordan in September 1970, in introducing economic and social reforms and in allowing the opening of the American Interest Section in Baghdad in 1972. Those actions raised some optimism among State Department officials, who anticipated some moderation in the country regarding the Israeli-Palestinian conflict. That did not happen. Iraq unhesitatingly sent large forces to the front with Israel in 1973. Since then, it has expressed a firm objection to all ceasefire agreements with Israel. Iraqi pragmatism had tactical aims. The Ba'th amplified the radical rhetoric, in order to remove any doubt about the Ba'th commitment to the Arab cause.

The Ba'th rejected UN Security Council resolutions 242 and 338, which ended the Six-Day War and the Yom Kippur War, respectively. The party also opposed the Nixon administration's Rogers Plan in 1969 that meant to end the state of belligerence – a plan that Jordan and Egypt supported. The Ba'th viewed these three moves as an American scheme to eliminate the Palestinian problem, so it called on the masses to join in 'a continuous revolution' (*al-Thawra al-Da'ima*) until the liberation of Palestine was achieved.[13] During Kissinger's shuttle diplomacy (1974–5), Iraq warned two of his hosts, Syria and Egypt, against reaching what it termed a 'submissive agreement' that might imply any recognition of Israel.

The Total Rejection of Settlement with Israel

The Ba'th portrayed American diplomatic efforts to find a peaceful solution to the conflict as a strategy to promote US influence and interests in the region ahead of the Arabs'. Iraqi rhetoric reflected conspiratorial thinking, portraying the US as an aggressive nation, hostile to the Arabs with a hidden agenda to destroy the Iraqi regime. In October 1975, when the classified clauses of the Sinai Agreement were leaked from the Senate Foreign Relations Committee, a Ba'th newsletter published an alarmist article, arguing that these classified American pledges to supply oil to Israel and provide military upgrades might enable Israel to reach nuclear capability. Moreover, it continued, the EarlyWarning Systems operated by American technicians in the Sinai hid a surveillance and espionage base, tasked to monitor Arab and Mediterranean forces.[14] As a matter of fact, the Early Warning Systems, staffed by American civilian technicians, were positioned on both the Egyptian and the Israeli sides. The systems contained seismic surveillance equipment tasked with alerting the UN peacekeeping forces to any military land forces approaching.[15]

This rejectionist attitude positioned Iraq as more radical than the Syrian Ba'th. Iraq demanded that any peace solution relate to all of Palestine, stating that Israel had no right to exist. The Palestinian commentator Fuad Jaber argued that the Iraqis adopted the Vietnamese model as the winning strategy. Iraqi newspapers closely followed the process that led to a complete American withdrawal following that country's war, and expressed sympathy and empathy for the North Vietnamese as victims of American imperialist aggression.[16]

The Vietnam War was covered frequently in the Iraqi media, in keeping with the party's anti-American propaganda campaign and with the general support of left-wing resistance movements. However, Jaber's argument that the Ba'th adopted this model against Israel does not reflect Iraqi conduct. The Ba'th was building a strong military power and was embarking on a program to develop weapons of mass destruction. Like in Syria, the Iraqi Ba'th party's goal was to reach a strategic balance with Israel, something not feasible through guerilla warfare alone.

At the Rabat Summit in October 1974, Saddam gave his consent to a 'phased plan' to spur Israeli withdrawals in stages and ultimately liberate

Palestine in stages – as long as no recognition of Israel occurred. This position, though, required clarification for the Iraqi public. An editorial published in *Al-Jumhuriyya* following Saddam's comments linked the 'phased plan' as being fully consistent with the Ba'th strategy for Palestine since the 1968 revolution. The editor stressed that Iraq 'had no intention to give up any principle, or abandon any right or part of the occupied land ... Israel must withdraw, as a first stage, to the 1967 lines within the UN or other framework, provided it does not involve any Arab recognition of Israel.'[17] In fact, this statement recognised, in principle, the right of the Palestinians to their own national rule (*sulta wataniyya*) and considered the phased-plan strategy as the means to achieving this goal.[18] Other articles in Ba'thi publications following the Rabat Summit emphasised the solid rejectionist principles of the Ba'th and armed struggle as the sole path to liberating all of Palestine.[19]

According to Baram, Saddam's statement had one purpose: to serve the urgent need of Iraq as it struggled with the Kurdish rebellion and the Iranian military. The comments meant to draw Arab support by giving the Arab League legitimacy to take political action on behalf of the Palestinians, without giving up any of the rejectionist principles: no recognition of Israel and opposing all political peace initiatives.[20]

Saddam's statement did not draw much attention in the State Department, though Lowrie conveyed to Washington his interpretation that Iraq was moving away from radicalism and approaching the centre of Arab consensus.[21] Saddam called for forming policy discreetly as a way of making progress. 'This strategy does have to be declared publicly. We will decide on when and what can be published, or what could not be disclosed', Saddam said.[22]

This statement reached the sympathetic ears of Lowrie, who quoted 'observers' in Baghdad as saying that Saddam's opposition to recognising Israel, along with his acceptance of the 'phased plan', indicated that the rhetoric about non-recognition of Israel was just lip service. Such reporting nourished a misperception in the State Department and elsewhere and was meant to encourage the administration to develop relations with Iraq. In that view, the Ba'th was pragmatic and would demonstrate flexibility regarding Israel as well.[23]

Rejectionist Ideology and the US

Iraq condemned US policy on Israel in three main areas: US economic and military support; political support, including exercising its UN Security Council veto against anti-Israel resolutions; and its peace initiatives that intended to reach bilateral agreements between Israel and states bordering it. Since Iraq shared no border with Israel, and had no territories occupied by it, the Ba'th could not condemn Arab states for negotiating ceasefire and disengagement agreements with Israel. What it did, though, was to condemn Syria for betraying the Arab cause. The radical rejectionist philosophy of the Iraqi Ba'th was a political asset not to be given up easily. It gained popular support in the Arab street and in the domestic arena. The condemning of the US and other states for supporting Israel became a fixed policy among Arab countries, Socialist countries and states in the Non-aligned Movement. Those countries' media, too, described all political initiatives on Israel's behalf as being a hostile, imperialistic conspiracy to penetrate the Middle East.[24] Following the nationalisation of the Iraq Petroleum Company in 1972, the special privileges granted to France as a payoff for anti-Israeli positions became the Iraqi model for using the oil weapon. Saddam exploited the 1973 oil crisis to encourage oil purchasers to adopt anti-Israeli positions. Saddam's claim of US economic dominance was meant to drive a wedge between Washington and Western Europe and Japan.[25] For example, Bernt Carlsson, the Swedish SG of Socialist International (SI), and his deputy Bruno Kreisky visited Baghdad in March 1976, and were received by Saddam Hussein.

On his return from Iraq, Carlsson told the American political counselor at the Stockholm embassy, that Saddam's attitude was unexpectedly moderate. Carlsson quoted Saddam as saying: 'We are not against the Jews. We condemn anti-Semitism where it exists. We are in favor of coexistence of various nationalities in Palestine and the identity of each people, but we do not accept a fait accompli ... We do not see a single positive element in the conduct of the enemy.'[26]

The American official, Counselor Johnson, remarked in his report to Washington that Carlsson seemed to be unfamiliar with Middle Eastern issues. Johnson mentioned that the SI decided not to publish Saddam's moderate words.[27] This was most likely to avoid embarrassing Saddam, assuming that the radical statements of the Ba'th were just lip service, to maintain their image in the Arab arena, and assuming that such publicity would compel Saddam to issue a denial. As the Geneva conference approached, Iraq initiated an alternative conference of radical movements in Barcelona in protest against the Socialist International participation in Switzerland.[28]

It seems that Iraq had realised that American support of Israel was an unchangeable given and attributed it to 'American Jewish pressures'.[29] This was explicit in interviews with foreign press and in interactions with Westerners, and Iraqi leaders projected realism, pragmatism, that was perceived as moderation. At the same time, Iraqi officials insinuated that criticism of the US was a political necessity, given Iraq's sensitivity to its domestic audiences. In a speech to 150 foreign correspondents on 18 July 1976, Saddam minimised Iraq's role in the Arab-Israeli conflict, stressing that Iraq had no border with Israel: 'As a state, we are not in a position to make decisions reflecting our views', he told them. 'We left the area to Syria, Jordan and Egypt, [though] we express our [general] views on peace and war ... But whether we are asked about our [specific] opinion on war and peace, our response is that we are confined geographically.'[30]

Activating the Palestinian Armed Struggle

Iraq-PLO: A Love-Hate Relationship

Until September 1970, the Ba'th took pride in its active support of the PLO. That included maintaining a large Iraqi expedition force in Jordan; financing PLO institutions, such as the Palestinian Red Crescent, that opened an office in Baghdad, and allowing Iraqi citizens to join the ranks of the PLO. Iraq kept an eye on the PLO, though, watching for any sign of moderation, such as considering involvement in a political process with Israel or withdrawal from the 'armed struggle' and refraining from attacking civilians. In a visit to Baghdad right after the Yom Kippur War, PLO chairman Yasser Arafat was told bluntly by al-Bakr and Saddam that Iraq opposed the Geneva Convention, stressing that Iraq would support the continuation of the armed struggle against Israel from Iraqi soil.[31] In June 1974, the Palestinian National Council issued a resolution in which it committed to focusing the armed struggle on Israel and the territories; that indicated an intention to cease attacks against civilians including hijacking civilian aeroplanes and attacking airports and embassies. As a result, Arafat was invited to speak before the UN General Assembly.[32]

The PNC resolution was a slap in the face for the Ba'th, whose main concern was stopping Arafat from conceding the principle of the armed struggle against Israel in all arenas and even negotiating secretly with the US and Israel. Iraq increased its financial support for the PLO, while monitoring its political activity. It issued diplomatic passports to Arafat's entourage to travel to New York, but signaled that it would not accept any PLO concessions or moderation. Iraq became even closer with radical Palestinian organisations that defied Arafat's leadership.[33] Iraq fiercely rejected the idea of any PLO contacts with left-wing Israeli citizens, like a meeting in Prague in May 1977 between PLO members and members of the Israeli Communist Party, an anti-Zionist party.[34]

Besides the deep controversies within the Palestinian camp, and Iraqi support for anti-Arafat groups, Arafat always received a formal, high-profile welcome when he visited Baghdad. Arafat had capricious relations with Arab leaders, calling them alternately either 'brothers' or 'traitors'.[35]

The United States could not ignore the public acclaim with which Arafat was always received by al-Bakr and Saddam Hussein. Iraq had been active diplomatically in a bid to gain international recognition of the PLO. After the PLO was invited to attend a UNESCO conference held in Paris (17 October–23 November 1974), the Iraqi Ministry of Foreign Affairs requested that all foreign legations in Baghdad encourage their governments to recognise the PLO as the legitimate representative of the Palestinian people.[36] Iraq was deeply involved in Palestinian politics, publicly and discreetly, including by exploiting internal rifts between Palestinian groups and their Arab supporters to increase their presence and influence. Only at the Baghdad Summit, convened following the Camp David peace agreement between Israel and Egypt, did Saddam settle his differences with Arafat, following years of Iraqi-directed violence against Arafat's leadership by proxy groups. To ensure the PLO's participation at the summit, he expelled the two leaders of Iraq-based rejectionist Palestinian organisations: Abu Nidal and Wadi' al-Haddad from Iraq.[37]

The Arab Liberation Front (ALF): A Palestinian Organisation Linked to Iraq

The ALF's name did not include the word 'Palestine.' The organisation was established in January 1968 by the Pan-Arab Command of the Iraqi Ba'th shortly after the Syrian Ba'th established *al-Sa'iqa*. ALF boasted at the time only 500 men, and ultimately grew to fewer than 1,000 members. Some were Palestinians, while others were Lebanese, Jordanians and Iraqis. ALF's leaders were trusted Ba'thi figures from the Pan-Arab Command, including Munif al-Razzaz, a Jordanian of Syrian descent; Abd al-Wahab al-Kayali, a Palestinian; and Abd al-Rahman Ahmad.[38] ALF lost ground following the Black September crisis in Jordan in 1970, but gradually gained support as Iraq increased its involvement in Lebanon.[39]

The Ba'th defined the ALF's mission as being consistent with Ba'th ideology, 'encouraging cooperation among Palestinian groups, and between the Palestinian revolution and the Ba'th, by steadfastness and armed struggle.'[40] ALF was an instrument to promote Iraqi influence in Lebanon and, in particular, Syria, which held Lebanon under Syrian influence.[41] ALF received financial support, weapons and training from Iraq, took instructions from Baghdad and served Iraqi interests that were not necessarily related to

Palestinian issues.[42] ALF was kept small because Baghdad feared that a strong Palestinian group would be difficult to control. ALF members were not allowed to carry arms and wear uniforms publicly in Iraq, and their movements were monitored.[43] ALF was represented in the PNC under Arafat even after the PLO offices in Baghdad were closed in 1974. ALF had carried out a limited numbers of attacks inside Israel, including in the Upper Galilee communities of Kfar Yuval in 1975 and Misgav Am in 1980.[44] The other Palestinian groups considered ALF to be serving mostly Iraqi interests,[45] as indeed the ALF served, primarily, Iraqi interests, demonstrating that Baghdad held influence in the Palestinian arena in Lebanon for the patrons. Keeping ALF financially and politically was an uneasy and costly task, since Iraq had no direct ground access to southern Lebanon, which was under the watch of the Syrian Ba'th.[46]

Supporting Radical Palestinian Factions

Particularly following the passage of the PNC resolution in 1974, Iraq also supported, financially and militarily, radical Palestinian factions that rebelled against Arafat's authority, including the Popular Front for the Liberation of Palestine (PFLP), the Democratic Front for the Liberation of Palestine (DFLP), the PFLP – General Command (also known as the Jibril organisation) and other radical factions. This cooperation was public, and it amplified Iraqi involvement in Palestinian affairs and in Lebanon, and its defiance of Arafat's leadership. It also demonstrated Iraq's competition with the Syrian Ba'th.[47]

The leaders of these Palestinian organisations regularly traveled to Baghdad for meetings with the Pan-Arab Leadership of the Ba'th. In October 1974, Lowrie reported to Washington on the arrival of DFLP leader George Habash, the Jibril organisation's Tallal Naji and Samir Ghosha of the Palestinian Popular Struggle Front (PPSF). They had come to Baghdad for consultations prior to the Rabat Summit. (PNC Secretary General Khaled Al-Fahum had paid a visit to Baghdad earlier.)[48]

A joint statement published at the end of the visit 'condemned all formulas connected to a so-called settlement, which aim at recognizing the Zionist entity and freezing the Palestinian conflict'. The statement was a defiance of Arafat and the PNC resolution. It was also a reminder to Washington of Iraq's close relations with rejectionist, far-left Palestinian factions close to the Soviet bloc, since it stressed the necessity 'of cementing ties of friendship with forces of revolution, particularly Socialist countries.'[49] In addition to providing financial aid and allowing the groups to run training camps on Iraqi soil (the camps operated until the 1990s), Saddam maintained direct contacts with their leaders – and took pride publicly in saying so.

Nevertheless, intelligence and operational communications between the Iraqi security services and the radical Palestinian factions remained discreet and highly classified. The purpose was practical, to create ambiguity within the groups, enabling Iraq to communicate with rival factions and manipulate controversies; and to facilitate deniability. Iraq could claim to support an organisation's cause, while renouncing any link to it should the organisation perpetrate a terrorist attack.[50] The kidnapping, by the Brazilian terrorist Carlos the Jackal, of OPEC ministers in Vienna in December 1975 caused embarrassment to Baghdad when the participation of Iraq-based Wadi' al-Haddad was exposed.[51] The use by Iraq, Syria and other states of Palestinian proxy factions to carry out terrorist attacks became common and led to the term 'state-sponsored terrorism' being used from the late 1970s. Most terrorist attacks by these radical factions were directed at Arab targets, some of them common enemies of Iraq, such as individuals suspected of tendencies towards moderating their views and those who might agree to join peace negotiations. Most of those were Syrian Ba'th and PLO members.

Abu Nidal: Joint Interests and Denial

Sabri Khalil al-Bana, known as Abu Nidal (Father of the Struggle), arrived in Baghdad in August 1970 as the PLO's representative. He integrated in the Palestinian community there and established close relations with Ba'thi leaders. The following year he resigned from the PLO, adopted a radical-rejectionist ideology compatible with that of the Iraqi Ba'th, and established a headquarters for his new group, The Revolutionary Council, mostly known as ANO – the Abu Nidal Organization in Baghdad. For more than a decade, the Iraqi Ba'th granted him a home, logistical support and, most importantly, security. In return, he carried out various 'services' for the Ba'th leadership, as a contractor for terrorism – but one for whom Iraq could claim deniability. Abu Nidal was most valuable in conducting operations outside Iraq, mostly in Europe.

For those activities, Iraq issued diplomatic passports for Abu Nidal's men, shipped weapons through the diplomatic mail and allowed the use of its diplomatic vehicles in Greece, Turkey, Cyprus and France. The men were tasked with following anti-Ba'th activists and other expatriates who could be recruited. *Le Monde* reported that Abu Nidal was given a budget to offer Iraqi scholarships to Palestinian students all over Europe; those students were ready to act when called upon to commit terrorist attacks.[52] With his Iraqi benefactors, Abu Nidal also operated a radio station called Voice of Palestine and a news agency called WAFA (the Palestinian News Agency) that bore a name identical to the official agency of the PLO.[53]

Abu Nidal was mostly loyal to his Iraqi hosts, and some of the terrorist attacks he committed were directed from Baghdad. He was keen to maintain his independence. It is not clear to what extent other party members helped to choose the targets of attacks and the details of the operations.[54] He also maintained his contacts in other radical states, such as Syria and Libya. According to journalist Patrick Seale, Abu Nidal was close to Sa'dun Shaker, Iraq's head of security; to the senior Ba'thi and member of the Ba'th Regional Command Tariq Aziz, to Al-Bakr; and, to a lesser extent, to Saddam, most likely due to their similar personalities. Saddam likely was anxious about Abu Nidal's independence. That anxiety may explain Saddam's expelling him from Iraq in 1978 as a gesture to Arafat, who was Abu Nidal's arch rival. During his stay in Iraq from 1971 until 1985, Abu Nidal committed seventy-two terrorist attacks, which were 21 percent of all Palestinian-executed terrorist attacks throughout that period.[55] While some attacks on Syrian targets could have been coordinated with Iraq,[56] Abu Nidal's alleged assassination attempts in Saudi Arabia and Morocco did not serve an Iraqi interest, but Abu Nidal's alone.

The assassination attempt on Shlomo Argov, Israel's ambassador in London, provides an interesting example of joint cooperation to commit terrorism in the service of Iraq. In June 1982, Iraq was locked in a painful war with Iran, humiliated for not responding to the Israeli attack a year earlier on the nuclear French-made facility Tamuz (aka OSIRAK), and unable to cope with Syria in Lebanon. According to one theory, Saddam was drawing a sophisticated plan to assassinate the Israeli ambassador in London Shlomo Argov by Palestinians and assumed that Israel would surely strike back against the PLO in Lebanon, igniting regional war involving Syria over Lebanon. That war, according to Saddam, would compel the Islamic Republic of Iran to ease the military pressure from Iraq and focus on the Syrian war against Israel. Indeed, that scenario was nearly fulfilled – it launched Israel's invasion of Lebanon, where Israeli forces would be mired for nearly two decades. However, Saddam's second assumption – that Iran would respond to Iraq's proposal to stop the fighting and send troops to the Lebanese front with Israel – proved totally wrong. Another theory about the Iraqi motive for the London attack by Abu Nidal was to present Assad with a difficult decision: either to assist the Palestinians in Lebanon, and be defeated by Israel, or to be exposed as betraying his commitment to the Palestinians. In any case there was more than one motive for Iraq to initiate the Abu Nidal attack in London. Scotland Yard's investigation confirmed that the plan and the weapons originated in Baghdad. The close cooperation between Abu Nidal and Iraq, which lasted for more than a decade, continued after Abu Nidal relocated his base from Baghdad to Syria[57].

The US administration closely followed Palestinian affairs, controversies and alliances, including Iraqi support for the rejectionist factions. Although radical Palestinian organisations carried out most of the attacks against American and Israeli targets beginning in 1974, Washington viewed the groups' cooperation with each other as an instrument for consolidating Iraq's status against Syria and the PLO, even though it harmed American citizens and interests.[58]

Though Lowrie was aware of the visit of Libyan prime minister Abd-al-Sallam Jallud in Baghdad in June 1975 and the militant anti-Israeli rhetoric he shared openly with Iraq, following his meetings with Al-Bakr and Saddam Hussein, he preferred to cable Washington the analysis of the Egyptian ambassador to Iraq Abd-al-Mun'em al-Naggar, suggesting that the militant statements against Israel and the PLO were intended to appease Saddam's opponents. Ambassador Naggar stressed that the Ba'th leadership was flexible and would not resist the Egyptian-Israeli arrangement in the Sinai.[59] Lowrie continued to send optimistic evaluations of what was said to be Iraq's trend toward moderation, although the Iraqi Ministry of Foreign Affairs political director, Ibrahim al-Wali, insisted, in a meeting with Lowrie who asked for clarifications, that his country's position correlated with the radical, rejectionist Palestinian factions who opposed Arafat.[60]

The attack by the Abu Nidal organisation on the Intercontinental Hotel in Amman in October 1976 should have alerted Washington to the modus operandi of a proxy terror organisation, operating as it did on the order of its sponsor, Iraq. The attack did not intend to overthrow Jordan's King Hussein, an important US ally, but to deliver a warning that he should have rebuffed the US desire to see him cooperating with Syria to isolate Iraq. This took place near the end of the Ford presidency. The US administration was then holding frequent discussions with Syria on the crisis in Lebanon, encouraging the warming of relations between Syria and Jordan. In November, Washington hosted a meeting with Jordanian and Syrian delegates on civil aviation, with the intention of paving the way for direct flights from both Damascus and Amman to New York. King Hussein briefed the US ambassador in Amman, on progress in his relations with Assad, anticipating American aid as well. Zaid Rifa'i told Ambassador Thomas Pickering that Assad, in order to get the support of the Syrian Ba'thists, had to present his rapprochement with King Hussein as a Syrian need to cope with both Israeli and Iraqi threats.[61]

The US learnt that the Abu Nidal attack in Amman was initiated by Baghdad. The US had been well aware of the sensitivity of these inter-Arab political processes and, in particular, the Jordanian-Syrian talks, and kept most correspondence highly classified.[62] The King provided Pickering with all of Jordan's investigation reports, including evidence that one of the Intercontinental Hotel terrorists had survived. The attack, according to Jordan's investigation, was perpetrated by Palestinians recruited outside Jordan by the Abu Nidal organisation, trained in Iraq and sent to Jordan. There, they received instructions directly from Baghdad. Jordan expelled four Iraqi diplomats for their direct involvement in the terrorist attack. Iraq took its punishment and did not reciprocate.[63] The King did not share with Pickering the report's finding that the terrorists demanded that he, the King, should withdraw his support in the Arab League that allowed a Syrian presence in Lebanon. This decision was welcomed by the US and insulted Iraq. King Hussein also did not tell Pickering that, after the Amman attack, a personal courier arrived from Baghdad carrying a suitcase containing $20,000 in cash as, in the courier's words, 'a personal gift from brother Saddam', with a promise that further gestures would follow. This was a gang-style warning to the monarch that his dialogue with Assad, under American auspices, along with his support of Syria in the Arab League, would not be tolerated – that he had to choose between friendship with Iraq (with its financial benefits) or becoming a target of proxy terrorism.[64]

King Hussein continued the dialogue with Syria and visited Damascus in November. In December, an attempt was made on the life of Syrian Foreign Minister Abd al-Halim Khaddam. The attack resembled the Amman Intercontinental Hotel attack in Jordan a month earlier, perpetrated by Abu Nidal under instructions from Baghdad.[65] Consequently, the King stayed away from Syria, as Iraq demanded, and received aid from the US – and discreetly from Iraq as well. Ford and Kissinger seemed to have underestimated the intensity and the depth of Iraq's resistance to any attempt to isolate Iraq from the political process, and from Jordan, Lebanon and Syria. Iraq's reaction was so fierce that they used terrorist attacks to present this message.

Iraq needed Jordan on her side not just politically – not too close to Syria – but also strategically – as an outlet to the Red Sea through the port of Aqaba. Beginning in the early 1970s, Iraq invested in Jordanian infrastructure, in particular in connecting roads that reached Aqaba that proved essential for Iraq in the 1980s during the Iraq-Iran war.[66]

The US did not consider Iraqi support for, and close cooperation with, radical Palestinian groups as a serious threat, though those groups acted against American interests by destabilising US allies and by opposing moderate trends in the Arab world. Iraq's involvement in terrorism was known to the intelligence community and State Department, and was mentioned by name in congressional open hearings over counterterrorism legislation.[67]

Terrorism and Iraqi Diplomacy

Iraq supported, and was directly involved in, terrorist acts carried out by proxy organisations. This, despite Iraq's being a signatory to three international charters against aviation piracy and hijacking. Iraq spoke highly, denouncing terrorism in general and specific attacks, including attacks attributed to Abu Nidal.[68] In that way, Iraq nurtured the image of a respectable, law-abiding state. Iraq liked to portray itself as a victim of terrorism, mostly through Syrian attacks when Israel intercepted a passenger plane in August 1973, mistakenly assuming that George Habash of the PFLP was on board; passengers were safely released. Iraqi Ambassador to the UN Abd al-Karim al-Shaikhli protested that the US, by casting a veto on a UN Security Council resolution condemning Israel, encouraged Israeli aircraft piracy.[69] Another opportunity to sustain its image as a victim occurred when the Jewish Defense League threw firebombs at the Iraqi Mission to the UN in New York in April 1975.[70] Iraq was then active diplomatically in the UN as a non-permanent member on the Security Council. Iraq sponsored anti-Israeli resolutions, including an initiative to expel Israel from the UN. Iraq took pride in the passage of the General Assembly resolution that equated Zionism with racism, which it portrayed as a historic day in UN history because it overcame US opposition.[71]

US officials did not consider Arab reports of Iraqi involvement in terrorist attacks credible, though Saudi and Kuwaiti investigators held Iraq responsible for the Abu Nidal attack on the Saudi embassy in Paris in September 1973.[72] The Jordanian ambassador in Baghdad informed Lowrie that Iraq was behind the hijacking of a KLM plane on 25 November 1973. In his report to Washington, Lowrie commented that the Jordanian information was biased, tainted by the country's hostility to the Iraqi Ba'th.[73] Arab states and the PLO expressed doubts regarding the sincerity of an Iraqi statement denouncing the November 1973 hijacking of a British aircraft flying from Tunis to Kuwait, insisting that Iraq was responsible for the attack.[74] Arafat sent a message to the State Department through the ambassador of the Ivory Coast in Washington, stating that Iraq and the Soviet Union were responsible for the terrorist activity of the radical, rejectionist Palestinian organisations.[75]

While being aware of Iraqi support of those groups, the US was a target. Khalid Al-Jawhari, a member of Black September, was arrested in February 1973, during a planned terrorist attack against Israeli targets in New York when Prime Minister Golda Meir was visiting.[76] Yet only following the kidnapping and murder of American and Belgian diplomats in Khartoum, Sudan, on 1 March 1973, did the administration adopt a strategy against terrorism. It was difficult to find evidence that linked Iraq to these terrorist attacks, especially because splinter groups were involved. The Iraqis had kept communication with these organisations confidential; moreover, these groups received financial support from several Arab states. The Iraqi Ba'th was also intensively promoting propaganda, and its diplomats presented a positive image of the country. Indeed, even while Iraq was unabashedly rejectionist regarding the Middle East conflict, evidence was hard to come by to tie it to terrorist attacks. The State Department hoped that improving relations would moderate Iraqi rejectionism, as well as serving to lessen Iraq's political and financial support of radical, rejectionist organisations.

The American Approach to Palestinian Terrorism

The US intelligence community and the military were more aware of Iraq's sponsoring of terrorism than were other parts of the administration. It was the case that America's friends and allies in the region – Israel, Jordan and the Gulf states – had been making, and passing estimates and information.[77] Nevertheless there were other views. A study prepared for the CIA by an external researcher on international terrorism concluded that Palestinian terrorism posed a minor threat to US interests, compared to the threat posed by Marxist-influenced terrorism against Latin American governments.[78] Anti-terrorism legislation in Congress progressed slowly. Still, Black September's assassination of the American and Belgian diplomats in Khartoum in March 1973 shocked the administration to the extent that negotiations were held with the terrorists to release the hostages, thus breaching Washington's policy of not making concessions to terrorists – even by meeting them. The policy contrasted with that of European states, which preferred to release terrorists, thinking that doing so would, oddly enough, spare it from terrorists' revenge attacks.[79]

Furthermore, the administration initiated back-channel communications with the PLO shortly after the Khartoum killings, despite knowing that Arafat was involved in the operation.[80] James J. Welsh, a National Security Agency agent, then revealed a cover-up by the State Department. He claimed that the NSA intercepted communications a day before the attack, which indicated that Arafat and the PLO were involved in its planning. Welsh argued that the State Department ignored the information and then covered up the failure. Most important about the revelation, of course, was its implication that the terrorist attack could have been prevented. In later years, according to Welsh, the US deliberately ignored Arafat's role to avoid interrupting the American communication with the PLO.[81]

November 1973, however, showed the beginning of a back-channel dialogue between the US and the PLO, conducted by senior officials on both sides: Vernon A. Walters, the deputy director of the CIA's for Intelligence (DDI), and Khaled Hasan, one of Arafat's senior deputies.[82] The dialogue was enhanced following the PNC's phased-plan resolution and the statement to focus the 'armed struggle' on Israel, meaning halting the participation in international terrorist attacks and confining operations to Israel only. Libya, Iraq and the Palestinian rejectionist organisations opposed the PNC vote and rejected any political dialogue with the US.[83]

Counter-terrorism Legislation: Congress vis-à-vis the Administration

To cope with air piracy, Congress introduced legislation in the form of the Anti-Hijacking Act of 1974. It was an addendum to the Hague Convention of 16 December 1970, known as The Convention for the Suppression of Unlawful Seizure of Aircrafts.[84] Only in January 1979, the US Export Administration Act of 1979 (P.L. 96-72; September 1979) set export restrictions on certain states for national security or foreign policy reasons i.e. sponsored terrorism. Senator John Heinz (R-PA.), a sponsor of antiterrorism legislation, said, in a 1977 hearing, that Iraq had become a major base for radical Palestinian terrorist groups. Moreover in addition to financial support, Iraq maintained a separate training facility for Palestinian terrorists, which was the main base of the PFLP and the Abu Nidal group.[85]

The Omnibus Antiterrorism Act of 1977 required inter alia reorganisation in the White House and the executive branch to establish a mechanism to cope with international terrorism. It also required the State Department to publicly issue a list of states that supported terrorism – a practice that continues to this day.[86] Only then was Iraq formally defined as a state sponsor of terrorism, making it ineligible for US export benefits and other benefits. Public hearings in both houses of Congress shed light on differences and controversies within the White House regarding Iraq. Congress demanded that the administration take measures against Iraq – primarily, deny US-made technologies that the Iraqi Ba'th wanted to acquire. The Department of State and the Office of the US Trade Representative

(USTR) strongly opposed the imposition of any economic sanctions against Iraq.[87]

A Senate hearing held in September 1977 on international terrorism introduced a grim picture of an already grim topic. Speakers noted an increase in the number and sophistication of terrorist attacks perpetrated by 'rejectionist Palestinian organisations', such as the attempted launch of a missile (at an El Al aircraft at Paris' Orly Airport by 'Carlos the Jackal' who collaborated with the Iraqi based Wadi'i al-Haddad of the PFLP-EO), and the stealing of 15 Law shoulder missiles from a US Army facility in southern Germany. The testimonies pointed to Libya as a major sponsor of these attacks, although Iraq was said to have increased its support for these radical groups and to have become the main sponsor of the 'Black June', a name used by Abu Nidal for certain operations, that attacked Syrian and Jordanian targets in 1976.[88] The State Department had a different view on Iraq's link to terrorism. A report submitted to the committee reiterated the administration's view that Libya was a key supporter of radical Palestinian organisations, rather than Iraq, but indicated that, while Iraq publicly backed these groups, there was no clear evidence of the nature of this support, financial, military, logistical and for training.[89] The minimising of Iraq's role in sponsoring terrorism appears repeatedly in most US analyses and briefings of the period, including the National Intelligence Estimate, which integrates the reports of all agencies in the US intelligence community.

For example, the Special National Intelligence Estimate of 1981 surveyed the linkage between the USSR and terrorist groups worldwide. It stressed the role of Libya and the pro-Soviet orientation of its leader, Mu'ammar Qadhafi, but Iraq was not mentioned at all.[90] The administration, particularly the State Department and USTR, were reluctant to label Iraq a terrorist state, fearful that doing so would harm bilateral relations and affect trade. This policy was supported by the American energy lobby, grain lobby and other industries, which were eager to compete with Europe and Japan for the huge opportunities in Iraq in infrastructure projects, in the oil industry allocated by the Ba'th for development. Indeed, President Carter's secretary of state, Cyrus Vance, testifying before the Senate Government Operations Committee, voiced his department's objection to imposing restrictions on American exports to Iraq.

'There were some indications that Iraq might be willing to change its position', Vance said on 14 September 1977; 'It has come out against skyjacking. It has indicated it was willing to consider other steps, which would move away from its past policies. In light of this, it was felt it would be premature at this point to take the step until we see what might be able to be resolved.'[91]

Libya had been under US sanctions since 1973, while Iraq was added to the US's terrorism-sponsor list only in 1979. During most of that period, Iraq was entitled to procure American civilian goods, including advanced technologies.

Congress was more attentive to security concerns, including those of Israel, which closely followed the Iraqi military build-up, as well as Iraq's connections with the radical rejectionist groups that operated against Israel.[92] Speaking before the Senate Foreign Relations Committee in October 1977, US Air Force Major General (ret.) George Keegan spoke of the scope and quality of the Iraqi military buildup. The huge stockpiles of Soviet military equipment, including artillery, which once deployed in western Iraq, close to the Jordanian border, could pose a serious threat to Israel. He added that a Saudi Arabia equipped with American-made, state-of-the-art equipment could then join forces with Iraq on Israel's eastern front.[93]

US defense and intelligence agencies were also sluggish in formulating strategies against terrorism. Following the attack on the Israeli delegation to the Munich Olympics, Nixon established coordinator teams on counter-terrorism. Only in 1976 was the CIA tasked with collecting intelligence on terrorist activities overseas. In September 1977, National Security Advisor Zbigniew Brzezinski organised a working group in the National Security Council to address global terrorism.[94]

During this period, Iraq expressed interest in expanding trade with the US, along with its military-procurement deals with European states. A cable from the Baghdad legation urged Washington to respond favorably to Baghdad's request for American military technologies, a gesture he said would lead to resuming full bilateral relations.[95] Reviewing the list of military-related items requested by Iraq and rejected by the US, according to the Foreign Military Sales Act of 1968 (P.L.60-629 and the International Security Assistance and Arms Export Control Act of 1976 (PL 94-329) indicates great Iraqi interest in, and admiration for, American military technology, since Baghdad could have done its purchasing in France without any limitation. The list included radar systems and related accessories, equipment to obstruct and intercept communications and armoured ambulances.[96] The State Department opposed legislators' suggestions to limit civilian equipment that could be used by the army, such as aircraft, and to block federal credit granted by the Export-Import Bank. The department's repeated argument was that expanding trade could moderate Iraqi positions and enable the resumption of relations.[97]

The apparent role and influence of Jewish and pro-Israel legislators in Congress in trying to restrict exports of arms to Iraq, as well as to the US's ally Saudi Arabia, did not go unnoticed in Baghdad. Senators Jacob Javits and Carl Levin, Representative Abraham Ribicoff – all Jewish – along with Heinz hammered away at Iraq's involvement in international terrorism, and pressured administration witnesses in the various legislations against terrorism as mentioned above, as well as anti-boycott legislations that will be discussed later in this chapter, to impose sanctions on Iraq, as had been applied to Libya. Moreover, in July 1979, Congress activated the Fenwick Amendment, requiring early public notification of the USTR and State Department Bank when considering the granting of export licenses over $7 million to a state sponsor of terrorism i.e. Libya, the People's Democratic Republic of Yemen, Syria and Iraq. It did so to tighten control over Iraq, after several members of Congress learned that the administration had approved the export to Baghdad of gas turbines for engines.[98]

Since the Iraqi Ba'th , and in particular Saddam, were closely following American politics and, in particular, legislation that concerned their procurement request from the US, they must have noticed the activity of AIPAC in Capitol Hill and the White House, as well as the influence of Jewish and pro-Israeli legislators to limit technological trade to Iraq. Publically the regime refrained from anti-Semitic statements, invited Jews who left Iraq to return, and focused its attacks on Israel. The Iraqi regime saw this as solid evidence of a Jewish-Zionist hold on Capitol Hill and the White House.

Practically, export controls over Iraq did not last long. Still, they caused delays. Carter exercised his right to issue waivers on a case-by-case basis and gradually loosened restrictions, allowing the export of military supplies to Iraq. In 1982, Iraq was formally removed from the list of states sponsoring terrorism, and American companies could sell arms to Iraq. By then, of course, Iraq was at war with Iran.[99]

American Initiatives to Solve the Arab-Israeli Conflict

The US's search for a solution to the conflict started as early as June 1967, when President Johnson announced his five principles for peace in the region: firstly, that every nation in the area has a fundamental right to live, and to have this right respected by its neighbours; secondly, on justice for the refugees … there will be no peace for any party in the Middle East unless this problem is solved; thirdly, maritime rights must be respected … the right of innocent maritime passage must be preserved for all nations; fourthly, there must be a limit on the arms race in the Middle East; fifthly, respect for political independence and territorial integrity of all the states of the area. The Nixon administration followed this policy at the UN and elsewhere with its Rogers Plan. In 1971 and 1972, Kissinger, in consultation with Sadat, sponsored a plan calling for an Israeli withdrawal from the Sinai in return for an arrangement that was less than a peace treaty. It was rejected by Israel, with the US understanding that Israel preferred the status quo.[100] In late February 1973, Sadat offered a proposal through his National Security Adviser Affairs Hafez Isma'il to Kissinger to reach a separate arrangement with Israel in return for Israel's withdrawal from Sinai. Nixon regarded the Egyptian offer as a breakthrough, a historical opportunity to preempt war and promote US strength vis-à-vis the USSR in the coming summit in June.[101]

In March 1973, Kissinger sought to persuade PM Golda Meir to respond favorably, but she fiercely rejected an Israeli withdrawal as a pre-condition for negotiations. However, former army generals Yitzhak Rabin, then serving as ambassador in Washington, and cabinet ministers Dayan and Yigal Allon did not utterly reject the idea, but they were overruled by Meir. Through April 1973, Israel and Egypt exchanged messages through Kissinger, and Kissinger met secretly with Sadat's National Security Adviser Hafiz Isma'il. Kissinger did not share the information even with Rogers, and Meir excluded most of her cabinet members from the process as well.[102]

In the following years, Meir was severely criticised domestically for misjudgment of the proposal, which, critics believed, could have avoided the trauma of the 1973 war. But she doubted the sincerity of Sadat. She was certain that the US would support Israel, anyway, and was confident that the IDF was capable of fighting off any Egyptian attack.[103]

Kissinger tried tirelessly to persuade Meir to agree to negotiations. Nixon even exerted pressure by delaying the sale of fighter planes to Israel – to no avail. As the April 1973 meeting between Kissinger and Isma'il approached, the initiative seemed deadlocked, and then it faded away.[104] Kissinger accepted that Israel would stick to the status quo. Retrospectively, Kissinger put the blame on the Egyptians for not maintaining the secrecy that is essential in such a sensitive process.[105] 'In Vietnam, the settlement got us out; in the Middle East, the settlement will draw us in, in order to protect what we have imposed', he told British under Secretary of State Thomas Brimelow.[106]

From Sadat's perspective, he took an exceptional risk by proposing a separate agreement, even with a deadline of 1 September 1973 to retrieve the territories peacefully. He was disappointed that the US did not bring about an Israeli withdrawal from the Sinai.[107] Sadat was determined to regain the peninsula, but his proposal caught both Israel and the US by surprise. The US had no choice but to remain involved to preserve American strategic interests to protect its energy resources and deter Soviet encroachment. The active role of Kissinger in mediating Israeli ceasefires with Syria and Egypt, and his meetings with Sadat, Assad and Meir, created a unique opportunity for US diplomacy to produce a solution to the conflict.

Washington, after all, was the only player with the leverage to bring about an Israeli withdrawal. It had cooperated with the Soviet Union to reach a ceasefire agreement and help pass UN Security Council resolution 338, based on UNSC resolution 242 following the 1967 war. (The two resolutions have become, ever since, the basis for all subsequent peace processes in the Arab-Israeli conflict.) Kissinger created the step-by-step policy and gradual process towards the Geneva Convention that left the USSR participating mostly in a protocol role.[108]

Kissinger was neither discouraged by the rejectionist statements coming from Iraq and Libya, nor by the conclusion issued by the Algiers Summit in late November1973 rejecting any secret arrangements or negotiations until Israel withdrew from all occupied territories.[109] This step-by-step policy gained momentum in October 1973 after the US succeeded in pressing Israel to lift the IDF's siege on the Egyptian Third Army west of the Suez Canal, and later when disengagement agreements were signed between Israel and Egypt (January 1974) and between Israel and Syria (May 1974). Kissinger was determined to attain Israel's further withdrawals in the Sinai, from the Gidi and Mitla strategic passes, and to have the Egyptians regain their oil fields. Kissinger insisted that Israel should have made a unilateral gesture in withdrawing from these passes, given that Sadat proposed an interim agreement without pre-conditions that included a timetable for Israel's withdrawal. He blamed Israel for its insistence on keeping a six-mile security strip in the Sinai.[110] In January 1975, US intelligence reports warned of a possible escalation between Syria and Israel that could evolve into a full-scale war with Soviet involvement.[111]

Administration officials, and President Ford himself, reiterated the danger of another war in the Middle East as harming essential American interests.[112] Kissinger exerted significant pressure on Israel to accept the Egyptian-American terms for a Sinai withdrawal. Kissinger feared that renewal of war with Syria would mean the collapse of his peace initiative and Sadat's fall as a major Arab leader who had turned away the Soviets and accepted American dominance in the process. Kissinger was hoping that other Arab states would follow Sadat's strategic turn. At that point, American foreign policy sought to develop closer relations with Arab states, including the non-conservative Syria, Algeria and Iraq.

1975: The 'Reassessment' Crisis with Israel

Kissinger, backed by Ford, initiated a crisis with Israel. On 21 March 1975, as Kissinger was arriving in Jerusalem from Cairo, Ford sent a dramatic message to Rabin, stating that a breakdown of his mediation efforts between

Israel and Egypt, as a result of Israel's position, would bring about the US's reassessment of its policy towards Israel.[113] The following day, Kissinger instructed all the heads of US missions in Arab capitals to notify the host governments of the suspension of the Israeli-Egyptian talks and of the US's initiation of a major reassessment of its policy towards all parties. The message praised Sadat, who, Kissinger wrote, 'had demonstrated great statesmanship in seeking to lead the Arab world toward honorable peace'. The wording implied that Israel bore responsibility for the failure of diplomacy.

Lowrie conveyed Kissinger's message to Jallal al-Samra'i, the political director general of Iraq's Ministry of Foreign Affairs. Al-Samra'i refrained from comment, except to say that he would pass the message to Foreign Minister Hammadi.[114] The lack of any response by the Iraqi official to such a dramatic message, not even a response couched in words of diplomatic courtesy, could be attributed to the atmosphere of fear and anxiety that prevailed within the bureaucracy, given that all policy guidelines were approved by the Ba'th Party. Indeed, Iraq withheld a reaction to the American message, except in sarcastic op-ed pieces in the state-owned and Ba'th controlled media that claimed that there was no real change in US policy.

This attitude reflects the dilemma of the Ba'th regarding the peace process. On the one hand, Iraq had endorsed the phased plan since 1974; on the other hand, welcoming US pressure on Israel to reach a settlement with Egypt would imply support for recognising Israel. At that time, Iraq was developing closer economic relations with Egypt and ignored Sadat's involvement in the process to reach agreements involving Israel.

Washington's 'reassessment' policy marked its most severe crisis with Israel since the Eisenhower administration was caught by surprise when Israel joined the British-French operation in 1956, imposed an arms embargo on Israel and demanded immediate Israeli withdrawal from the Sinai. The toll of that embargo in 1975 was extremely high: the freezing of Israel's military procurement, including of the F-15 aircraft, the delaying of economic aid and the holding of unusually harsh discussions with Israeli leadership. The US had no intention of abandoning Israel either in 1956, or in 1975, but it was exerting psychological and practical pressure on its leadership to be more forthcoming and make what Washington considered to be necessary concessions to Sadat who had turned away from the Soviets and relied on American mediation. Israel rejected the Egyptian pre condition that, in return for IDF withdrawal from the strategic passes and the Sinai oil fields, Egypt would make just a general statement of 'non-belligerency'. Israel demanded a peace treaty with Egypt, including and freedom of navigation in the Suez Canal.[115]

Although this 'reassessment' crisis had been planned, it was not merely a tactical, manipulative move. Rather, it reflected the administration's rage at Israeli rigidity. In closed sessions in the White House, Israel was portrayed as inflexible, excessively anxious regarding its security and with an unlimited appetite for state-of-the-art military technology. Kissinger told Ford that it was a mistake to transfer that scope of weapons to Israel when the Jewish state reciprocated by demonstrating ingratitude. 'I have never seen such cold-blooded playing with the American national interest', he said. 'Every Arab was looking to us; we had moved the Soviet Union out of the Middle East; even Iraq was being moved. What they have done is destroy this.'[116]

The administration was also infuriated by the Israeli influence in Congress, derived from the growing political power of American Jews, who, the administration also believed, were committed to pressuring the administration to force the Soviet Union to allow its Jews to emigrate; in the view of some US officials, such lobbying could obstruct US-Soviet relations.[117] Kissinger even expressed to foreign leaders his anger at Israel. He did so even to Tunisian Prime Minister Hedi Amara Nouira, and told King Hussein of Jordan that if Israel had accepted Hussein's previous proposal, the Rabat resolution, which transferred the sovereignty rights in the West Bank from Jordan (and Gaza from Egypt) to the PLO, would have been circumvented.[118] Vice President Nelson Rockefeller informed an Egyptian parliamentary delegation that foreign aid to Israel would decline following new legislation on election funds that would significantly weaken Jewish influence in Capitol Hill.[119]

The administration did not anticipate the intensity of the criticism of its reassessment policy, coming mostly from Congress and the media, claiming that the move might weaken the credibility of the US globally.[120] On 21 May, a letter signed by seventy-six US senators criticised the administration for blaming Israel for the suspension of the talks and for threatening to withhold aid to Israel. In the letter, the contents of which were published in many articles, the senators urged Ford to respond to Israel's military and economic needs for the sake of American national interests.[121]

Public support for Israel by then had become bipartisan, thanks to the lobbying work on Capitol Hill of the American Israel Public Affairs Committee (AIPAC). Kissinger told British Prime Minister Harold Wilson that the letter, initiated by Senators Jacob Javits (R-N.Y.) and Henry Jackson (R-Wash.), resulted from an Israeli campaign in Congress against the administration, using the American Jewish community.[122] The administration might have been well served to know that its reassessment policy had almost no effect: public opinion polls indicated that Americans' support for Israel did not significantly decline as a result of the policy, and that support for the Arabs remained very low; according to the Roper Report in April 1975: 43 percent of the American public supported Israel but only 7 percent supported the Arabs. Regarding Israeli security and Washington's provision of military assistance, the gap was even wider, since it was well known that the USSR was arming the Arab states. A Gallup poll indicated, in April, that there was 54 percent support for arms transfer and 37 percent against it. The Yankelovich poll of August 1975 found that 52 percent were certain that the Arabs intended to eliminate Israel, while only 17 percent assumed that the Arabs had peaceful intentions.[123]

Reluctantly, the administration pulled back. In August 1975, the US extended a generous economic and military aid package to Israel, and committed to not recognising the PLO, in return for Israel's withdrawal from the Sinai passes. Kissinger and his team could now move forward towards negotiating an interim agreement between Israel and Egypt, which was signed on 4 September 1975. This process became a pattern for the following negotiations (in 1977 with Egypt and in 1982 with Jordan and the PLO). The American mediator also granted guarantees and incentives to both parties, as an integral part of the peace process.[124]

American Jews enjoyed special influence with the Ford administration. One of them, Max M. Fisher, had been the unofficial liaison between the American Jewish community and Ford. Fisher, a Michigander like Gerald Ford himself, was a frequent visitor to the White House to meet with Ford and Kissinger. Fisher played a major role in the resolution of the 1975 crisis, including by presenting Israel's position to the White House. [125]In a conversation with Kissinger, on 24 March 1975, Fisher demanded an immediate meeting to be briefed about the crisis. He also insisted that the administration not blame Israel alone for the failure in the negotiations.

The administration continued to try and approach the Arab states, in particular following the signing of the interim agreement. In a toast for the Arab heads of missions to the UN, Kissinger said openly: 'We are prepared to work with all the parties toward a solution of all the issues yet remaining – including the issue of the future of the Palestinians.'[126] In November 1975, State Department Deputy Assistant of Secretary of State Harold Saunders, made a statement to the House Committee on International Relations Subcommittee on the Middle East. Responding to Chairman Lee Hamilton, who pushed him on the question of why the US was not talking to the PLO or bringing it into the process, Saunders answered: 'The Palestinian dimension of the Arab-Israeli conflict is the heart of that conflict.' This statement was later known as 'The Saunders' document'. He even raised the possibility of negotiations between Israel and the PLO, if the latter renounced terrorism and recognised Israel.[127] The Saunders statement provoked debate in the American and Middle Eastern media. Saudi Arabia and Egypt welcomed what they saw as a new American position. Palestinian rejectionist newspapers, like *Al-Hadaf* (aligned with the PFLP), *Ila Al-Amam* (Jibril) and *Al-Tha'ir al-'Arabi* (the Iraqi ALF), described Saunders' words as a dangerous conspiracy to impose an American-Israeli arrangement.[128]

Iraqi media and officials closely followed American affairs,[129] including American military support for Israel. Ba'th propaganda explained the military strength of Israel on that basis. The Ba'th also amplified the Israeli-American threat to create a sense of unity and to justify harsh measures against the party's opposition elements. Iraq reacted with great scepticism to the idea of American pressure on Israel to withdraw from occupied territories. The Iraqi daily *Al-Jumhuriyya* claimed that 'all partial arrangements assigned to serve US and Israeli interests are bound to fail, [and] highlight the Ba'th way that calls for an "all-Arab united struggle"' (*al-nidal al-qawmi, al-shamil wal-muwahad*).[130] Vicious criticism of the US appeared in response to the Middle East trip of Senator George McGovern (D-SD), whom Kissinger asked to clarify the re-assessment policy. The article in the Iraqi *Al-Jumhuriyya* responded to McGovern's interview with the Lebanese Journal *Al-Nahar*. The Iraqi paper described the reassessment policy as 'a sickening method to exert diplomatic pressure by creating an illusion [of] a reassessing of American positions.' The article added that 'the only option left for the Arabs to defend themselves against America is to return to the national armed struggle, using all Arab resources against the US ... until the whole of Palestine is liberated'.[131] Iraqi animosity towards the US gained further momentum following open statements and reports on a US-Iranian 'contingency plan' to take over the oil fields by force.

The Iraqi press protested the inflammatory statements of US officials in 1975, that any future Arab oil embargo would generate a harsh American response, including a military one. Kissinger said, in early January, to the *Business Week* that the US 'would consider using military force in the Middle East under circumstances of grave emergency – if say, the industrialized world became threatened with economic strangulation'. Defense Secretary Schlesinger warned that America would be 'less tolerant' of a new oil embargo and was reserving military force as one possible response, according to *The Daily Telegraph* of 20 May 1975. These statements were portrayed in *Al-Jumhuriyya* as evidence of US hypocrisy, and that the US had no intention of abandoning Israel.[132]

Bilateral Relations through the Arab-Israeli Prism

The administration hoped that the US's success in brokering Israel's withdrawal from territories in the interim agreement (known as Sinai II, of September 1975) would encourage the Iraqi Ba'th to be open to launching warm bilateral relations with Washington and to gradually move away from the USSR and join what seemed to be Arab mainstream approach to the conflict.[133]

The long-awaited meeting between Kissinger and his Iraqi counterpart, Sa'dun Hammadi, was held in secret on 17 December 1975 at the residence of the Iraqi ambassador in Paris. The meeting did not bring about a diplomatic breakthrough, and Iraq maintained its rigid and unchangeable position towards the Arab-Israeli conflict. Hammadi presented the well-known Ba'th rejectionist position that Israel was not a legitimate entity, that it had been established by force and that Iraq rejected any political arrangement to allow Israeli rule. Kissinger mentioned that the US could not negotiate the existence of Israel, but could 'reduce its size to historical proportions'. Kissinger's words implied an unprecedented change of policy towards Israel. Hammadi conveyed Iraqi concerns over US policy in support of the Kurds, and against American and Israeli involvement in Lebanon.[134] But Hammadi, apparently, wouldn't further discuss the Palestinian-Israeli conflict, most likely because he lacked the authority to do so. His attitude underscored the unbridgeable gap between the two sides.

From the American perspective, the meeting was a failure. Talking points prepared by the State Department for the Kissinger Hammadi meeting listed three main subjects: (1) promoting bilateral relations, reiterating US willingness to discuss resumption of relations; (2) Arab-Israel: explaining the US belief that negotiation for a settlement was the only realistic way to deal with the problem, though the US was prepared to agree to differ with Iraq; (3) the UN and Israel: the US believed that suspension of Israel from the General Assembly of the United Nations was wrong and would work against it.[135] Kissinger failed to discuss the need for negotiated settlement between Israel and the Arabs, in particular following the successful Interim Agreement between Israel and Egypt. The significant topic of bilateral relations was rejected by Hammadi, and the status of Israel in the UN and the Arab call to expel Israel following UN resolution 3379 (*Zionism is Racism*) was not even raised.

But the administration should have known that the Sinai II agreement, which had been denounced in Iraq, wouldn't alone serve to elevate relations. For example, two months before the Paris meeting, on 4 September, the Pan-Arab Command of the Ba'th Party issued a white paper on the party's solution to the conflict calling for the creation of an Iraqi-Syrian-Jordanian front against Israel. As to the Sinai, the document suggested the same form of unconditional evacuation of forces as that which followed the 1956 war.[136] Other articles in the Iraqi press – including one written by Iraqi author Badi'a Amin in the political and cultural magazine *Aafaq Arabiyya* – attacked Sadat for turning to a non-Arab mediator, the US, to lead the process.[137]

From Baghdad's perspective, the meeting achieved a key goal, since the US had courted Iraq. The meeting reflected a clearly asymmetrical pattern for the relations. While the US was forthcoming on forging closer political relations, Iraq was interested in expanding trade relations only; it was clear a priori that the US would not abandon Israel, so Iraq could always use its rejectionist position to evade resuming relations. On 10 January 1976, the English language Iraqi newspaper the *Baghdad Observer* published an article that described a new American approach towards the Arabs. The article maintained that the US concluded that relying on Israel alone did not serve American interests, so it approached the Arabs with a plan to allow a mini-Palestinian state, while continuing to support Israel. The new Head of Baghdad Interest Section Marshall Wiley, who was unaware of the secret meeting in Paris, called the article another positive signal from Iraq to the US.[138]

Iraqi 'Pragmatism' towards Israel: American Misperception or Iraqi Deception?

The State Department's optimism regarding expanding relations with Iraq after the March 1975 Algiers agreement was well substantiated. In April 1971, the political director general of Iraq's Ministry of Foreign Affairs, Ibrahim al-Wali, told Arthur Day, the newly appointed director of the State Department's Bureau of Near Eastern Affairs, that his country's chief goal was to end its isolation, following the war over Kurdistan that consumed major national resources. The new approach, he said, was based on realism and pragmatism.[139]

The stated focus on pragmatism, including launching vigorous development programs and diplomatic efforts to end international isolation, allegedly indicated an Iraqi acceptance of the US's support for Israel being unchangeable. At the same time, Iraq continued to offer its rejectionist rhetoric perceived by Americans as lip service for image purposes.[140] Both Lowrie and Wiley, who cumulatively headed the Baghdad Interest Section from 1972 to 1977, endorsed the idea that Iraq was on the path to moderation, eager to pursue modernisation and would not oppose a peace process. Legislators, politicians and businessmen who visited Iraq concurred with this view and promoted relations with Iraq. Senator William Fulbright (D-Ark.) reported to the White House that officials he met in Baghdad stated that the Ba'th would not hamper an arrangement with Israel.[141] Senator Ted Kennedy (D-Mass.) told Kissinger that both President Al-Bakr and Foreign Minister Hammadi stressed that Iraq was not interested in war and would not oppose a political arrangement, since such opposition was bound to fail.[142] The British ambassador in Baghdad, J.A.N. Graham, concurred.[143]

However, Congressional and trade missions to Iraq noted the regime's radical position towards Israel, compared to other Arab countries. Senator Adlai Stevenson (D-Ill.), on a visit to Iraq in early 1976, was appalled when one of his hosts said that he did not see any reason for Israel to exist and that Israel's size should be 'reduced ... to historical proportions'. Still, Stevenson was impressed by Iraq's interest in improved trade relations with the US.[144] The administration, too, understood that Iraq would stick to its stated policy of rejection, while not obstructing the process.

Iraqi media covered Kissinger's frequent shuttle-diplomacy visits to Cairo, Damascus and Amman, and criticised the US-led process. Still, it avoided attacking Egypt directly and the ultimate Arab target of Iraq's propaganda attack was Syria.[145] The media's more favorable attitude toward Egypt – which, like Syria, had signed disengagement agreements with Israel, and maintained close relations with Washington – reflected the tactical flexibility of the Iraqi Ba'th, which placed national interests before ideology. The American assessment of the party, though, reflected a fundamental misunderstanding of the ongoing struggle of the Ba'th to gain legitimacy in the Arab arena. The Iraqi Ba'th had no incentive to change its radical position and to resume relations with the US – and that position gave it legitimacy, in particular *vis-a-vis* Syria, which had to cooperate with the US to achieve the ceasefire and border arrangement with Israel, and which exchanged ambassadors with Washington. Moreover, Iraq could expand economic relations with the US without changing the low status of the diplomatic legations in Baghdad and Washington or turning away from the USSR. Hence, the American hope for a breakthrough in relations with Iraq was senseless.

The Iraqi-Syrian Rivalry and the US

Kissinger's shuttle diplomacy in the search for a peaceful solution was the core controversy between the Iraqi and Syrian Ba'th regimes. The rivalry exceeded both regimes' ideological boundaries and turned into a fierce, personal power struggle between Saddam and Assad. Both regimes accused each other of cooperation with the US. Syria blamed Iraq for making territorial concessions to Iran in the Algiers agreement, including on Arabistan (Iraninan Khuzistan) submitting to alleged American pressure to reach the Algier's agreement. Syria asserted that Iraq diplomatic approaches to Iran and Turkey, both US allies, indicated a disloyalty to Arab nationalism. Even the construction of an Iraqi pipeline via Turkey was portrayed as an 'Iraqi anti-Syrian conspiracy, encouraged by the US.'[146]

Iraqi propaganda used the same coin – American influence – to reciprocate. Iraqi media attacked every exchange between Damascus and Washington, including Kissinger's frequent visits in Damascus and Nixon's meeting with Assad in June 1974.[147] Both sides resorted to personal defamation; Iraq claimed that Rif'at Assad, the president's brother, received $12 million from the CIA.[148] On Lebanon, Iraq accused Syria of 'serving the American Zionist conspiracy against the national and Palestinian forces.'[149]

The most serious charge Iraq leveled against Syria was that it betrayed the Palestinians. Iraq observed with great concern the signals that Syria was considering signing a separate agreement with Israel, mediated by the US. Following the dramatic visit of Sadat to Jerusalem in 1977, the Iraqi newspaper *Al-Jumhuriyya* published an article entitled 'The Damascus Rulers are Happy, in Spite of their Statements.' Further commentaries placed a photo of Assad next to that of Sadat, calling both traitors.[150]

From an American viewpoint, Syria and Iraq had the same starting point. Both severed relations with the US in June 1967, and established Ba'thi radical, socialist regimes with a strong affiliation with and dependence on the Soviet Union. Iraq had the image of being more pragmatic and 'civilian'. Lowrie, the first head of the US interest section, arrived in Baghdad in November 1972, while the first head of legation in Damascus, Thomas Scotes, arrived in Damascus in February 1974, though full diplomatic relations with Syria resumed in June 1974, with the arrival of Ambassador Richard Murphy in August of that year. Full diplomatic relations with Iraq were resumed only a decade later, in November 1984.[151]

The US's mediation efforts to end the Yom Kippur War focused American attention on Syria, as a major confrontation state sharing a border with Israel. At the same time, Iraq was pushed aside, due to its radical statements against the ceasefire and the disengagement agreements, while the Carter administration would establish a rapport with Assad, hoping that he would eventually become a partner for peace. Vance was encouraged when Khaddam, his Syrian counterpart, agreed to American proposals to participate in further negotiations and set a date, 9 May 1977, for a Carter-Assad meeting that took place in Geneva.[152] Both the Ford and Carter administrations shared the expectation that Syria would eventually join the peace process in a bid to retrieve from Israel the occupied Golan. Both Syria and Iraq recognised the significant role of the US in the region and left open channels to the US. Both sent double meaning signals for openness and readiness for general cooperation, though Iraq never expressed any inclination to pull back from its rejectionist position, known in the Ba'th lexicon as *summud* (steadfastness).

Carter was deeply disappointed by Iraq's rejectionist attitude to the Israeli-Egyptian negotiations. Iraqi leaders called Sadat a traitor, demanded his death and denounced the role of the US in facilitating the peace process.[153] Yet, America's sober view of Iraq as a regional threat did not last long. The dramatic events that led to the fall of the Shah created a new reality that shed a different light on Iraq, as a potential ally since the Iranian close ally became an enemy. Brzezinski recommended sending signals to Iraq of the US possibly providing military aid if Saddam attacked Iran. The impulse to aid Iraq against Iran gained support in the NSC and at the Pentagon when Baghdad initiated war with Tehran in September 1980.[154]

Civil War in Lebanon

The Lebanon crisis that broke out in 1975, caused by the demographic changes as a result of an influx of Palestinian Muslims into Southern Lebanon, and the violation of the traditional sectarian balance that prevailed in Lebanon, was about to turn into civil war. Iraq was involved in Lebanon since Lebanon was the main arena of the Palestinian organisations, and therefore the place to show Arab national political activism. In addition, Lebanon was viewed by Syria as a Syrian historical sphere (Greater Syria). The Lebanese civil war placed the US and Iraq in opposition. America's main concern was that the sectarian conflict in Lebanon would deteriorate and turn the prosperous, moderate country into a radical, anti-Western state that would present risks to Israel from the north. The US sought solutions to the civil war that would restore the historical balance between Christians and Muslims and push away the radical elements within Lebanese and Palestinian-emigrant societies. Baghdad was involved through the regional pro- Iraqi Ba'th and used as a channel to Iraqi involvement in Lebanon, mostly through radical Palestinian groups, but also by connections to other sectors of Lebanese society. The purpose of Iraq's involvement in Lebanon and in the Palestinian arena was to gain prestige and influence as the Iraqi Ba'th stated goal representing Arab Nationalism, and practically to avoid Syrian dominance, since Asad perceived Lebanon as his backyard and historically natural sphere of influence ('Greater Syria').

Iraq perceived the US's involvement in Lebanon as a threat against all radical groups and Iraq itself. *Al-Jumhuriyya* described American officers as arriving in Beirut to assist Syria, and warned against the interference of the US Navy's Six Fleet in the crisis. Another article warned against even indirect American involvement in Lebanon by facilitating the flow of arms to 'Israel and the other American agents – the sectarian reactionary parties'.[155]

The US considered restraining Syrian military activity in Lebanon, fearing Israeli air raids in response. As sectarian violence escalated, that view changed. Former US Ambassador to Jordan L. Dean Brown was sent to Lebanon in late 1976 to mediate a solution, and reported that Syria shared the US's interest in preserving the delicate status quo, in opposing radicalisation, and in opposing the pro-Iraqi Ba'th and the other radical groups supported by Baghdad.[156] In an April 1976 meeting at the White House, a delegation of American Christians of Lebanese descent urged Ford and Kissinger to save Lebanon.[157] The next month, the former president of Lebanon, Charles Helou, met Scowcroft and Sisco and urged the US to save Lebanon from the 'genocide and sabotage' being perpetrated by radical elements inside the country and sponsored by external elements in Libya and Iraq.[158] American support for Syrian presence in Lebanon served an additional purpose, distancing Syria from the influence of radical states, including Iraq, and thereby enhancing the possibility of a peace process. In a closed meeting with Ford, Kissinger said the following:

> We have no illusion about Assad, but we want to keep Syria split from Libya and Iraq and the USSR. If a radical crescent involving Iraq, Syria, a PLO-controlled Lebanon and Libya comes into being – following the overthrow of Assad – it will be very bad for Egypt ... We do not want a radical bloc in the north. We want an eventual reconciliation of Egypt, Syria, Saudi Arabia and Jordan so a peace process can be resumed.[159]

On 16 June, the US ambassador-designate to Lebanon, Francis E. Meloy, and the embassy's economic counselor, Robert O. Waring, were gunned down in a Beirut street by the PFLP, a radical group supported by Iraq. Ford stated in his eulogy that the US was determined to carry on in its efforts to broker peace in Lebanon.[160] The US then viewed Syria as enforcing law and order, confronting radical Palestinian groups that threatened to take over Lebanon, and saw that the Soviets might find an excuse in the case of a vacuum to interfere in Lebanese affairs. [161]

The Iraqi regime resented America's support of Syria in Lebanon. Iraq sent a 'volunteer force' to Lebanon, comprised of Iraqis, Lebanese and Palestinian residents of Iraq. The force participated in skirmishes against Syria in the Lebanese cities of Beirut, Sidon and Tyre, and trained other radical groups. However, an Arab League resolution compelled the force to leave Lebanon.[162] This humiliating defeat had a deep impact on Saddam, so much so that, in 1991, one of the conditions he raised for negotiating a withdrawal of Iraqi forces from Kuwait was Syria's withdrawal from Lebanon. The British ambassador in Baghdad J.A.N. Graham concluded that Iraq's involvement in Lebanon was an expression of a rejectionist position. In fact, the main motive had been Iraqi determination to teach Syria a lesson.[163]

The Baghdad Rejectionist Summit: Defying America

Saddam portrayed himself as an Arab leader representing a steadfast, rejectionist front against the normalisation process with Israel, in clear defiance of the US, which had invested itself diplomatically and rewarded Israel (and later Egypt, too) generously. From the Ba'th point of view, the peace accord between Egypt and Israel was a major disaster. In its view, the US succeeded in recruiting a major Arab state to sign a separate treaty with Israel, thereby destroyed the Arabs' rejectionist consensus. Saddam brilliantly seized the opportunity right after the signing of the Camp David Accord and arranged an Arab League Summit in Baghdad in November 1978. He presented himself as the Arab leader who stood for genuine Arab nationalism. Defying America was an asset he could not give away. All the while, he maintained business as usual with the US Interest Section, even expanding trade relations.

At the summit, the Iraqi Ba'th pledged to cease support for subversive movements in Yemen, Oman and Syria, and reassured Jordan and Kuwait that Iraq would refrain from subversive activity in their territory as well.[164] To appease Arafat, Saddam evicted such radicals as Abu Nidal and Wadi' Al-Haddad from Iraq, though Saddam kept in touch with them and continued to use their services in later years. These organisations had been involved in international terrorism and assassinated Arab targets. These new developments of appeasement policy in the Arab arena were stated in Ba'th speeches and publications, which emphasised Iraq's consistent commitment to the Palestinians, including in the Rabat resolutions in 1974. Furthermore, the Ba'th was careful to avoid attacking Egypt as a whole, instead reserving criticism for Sadat's 'treason' and the collaboration of Hosni Mubarak, his successor as president. The purpose of the Baghdad summit, as defined by the Ba'th, was to express a united rejection of the Camp David Accords for being no more than a 'Zionist American conspiracy against the Arab nation, while keeping Egypt in the Arab bosom'.[165] At the report of the Ninth Congress of the Ba'th Regional Command in 1983 Saddam explained that the purpose of the 1978 summit resolution had not been to target Egypt, but, rather, to dissuade other Arab states from joining the peace process with Israel.[166]

These tactics correlated with Saddam's personality and ambition to become a historical Arab figure, such as Nebuchadnezzar or Nasser.[167] Saddam's bold act in confronting the US as the sponsor of the peace process, and his working to block negotiations meant to conclude further peaceful treaties with other Arab states, were a show of force and a matter of pride. Saddam admired power and viewed the US as the greatest superpower on Earth. He admired American technology and understood the US's dominance in the world economy. A cartoon in *Al-Jumhuriyya* portrayed the Baghdad summit as a huge bomb that caused the US to flee.[168] Tariq Aziz himself, who was then Deputy Prime Minister and an RCC member, told the team of US newspaper columnists Rowland Evans and Robert Novak with obvious glee: 'US sponsorship of the Camp David Accords has enabled Iraq to use oil money and Ba'athist ideology to envision political dominion of the Persian Gulf.'[169]

The Carter administration celebrated the treaty as the first step towards comprehensive peace between the Arabs and Israel. That was a natural conclusion of Carter's utopian view that the other Arab states bordering Israel would realise 'the fruits of peace' – Israeli withdrawal from territories and economic prosperity and join the process. So Carter was surprised and upset by the rejectionism emanating from the Baghdad summit, in particular from Jordan and Syria, who both denounced the Egyptian move.[170] Syndicated well known Washington based writer Joseph Kraft observed accurately that Carter had been mistakenly focused on the negotiations with Sadat, and had underestimated the intensity of the Arab resistance to the treaty.[171]

Iraq-US and the Arab Boycott

The Arab boycott of Israel[172] had been an integral part of Iraqi foreign policy ever since the Arab League adopted it some decades before. The Ba'th regime, as a flag waver of anti-Israel rejection, could not afford any concession on this issue. The director of the Arab Boycott Bureau in Baghdad Abd al-Karim al-Tai' had been a senior official of Iraq's Ministry of Foreign Affairs.[173] The Arab boycott contradicted the American principles of free trade and anti-discrimination. In 1974, Congress demanded that Ford's administration enforce these anti-boycott principles and initiated new legislation accordingly.[174] The process created obstacles to expanding trade with Iraq, in particular the signing of new contracts. Carter, the Democrats' nominee for president in 1976, criticised Ford for not acting toughly against the boycott, with Ford blaming Congress for being too slow in the legislation process; Ford did issue a regulation allowing the US to publish a list of companies that complied with the boycott. In 1977, Carter initiated an anti-boycott provision in the Export Control Act which referred to companies as well as to individuals. Senator Ribicoff introduced enforcement and punitive measures, such as barring companies complying with the Arab League boycott from receiving tax benefits. Moreover, the law banned companies from abiding by any restrictions against 'friendly states' based on race, religion, gender or nationality.[175]

The US legislation was in conflict with Iraqi policy, appearing in all Iraqi international tenders, that disqualified from international contracts companies that had trade relations with Israel, but companies 'controlled' by Jews. Iraqi provision, besides being morally problematic, was impractical, given the Jewish presence in corporate America. Wiley was asked to approach the Arab Boycott Bureau to settle the matter. He met with Al-Khargouli, the Economic Director General of Iraq's Ministry of Foreign Affairs, who argued that Congress's anti-boycott legislation displayed a misreading of the Arab boycott as being racially discriminatory against Jews. Al-Khargouli said that the boycott was as legitimate as the US's boycott of Cuba.

In an attempt to find a compromise in a contract with the US Department of Defense, the Iraqis suggested ambiguous language for their own policy. The language would not mention Israel, but would ban trade with 'countries that the Republic of Iraq has already boycotted or who's manufacturing and trading firms it no longer deals with'. The State Department rejected the proposal, since it clearly meant Israel and remained at odds with the Anti-Boycott provision of the Export Control Administration Amendment of 1977.[176] Knowing that anti-boycott legislation would obstruct new deals, the Baghdad Interest Section sent a message to Washington, urging lenient treatment of Iraq regarding the anti-boycott regulations: 'It is unthinkable that the Ba'th regime would respond pragmatically with an eye solely or even mainly to Iraq's economic interest if the US were to enact *the House International Relations Committee* Amendment ... Certainly, GOI [the government of Iraq] would not rewrite their laws to make it possible for US firms to avoid having to face boycott language.'[177]

The Iraqis viewed the American anti-boycott legislation as a hostile campaign against Iraq and the Arabs. These regulations threatened to freeze US Export-Import credit lines for Iraq and halt the supply of spare parts for the oil industry, and were perceived by Iraq as extortion.[178] A special session of the Arab League was convened in Baghdad in November 1976 to deal with the implications of the American legislation. Muhammd Mahjub, who chaired the forum, stated that the American legislation would harm mostly the US. He added that the Arab Boycott Office would intensify the investigation of long-term contracts to include shareholders and sub-contractors to ensure the implementation of the boycott of Israel. Wiley claimed that the legislation had a negative effect on the US's reputation and credibility as a business partner, for, in his view, submitting to 'Zionist pressures.' [179]The British attaché reported that the Ba'th was spreading a rumour that Al-Bakr intended to bar all American firms from partaking in Iraqi bids when the legislation was completed. The British official cast doubt on whether the Ba'th would execute this threat, since Iraq depended on US parts and components to maintain its Boeing aircraft fleet and other equipment.

Iraq's intention to retaliate against American companies was more than rumour. After learning that Westinghouse had bid to construct a plant in Israel, the Ba'th barred it from bidding on the construction of a petrochemical plant in Iraq.[180] By contrast, Kuwait and Jordan signed contracts with Westinghouse, which had long been active in Arab states and had even won the bid to construct a nuclear power plant in Egypt.[181] Iraq was a hardliner in implementing the boycott, and was the only state that required a company's 'negative certificate of origin' and an official statement, or by detailed questioner signed to the effect that the company had no link to Israel, including maintaining agents and representatives there, and even shareholders.[182] When ratifying international charters, such as the Extension of the Wheat Protocol [the formal name was: Protocols of the Further Extension of the International Wheat Agreement, the Food Aid Convention constituting the Wheat Trade Convention 1971],[183] Iraq insisted on adding this clause: 'Entry into the above protocol by the Republic of Iraq shall, however, in no way signify recognition of Israel or be conducive to entry into any relations therewith.'[184] US corporations and investors opposed the anti-boycott legislation, anxious that they would lose business opportunities in Iraqi development plans and that existing contracts would be terminated. Some firms hired lobbyists to oppose the legislation in Congress.[185]

Retrospectively, the anti-boycott legislation did not have a significant effect on US trade with Iraq or other Arab states. To be sure, the Arab League resolution on the boycott had been enforced voluntarily by the Arab states. Yet, in spite of the American legislation to enforce export controls on states that sponsored terrorism and applied the Arab Boycott, such as Iraq, the volume of trade between Iraq and the US did not decline. According to New York based American Jewish Committee analysis, the reason trade with the US did not grow as anticipated was mostly because of Iraq's decision to purchase from states that had imported Iraqi oil. In any case, the demand to include boycott-compliance language in every contract became obsolete, and from 1978 onward most Arab states did not include the Arab Boycott clauses in international contracts.[186]

Statistics indicate that US-Iraq trade gradually grew, in spite of the congressionally mandated anti-boycott and anti-terrorism limitations.[187] Iraq seemed to have quietly found ways to sign contracts without formally renouncing the boycott. In late October 1978, the director general of Iraq's Ministry of Health told a visiting trade mission of American Health Industries that Iraq preferred US medical technology, which it considered far superior to that of Eastern Europe. He added that his office would seek a boycott exemption for firms producing superior equipment.[188] The US State and Commerce Departments assisted American companies in receiving legal exemptions, including waivers extended by the president, to carry out their contracts. The boycott rules on both sides included no restrictions on training and exempted the telecommunication industry that was allowed to operate in the Middle East with states that complied with the Arab Boycott. In September 1976, Iraqis were invited to an international workshop on remote sensing, held in Sioux Falls, South Dakota.[189]

For the Ba'th, the self-proclaimed leader of the Arab rejection front against Israel, the Arab boycott held important symbolic value, so Iraq had no interest in appearing to violate the boycott.[190] In fact, the boycott had been so embedded in the national Iraqi consciousness that even after the fall of Saddam in 2003, the Iraqi transitional government notified the Arab Boycott Bureau in Damascus that Iraq remained committed to the policy and would not allow the import of Israeli goods.[191]

Marshall Wiley: An Arabist and a Businessman

Marshall W. Wiley, head of the US Interest Section in Baghdad from October 1975 to May 1977, was born and raised in the Midwest, in Rockford Illinois, and served in the navy. He was first exposed to the Middle East when he was posted to Israel (1954–7) to work on a project overseen by the US Agency for International Development (USAID). Israel had been absorbing Jewish refugees and tripled its population in its first decade, but Wiley was moved by the plight of the Palestinian refugees. He joined the US Foreign Service in 1958, learned Arabic and specialised in the Arab world. Wiley was a great supporter of US-Arab relations and, as head of the US Interest Section in Baghdad, he viewed economic relations with Iraq as leverage the US could utilise to moderate Iraq's radical positions. In spite of Iraq's fierce rejection of Kissinger's shuttle diplomacy, Wiley, who had good insight into the Ba'th's ideological commitment, estimated that it would not act against the peace settlement.

In the Baghdad office, Wiley hosted more American visitors and met more senior officials of the Ministry of Foreign Affairs than did his predecessor Lowrie. His reports conveyed meticulously the Iraqi message, and reflected a deep understanding of Iraqi views. However, his interpretations, analysis and predictions were overly optimistic. For example, he explained Iraq's anti-American rhetoric and rejectionist position as being solely to rally domestic support, and maintained that Iraq, as a civilised nation, could not possibly have sponsored terrorism, except in resistance to Israel. In an interview in 1989, he continued to accept, at face value, Iraq's explanation that it had hosted Abu Nidal and his men in Iraq solely to control and confine his terrorist activity. Wiley considered US support for Israel to be the main stumbling block to improving relations with the Arab world and with Iraq in particular. He welcomed the Saunders Statement recognising the role of the Palestinians in a future settlement, as a step in the right direction, though not enough. He called for more American recognition of Palestinian grievances and more understanding of Iraqi and Arab positions in the UN, which he said were based on a profound sense of historic injustice on Palestine[192].

Wiley was proud to be an expert on the Middle East, and considered unfair his branding as an 'Arabist', in the negative sense of being anti-Israeli and pro-Arab. While in Iraq, he developed an admiration of Saddam, and portrayed the regime's violence against its domestic opponents as an essential tool and as part of the political culture. Following his retirement from the Foreign Service in 1981, he expressed support for Iraq in its war with Iran (1980–8), and opposed the imposition of economic sanctions on Iraq even after the chemical attack on the Kurds of *Halabja* in 1988. He even found some justification for the Iraqi invasion of Kuwait in 1990. When full relations between the US and Iraq finally resumed in 1984, Iraq was in a desperate state of war, and Wiley's connections in both Washington and Baghdad proved valuable, since American equipment and products were flowing to Iraq and Wiley could use his connections in both Washington and Baghdad. In 1985, Wiley established the US-Iraq Business Forum, whose members represented major American corporations. It soon became a powerful lobby for the expansion of US trade with Iraq, including military supplies and technologies. The forum was active until 1991, when Iraq invaded Kuwait and the US military launched Operation Desert Storm. Wiley did not hide his criticism of AIPAC when it raised concerns during the activity of the Forum in the 1980s, regarding the US's arming of Iraq, and caused delays in Congress.[193]

Jews, Zionism and Anti-Semitism

Israeli analyst Yehoshafat Harkabi maintained that Arab anti-Semitism was primarily ideological and political, targeting the very existence of the State of Israel, and not directed at the Jewish people worldwide. As a result of the frustration over the failures to defeat Israel, Arab political literature kept alive the idea of Israel's destruction as an Arab national goal, Harkabi said. The line between Zionism and Judaism would become blurred, and they frequently overlapped.[194] The attitude of Saddam toward Jews in general, and Iraqi Jews in particular, and their relations with Israel and the Arab-Israeli conflict, is based on some well-known Ba'th principles. The Iraqi Ba'th added an accusation that the Jews became a stumbling block in preventing Saddam from gaining regional leadership and international recognition. The Ba'th emphasised, though, that Saddam was not an anti-Semite, and it repeatedly noted that he hated neither the Jews nor the Jewish religion – merely Zionism, which claimed Palestine as the Jewish national home.

However, Ba'th writings, opinion articles and cartoons in the press indicate deep-rooted anti-Semitic elements (originating in Europe) regarding the supernatural powers of Jews around the world, in particular in the US, that enabled Israel to exist.[195] These concepts were so common in the Ba'th that Foreign Minister Shadhil Taqa, upon meeting Senator James Abourezk (D-S.D.), an Arab American and a Christian, in January 1974, related what he considered to be the truth about bi-partisan Jewish political influence on the administration: 'Though there are fewer Jewish members in the Republican Party, the structure of the US system enables Zionist influence to remain strong ... and even if the president attempted to change policy, Zionists would drown him in Watergate.'[196] Khairalla Talfah, an uncle of Saddam, said the following in 1980, during the Iran-Iraq war: 'Three whom God should not have created: Persians, Jews and flies.'[197] Saddam admired Talfah, who participated in the Rashid Ali al-Kylani rebellion against the British in 1941, and who was inspired by Nazi propaganda. An anti-Jewish pogrom in June 1941 known as *Farhud*, had been described by Iraqi nationalists and later on by Ba'thi writers, as revenge for the Jews' betrayal in supposedly assisting the British occupier.[198]

When the Ba'th assumed power in July 1968, the small Iraqi Jewish community had been struggling to make a living and generally was uninvolved in politics. However, perhaps the Ba'th bore a grudge against Jewish activism in the Communist Party and in the Zionist underground two decades earlier. The regime conducted show trials, followed by the public hanging of nine Jews in January 1969 alongside others deemed to be traitors. The trials and executions were meant to project power and deter opposition – even though Jews remained involved in politics. Mostly, they sought to appease the masses, frustrated and humiliated by the 1967 defeat to Israel.

The public hanging and abuse of corpses were not unprecedented. When the monarchy was toppled by Abd al-Karim Qasim in 1958, the corpses of the regent and of the veteran politician Nuri Sa'id was dragged along the streets. The Ba'th leadership was unprepared for the magnitude of the universal shock in reaction to the executions. Past governments in Iraq had taken harsh measures against Assyrians, Kurds, Shi'is, communists and other individuals, but those did not trigger such public outrage and denunciations. And while those executed by the Ba'th included prominent figures, the negative outcry referred mostly to the Jews. The campaign against the persecution of Iraqi Jews was led by American Jewish organisations, and the regime saw it as a show of force against Iraq, just as it viewed American support of Israel as a conspiracy of Jewish power. While European-based anti-Semitism reached the Arab world – the long-discredited *The Protocols of the Elders of Zion* had been translated into Arabic and was considered a credible historical source – the Ba'th did not use anti-Semitic language when referring to Iraqi Jews or to other Jewish communities, except Israel. Being secular, the regime aimed to demonstrate a tolerant, pluralistic approach to ethnic and religious minorities, including Jews.

This was also consistent with the Iraqi idea for the solution of the Palestinian problem, namely, the return of all (Israeli) Jews in Palestine to their countries of origin, including to Iraq, and the return of all Palestinians to their homes all over Palestine meaning the cessation of the State of Israel.[199]

It's unclear to what extent Saddam's attitude toward Jews affected his policy towards the US. He consistently evaded the issue. Saddam did not consider himself an anti-Semite, or anti-Jewish. He grew up in Tikrit and not in Baghdad, where the country's large Jewish community flourished in the 1940s, but it was likely that he did not have a great deal of contact with Jews since many had left Iraq. However, according to an Iraqi Jewish source interviewed by Baram, a Jewish family saved Saddam's mother, a widow pregnant with Saddam, when she intended to commit suicide or abort the fetus; the Jewish family gave her shelter and medical care.[200] One can see the lack of public statements by Saddam against Jews and the intensive effort to refute allegations of harassment and oppression of individual Iraqi Jews, since Jews had allegedly saved his family, as a personal commitment, based on ancient Arab and tribal respect and dignity towards those to whom one has a moral obligation.

His attitude toward Israel and American Jews, who he believed were exerting pressure on the US administration, was another matter entirely. He fell back on anti-Semitic conspiracy theories that attributed monstrous, unnatural powers to world Jewry. These theories commonly appeared in Arab publications.

Saddam's conviction that Jews possess supernatural powers was established from the horse's mouth in a recording of RCC session in the 1990s, captured by the US army in 2003. Saddam ordered a thorough study on the source of these mythical powers of the Jews from the book[201] Protocols of the Elders of Zion, which had first been translated into Arabic in the 1920s in Cairo, and has been available ever since in the Arab world. The Ba'th firmly denied accusations of being anti-Semitic or anti-Jewish, and was most likely shocked by the swift and comprehensive Jewish reaction.

Political Activism for Iraqi Jews

American Jewish organisations led the campaign for Iraqi Jews, while Israel followed the campaign cautiously and discreetly.[202]

American Jewish organisations had been assisting vulnerable Jews globally for decades. The relevant effort had begun in the early 1970s on behalf of Soviet Jewry including groups that were not oriented towards Zionism and did not encourage immigration to Israel in particular – but cooperated to pressure the Soviet Union to stop the persecution of its Jews and allow them to leave and to settle elsewhere. When it came to international Jewish advocacy to assist the Jews of Iraq, it is likely that the Ba'th was not aware of nuanced differences between the organisations – only that they all seemed to cooperate and coordinate. Their activities were both public (organised protests, signing of petitions and media coverage) and discreet (meeting members of Congress, administration officials, representatives of international organisations, diplomats). Iraq claimed that the organisations were recruited by Israel and were acting on its behalf.

The Committee of Concern for Jews in the Arab Lands was established in New York City shortly after the Iraqi executions of Jews in 1969. It was headed by a Lucius D. Clay Jr., a non-Jewish decorated four star Air Force General. The organisation had active branches in Paris and London, supported by Jews and non-Jews alike.[203] The American Jewish Committee (AJC) was at the forefront of political action, led by George E. Gruen, head of its Middle East Department, who coordinated efforts with other Jewish organisations in the US and abroad.[204] Meetings were held with such figures as UN Secretary General Kurt Waldheim, US Assistant Secretary of State Joseph Sisco and World Bank President Robert S. McNamara (since the bank was active in both Syria and Iraq).[205] Most political activity took place on Capitol Hill, where bipartisan support in both houses produced resolutions denouncing Iraq. On 30 January 1969, Rep. Leo J. Ryan Jr. (D-Calif.) proposed legislation to provide asylum to Iraqi Jews who wished to immigrate to the US.[206] On 6 February, the House of Representatives passed a resolution denouncing the executions and calling for a special session in the UN Security Council to deal with Iraq's violation of the UN charter.[207] Some legislators who approved the resolution thought beyond limiting the resolutions' implications to Iraq. Rep. Lee H. Hamilton (D-Ind.) proposed urging France to advocate on the matter with the Iraqi leadership, with which it was close.[208] This proposal was based on the perception that diplomatic approaches could change even radical states to moderate their policy. Following the Yom Kippur War, similar follow-up work extended to Jewish communities in Syria, Egypt and Yemen.[209]

Interest deepened in the conditions under which Iraqi Jews lived. Human rights organisations abroad compiled information on Jews who were arrested or even disappeared, and on Iraqi Jews' requests for exit visas that were rejected. Coordinated by the AJC, those organisations were involved in political action in Congress and the White House, at the UN offices in New York and Geneva.[210] Amnesty International sent a prominent figure, Sir [Michael] Osmond Williams to Baghdad; UN Secretary General Kurt Waldheim dispatched, in January 1970, Ismet Kittani, an Iraqi Kurdish UN official who worked for the Secretary General of the UN in New York; the United Nations High Commissioner for Refugees UNHCR Aga Khan visited Iraq in April 1973; a diplomat in the Iraqi Interest Section, Khalid al-Hashimi, was approached informally by an Indian mediator, who presented a proposal to redeem each Iraqi Jew allowed to leave at $10,000 per person (this single discreet proposal, reported to Israeli authorities, most likely did not materialise but indicated the determination and the efforts made by the American Jewish community to save Iraqi Jews.)[211] Discretion was essential to avoid Iraqi harassment of the remaining Jews. A widow and her young children waited desperately for permission to leave, but a letter to the editor published in the *New York Times*, written by her relative, resulted in further delay in the issuing of her exit visa.[212]

The matter of Iraqi Jews wishing to depart was sensitive for the regime in another way, too. Many of those leaving intended to come to Israel, and publicity could have harmed the whole operation. The Ba'th apparently turned a blind eye to many Jews escaping via Iran.[213] In March 1973, Khan returned to Baghdad to inquire about the fate of ten Jews who had been arrested and disappeared; these ten unaccounted for Jews are presumed dead, though others who had been executed had their bodies returned to their families (1970–4). Al-Bakr was surprised at Khan's mission and promised to find out as he was concerned that the image of Iraq would take a hit.

It seems that arrests and interrogations were a common routine of the internal security services, although it is likely that neither Al-Bakr, nor his deputy Saddam Hussein were updated with the actual details.[214] The International Committee of the Red Cross, though, refused to act.[215]

In the summer of 1973, the widows of two Jews who had been hanged in Baghdad in 1969, Simha Horesh and Odile Dallal, who managed to leave Iraq, spoke at the UN's New York headquarters. They also spoke at demonstrations in the city and were interviewed by the American media – all while hiding the fact that they had settled in Israel, thereby sparing Jews in Iraq further harassment. Linda Menuhin, daughter of the lawyer Yakov Abd-al-Aziz, who was kidnapped in Iraq in 1972 and presumably murdered, also came to New York to demonstrate and protest the fate of her father.[216]

Following the Yom Kippur War, organisations rallied to assist Jewish communities in Syria, Egypt and Yemen.[217] The campaign reflected a real concern for the remaining Jews in Arab countries as a result of the war, as it had happened in 1948 and 1967.

The State Department's Initial Reluctance to Act on Behalf of Iraqi Jews

There was no American diplomatic presence in Baghdad when the show trials and executions were conducted. The State Department, which had no diplomatic presence until November 1972 had to convey the message of denunciation through the Belgian embassy, was anxious that Israel would retaliate militarily against Iraq.[218] The US was already working with Jordan's King Hussein to bring about the release of an American engineer arrested in Iraq for espionage, and the goodwill of the Iraqi authorities was needed.[219] The White House and Congress demanded diplomatic action. Under congressional pressure, the State Department was urged to ask Canada, Italy and France – all with embassies in Baghdad – to act on behalf of Iraqi Jews. The State Department was reluctant to act, sceptical about the effects of such a move, since the Ba'th denied that any discrimination existed against the Jews. The Ba'th trotted out the chief rabbi of Iraq, who repeated the Ba'th statement about non-discrimination. A State Department INR report stated that the trial indicated the weakness of the Ba'th, which, it claimed, acted against the eight Jews in retaliation for Israeli air raids on the Iraqi expedition force in Jordan.[220] The governments of Canada and the Netherlands had been more forthcoming than the US in granting refugee visas immediately to Iraqi Jews. The State Department's first laconic response was that the immigration quota had been filled, though, later on, this policy changed.[221]

In 1973, the number of Jews who were unaccounted for reached twenty-five. The State Department instructed US embassies in friendly nations to stop follow-up on Iraqi Jews. It pursued the case on humanitarian grounds at the UN and UNHCR.[222] State Department officials cabled John A. Scali, the US ambassador to the UN, saying that, due to instability in Iraq, US interference might be counterproductive. Consequently, America's European allies were reluctant to interfere in an Iraqi domestic issue and anger the Iraqis – especially since most of that country's Jewish community had already been allowed to emigrate. The cable concluded that 'Only moral pressures, as those coming from neutral international figures like the Secretary General, may have some alleviating effect.'[223]

The Growing Influence of American Jews

In the 1970s, the American Jewish community was much stronger than in 1948, when Jews in Arab lands were persecuted upon the establishment of Israel and became refugees. Most American Jewish organisations had begun as philanthropic organisations in the early 20th century and had established a tradition of a moral obligation to assist and rescue Jews in danger, wherever they were. The Six-Day War of 1967 contributed to Jewish confidence, pride, and solidarity – and possibly to inter-organisational cooperation, too.[224] Thus, various groups joined in protests over the execution of Iraqi Jews.

That experience would be a building block for the effort, begun a few years later, to advocate on behalf of Jews persecuted in the Soviet Union. Cooperating discreetly with Israel and wielding its political power in Congress, American Jews worked to help Soviet Jews. They lobbied for legislation that pressured the Soviet Union and spoke out publicly to demand that Soviet Jews be allowed to emigrate. Such political action towards the Soviet superpower presumably impressed Al-Bakr and Saddam, both of whom closely followed American politics, and amplified their image of Jews as having demonic, mythical powers. No doubt, they, like other Arab leaders and citizens, were concerned that an influx of Jews would further tilt the demographic balance in Israel. Khan reported to the Jewish representatives of the AJC, American Jewish Joint Distribution Committee (JDC) and the Hebrew Immigrant Aid Society (HIAS) that, on 29 January 1969, he had approached the Iraqi ambassador in Geneva immediately after the executions, asking for explanation of the public hanging and the abuse of Iraqi Jews. The embarrassed ambassador urged Khan to wait before taking action against Iraq, since the situation in Baghdad was chaotic, and promised that such trials and executions would not happen again.[225]

(Indeed, all public executions were not repeated and the next executions were held in prison.)

The promise went unfulfilled, as Iraq's arrests of its citizens on espionage charges continued. In the summer of 1969, most such defendants were Muslims and Christians, along with two wealthy Jews whose entire property was confiscated by the regime.[226] The condemnation and mass demonstrations, initiated by Jews abroad, demonstrated to the Ba'th the solidarity, coordination and political influence of Jews around the world, in particular those in the US.

In response, Iraq sought to defend its international image, and it later allowed Iraqi Jews to leave. In March 1970, Interior Minister Salih Mahdi Ammash announced the cancellation of laws allowing for discrimination. Shortly after, the English language *Baghdad Observer* newspaper spoke of the good financial conditions of the Jewish minority. The British embassy in Baghdad reported back home about the Ammash statement, which appeared immediately after the visit to Baghdad in January of Lord George Brown, the former Foreign Secretary, and the visit of Canada's Teheran-based ambassador to monitor the situation of the Iraqi Jews.[227]

In April 1971, the Iraqi weekly magazine *Alif Baa'* ran a story about the release from detention of seven Jews – publishing their names and photos – who had been caught in the Kurdish area while allegedly trying to leave Iraq illegally and smuggle money out. The magazine blamed 'the Zionist and American media, for spreading lies on the conditions under which Iraqi Jews lived'.[228] Iraqi Jewish dignitaries had been asked to publish statements praising the regime's attitude to Jews. When the elderly chief rabbi, Sasson Khadduri, spoke on Iraqi TV, Iraq's ambassador to the UN requested that the transcript be included in the UN archives. Foreign correspondents were invited to tour the Jewish school and interview local Jews, and a propaganda booklet on Iraqi Jews was published in English.[229] When Khadduri died in May 1971, senior Ba'thi officials, including the Minister of Justice, attended his funeral.[230]

The regime allowed and assisted in the transfer of old religious books from Baghdad to Jewish communities in the West. The transfer often occurred via diplomatic mail, and it happened after the New York-based American Sephardi Federation in New York, and similar organisations in Jewish communities in Europe, appealed for these books.[231] The regime considered its assistance to be a gesture to the Jews and evidence of the generosity of the Ba'th. In December 1975, the president of the Jewish community in Baghdad, Naji Alias, sent a letter to the Minister of Information, expressing gratitude for the government's assistance in shipping an 1891 Torah scroll to the Jewish community in Stockholm. The scroll was to be handed over in an official ceremony by an Iraqi embassy official in the Swedish capital.[232] However, the Torah Scroll apparently was never sent or never reached the Jewish community of Stockholm.[233] The whole episode, including the letter, seems to have been a hoax the Ba'th cooked up for public relations purposes.

The Ba'th continued to stress that the government applied no discrimination against those it called 'law-abiding' Jews. In European capitals, Iraqi embassy officials published statements in full-page advertisements in the leading newspapers, denying any persecution or harassment of Jews. The advertisements stated that claims to the contrary were merely Zionist propaganda, intended to divert the world's attention from the crimes committed by Israel.[234] Saddam, in an interview with Paris's newspaper *l'Express*, firmly denied that any persecution of Jews on religious or political grounds was taking place in Iraq. He also stated that no Jews were under arrest.[235]

Diplomatic pressure on Iraq resumed, though, following the murder of the Jewish *Qashqush* family on 12 April 1973. The common assessment is that the Jewish family was murdered as revenge by security forces for an Israeli raid on Iraqi forces in Jordan that killed Iraqi soldiers.[236]

According to a Belgian embassy report, the Iraqi regime increased the number of exit visas it issued to Jews, and also turned a blind eye to Jews' illegal escape to Iran, with the assistance of Kurdish smugglers.[237] The Ba'th apparently had decided to let Jews leave the country, since they had become a burden and were harming Iraq's image. It is clear that the international protest and the diplomatic pressure, driven by American Jews, facilitated this decision. Salih Citiat, who had left Iraq by then, told an American official that the regime was expressing more goodwill toward minorities since the attempt to overthrow the Ba'th by Nazem Kezar.[238] It seems that the regime was so shocked by the coup attempt by the head of security, that they decided to focus on real internal security threats, and dealing with Iraqi Jews was a burden.

Except for a brief halt during the Yom Kippur War, Iraq's lenient emigration policy continued through 1974.[239] Iraq seemed to have been impressed by the actions taken by Jewish organisations abroad – enough so to seek to understand how they operated. The economic attaché at Iraq's embassy in Vienna, Hussein A-Saffar, sent a letter to an official of the city's JDC office there, requesting information about the New York-based global organisation.[240] At the time, Austria was a key transit station for Soviet Jews emigrating to Israel and the United States, and numerous Jewish groups had been involved in the effort.

Zionism is Racism: UN Resolution 3379

In November 1975, the UN General Assembly adopted Resolution 3379, defining Zionism as a form of racism. It was a significant diplomatic victory for the Arab bloc. *Al-Jumhuriyya* wrote that the resolution had defeated 'the American influence', while 'isolating the Zionist entity'.[241] Simultaneously, the RCC announced in the Western media that it was inviting all Jews who had left Iraq after 1948 to return to their homeland and regain the full rights of any citizen, based on the Iraqi constitution, the UN Charter, and the Universal Declaration of Human Rights.[242]

The statement clearly was a public relations effort to demonstrate that Iraq was not hostile to Jews. It painted an idyllic picture of Jewish-Arab relations before Israel came into being.[243] Saddam later admitted, in an interview with Egyptian journalist Sakina Sadat, that the purpose of inviting Iraqi Jews was to improve Iraq's international image. He added that the idea was linked in principle to his notion that all Jews who settled in Israel after the country's founding in 1948 should return to their countries of origin.[244] Indeed, in May 1976, Iraq introduced to the media an Iraqi-born Jew, Yusuf Salih Nawi, and his family, who had arrived from Israel, complaining that Israel discriminated against Jews from Arab lands. He announced that he considered himself a Jewish Arab opposed to Zionism. Nawi reportedly returned to Israel after a year.[245]

In allowing Jews to leave, Iraq got rid of one problem, while also benefiting from taking over the properties of those who departed. Even after being granted exit visas, Jews often faced harassment. From Saddam's perspective, that was fine. The Jews who were leaving represented 'Jewish power' from abroad that made him anxious.[246]

US-Israel Special Relations

Iraq's leadership held the US responsible for Israeli military supremacy, but it is also an interesting prism through which to examine the impact of Israel and the conflict on US-Iraqi relations and mutual perceptions. The first direct confrontation between the IDF and Iraqi forces under the Ba'th occurred on the Golan Heights in October 1973. An Iraqi armoured brigade managed to delay an IDF counter-offensive towards Damascus. Iraqi propaganda described the battle as a heroic victory that saved Damascus. However, after the war, the Ba'th initiated a thorough investigation of the performance of the Iraqi force which produced practical lessons that were applied in the buildup and modernisation plan of the Iraqi army in the following years.[247] The Ba'th recognised the IDF's military superiority and was reluctant to fight Israel, as long as the strategic balance favoured the enemy. Moreover, the Israeli military conducted successful operations against terrorists outside Israel, including the 'Aviv Ne'urim' (Spring of Youth) operation in 1973 in Lebanon, in which the IDF annihilated the perpetrators of the terrorist attack on the Israeli Olympic mission in Munich in 1972 and the rescue of aeroplane hostages held in Entebbe, Uganda (1976).[248]

The Ba'th also recognised the superiority of Israel's military intelligence and undercover capabilities. It knew, for instance, that Israel built alliances in Lebanon with ethnic groups, mostly Christians, and that Israel had maintained a presence in the Kurdish area, where it assisted Barzani – something so embarrassing to the regime that the Ba'th refrained from admitting it publicly.[249]

Iraq was also insecure about Israel's supposed possession of nuclear weapons, augmented by the Israeli policy of ambiguity on the matter. The common assumption worldwide was that Israel had the capability of producing fissile material, possessed nuclear weapons and was the driving force for building its own nuclear facilities. Following the Israeli air raid on the Iraqi reactor in 1981, Saddam Hussein considered Israel a 'nuclear Zionist threat' to Iraq.[250]

Mutual Misperception of the Arab-Israeli Conflict

The Arab-Israeli conflict was a fundamental strategic issue facing the US and Iraq, yet their perceptions were asymmetrical. They stemmed from different interpretation of facts and events, due to their different cultures, ideologies and images. The US and Iraq had different motives for considering the Middle East conflict a major policy issue, and they had different goals regarding the conflict. The US, in particular during the Carter administration, believed that the economic and territorial benefits of a bilateral peace treaty – as was signed by Egypt with Israel – would stimulate other Arab states to follow. The US did not understand the intensity and the hostility of the Ba'th towards Israel. Nor did it grasp Iraq's power over other Arab states as being unpopular and subversive. The self-image of Iraq as the vanguard of Arab nationalism started as early as the 1930s, when the state was established. Iraqi officers adopted Arab nationalism and supported the Palestinians. This national concept had been developed further by well-known Iraqi nationalist intellectual Sati' Al-Husri and the national discourse in the *Al-Muthana Club* that inspired young nationalists in the spirit of fascism since the 1930s. The Iraqi Ba'th party integrated the principles of the Ba'th and Pan Arabism with Iraqi patriotism.[251]

An ideological and emotional commitment to Arab nationalism had been the raison d'être of the Iraqi Ba'th, the core of its legitimacy, in particular vis-à-vis Syria. The party, therefore, could not have compromised or shown flexibility towards Israel. A survey of Ba'th statements since 1968 indicates that any Iraqi involvement with rival Syria, Iran or the Kurdish revolt was defined as a distraction from the country's main nationalist goal of the Palestinian issue. US analysts, meanwhile, were aware of the Ba'th rejectionist statements, but were misled by the party's tactic of expressing interest in purchasing American goods, sending ambiguous signals of being willing to moderate their rejectionist position and dangling the bait for the US that resuming relations with Iraq was close. Iraq's policy of ambiguous flexibility was successful: it held out the false hope that Iraq would not stand in the way of a negotiating process, even one that would result in an Israeli territorial withdrawal. The US failed to understand that rejecting the Israel-Egypt peace treaty was an asset to the Ba'th. With the Arab world in shock over Egypt's signing a separate peace, Iraq's Ba'th rushed in to fill the vacuum and took the lead in blocking any other Arab country from recognising Israel.

The Americans viewed a peaceful solution of the Arab Israeli conflict as an essential American national security interest. Sadat promised that other Arab states would follow his lead, and that peace would bring prosperity and stability to the Middle East. The Iraqi Ba'th misperceived American policy, which, since June 1967, had been deeply committed to a Middle East peace process. To the Iraqi way of thinking, US policy was motivated by economic considerations, mostly oil, and by deterring the Soviet Union. The US underestimated Saddam's determination not to allow any solution in the Middle East without Iraq, and his ability to appeal to the Arab emotional national psychic.

In the absence of a meeting point or a tangential line between the US and Iraq, in particular regarding the conflict, their relations remained stagnant. Iraq continued to attack US policy in the region as being one of an imperialist aggressor and supporter of Israel. At the same time, it repeatedly courted the US by increasing its purchase of US-made technology (see details in Appendix I). After the 1973 war and the 1979 signing of the Israeli-Egyptian treaty, the Iraqi regime returned to maintaining routine relations with the US through the Baghdad Interest Section. It was a sophisticated, pragmatic approach. The US failed to understand that Iraq had no intention of upgrading relations as long as Iraq remained strong and unthreatened. Indeed, full diplomatic relations and exchange of Ambassadors resumed only in 1984, when Iraq was on the verge of collapse and Iranian forces invaded the strategic area of Fao.

The peace process was pushed to the back burner in 1978, when the Shah, the US's ultimate ally, was forced to leave Iran. That reoriented Washington's focus on Iran and the Persian Gulf. Iraq emerged as a significant factor in the Gulf, yet the administration did not inquire more deeply into the essence of the Ba'th and Saddam – and his perceptions and intentions.

Notes

1. For example: Saddam Hussein told his biographer Amir Iskandar, that just before the Ba'th coup in July 1968, he had to recruit Hamad Shihab, Commander of the Baghdad Armoured Brigade to join the coup against Aref. The only argument that finally convinced Shihab to cooperate was that his oath of allegiance (Bay'ah) to Aref was inferior to his allegiance to the Arab honour and Iraq, since the treason of Aref led to the disastrous defeat in June 1967. Amir Iskandar, *Saddam Hussein the Fighter, the Thinker and the Man* (Paris: Hachette Book Group, 1980), p. 108.
2. On the interaction of the Iraqi Ba'th and Saddam Hussein with Egyptian president Gamal Abd-al-Nasir and Nasserism: A. Baram, 'Saddam Husayn and Nasirism, 1968–2000', *Orient*, 41(3) (2000), pp. 461–71.
3. Ofra Bengio, 'Crossing the Rubicon: Iraq and the Arab Israeli Peace Process', *Midde East Review of International Affairs*, 2(1) (March 1998), pp. 32–41.
4. A. Ben Zvi, *From Truman to Obama, The Rise and the Early Decline of American-Israeli Relations* (Tel Aviv: Yedi'ot Ahronoth, 2011), pp. 106–41.
5. In February 1928, a violent demonstration had been held in Baghdad protesting the visit of Sir Alfred Mond (later known as Lord Melchett) and the pro-Jewish policy of the British Government . S. Longrigg, *Iraq, 1900–1950 – A political, social and economic history* (London: Oxford University Press, 1953), pp. 192–3.
6. M. Khadduri, *Socialist Iraq – A Study in Iraqi Politics since 1969* (Washington: Middle East Institute, 1978), p.168.
7. ABSP, Michel Aflak, *Choices of texts from the Ba'ath Party founder's thoughts* (Firenze: Cooperativa lavoratori, 1977).
8. Al-Bakr, *Mithak al-'Amal al-Watani (The National Charter)*, 15 November 1971, pp. 3–6. The historical concept that Israel was created by the colonial powers, and therefore could not survive without their support became an integral part of the Ba'thi doctrine as reflected in almost every Iraqi reference to Israel and the Palestinian issue. For example: 'Qadiyyat Filastin fi Turath Al-Ba'th', *Al-Thawra Al-Arabiyya*, 4:6–7, 1973, pp. 65–71; Hassan Tawelba, *The Ba'th and Palestine* (Baghdad, 1982), p. 23.
9. Fuad Matar, *Saddam Hussein – The Man, the Cause and the Future* (London: Third World Center, 1981), pp. 234–5. Interiew with the author, 17 July 1979.
10. *Qadiyya Filstin in al-Thawra al-Arabiyya*, 4:6–7, p. , 67 quoting *Nidal al-Ba'th*, 1: 21 (December 1973).
11. A. Baram, 'Qawmiyya and Wataniyya in Ba'thi Iraq: The Search for a New Balance', *Middle Eastern Studies*, 19:2 (April 1983), p. 194.
12. ABSP, *Revolutionary Iraq 1968–1973 – The political report adopted by the Eighth Regional Congress of the Ba'ath Socialist Party-Iraq* (Baghdad,1974), pp.198–204; Saddam repeated the need to postpone the next war with Israel, before Iraq gained capabilities for coping with Israel, to the Egyptian correspondent Sakina Sadat, 19

January 1977. Saddam Hussein, *Social and Foreign Affairs in Iraq* (London: Croom Helm, 1979), pp. 87–110.

13. *Al-Jumhuriyya*, editorial, 2 September 1970. Quoting a statement of Shibli al-'Aysami, Deputy of Michel 'Aflaq, Secretary General of the Pan-Arab Command of the Ba'th Party; *Al-Jumhuriyya*, 28 July 1970.

14. 'Viewing the secret obligations attached to the Sinai Agreement' (*Adwa' 'ala al-ta'ahudat al-sirriyya al-mulhaqa bi Ittifaq Sina'*), *Al-Thawra Al-Arabiyya*, 1:8, 1976, pp.101–20; Kissinger testified before the Senate Foreign Relations Committee, 7 October 1975, admitting that some arrangements agreed by both Egypt and Israel (MOUs) had not been published. Israel *MFA Foreign Relations III* (1974–7).

15. Barry Cherniavsky, *Early Warning Systems and the American Peacekeeping Mission: The Case of the Sinai II Agreement between Egypt and Israel*, Incidental Paper I-81-6 July 1981 (Cambridge Massachusetts: Center for Information Policy Research, Harvard University).

16. Fuad Jaber, 'The Arab Regimes and the Palestinian Revolution 1967–1971', *Journal of Palestine Studies*, 2:2 (Winter 1973), p. 80; *Al-Jumhuriyya*, 3 April 1975.

17. *Al-Jumhuriyya*, 29, 30 October 1974.

18. A. Baram, *National Integration and Exclusiveness in Political Thought and Practice in Iraq under the Ba'th1968–1982* (Jerusalem: Hebrew University, 1986), p.139.

19. 'Al-nidal al-filastini, al-wad' al-rahin wa tariq al-khilas al-watani', in *Al-Thawara al-Arabiyya* (March 1975), pp. 22–32.

20. A. Baram 'Qawmiyya and Wataniyya in Ba'thi Iraq: The Search for a New Balance', p. 194.

21. Baghdad 759 (Lowrie), 4 November 1974.

22. *Al-Jumhuriyya*, 30 October 1974.

23. *Ibid.*

24. Sampling: *Al-Jumhuriyya*, 21January1974, Anti-American headlines: 'Kissinger's new conspiratorial mission for the Arab region', 19 February 1974: editorial portrays the disengagement agreement as an American imperialistic threat, 8, 10 May 1974: opinion articles contain personal attacks on Kissinger.

25. Saddam Hussein address, 12 June 1975. In Saddam Hussein, *Al-Mukhtarat*, vol. 5, Chapter 1.

26. Stockholm 2366 (Johnson), 29 April 1976.

27. Stockholm 2103 (Owens), 15 April 1976.

28. Madrid 9115 (Stabler), 12 December, 1976. Stabler commented that Iraq most likely supported that conference financially.

29. On the enormous power of American Jews: M.S.Al-Samraa'i, *Istiqlaliyyat al-Siyyasa al-Kharijiyya al-Iraqiyya* (Iraqi Independent Foreign Policy), Baghdad 1985, pp. 170–1; *Al-Junhuriyya*, 27 October 1975.

30. Saddam Hussein in Press Conference, 18 July 1976. S. Husssein, *Al-Iraq wa- al-Siyasa a-Dawliyya*, pp. 239–40.

31. Fuad Matar mentioned as an anecdote that the Iraqi security, reluctantly allowed Arafat to carry his gun during his meeting with Saddam. *Al-Nahar*, 15 November 1973.

32. In June 1974, the PNC adopted, for the first time, the 'phase plan' (*Khutat al-Marahil*) that accepted phases for Israeli withdrawal, without recognition of Israel, or giving up on any Palestinian territories. 'Twelfth Palestinian National Council Political Program', Cairo, 9 June 1974, Israel *MFA Foreign Relations III* (1974–7).

33. Arafat's entourage to the UN General Assembly in New York was carrying diplomatic passports from Iraq and the Republic of Southern Yemen: Beirut 12802 (Godly), 24 October 1974.

34. Bengio, 'Iraq', *MECS* 1(1976–7), p. 415.
35. Arafat was using an executive jet, made available by Iraq, for his multiple trips to Arab capitals. Dani Rubinstein, *Arafat* (Tel Aviv: Zmora, 2001), pp. 48, 81–2.
36. Baghdad 620 (Lowrie), 24 September 1974.
37. Abu Iyyad told Patrick Seale that Saddam Hussein promised him that he intended to stop Abu-Nidal's activities against the PLO to atone/compensate for Iraqi non-intervention at the Black September crisis in Jordan 1970. P. Seale, *Abu Nidal – A Gun for Hire* (New York: Random House, 1992), p. 112; on Abu Nidal operations from Baghdad see: Y. Melman, *The Master Terrorist* (New York: Adama Books, 1986), pp.125.
38. H. Cobban, *The Palestinian Liberation Organization – People, Power and Politics* (New York: Cambridge University Press, 1984), pp.163–4.
39. 'al-barnamaj al-siyyassi lil jabha al-arabiyya al-musharika li-thawra al-filastiniyya', *Al-Thwra al-Arabiyya*, (4: 6–7, 1973), pp. 164–70.
40. 'Jabhat al-Tahrir al-Arabiyyatastaqbil 'ammha al-sabi'', *Al-Thawra al-Arabiyya* (2:7, 1975), pp. 35–9.
41. 'fi dhikra al-rabi'a li-ta'sis Jabhat al-Tahrir al-Arabiyya', *Al-Thawra al-Arabiyya* (4:6–7, 1973), pp. 75–81.
42. During the Iran Iraq war, Baghdad instructed ALF to set aside targeting Israel and attack Syrian forces in Lebanon. The source an Iraqi officer who was in command of ALF operations in Lebanon. Debriefed by A. Baram, 1986.
43. *WP*, 22 February 1970.
44. The northern Israeli village Kfar Yovel was attacked in June 1975; two of the hostages and one IDF soldier were killed. The Kibbutz Misgav 'Am was attacked in April 1980; children were kept hostage. Three Israelis were killed.
45. J.W. Amos, *Palestinian Resistance: Organization of a Nationalist Movement* (New York: Pergamon Policy Studies, 1980), pp.107–10.
46. A. Baram, *National Integration and Exclusiveness*, pp.116–17.
47. *Ibid.*, pp. 125–46.
48. Baghdad 620, 691 (Lowrie), 18 September, 12 October 1974.
49. Baghdad 701 (Lowrie), 16 October 1974; *Al-Jumhuriyya*, 12–14 October 1974.
50. Wadi' Haddad was initially commander of operation for the PFLP, arriving in Iraq in 1972, and was coordinating activity with International terrorists groups such as Bader Meinhoff and Carlos. He was buried in Baghdad in 1978 with full military honour. P. Seale, *Abu-Nidal*, pp. 95,105,111; C. Coughlin *Saddam: King of Terror* (New York: Harper Collins, 2002), pp. 142–3.
51. The purpose of the Baghdad visit of rejectionist leaders on 30 December 1975 was to discuss coordination for engagement within the rejectionist front, and guarantee the continuation of Iraqi support of the radical front. Baghdad 003 (Wiley), 6 January 1976.
52. Seale, *Abu Nidal*, p. 105; Y. Melman, *The Master Terrorist*, p. 71.
53. Kameel B. Nasr, *Arab and Israeli Terrorism: The causes and effects of political violence 1936–1993* (Jefferson NC: McFarland, 2007), p. 93.
54. According to Seale, some of the deadly attacks by Abu Nidal on individuals that expressed moderation had been coordinated with Baghdad. Seale *Abu Nidal*, pp. 164, 166. To name a few moderate targets: PLO Sa'id Khamami in London, Azz al-din Qalaq and Adnan Hammad in Paris.
55. Following the Iraqi reconciliation with Arafat in 1978, Abu Nidal shuttled between Damascus and Baghdad. In 1984, when Iraq resumed relations with the US, he moved to Damascus, and then in 1987 to Libya. He returned to Iraq in the late 1990s, and died

in 2002. Ariel Merari and Shlomi Elad, *The International Dimension of Palestinian Terrorism* (Tel Aviv: Hakibbutz Hameuchad, 1996), pp. 45–6.

56. Ambassador Richard Murphy reported that the attack on the Semiramis Hotel in Damascus had been planned in Baghdad, while two of the perpetrators were Palestinians who lived in Baghdad. Damascus 6492 (Murphy), 27 September 1976.

57. Israeli Intelligence immediately identified the weapon, micro submachine gun, as used by Abu Nidal, dispatched from Baghdad. This was confirmed later by Scotland Yard. Z. Schiff & E. Yaari, *War of Deception* (Tel Aviv: Shocken, 1984), pp. 12–13.

58. Beirut 14376 (Houghton), 3 December 1974; DIA, *International Terrorism, A Compendium (Secret)* Vol. II, July 1979, pp. 15–17, *DNSA*.

59. Baghdad 656 (Lowrie), 21 June 1975.

60. Baghdad 718 (Lowrie), 5 July 1975.

61. Amman, 6689, 6691, 7128 (Pickering), 4, 4, 29 November 1976; State 283127, 18 November 1976; Baghdad 1919 (Wiley), 28 December 1975. Zaid al-Rifa'I was close to the King and his contact with the US.

62. This information is indicated by a collection of cables not yet declassified except for the subject heading. For example Amman 12 October, 24 November, 5 December, 1976, all relating to secret Syrian-Iraqi dialogue, encouraged by the US. Electronic Telegrams Withdrawal Cards, 1976, *NARA AAD*.

63. Amman 07051 (Pickering), 24 November 1976.

64. The source: an Israeli senior intelligence officer, as told to A. Baram in 1986; Thomas Pickering confirmed that the US was aware that the terrorist attack was an Iraqi warning to the King, yet he did not know about the cash suitcase delivered to the King, but this tactic of Saddam was not surprising. Pickering to Barukh Binah 13 June 2013, Washington DC.

65. Amman 6992 (Pickering), 22November 1976; Damascus 8357 (Murphy), 22 December 1976; Rifa'I to Pickering, Amman 7536 (Pickering), 22 December 1976.

66. A. Baram, 'Ba'athi Iraq and Hashemite Jordan: From hostility to alignment', *Middle East Journal*, 45(1) (Winter 1991), pp. 51–70, Note 17 (an interview with Western diplomat, 1981); Iraqi Aqaba loan, *FRUS XXVII*, p. 895.

67. J.P. Smith, 'Evidence Indicates Iraq Encourages Terrorism', *WP*, 6 August 1978.

68. For example, Iraqi denunciation of the hijacking of a British aircraft to Dubai, 22 November 1974. *Al-Thawra* editorial, 24 November 1974; Cairo 9549 (Eilts), 25 November 1974.

69. USUN 078364 (Scali), 14 August 1973. The Lebanese aircraft was chartered by Iraq, on the way to Baghdad.

70. USUN New York, 1178, 1206, 15 April 1975.

71. *Al-Jumhuriyya*, 13 November 1975.

72. Jidda 3987 (Thacher), 16 September 1973; Kuwait 3381 (Stoltzfus), 17 September 1973.

73. Baghdad 674 (Lowrie), 8 December 1973.

74. Arab press in Lebanon, Egypt, and Syria, as well as Western press carried reports on Iraqi involvement supporting the hijackers. *Al-Thawra* (Syria), 24 November 1974; Cairo 9491(Eilts), 23 November 1974; Beirut (Houghton), 24 November 1974.

75. The message was delivered by PLO delegation headed by 'Issam Sirtawi, then was reported to Under Secretary Newsom and his deputy Davis. State 249029 (Rush), 22 December 1973.

76. Maggie Haberman, *New York Post*, 3 February2003; a secret message from Acting Director FBI to the White House Situation Room, 8 March 1973, *Nixon Presidential Library*.

77. MOC, Kissinger, Helms, Atherton, Eilts, Pickering, 7 August 1976, *DNSA*.

78. The study described the Palestinian activity as mostly defensive; during the period 1968–75 out of a total of 913 terrorist events, only 148 attacks were carried out by Middle Eastern terrorists, compared to 150 attacks by Latin American terrorists, David L. Milbank, 'International and Transnational Terrorism: Diagnosis and Prognosis', *Research Study prepared for the CIA*, PR 76 10030, April 1976, http://www.higginsctc.org/patternsofglobalterrorism/1976PoGT-Research-Study.pdf, last accessed 13 August 2017.

79. Public Law 92-539, 1972; 'No concessions policy' Memorandum from Secretary Rogers indicated that the attack had been handled by *Black September* HQ in Lebanon, but did not mention Arafat. Memorandum from Secretary Rogers to President Nixon, 11 April 1973, *FRUS XXV* #46; according to Jim Hoagland, the US alerted France on the arrival of Abu Da'ud of *Black September* to Paris carrying an Iraqi passport under a false name. He was arrested upon arrival but released later. *WP 14* January 1977.

80. Backchannel message from Egyptian Presidential Advisor (Ismail) to Kissinger, Cairo, 20 March 1973, *FRUS XXV* #41, notes 3, 4.

81. Welsh, NSA agent intercepted Arafat's conversations dealing with the planned attack on the Saudi Embassy in Khartum, as evidence for Arafat's active involvement in the 'Black September' attack that killed the diplomats. This information, according to Welsh, had not been disseminated and censored until declassified in July 2011. On Welsh and his campaign's investigation of the issue see Amir Oren, *Haaretz*, 26 August 2011; Joseph Farah, 'Is US hiding Arafat murders'? 17 January 2001; 'Ex-NSA op asks Congress to probe Arafat murders' 17 April 2001, *WND*, http://www.wnd.com/news/article.asp?ARTICLE_ID=21365, last accessed May 2014.

82. Backchannel message from DD/CIA (Walters) to Secretary Kissinger, 4 November 1973, *FRUS XXY* #318.

83. *NYT*, 26 September, 6 October 1974; *LAT*, 27 September 1974.

84. Anti-Hijacking Act of 1974 'Implementing the Convention for the Suppression of Unlawful Seizure of Aircraft', The Hague 1970.

85. US Export Administration Act of 1979 (P.L. 96–72; September 1979); Senator Heinz in US Senate Hearing before the Subcommittee on Foreign Assistance of the Committee on Foreign Relations on International Terrorism, 14 September 1977, *GPO* 1977 .

86. H.R.406 – Omnibus Antiterrorism Act of 1977; The Foreign Intelligence Surveillance Act of 1978 (Public Law 95–511, October 1978).

87. International Security Assistance and Arms Export Control Act of 1976 (PL 94–329; 90 Stat. 734); David Tucker, *Skirmishes at the Edge of Empire* (Westport CT: Praeger, 1977); Ribicoff's proposal to publish lists of states sponsoring terrorism: *Congressional Record*, Vol. 123 no. 172, 25 October 1977 (S 2236).

88. US Senate Hearing before the Subcommittee on Foreign Assistance of the Committee on Foreign Relations on International Terrorism, 14 September 1977, *GPO* 1977.

90. 'Soviet support for international terrorism and revolutionary violence', *CIA SNIE* 11/2-81, 15 May 1981.

91. United State Senate, Committee on Government Affairs, 95th Congress, second session, 23 January 1978, S. 2236, *DDRS*.

92. US Senate Hearing before the Subcommittee on Foreign Assistance, Committee on Foreign Relations on International Terrorism, 14 September 1977, *GPO* 1977.

93. Major General (Ret.) George J. Keegan, USAF, 'Middle East Strategic Problems', Hearing before the Subcommittee on Near Eastern and South Asian Affairs, Senate Committee on Foreign Relations, 3 October 1977, *GPO* 1997.

94. 'Terrorism Analysis in the CIA: The Gradual Awakening 1972–1980, n.d. (partially sanitised); Studies in Intelligence, *National Security Archive*, Electronic Briefing Book No. 431, posted 4 June 2013, www.gwu.edu/~nsarchiv/NSABB/NSAEBB431, last accessed April 2014.

95. Baghdad 898 (Killough), 30 August 1975.

96. These items had been rejected before antiterrorism legislation, based on previous legislation that committed the State Department to bar export of military related items to states that have no full diplomatic relations with the US; US Senate, Omnibus Antiterrorism Act of 1979, Hearing before the Committee on Government Affairs, 30 March, 7 May 1979, *GPO 1979*, pp. 63–5.

97. Senator Heinz to Secretary Vance, US Senate, Committee on Government Affairs, 95th Congress, 23 January 1978. Secretary Vance's argument was that the aircraft deal was signed legally in 1976–1967 prior to the Export Control Act (S. 2236).

98. D.Tucker, *Skirmishes at the Edge of Empire*, p. 88; Fenwick Amendment to Export Control Administration, December 1979; John F. Murphy and Arthur T. Downey, 'National Security, Foreign Policy and Individual Rights: The Quandary of US Export Controls', *The International and Comparative Law quarterly*, 30(4) (October 1981), pp. 779–834.

99. *WP*, 19 March 1982.

100. Y. Kipnis, *1973, The Way to War* (Tel Aviv: Kinneret Zmora Bitan Dvir, 2012), pp. 64–73.

101. *FRUS* XXX#38.

102. Actually the Egyptians did not offer normalisation with Israel in return for withdrawal, just their readiness to start negotiations with Israel towards recognition and a separate peace treaty at the end of the process.
    Memorandum from Kissinger to the President, 25–6 February 1973, *FRUS XXV* #28; K. Stein, *Heroic Diplomacy: Sadat, Kissinger, Carter, Begin and the quest for Arab-Israeli peace* (Hebrew edition, Tel Aviv: Maarachot, 2003), pp. 88–9; Kissinger, *Years of Renewal*, p. 221.

103. Kipnis criticises PM Meir's persistent objection to any retreat from the Suez Canal; she also ruled out Dayan's suggestion for partial withdrawal that would allow Egypt to reopen the Canal for navigation, as well as not sharing the dialogue with Egypt with MFA and most of the intelligence community. Y. Kipnis, *1973, The Way to War*, pp. 62–3, 73–9, 95–6.

104. Memorandum from Kissinger to the President: 'Meeting with Hafiz Ismail', 20 May 1973, *FRUS XXV* #63.

105. The Egyptians leaked the information to the Saudis, and then to all diplomatic community in Cairo. Kissinger, *Years of Renewal*, p. 224.

106. Kissinger conversation with Under Foreign Secretary Thomas Brimelow, 5 March 1973. Ibid., pp. 221–2.

107. U. Bar-Joseph, 'Last chance to avoid war: Sadat's peace initiative of February 1973 and its failure', *Journal of Contemporary History*, 41(2006), pp. 545–56.

108. W. Isaacson, *Kissinger – A Biography* (New York: Simon and Schuster, 2005), pp. 525–6; Ben Zvi, *From Truman to Obama*, pp. 27–128.

109. Kissinger, *Years of Renewal*, pp. 756–7; K. Stein *Interviews with Saunders and Sisco* (1992); Stein, *Heroic Diplomacy*, p.160.

110. Israel demanded an Egyptian declaration of an end to the belligerence situation, facilitation in Arab Boycott restrictions and right of passage through the Suez Canal. Stein, *Heroic Diplomacy*, pp. 214–15.

111. Goldstein & Zhukov, 'Tales of two fleets, A Russian perception on the US naval standoff in the Mediterranean', *US Naval War College Review*, 7(2) (Spring 2004), pp. 27–63; *Haaretz*, 22 April 2004.

112. President Interview with European Journalists, 23 May 1975; President's greeting remarks, Annual Boys Nation Convention, 23 July 1975; President interview to PBS, 7 August 1975, *APP*.

113. According to Isaacson, Kissinger was behind Nixon's letter and the 'reassessment', W. Isaacson (2005), pp. 631–2; Rabin himself considered the dramatic statement of the President as a pre-planned move, initiated by Kissinger; Rabin added that the reassessment message created such an objection that even cabinet members who were inclined to accept the Egyptian offer voted against it . I. Rabin, and D. Goldstein, *Pinkas Sherut* (Hebrew, Tel Aviv: Sifriyyat Maariv, 1997), vol. II, pp. 458–61.The President's letter was leaked to the press, and increased the discontent towards Israel in the White House. B. Reich, *Quest for Peace – United States-Israel Relations and the Arab-Israeli Conflict* (Piscataway NJ: Transaction Books, 1977), pp. 33–4; MOC Ford, Kissinger, Rabin, Washington, 11June 1975, *FRUS XXVI* #183.

114. Jerusalem 6658 (Kissinger), 22 March 1975; Baghdad 304 (Lowrie), 27 March 1975.

115. Stein *Heroic Diplomacy*, pp. 214–15.

116. MOC, Ford, Kissinger, Scowcroft, 24 March 1975, *Ford Presidential Library*.

117. MOC, Ford, Kissinger, Scowcroft, 25 April 1975, *Ford Presidential Library*.

118. MOC, Ford, Kissinger, Scowcroft, Keating, Murphy, Eilts, Atherton, 14 April1975. *Ford Presidential Library*.

119. MOC, VP Rockefeller, Egyptian Parliamentarians. 1 May 1975, *Ford Presidential Library*.

120. Kissinger Remarks to State Legislators, 25 April 1975, *Ford Presidential Library*.

121. Ben Zvi, *From Truman to Obama*, p. 135.

122. MOC, Ford, Kissinger, Scowcroft, 8 May 1975, *Ford Presidential Library*.

123. A. Ben-Zvi, *The United States and Israel* (New York: Columbia University Press, 1993), pp.100–1;E. Gilboa, *American public opinion toward Israel and the Arab-Israeli Conflict* (Tel Aviv: MOD Publishers, 1993), pp. 63–71. Nadav Safran, *Israel the Embattled Ally*, (Cambridge MA: Harvard University Press, 1981). pp. 548–9.

124. Ben Zvi, *From Truman to Obama*, pp. 135–8.

125. Max Fisher raised one third of the donation for Nixon's presidential campaign in 1968. He refused a White House position, but functioned as senior advisor to the President on Jewish affairs and Israel. Y. Melman & D. Raviv, *Shutafim Lidvar Ma'ase* (Tel Aviv: Sifriyyat Maariv, 1994), pp. 132,150.

126. Secretary Kissinger 'Furthering Peace in the Middle East', A toast given on 29 September 1975, by the US Mission to the UN in honour of the heads of delegations and Permanent Representatives to the UN of member nations of the Arab League, *Department of State Bulletin*, 73 (20 October 1975), pp. 581–4.

127. Harold H. Saunders, Statement before the House Foreign Affairs Subcommittee on the Middle East, 12 November 1975, http://www.mideastweb.org/saunders.htm Last accessed February 2013.

128. Quoted in Marwan Buheiry, 'The Saunders Document', *Journal of Palestine Studies*, 8:1 (Autumn 1978), pp. 37–8.

129. For example: 'al nizam al-siyyasi lil wilayat al-muttahida' (The political structure of the US) in '*Aafaq Arabiyya*, 5 October 1978, pp.53–46.

130. *Al-Jumhuriyya*, 25 March 1975.

131. *Al-Jumhuriyya*, 4 April 1975. The article responded to the Al-Nahar (Lebanon) report on Senator George McGovern's trip in the region. He was visiting the region as Chairman of the Senate Sub Committee for the Middle East, and followed Kissinger's request to increase pressure on Israel within the reassessment policy, in his meeting with Sadat and Arafat. See Kissinger cable to the Senator: Cairo 70773, 28 March 1975; Beirut 4136, 1 April 1975.

132. *Al-Jumuriyya*, 29 April, 20 May 1975; *The Daily Telegraph*, 20 May 1975, and *The Buisness Week* of January quotes are in 'The US and the Persian Gulf: The Logic of Intervention' in *The Harvard Crimson*, 12 February 1976, http://www.thecrimson.com/article/1976/2/12/the-us-and-the-persian-gulf/?page=1, last accessed June 2012.

133. Lowrie added that the Sinai II would contribute to the US peace initiative. Baghdad 501 (Lowrie), 9 May 1975.

134. MOC Sa'dun Hammadi, Salih Mahdi Ammash, Henry Kissinger, Isa Sabbagh, Peter W. Rodman, 17 December 1975, Iraqi Ambassador Residence, Paris, *DNSA*; K. Stein, 'Henry Kissinger to Iraq in 1975: "We can reduce Israel's size"', *Middle East Quarterly* (Fall 2006), pp. 71–8.

135. State 42906 (Ingersoll), 31 August 1975.

136. *Al-Jumhuriyya*, 4 September 1975; *Baghdad Observer*, 5–6 September 1975; Baghdad 934 (Killough), 8 September 1975.

137. Baghdad 920 (Killough), 5 September 1975; Badi'a Amin, 'Ihtimalat ma ba'd Tawqi' Ittifaqiyyat Sina"' (The Odds of the Sinai Agreements), *Aafaq Arabiyya*, 5 January 1976.

138. Baghdad 029 (Wiley), 13 January 1976.

139. Baghdad 454, 656 (Lowrie), 26 April, 21 June 1975.

140. The repeated idea to postpone the confrontation with Israel, until Iraq would be able to reach military balance with Israel, was not mentioned in the available US documents, perhaps not considered important.

141. MOC, Washington, Ford, Fulbright, Scowcroft, 2 July 1975, *Ford Presidential Library*.

142. MOC, Kissinger, Kennedy, Atherton, Hunter, 10 June 1975, *DNSA*.

143. British Embassy Baghdad (Graham), 29 May 1975, FCO 8/2544, *TNA*.

144. MOC, Ford, Fulbright, Scowcroft, 2 July 1975, *Ford Presidential Library*, l; Baghdad 630 (Killough), 11 June 1975; Baghdad 640 (Lowrie), 14 June 1975; Arthur Siddon, *Chicago Tribune*, 29 February 1976; 'Report by Senator Adlai E. Stevenson on his trip to ;the Middle East', 10–25 February 1976, submitted to the Senate Committee on Banking, Housing & Urban Affairs, *GPO*, April 1976.

145. *Al-Jumhuriyya*, 6 March 1975.

146. British report on Syrian attitude to the visit of Philip Habib in Baghdad. British Embassy Damascus (A.J. Colquhoun), 30 May 1977, FCO 8/3011, *TNA*.

147. *Al-Jumhuriyya*, 22 February 1977. Headline: 'Syrian close relations with the US towards appeasement with the enemy'. *Al-Jumhuriyya*, 27 April 1976, Palestinian Rejection Front warns Syrian preparation to end the conflict with the enemy, Syria assists American Imperialists to protect separatists' elements in Lebanon.

148. Baghdad Radio, 6 September 1977 in Kienle, Ba'ath v. Ba'ath, 120–12.

149. US-Syrian cooperation in Lebanon: *Al-Jumhuriyya*, 10 July, 15 August 1975, 21 April, 3 August 1976, 10 July 1977.

150. 'Falasifat al-Khiyana' (The philosophy of treason), *Al-Jumhuriyya*, 25 November 1977.

151. US Department of State, Office of the Historian, *A Guide to the United States' History of Recognition, Diplomatic, and Consular Relations, by Country, since 1776: Syria*, http://history.state.gov/countries/syria, last accessed 13 august 2017.

152. Khaddam interview with K, Stein, 18 July 1993; Stein, *Heroic Diplomacy*, p. 231; C. Vance, *Hard Choices: Four Critical Years in Managing America's Foreign Policy* (New York: Simon and Schuster, 1983), p. 170.

153. President Carter, Q&A with reporters, 6 January 1978, *PPP*; Carter Diary, 23 November 1977; Carter, *Keeping Faith*, p. 298.

154. Brzezinski, *Power and Principle, – Memoirs of the National Security Adviser 1977–1981* (New York: Farrar Straus & Giroux, 1983), p. 506; James G. Blight et al., *Becoming Enemies, U.S-Iran Relations and the Iran-Iraq War 1979–1988* (Plymouth UK: Rowman & Littlefield, 2014), pp. 260–1.

155. *Al-Jumhuriyya*, 24 September 1975, 22 January 1976.

156. MOC, The White House, President Ford, Ambassador D. Brown, Scowcroft, 27 April 1976; NSC Meeting, Ford, Kissinger, Rumsfeld, Bush (DCI), 7 April, 1976, *Ford Presidential Library*, digital; Briefing Memorandum from State (Saunders), 'Will the Syrian presence in Lebanon inevitably lead Lebanon to the left?' 14 April 1976, *Ford Presidential Library*, Country Files, the Middle East and South Asia, Box 24.

157. MOC, Ford, Scowcroft, Saliba – 'Standing Conference of American Middle Eastern Christian and Moslem Leaders', 15 April 1976; President Cabinet Meeting, 18 June 1976. *Ford Presidential Library*, digital.

158. MOC, Scowcroft, Sisco, Charles Helou, 4 May 1976, *Ford presidential Library*, digital.

159. MOC, Kissinger, Helms, Atherton, Eilts, Pickering, 7 August 1976, *DNSA*.

160. President Ford Remarks on the Assassination of US Officials in Lebanon, 16 June 1976, www.arlingtoncemetery.net/rowaring.htm, last accessed October 2014.

161. MOC, Ford, Kissinger, Scowcroft, 19 July 1976, *Ford Presidential Library*, digital.

162. P. Malovany, *The Wars of Modern Babylon* (Tel Aviv: Maarachot, 2009), p. 93; R. Avi-Ran, *Syrian involvement in Lebanon 1975–85* (Tel Aviv: MOD, 1986), pp. 74–5; Beirut 8438 (Lane), 13 November 1976.

163. Ambassador J.A.N. Graham, 'Iraq: Annual Review for 1976', 6 January1977, FCO 8/3008, and *TNA*.

164. Baram, 'Ba'thi Iraq and the Hashemite Jordan: From Hostility to Alignment', *Middle East Journal*, 45:1 (Winter 1991), p. 54, Footnote 17 (An interview with Western diplomat, London, September1981).

165. *Al-Jumhuriyya*, 7 November 1978.

166. Arab Ba'ath Socialist Party, *The Central Report of the Ninth Regional Congress, June 1982*, Baghdad, 1983; A. Baram, *National Integration and Exclusiveness*, p.146.

167. Jerrold M. Post, *Leaders and Their Followers in a Dangerous World* (Ithaca: Cornell University Press, 2004), p. 219.

168. *Al-Jumhuriyya*, 7 November 1978.

169. Rowland Evans & Robert Novak, 'Not-So-Neighborly Iraq', *WP*, 24 December 1979.

170. Stein, *Heroic Diplomacy*, pp. 297, 302, 304.

171. Joseph Kraft, 'Arab Double Talk', *WP*, 2 November 1978.

172. Martin A. Weiss, 'Arab League Boycott of Israel', *CRS Report to Congress*, Updated 27 August 2008.

173. Wiley describes the Iraqi director, Abd al-Karim al-Tai', a career diplomat, soft spoken, graduate of the University of Southern California. Baghdad 026 (Wiley), 13 January 1976.

174. Baghdad 889 (Killough), 25 August 1975.

175. Baghdad 1574 (Wiley), 22 October 1976.

176. Quotation from an Iraqi contract, rejected by the US: 'Tenderer should not import these goods from countries that the Republic of Iraq has already boycotted or whose manufacturing and trading firms it no longer deals with'. Baghdad 1252 (Killough), 31 August 1976; State 118174 (Robinson), 4 September 1976.
177. Baghdad 1288 (Killough), 7 September 1976.
178. *Ibid*. Quoting *Al-Thawra*, 5 September, and *Baghdad Observer*, 4 September 1976.
179. Baghdad 1745, 1753, 28 November 1976. The latter quoted the senior executive at the Iraqi National Oil Company to an American energy company executive during his visit in Iraq.
180. British Embassy Baghdad, P. Rogan: 'Iraq/USA Relations', 9 May 1977; 'Iraq Trade Promotion', A.J.D. Stiring, Department of Trade, London, 31 May 1977, FCO 8/3011, *TNA*; The British Embassy followed the subject, since US oil corporations had British partners that could be affected.
181. State 269213 (Kissinger), 2 November 1976; State 253344 (Kissinger), 13 October 1976.
182. Charlotte A. Phillips, 'The Arab Boycott of Israel – Possibilities for European Cooperation with US Anti-Boycott Legislation', *CRS* 215F, May 1979. West European states, though they opposed the Arab Boycott, did not follow the US legislation and possible risk to their trade relations with Arab oil producers.
183. Department of State, *United States Treaties and other International Agreements*, Vol. 27:1, January 1976.
184. State 288095, 24 November 1976.
185. For example: Casper Weinberger, Director of the Office of Management and Budget under the Nixon-Ford administration, was hired by *Bechtel Group Inc.*, http://projects.publicintegrity.org/wow/bio.aspx?act=pro&ddlC=6, last accessed April 2014.
186. American Jewish Committee, 'The Impact of Arab-Boycott Laws on US Mideast Trade', May 1979, http://www.ajcarchives.org/AJC_DATA/Files/778.PDF, last accessed April 2014.
187. In 1977, US export to Iraq declined from 381mn to 210 mn USD, but in 1980, US export reached 720mn. See Appendix I, *International Trade by Commodities Statistics* (ITCS), SITC/CTCI Rev. 22, 1961–1990, Historical. CDRom, University of Chicago; US Trade with the Middle East, *Middle East Economic Digest* (*MEED*), 20:37, 10 September 1976, p. 9.
188. Baghdad 2259 (Peck), 31 October 1978.
189. State 204113 (Kissinger), 17 August 1976.
190. Martin A. Weiss, 'Arab League Boycott of Israel', *CRS* Report to Congress, Updated 27 August 2008.
191. AP correspondent quoted in Haaretz, 29 April 2004.
192. Baghdad 070 (Wiley), 20 January 1976; Baghdad 214 (Wiley), 17 February 1976; Marshall W. Wiley Interview, 18 April 1989, *ADST*.
193. R. Kaplan, *The Arabists, – The Romance of an American Elite* (New York: Free Press, 1993), pp. 255–7.
194. Y. Harakabi, 'Revival of Arab antisemitism' in *Anti-Semitism Through the Ages*, S. Almog (ed.) (Jerusalem: The Shazzar Center, 1980), pp. 259–247.
195. For example: Hasan al-Bazzaz, 'nufuz al-aqaliyya al-Yahudiyya fil-ahzab wal-intikhabat al-amrikiyya' (The Impact of the Jewish minority on the political parties and the US elections), *Aafaq Arabiyya*, 1–6 September 1975, pp. 50–61.
196. Baghdad 003 (Lowrie), 6 January 1974.
197. Talfah words from 1981 were quoted in Congressional hearing in 1990: Jerrold M. Post, 'Explaining Saddam Hussein: A psychological Profile', Testimony presented to the

House Armed Services Committee, December 1990, http://www.au.af.mil/au/awc/ awcgate/iraq/saddam_post.htm, last accessed: December 2013.
An example for a book written by then Saddam confidant Fadil al-Barrak, on the history of the Iraqi Jews, blaming them for treason and ingratitude. Fadil Al-Barrak, al *madaris al-yahudiyya wal-iraniyya* (Baghdad, 1985).

198. The nationalist figures that lend this anti-Jewish trend in the 1930s were Sati' al-Husri, Muhammad Fadil al-Jammali and Sami Shawkat, R. Spector-Simon, *Iraq between the Two World Wars – The Militarist Origin of Tyranny* (New York: Columbia University Press, 2003), pp. 37–43; S. Binah, *The Anti-Jewish Farhud* (New York: CUNY, 1989), pp. 37–47.

199. Saddam Hussein interview to the Egyptian journalist Sakina al-Sadat, 19 January 1977, 'Détente and the Arab-Zionist conflict', in Saddam Hussein, *Social and Foreign Affairs in Iraq* (London, 1979).

200. J. Post & A. Baram, *Saddam is Iraq: Iraq is Saddam* (USAF Counter-proliferation Papers, Future Warfare Series, No. 17, January 2002. (Maxwell Air Force Base, Alabama, 2002 http://www.dtic.mil/cgi-bin/GetTRDoc?AD=ADA424787&Location=U2&doc= GetTRDoc.pdf) The details of Saddam's pre-natal and early childhood history are based on A. Baram interview with Nasimah, an elderly member of the Jewish family who saved Sabha's life and looked after her just before and after she gave birth to Saddam, conducted in Tel Aviv on 2 February 1991. These details were confirmed again by Nasimah's son, Yigal, in a telephone conversation on 1 July 2002. The story is not mentioned in Iraqi publications describing the childhood of Saddam Hussein, but confirmed in the biography by Amir Iskandar, *Saddam Hussein – Munadilan wa Mufakkiran wa Insanan* (Paris: Hachette, 1980), pp.15–19.

201. The Pentagon collection of Ba'athi documents, CRRC SH- SHTP-A-001-215 ~1990s, n. d.

202. Coordinate activity of Israel and AJC: in November 1972, Y. Ben Ahron, Political Councilor at the Embassy of Israel, and G. e Gruen of AJC approached State Department, asking to check reports on renewed harassment and arrests of Iraqi Jews. State 201125, 3 November 1972, FRUS E-4#327; Interview with Ben Ahron, Jerusalem, 24 August 2011.

203. The London branch of the 'Committee of Concern' was headed by Lord Wells-Pestell, who arranged a meeting with FM Sir Alec Douglas Hume, 8 December 1970.
J.P. Tripp, 'The British Committee of Concern for Jews in the Arab Lands', 20 July 1970, FCO 17/1327; J. Godber FCO to Lord Wells-Pestell, 10 February 1971, FCO 17/1263 *TNA*.

204. Dr George E. Gruen, Director for Middle East Affairs of the American Jewish Committee.

205. AJC Activities on Behalf of the Jews in Iraq and Syria, 6 February 1973, *AJC Archives*, FAD 1972–1973.

206. Congressional Record – House, 30 January 1969.

207. H. Res. 227, 91st Congress, 6 February 1969.

208. Lee H. Hamilton (D. Indiana), 'The plight of the Jewish communities in Syria and Iraq', 8 May 1973, *Congressional Record*, 93rd Congress, 119:69.

209. A. Karlikow, G. Gruen, 'Jews in Syria, Iraq and Egypt', 9 November 1973, *AJC Archives* FAD 1972–1973.

210. Melamet, WJC, 7, 12, 13, 14, 21, 22 April 1971; Kaplan (Paris), 6, 13, 15, 30 April 1971; 3 November 1972, CZA, C 10/3671.

211. MFA-Jerusalem, S Hillel, Deputy PM Yigal Alon, Director of Mossad Zvi Zamir, Director of Jewish Agency Yehuda Dominitz. 18 March 1969CZA S-1002.

212. Interview with the widow of one of the victims, April 2009. The letter was published in *NYT*, 15 October 1969, and added to the *Congressional Record*.

213. Melamet to Armand Kaplan, WJC, 26 April 1971, AJC Archive.

214. Interview with Maurice Shochet, Washington DC, 23 May 2013.

215. Roth (London) to Melamet, Kaplan, WJC, 29 October 1973, *Ibid*.

216. MFA (Israel) Circular 593 (Divon) to NY, Washington, 12 June 1973; Paris 593 (Amir), 8 July 1973; NY 414 (Abillea), 21 September 1973.

217. A. Karlikow, G. Gruen, 'Jews in Syria, Iraq and Egypt', 9 November 1973, *AJC Archives*, FAD 1972–1973.

218. Tel Aviv 321 (Barbour), 27 January1968, *NARA* RG 59, 1967–1969. See Chapter 1.

219. William Touhy 'Rooftop Arial Blamed for Arrest of US Oil Engineer in Baghdad', *LAT*, 5 February 1969; Memorandum from State (Richardson), 13 January1969, FRUS E-4 #247; State (Leddy), 7 February1969, FRUS E-4 #250.

220. INR/ Research Memorandum (Hughes) to Secretary Rogers, 14 February 1969, *FRUS* E-4 # 251; Israeli air raids on the Iraqi forces in Irbid, Jordan in December 1968,'*Operation Ninve*' and *Galit* intended to contain the Iraqi shelling towards the Jordan Valley. S. Shay, *The Iraqi-Israeli Conflict, 1948–2000* (Tel Aviv: Maarachot, 2002), pp. 66–8.

221. The Canadian Ambassador arranged, in early 1972, exit visas for Jews under sixty years old. B. Gold, G. Gruen, 'Syrian and Iraqi Jews', 6 January 1972 (Confidential), *AJC Archives*, FAD 1972–1973; USUN (Buffum), 14 July1970, *Nixon Presidential Library*, RG 59 POL 27 Iraq; Embassy of Israel Washington (Ben Ahron) to S. Hillel, 12 February 1969, *ISA* 6557/20.

222. State Circular 84779, 4 May 1973; Rome 3615 (Volpe), 8 May 1973; State Circular 20112, 5 November 1972, *FRUS* E- 4 #327.

223. State 103226 (Rush) to USUN (Scali), 30 May 1973.

224. Ralph Goldman interview, 28 August 2008, JDC-Jerusalem.

225. Leonard Seiderman (Geneva) to Gaynor Jacobson, HIAS New York, 6 February 1969; Theodore Feder, 'Meeting with the UNHCR on the Question of the Jews in Iraq', 29 January 1969, *JDC Archives*.

226. N. Qazzaz, *The End of A Diaspora* – Iraqi Jews 1951–2000 (Or Yehuda: Babylonian Jewish Heritage Center, 2011), pp. 156–7.

227. INA, 3 March 1970; *Baghdad Observer*, 4 March 1970; J.S. Symons, British Embassy Baghdad, 14 February–7 March 1970, *FCO* 17/1327; Ambassador H.G. Balfour Paul, 'Treatment of Jews in Iraq', Diplomatic Report 529/70, 24 November 1970, *FCO* 17/1263, *TNA*.

228. *Alif Ba'* (21 April 1971), pp. 4–5.

229. N. Qazzaz (2011), pp. 143–6.

230. Sassoun Khadduri, *ra'i wa ri'aya* – *sirat hayat al-hakham Sassoun Khadduri* (The Biography of the Rabbi Sassoun Khadduri – Arabic) (Jerusalem, 1999), pp. 187, 209.

231. Basri, Baghdad to Dr Gaon, London in Shemesh to Dominitz, 25 February, 20 May 1972; Revd Louis Gerstein, to the Administrative Committee for Iraqi Jews, Frank Iny School, Baghdad, 29 June 1972, CZA S 6/10317.

232. Reuven Naji Alias, President of the Jewish Community (Rai's A-Tai'fa Al-Musawiyya) of Iraq to Iraqi Minister of Information, Baghdad, 18 December 1975 (Arabic), *JDC Archives*, New York; A. Karlikow to AJC New York, 9 July 1970, *JDC Archives*; Karlikow to Gruen, 20 January 1972, *AJC Archives*; Shemesh to Dominitz/Jewish Agency (381), 1 October 1971; *The Torah books that remained in Iraq*, 21 July 1972 (977), CZA S 6/10317.

233. When last checked by author at the Stockholm Jewish Synagogue, no trace of any gift or correspondence was found regarding scrolls from Baghdad, June 2016.

234. State 046751 to Baghdad, 14 March 1973; NY/UN 34 to MFA Jerusalem, 2 May 1973, CZA S-6/10321.

235. Baghdad 0113, 13 March 1973; Paris, 15 March 1973.

236. Maurice Shohet interview, June 2013, Washington DC.

237. Brussels 2183 (Straysz-Hope), 20 April 1973.

238. Tehran 5313 (Heck), 28 July 1973.

239. Madrid 6170 (Rivero), 25 October 1973; Nives Fox to Gruen, 29 May 26 June, 1974; Karlikow to Gruen, 6 June 1974, *AJC Archives*.

240. Letter from the Embassy of Iraq Vienna to JDC, 24 January 1973, *JDC Archives*.

241. *Al-Jumhuriyya*, 13 November 1975.

242. The advertisement of the Iraqi Embassy to Bonn was published in *Frankfurter Allgemeine Zeitung*, 13 December 1975; The Embassy in London published at *The Guardian*, 4 December 1975; on 10 December 1975, the Guardian published the letter of the Iraqi Ambassador Abd-al-Malik al-Yasin stating that the Zionists were to be blamed for the grim fate of Iraqi Jews.

243. Abraham Karlikow, Paris to George Gruen, New York, 8 December 1975, *AJC Archives*.

244. Ibrahim al-Bahrawi, 'Al-Qarrar al-Iraqi bi I'adat al-Yahud al-Iraqiyyin' (The Iraqi resolution on the return of Iraqi Jews). *Aafaq Arabiyya*, 6: (March 1976), pp. 2–3; Saddam Hussein interview to the Egyptian journalist Sakina al-Sadat, 19 January 1977 in S. Hussein, *Social and Foreign Affairs in Iraq* (1979), p.109.

245. Nawi returned from Iraq to Israel a year later. *La Swisse*, 31 May 1976.

246. For Jewish property confiscated in Iraq see Itamar Levine, *Locked Doors –The Seizure of Jewish Property in Arab Countries* (Tel Aviv: Maarachot, 2001), pp.121–38.

247. A.Yaniv, 'Israel faces Iraq: The politics of confrontation' in A. Baram & B. Rubin (eds), *Iraq's Road to War* (London: Macmillan, 1994), pp. 234–51; *Dawr al-Jaysh al-Iraqi fi Harb Tishrin 1973* (The role of the Iraqi Army in the October 1973 War) (Beirut 1975).

248. Idi Amin, President of Uganda who supported the terrorists, received a generous welcome on his visit to Iraq in May 1974. *Al-Jumhuriyya*, 6 May 1974.

249. Y. Melman & D. Raviv, *Imperfect Spies* (Tel Aviv: Sifriyat Maariv, 1990), pp.133–5; another blow to Iraqi prestige occurred before the Ba'th coup in August 1966, when an Iraqi fighter pilot Munir Roufa, defected and landed in Israel. It gave Israel the benefit of being the first in the West to examine a Soviet-made MiG 21 model.

250. Saddam Hussein, *On Zionist Aggression against Iraqi Nuclear Installations* (Baghdad, 1981), p.15.

251. E. Beery, *The Officer Class in Politics and Society of the Arab East* (Tel Aviv: Sifriyat Poalim, 1966), pp. 219–21; M.I. Eppel, 'The Elite, the Effendiyya, and the Growth of Nationalism and Pan-Arabism in Hashemite Iraq, 1921-1958', *International Journal of Middle East Studies*, 30(2) (1998), pp. 227–50; Spector-Simon, *Iraq between the Two World Wars*, pp. 76–114.

6

The Persian Gulf:
A Strategic Asset for Both Sides

The Persian Gulf has long been central to the US's relations with many Middle East countries, including Iraq. The waterway has held significant strategic value for the US since the Second World War – not only because of its importance for the export of oil, but as a buffer against Soviet influence.[1] Every US administration has understood that the Persian Gulf is a strategic asset, and the gulf became even more essential after the energy crisis following the Yom Kippur War.

Yet, until 1973, the US, then still engaged in the Vietnam War, maintained a limited military presence in the Indian Ocean. At that time, Kissinger focused on attaining détente with the Soviet Union. The US had relied on the Shah and on the Saudi monarchy to protect American energy interests through the flow of oil. But the Shah's fall in 1979, and the emergence of the Islamic Republic of Iran as a hostile anti-American power, as well as US disenchantment with détente, intensified the US's need to increase its military presence in the Persian Gulf.[2] Iraq had a very narrow outlet to the Persian Gulf, and all Iraqi maritime movement was exposed to threats from Iran, Iraq's archrival, in line with the historical enmity between Arabs and Persians. During this period, Iran had contacts with the Iraqi Shi'i community and had been meddling with opposition to the Ba'th, Kurds, Shi'is and others. Until 1979, Iran was a key US ally, meaning that Iraq was surrounded by America's Gulf allies.

1968 through the Algiers agreement of 1975: the Ba'th focused on its survival, including by suppressing the Kurdish rebellion. The Ba'th was involved then in subversive activities in Oman, Yemen, South Yemen and Kuwait.

1975–9: Iraq focused on economic development and modernisation and on becoming the number two oil exporter in the Middle East and more active vis-à-vis other regional oil producers. Iraq strived for Arab leadership and became a regional power.

In the second half of 1970, the US became increasingly involved in the Gulf, succeeding Great Britain, which had evacuated its traditional bases.

The emergence of Iran as an Islamic republic following the Shah's overthrow created a country hostile to both the US and Iraq – and a new reality in the Gulf. It also gave Iraq and the US the potential for developing a common interest.

Iraq as a Gulf State

In November 1971, just before the United Arab Emirates declared its independence, Iran annexed three strategic islands in the Strait of Hurmuz: Greater Tonb, Lesser Tonb and Abu Musa. Iran claimed that they were occupied by Britain in 1921 and had been administered ever since by the British ruled principality of Sharja, which was later incorporated with the UAE. Iraq considered Iran's annexation as an abuse of Arab sovereignty, and tried unsuccessfully to garner Arab support against the Iranian move. But it did not act militarily. Iraq temporarily severed diplomatic relations with the United Kingdom, condemned Iran and called on Arabs to preserve the Persian Gulf as an Arab waterway.[3]

Iraq stated that it was defending the Arab motherland against foreign enemies, using Arabism as the leitmotif in approaching Gulf States, suspicious of the Ba'th intentions.[4] Iraq did the same after the emergence of Ayatollah Khomeini and during its war with Iran in the 1980s. The Ba'th contended that Iraq was defending what it called 'the eastern flank of the Arab motherland' and was, therefore, protecting the Gulf States from Iranian aggression. In a press conference on 20 June 1980, just two weeks before war broke out with Iran, Saddam argued that Iraq was the only Arab state to relentlessly demand that Iran return the islands. While negotiating the Algiers Agreement with the Shah, he said he insisted that Iran evacuate the Gulf islands. (The islands, though, were not mentioned in the agreement. Saddam apparently made this claim to justify the excessive concessions he made to Iran in 1975.)[5] Iraq's ambition to become a regional power over an Iran that controlled the narrow maritime passage required cooperation with the Gulf States on political, economic and security issues.[6]

In the first half of the decade, the Iraqi Ba'th supported radical pro-Soviet and anti-American opposition groups in the Gulf. After 1975, Iraq toned down its propaganda attacks against what it termed the 'reactionary' conservative, pro-American monarchies. It increased diplomatic and economic exchanges, signed multilateral agreements on culture and heritage and hosted conferences of Gulf representatives. It partnered with Saudi Arabia to construct a road connecting the holy cities of Najaf, Iraq, to Medina, Saudi Arabia. Iraq also agreed to accept Saudi mediation of its dispute with Syria over the water supply of the Euphrates River.[7]

The flip side of the Ba'th pledge to defend the Arab Gulf was opposition to all foreign presence there, including the American, British and Soviet navies.[8] The US Interest Section in Baghdad welcomed Iraqi rapprochement with the pro-American Gulf States as an indication of the regime's flexibility and moderation.[9] But while Iraq ceased support for *Zuffar* rebels in Oman and even diplomatically recognised the UAE in January 1976, the mutual mistrust between Baghdad and the Gulf States went unchanged. [10] Gulf leaders suspected that the purpose of Iraq's apparently friendly approach was to serve its ambitions to dominate the Gulf and ensure that Iraq would not be left out of any regional security arrangements.

Withdrawal of Britain and East-West Containment

Great Britain's Labour government withdrew forces from the Gulf in January 1968 – a move that, while expected, was carried out earlier than the late 1971 date the US anticipated. The CIA assumed that Iran, Iraq, Saudi Arabia and even Egypt might try to gain strategic influence with Great Britain's departure, but America's greater concern was that the USSR would rush to fill the vacuum.[11] As long as British forces were present in the Gulf, the US could trust that its interests were protected. The Shah convinced both the US and Great Britain that he was the only regional power capable of keeping the Gulf safe and stable, especially if he received the American weapons needed to contain Soviet encroachment.[12]

The Gulf's sheiks and ruling families considered Great Britain a safeguard for their own security. The British withdrawal from the port of Aden in southern Yemen in 1967, followed by the takeover of the city of Aden by the Marxist National Liberation Front (NLF), might have served as a warning against a recurrence in other oil-producing principalities. A seminar held at Georgetown University in Washington DC, in early 1969, discussed the implications of the British withdrawal, suggesting several scenarios that might destabilise the pro-Western monarchies. Iraq was covered briefly, but not as a regional player. The most dangerous implications mentioned were the obstruction of the flow of oil and the increase of Soviet leverage in the Persian Gulf and the Indian Ocean.[13]

Prior to the Iranian capture of the islands from the UAE, the US and the UK conducted a diplomatic campaign to ensure that Iraq would not instigate an Arab-Persian confrontation with Iran.[14] The Americans had to persuade the British to support the Iranian claim of the islands, being that Tehran was the strongest, most reliable, pro-Western power in the Persian Gulf. The US ambassador to Tehran, Douglas MacArthur II, told British

Foreign Secretary Sir Alec Douglas Hume that Iran's presence in the Straits of Hurmuz would preempt Soviet access to the Gulf through the Iraqi port Umm Qasr.[15]

The British urged the traditional leaders in the principalities of Sharja and Ra's al-Khaima (currently UAE) that had a traditional claim over the islands before British occupation, to accept the Iranian presence on the three islands. This diplomatic effort produced an agreement between Iran and Sharjah with respect to the largest island, Abu Musa. The Iranian occupation of the sparsely populated two islands of Tunb occurred without the acquiescence of the ruler of Ras al-Khaimah.[16] Today, however, both Sharja and Ra's-al Khaima are part of the UAE.

Britain kept the Royal Air Force base in the Omani Masira Island till 1977. Since then Oman allowed the use of the base by both the UK and the US. Both the US and the UK believed that, in spite of its hostile rhetoric, Iraq would not pose a threat to American and British interests.

At this time, the UK was downsizing its military presence in nearby Yemen and Oman, while maintaining its diplomatic and commercial activities. The US seemed to be succeeding Britain – which it perceived as experienced in dealing in the Arabian Peninsula – as the dominant foreign power in the Gulf.[17]

US intelligence reports before the 1973 war focused on the Soviet threat to destabilise the Gulf, such as by taking over the Iraqi port of Umm Qasr.[18] Helms, the CIA director, told Nixon the following in a memorandum dated 22 February 1973:

> Proxy forces of the USSR and the Free World have been engaged since September 1962 in a continuing armed struggle for control of the southern regions of the Peninsula. At stake is the control of the maritime passages at the southern exits of the Red Sea and the Gulf and ultimately the oil of the Peninsula and the Gulf. Moscow appears prepared to continue to support this classic 'war of national liberation' and to escalate military pressures on Oman and the Yemen Arab Republic from Aden. The introduction of Cuban guerrilla and military specialists and more sophisticated Soviet arms is the most currently indication [sic] of Soviet intentions.[19]

Helms did not mention Iraq. It seems that his recommendation, expressed in the memo, to increase intelligence gathering, was implemented, because a year later Helms noted an improvement in the quality of intelligence on the Gulf. In a subsequent report (dated 6 April 1974), when he was ambassador to Iran, Helms pointed to the threat posed by Iraq. Helms thought that Iraq might invade Kuwait, especially following the end of the Kurdish rebellion. He wrote:

> As for Kuwait, the external danger continues to be from Iraq, which completely outclasses Kuwait in everything but foreign exchange, and could occupy the country very quickly if its forces were not tied down by the Kurds and if it could be sure Iran would not react ... if the Iraqis can free themselves of their Kurdish challenge and decide to seize Kuwaiti territory to protect their growing port of Umm Qasr.[20]

Helms's prediction that Iraq would radicalise even further after the end of the Kurdish rebellion ran contrary to the State Department's assessment that Iraq would move away from the USSR and toward the West. Helms apparently did not persist in offering insights on Iraq. In March 1975, he accepted the Shah's reasoning for ceasing support for the Kurds under the Algiers Agreement, and did not repeat his warnings of the Iraqi threat.

The British shared the State Department's view that Iraq did not pose a threat to other Gulf States, noting that Iraqi aggression was reduced as the Ba'th coped with domestic issues. Israel thought otherwise, seeing Iraq as a constant threat to Kuwait and to Israel, as well as being a potential inroad for Soviet infiltration. However, Israeli and Iranian assessments were considered by US intelligence officials as too alarming and even biased.[21] Following the end of the Arab oil embargo on 17 March 1974, American interests shifted to working to resolve the Arab-Israeli conflict as a major US interest. The notion was that a war between Israel and the Arabs might degenerate into war with Soviet involvement, which would increase the heat of the Cold War. [22]

In February 1976, the National Security Council released a study on US security policy toward the Gulf.[23] The report recommended strengthening relations with the Gulf States, enforcing technological and military capabilities and encouraging cooperation among Gulf States that would allow for a US military presence in the Persian Gulf. Indeed, in the late 1970s, the US increased military supplies to the Gulf monarchies and encouraged closer relations between the countries it considered pillars, namely, Iran and Saudi Arabia.[24] Iraq was mentioned only briefly in these discussions, not regarded by the administration, the foreign policy community, academia and think tanks as important or strong enough to endanger US interests.

In addition to arms transfers to friendly countries, the US planned to increase its military presence to protect the Gulf's oilfields if necessary. The idea was to create a wide strip of deployment, stretching from Afghanistan to the Horn of Africa, thus improving deterrence against the USSR. The US expanded its base in the Indian Ocean island of Diego Garcia. It needed access to Persian Gulf ports as well. Following secret negotiations with the ruler of Bahrain, the US was granted rights of docking at the former British naval base of Jufair, since then Oman allowed the use of the base to both the UK and the US. Those negotiations with Oman and Bahrain were mediated and facilitated by the UK.[25]

Both Republican and Democratic administrations supported arms sales to Iran and the Gulf states. The Soviet Union was behind the military buildup and modernisation of Iraqi forces, providing supplementary weapon systems and aircrafts. However, Iraq was interested, in addition to the Soviet mass buildup, in acquiring Western state-of-the-art military technology, mostly from France, but from the US as well. In the US, some criticism was raised against the volume and sophistication of weapons supplied to Iran and Saudi Arabia, on the grounds that the sales were accelerating the arms race in the Gulf. Moreover, the Soviet threat in the Persian Gulf had decreased following détente and the Ba'th statements that Iraq would not allow any interference of foreign forces in the Gulf including the Soviet Union. Senator Edward Kennedy proposed legislation, endorsed by AIPAC, to address the Israeli concern that advanced weapons systems sold to Saudi Arabia could be used against Israel if they fell into the wrong hands.[26] Still, the flow of US arms continued, in keeping with Washington's policy of deterrence by providing her allies with arms and maintaining a presence including participation in joint manoeuvres in the Persian Gulf and the Indian Ocean.[27] Although from the American perspective, Iraq was a minor player in the Gulf, Iraq closely followed the massive arms transfer to Iran and Saudi Arabia, and considered US plans to establish a military presence in the Indian Ocean and the Persian Gulf 'a conspiracy against the Arab nation'.[28]

The US approach to the Gulf seemed contradictory. Iraq had been marginalised by the administration for its alleged weakness, yet, from 1975 to 1979 – even though Iraq gained wealth, became politically stable and acquired enormous military force – the Ford and Carter administrations did not view it as a regional threat. Closer relations with US allies in the Gulf correlated with the misperception that Iraqi interest in economic development implied, of necessity, peaceful intentions, rather than aggression. The two administrations did not draw a lesson from the fact that Iraq neither distanced itself from the USSR nor moderated its rejection of the peace process. In short, the White House was misled by the apparent Ba'th charm offensive.

Iran, Iraq and the USSR

Iraq's historical rival, Iran, was key to American policy in the Persian Gulf. Up to 1975, the Iraqi Ba'th was in a state of continuous friction with Iran and on the verge of war. The countries' rivalry seemed unrelated to the US and centered on three matters: the Kurdish rebellion, controversy regarding the sovereignty of the Shatt al-Arab and anxiety that Shi'i Iran might incite the Iraqi Shi'i Ulama against the secular Ba'th Party. Furthermore, Iran maintained close relations with Israel, supplying oil to the Jewish state even during the regional embargo. Seeing Iran as an anti-Soviet pillar had begun in the Eisenhower administration following the Qasim coup in 1958.[29] Since then, and through the period of this study, Iran was considered a solid American ally, protecting American interests in the Gulf, deterring Soviet infiltration and keeping the Straits of Hormuz open. The US supplied Iran with all its security needs, including selling it state-of-the-art military technology, beginning with Nixon's promise to the Shah in 1972. The US supported Iran's decision to take over the islands, and accepted the Shah's decision to abandon the Kurds in 1975.

To justify his requests on the security-procurement front, the Shah portrayed Iraq as a Soviet surrogate that threatened oil production. He offered his services as a first responder to Soviet attack on the Gulf oil fields. In such a scenario, Iranian forces would take over Iraqi airports until the United States and its allies would be ready to confront the USSR.[30] At the same time, Iran and the Soviet Union shared a long border and economic interests. The Soviet Union was involved in constructing a natural-gas pipeline in Esfahan, Iran, a project larger than Soviet oil projects in Iraq. This had a calming effect on its policy in the Gulf, as the Soviets had a vested economic interest in Iran and, therefore, would hesitate risking the project with anti-Iranian provocations. For example the USSR did not object when Iran took over the islands and was neutral in the Iraq-Iran conflict.[31]

Iraq complied with the Algiers agreement with Iran, and acceded to the Shah's request in September 1978 to put Khomeini under house arrest in Najaf before expelling him from Iraq. Iraq and Iran seemed to share a concern over political Islam, in addition to their concern over subversive communist activity – in particular after the communists overthrew the regime of Mohammad Da'ud Khan in Afghanistan in 1978.[32]

US intelligence analysts failed to detect both the power that Iranian religious leaders held over the masses and the shaky domestic status of the Shah in the late 1970s. Moreover, the Carter administration was more sensitive than its predecessor to criticism of an unlimited arms transfer to

Iran, and of human-rights violations committed by the Shah against opposition groups.[33]

Saddam, however, viewed Khomeini's Islamic revolution as an American conspiracy. This argument, published in the Iraqi magazine *Aafaq Arabiyya*, was used for propaganda purposes. Saddam also recorded it in his own voice in a meeting with senior advisers in November 1979.[34]

Kuwait: Historical Claim and Strategic Necessity

The significance of Iraqi access to the Persian Gulf had risen sharply with the increasing production of oil and the volume shipped by super-tankers. Iraq badly needed to develop the port of Umm Qasr for the use of such tankers, and most importantly needed safe passage through the Straits of Hurmuz, controlled by Iran. For that purpose, Iraq asked for a land post on the Kuwaiti islands that overlooked the route from the islands towards the straits. Thus, since the 1950s, Iraq had sought ways to establish its presence in the Kuwaiti island of Warba overlooking the Shatt al-Arab. Negotiations between Iraq and Kuwait (the first Arab state to recognise the Ba'th regime) began in 1969.[35] Iraq had not ceded its territorial demands over Kuwait, based on the 1875 Ottoman ruling that included Kuwait as part of the Basra district. An August 1969 report presented by the CIA to President Nixon raised the probability of an Iraqi invasion of Kuwait that would include its taking over of the oil fields. Helms discussed this with the British foreign secretary in March 1971.[36] When Iraqi-Kuwaiti negotiations deadlocked, Iraqi forces assaulted the border checkpoint in Samita in March 1973.[37] Such a change in the status quo could have ignited a superpower confrontation. Seeking to keep the Gulf stable, the US asked Saudi Arabia and Iran to approach Iraq. The Soviet navy sent additional vessels to the Persian Gulf, but did not intervene in support of Iraq. Saddam paid a sudden visit to Moscow, most likely related to the situation with Kuwait, asking for Soviet support in the border dispute, indicating that the USSR would not be asked to actually take part in the border dispute. The Soviet navy presence was meant to signal to the US that it ought to remain neutral as well.[38]

Great Britain, in 1961, was prepared to send troops if Qasim had invaded Kuwait. Following the British example, in 1973, the US ambassador to Kuwait William Stoltzfus recommended that Washington respond favorably to Kuwait's request for American military equipment needed to upgrade the Kuwaiti forces.[39] Kuwaiti anxiety over Iraq's aggressive intentions persisted, and its foreign minister Sabah al-Ahmad told the British ambassador to Kuwait, Albert Thomas Lamb, that his main concern was that Iraq would not hold onto the small coastal strip south of Umm Qasr, but would seize the Kuwaiti islands of Warba and Bubyan. He described Iraqi ambitions regarding Kuwait as a 'cancer, implacable and spreading.' [40]The Kuwaitis complained that Iraq was engaged in subversive activity, destabilising the rule of the Emir. [41] After determining that the USSR would remain neutral, Washington referred to the Iraqi threat against Kuwait as a 'controlled conflict.' It relied on the mediation efforts of Iran and Saudi Arabia after Iraqi-Kuwaiti negotiations resumed.[42]

The Iraqi threat against Kuwait was not dealt with during the US's interagency discussions on policy toward the Persian Gulf. In December 1976, Tariq Aziz, who was then Iraq's minister of information, referred to the islands of Warba and Bubyan as 'administered by Kuwait', implying non-recognition of Kuwaiti sovereignty. Iraq did not accept the Kuwaiti rejection of Iraqi forces' using the islands as a strategic area to protect Iraqi maritime traffic in the Gulf, mostly against Iran. Saddam noted bitterly that, if war broke out with Iran, he would occupy the islands.[43]

US Deterrence versus Iraqi Anxiety

All of the US's National Security Studies memoranda on Gulf security issues in 1969–79 referred to containment of the USSR to ensure oil production and export, including by exerting military interference, if necessary.[44] The major trend throughout the decade was the growing US involvement in the Gulf, at the same time that Great Britain was pulling back. National Security Study Memorandum (NSSM) deliberations referred to Iraq briefly, mostly by defense and intelligence representatives, as the main client Arab state of the USSR that might threaten the Gulf monarchies.[45] In the early 1970s, British officials stated that the country would scale back its military presence in the Gulf. The US, trapped in Vietnam, could not then send troops to the area, because it would lack the political and public support for such a move. Rep. Lee Hamilton noted, in a Congressional hearing in 1972, that the presence of the US Navy in the Persian Gulf, the Indian Ocean and the Red Sea was essential for containing the USSR. Hamilton mentioned Iraq as the only non-US ally in the Gulf with a significant military capability; sponsored by the Soviets, Iraq was bound to resist US presence in the Gulf, he concluded.

During the House Committee hearing on 'U.S. Interests and Policy towards the Persian Gulf', in June1972, Iraq nationalised its oil industry, an action that underlined the hostile, anti-Western image of the Ba'th regime. American oil-industry representatives, testifying before the committee, expressed empathy for the Iraqi decision, arguing that the IPC had rejected all compromise to end the conflict with the Government of Iraq for a decade. Other witnesses from the administration and academia concluded that Iraq did not pose a threat to the oil industry or the flow of oil from the Gulf.[46] Despite US intelligence and Department of Defense data on Iraq's military buildup, those had been mentioned and presented in congressional sessions as a lever by those advocating US military sales to the Shah. [47]

Following the fall of the Shah and the emergence of the Islamic Republic, Brzezinski expressed concern that the USSR might take advantage of the instability in Iran to infiltrate the Persian Gulf, assist states such as Iraq, Syria, Libya and the PDRY, that depended on Soviet military supplies, and support terrorism. Brzezinski singled out Libya and ignored Iraq.[48] CIA Intelligence analysis, in December 1979, held that the major threat posed by an Islamic regime in Iran was not in exporting the revolution to the Gulf States, but rather in leaving Iran vulnerable to a pro-Soviet takeover. Iraq was mentioned as a possible ally against Iran and, therefore, export of US military technology might have encouraged this trend. [49] But other voices in the CIA identified Iraq's aggressive intentions against Iran and raised the opposite option. CIA officer George Cave, who served as deputy chief of station in Tehran in the 1970s and spoke Farsi fluently, argued that Iraq would have been more harmful to the US than an Islamic republic in Iran would be.

In October 1979, a month before Iranian students stormed the US embassy in Tehran and took American diplomats hostage, Cave was sent to Tehran, hoping to establish relations with the new Islamic leadership. US intelligence had observed Iraqi forces deploying along the Iranian border, training to cross the Shatt al-Arab. Cave carried this sensitive information to Iranian Foreign Minister Ibrahim Yazdi, telling him that the US believed that Iraq was planning to attack Iran within a year. Cave told Yazdi about CIA-operated signal intelligence (SIGINT) based in Ilam, which was built in 1973 at the request of the Shah to eavesdrop on Iraq. Communication intercepts had been downloaded, translated and analysed at the Ilam ground station. Cave suggested reactivating the station. Yazdi, though considered pragmatic, dismissed the American alert, by saying in Farsi of Iraq, 'They would not dare.'[50]

The administration perceived Iraq as oriented more towards the Arab states confronting Israel and less towards the Persian Gulf. Indeed, the State Department grouped the Iraq country desk with Lebanon, Jordan and Syria, not with the Gulf States. The Pentagon and the North Atlantic Treaty Organization (NATO) evaluated Iraq as militarily strong, dependent on the USSR and a potential threat to US interests in the Gulf.[51]

Energy and oil had been a fundamental subject both to American and Iraqi foreign and strategic policy. It remained marginal to their bilateral relations, though, since the US did not import Iraqi oil yet it was determined that the 1973–4 oil embargo should never happen again.

The administration considered Iraq a potential threat to the free movement of oil in the Persian Gulf. It is puzzling, then, why the Iraqi threat was not studied more or taken more seriously. Since Iraq and other radical states such as Libya called on other oil producers to use petroleum as a weapon, Washington devised contingency plans to protect the oil fields. Correspondence between Tehran and the White House dealt with US plans to protect Saudi and Kuwaiti oil fields. Helms, in a cable in October 1973, sketched out scenarios in which the Saudi monarchy was overthrown by pro-Soviet states in the region, particularly Iraq. The US viewed Iran as pivotal to its plans. It sent troops to protect both Saudi Arabia and Kuwait, with a massive US airlift. The US also provided additional weapons to Iran. [52]

Iraq perceived that the 'imperialist power' – by which it meant the US – had aggressive intentions in sending its troops to the area. That fear was deeply rooted in Ba'th thinking and writings, even without the knowledge of the existence of the above mentioned contingency plans. The party's platform warned 'against the threat of the US and the UK, to interfere in an attempt to change the Arab character of the Gulf.'[53] Iraq pointed to the US's alleged role during the Black September crisis in 1970, and again during the Yom Kippur War and its aftermath, saying that they were a cover for anti-Arab aggression. While the rhetoric was typical Ba'th propaganda, what was credible was the charge that the US military could intervene if oil supplies to the West were at risk. Rumours about such a contingency plan leaked when the Ford administration was trying to create a dialogue between supplier states and consumer states. Ford and Kissinger stated unequivocally that the US would not rule out military action in case of a hostile takeover of the oil fields that threatened the West's access to its essential source of energy.[54]

In 1976, the Congressional Research Service (CRS) issued a feasibility study on military involvement. In a Senate hearing on national fuel and energy policy, the CRS assessed the consequences of such a military move. The public discussion of the possibility of US military intervention in the Persian Gulf likely occurred to create deterrence. However, this chatter generated hostile responses by Arab states and by US allies elsewhere in the Middle East and in Europe. When the US aircraft carrier *Enterprise* left the Philippines on 6 January 1975, heading towards the Indian Ocean, both Iran and Egypt came out against a possible US military intervention in the Persian Gulf. In the *New York Times* and in Iraqi newspapers, retired US military officers voiced similar criticism.[55]

For Iraq, the public debate validated the Ba'thi argument that the US was representing 'a new imperialism', succeeding the 'old imperialism' of Great Britain – hostile to Arabs in general and Iraq in particular. Kissinger's statements were quoted conspicuously in Iraqi media as evidence of a US conspiracy against the Arabs.[56] In early January 1975, the Iraqi media linked the alleged American threat to Kissinger's diplomatic efforts for peace with Israel; later that month, the media published front-page reports on the American navy's constituting a threat to the Gulf and the Indian Ocean. The Iraqis suspected that the US, convening a conference of heads of missions in May 1973 in Tehran, as well as the appointment of Helms as ambassador to Iran, indicated that it was planning to act aggressively against Iraq. An editorial in *Alif Ba'* magazine maintained that Helms was appointed for his 'expertise in intrigues and conspiracies' to control American interests in the Gulf.[57]

The Iraqi press, including communist newspapers, criticised the negotiations between Great Britain and Oman to allow a US military presence on the island of Masira, calling them a provocation against Iraq.[58] In a speech at a Non-aligned Movement conference in Havana in September 1979, Saddam charged that the 'imperialistic powers' would seek to occupy the oil fields to exploit the resources of the poor states.[59] While the charge had domestic propaganda value, the regime's statements also reflected a genuine concern for the US's growing presence in such Persian Gulf emirates as Saudi Arabia, Bahrain and Oman. Iraq had avoided pointing at Iran in this context since the Algiers Agreement was reached in 1975, but Iraqi anxiety and fear of an external attack increased when the Islamic republic replaced the monarchy. The Iraqi Ba'th viewed the Islamic revolution as a joint venture between the US and Khomeini; indeed, its newsletter published an article on American military manoeuvres in the Indian Ocean and Persian Gulf.[60] In a session with his senior advisers in November 1979, Saddam said that the US was not just involved in the events in Iran, but was behind the overthrow of the Shah. Saddam said he saw Iraq as surrounded by an American military presence at sea and in its bases in the Gulf States.[61] In his 1992 book, the Iraqi journalist and historian Sa'd al-Bazzaz described what he called Iraq's 'collective paranoia' dating back to long-ago invasions. He wrote too, that Saddam was in a constant state of anxiety because of the enemies he believed were targeting him or Iraq.[62]

Lacking a Meeting Point

Observing US-Iraqi relations through the prism of the Persian Gulf reveals a distinctly asymmetrical picture, more evident than the other prisms in this study. When Iraq was mentioned in US deliberations on policy in the Persian Gulf, it tended to be in the context of containment of the USSR, and not of Iraq as an independent player in the Gulf. America's main concern regarding Iraq was that it would allow Soviet forces access to the Persian Gulf. The US was well aware of Iraqi subversive activities against the pro-Western regimes of Oman, Yemen and Kuwait. But following the signing of the Algiers Agreement, Iraq was relegated to low on the list of dangers to US interests in the Gulf. The US welcomed the cessation of Iraq's subversive activity in Iran and Oman, and viewed the Iraqi rapprochement in the Arabian Peninsula as a sign of moderation, in that Baghdad shifted its revolutionary focus to economics and trade.

Iraq's massive economic and military buildup in 1975–9, and its diplomatic and economic initiatives towards moderate Arab regimes and states of the Non-Aligned Movement, were designed to promote the country's diplomatic status as a strong and active player in the international arena, including vis-à-vis such powers as the US.

Why did the US ignore Iraq's aggressive intentions in the Gulf? In part, because America held a misperception of Iraq. There was no focus on Iraq, no study or integrated analysis on Iraq as an emerging power in the Persian Gulf. The US settled for ambiguous signals received from Iraq, Iraqi rapprochement with the Gulf States and Iraqi statements regarding non-alliance – interpreting them as Iraqi intentions to veer from the Soviet Union, in spite of its harsh rhetoric attacking the US military presence in the area. The absence of a serious debate in Washington regarding the Gulf could indicate negligence, or reluctance to deal with a state that had become an important business partner for Western enterprises and expressed an interest in US-made products. However, the reluctance to deal with the Gulf was due to public and congressional criticism of the US's massive arms transfers to Iran and Saudi Arabia that were seen as accelerating an arms race in the Middle East. Iraq was becoming a major oil exporter, and the Ba'th – specifically, Saddam – was duly impressed with the quality of the US's technology and military industry, which Saddam considered the backbone of America's global status. Yet, the US view of Iraqi economic growth as a positive development led it to mistakenly assume that Baghdad would become moderate to preserve its economic gains. Iraq viewed the strength and influence of the US, coupled with the statements and reports about contingency plans to protect the oil fields as a direct threat to the Gulf and particularly Iraq. But the economic mutual interest failed to create a political meeting point or even a realistic dialogue between the two countries.

Notes

1. On the strategic significance of the Persian Gulf since World War II: D.F. Winkler, *Amirs, Admirals and Desert Sailors: Bahrain, the United States Navy and the Arabian Gulf* (Annapolis MD: Naval Institute Press, 2007).
2. J.C. Hurwitz, *The Persian Gulf* (The Foreign Policy Association, 1979), p. 38.

3. *Al-Jumhuriyya* editorial, 15 September 1970; *Al-Thawra*, 27 December 1972; Saddam Hussein, *nidaluna wal siyyasa al-dawliyya* (Our struggle and foreign policy), 12 June 1975 in Saddam Hussein *Al-Mukhtarat*, Vol 5:1, p. 69; Iran invaded the Abu Musa Island on 30 November 1971, after reaching financial settlement with the Sheikh of Sharja, yet seized the Tunb Islands without the consent of the Sheikh of Ras al-Khaymah. Iraq requested to convene the Arab League and appealed to the UN Security Council – without success. Memorandum from State (Eliot) to Kissinger, 1 December 1971, *FRUS* XXIV #110.

4. Saddam Hussein, *On Current Events in Iraq: Q & A session with journalists*, 8 April 1974, pp. 100–1.

5. 'Iran-Iraq Treaty on International Borders and Good Neighbourly relations', in M. Khadduri, *Socialist Iraq, A Study in Iraqi Politics since 1969* (Washington: Middle East Institute, 1978), Appendix E, pp. 245–60; S. Hussein, *Iraqi Policies in Perspective*, Press Conference, 20 July 1980)Baghdad, 1981), pp. 67–8.

6. O. Bengio, 'Iraq Stepdaughter in the Gulf?' in J. Kostiner (ed.) *Gulf States: Politics, Society, Economics* (Tel Aviv: Dayan Center, Tel Aviv University, 2000), pp. 89–94.

7. A. Baram, *National Integration and Exclusiveness in Political Thought and Practice in Iraq under the Ba'th, 1968–1982* (PhD Dissertation, Jerusalem: Hebrew University, 1986), pp.169–70; Naomi Sakr, 'Economic relations between Iraq and other Arab Gulf States', in T. Niblock (ed.), *Iraq: The Contemporary State* (London: Croom Helm, 1982), pp. 150–67.

8. American diplomats were instructed to use the term 'Arab Gulf' in Iraq and 'Persian Gulf' in Iran.
R.F. Nyrop, *Area Handbook for the Persian Gulf States* (Washington DC: GPO, 1977), pp. 396–7.

9. Baghdad 335 (Wiley), 13 March 1976.

10. T. Niblock, 'Iraq Policies towards the Arab States of the Gulf, 1958–1981' in Niblock (ed.), *Iraq: the Contemporary State*, pp. 145–6.

11. 'The Persian Gulf States', NIE 30-1-67, 18 May 1967, *CIA*, http://www.foia.cia.gov/docs/DOC_0000997363/DOC_0000997363.pdf, last accessed August 2013.

12. J. Abdulghani, *Iraq and Iran, The Years of Crisis* (New York: Routledge, 1984), pp. 75–6.

13. *The Gulf: Implications of British Withdrawal*, Special Report Series No. 8, The Center for Strategic and International Studies (Washington DC, February 1969). The report mentioned briefly the possible scenario that both Iran and Iraq would renew historical territorial demands: Iran on the Straits of Hurmuz Islands, and Iraq over Kuwait.

14. J.R. Macris, *The Politics and Security of the Gulf: Anglo-American hegemony and the shaping of a region* (London: Routledge, 2010), pp. 194–8.

15. 'Abu Musa Concession dispute as it relates to the future', in Tehran (MacArthur), 25 May 1970, *FRUS* E-4 #68; London 2491 (Annenberg), 19 March 1971, *FRUS* E-4 #119.

16. Memorandum from Secretary Rogers to the President, 16 December 1971, *FRUS* E-4 #153.

17. For example, DCM Ronald Spiers noted that the US can benefit from residual British influence in the Gulf, though the US was the leading power, he advised Americans to avoid an overtly aggressive manner while exercising this influence. London 02410 (Spiers), 15 February 1975.

18. NIE-1-71, 1 April 1971, 'The Persian Gulf after the British departure', *FRUS XXIV* #96.

19. Memorandum from US Ambassador Designate to Iran (Helms) to President Nixon, 22 February 1973, *FRUS XXXVI* #166.

20. Tehran (Helms), 6 April 1974, Secret/Sensitive, Helms Collection, https://www.cia.gov/library/readingroom/docs/74_1503753.pdf, last accessed 14 August 2017.

21. Report prepared by Director of Central Intelligence Helms, 'Views on the Persian Gulf' (n.d.), *FRUS XXIV* #101. The Israeli argument was based on the visit of Soviet vessels in Iraqi ports. The undated document was written most likely in late June or early July, since it was sent to General Haig on 8 July 1971.

22. L.J. Goldstein & Y.M. Zhukov, 'Tales of two fleets, A Russian Perception on the U.S. Naval Standoff in the Mediterranean', *U.S. Naval War College Review*, 7:2 (Spring 2004), pp. 27–63.

23. National Security Study Memorandum (NSSM) 66: 'Policy towards the Persian Gulf', 12 July 1969; NSSM 181: 'U.S. Policy in the Arabian Peninsula and the Persian Gulf', 10 May 1973; NSSM 238: Executive Summery, NSC Memorandum from Oakley to Scowcroft, 18 September 1976, *Ford Presidential Library*, National Security Adviser Files, NSSM.

24. A special interagency group was formed: 'The Middle East Arms Transfer', to deal with arming the Gulf States, that focused mostly on Saudi Arabia and Iran. *Ibid.*, NSSM 238.

25. British Embassy Baghdad (Given) to FCO/MED, 26 October 1976, FCO 8/2623, *TNA*; State 84477 to London, 8 April 1976, *Ford Presidential Library*, NSC Files, NSSM 238; Manama 1220–1 (Cluverius), 7 June 1977.

26. E. M. Kennedy, 'The Persian Gulf: Arms Race or Arms Control?' *Foreign Affairs*, 54(1) (1975), pp. 14–35.

27. Legislation proposals to limit US arms transfer to Gulf States, including Iran, had been sponsored in various Committees, mostly by Democrats. For example, Senator E. Kennedy introduced Resolution S 795 to the Senate Foreign Affairs Committee: 'A bill to suspend all sales of defense articles and services for 6 months to Iran, Saudi Arabia, Iraq, Qatar, Bahrain, the UAE and Oman', 26 February1975, *Library of Congress*, thomas.loc.gov/cgi-bin/bdquery/D?d094:./temp/~bdTVNV, last accessed February 2012.

28. The quote by Saddam was published in the Ba'th bulletin *Al-Thawra al-Arabiyya* (March 1980), p. 74. See also Iraq's response to reports on US contingency plans to take over oilfields later in this chapter.

29. 'A Survey of U.S.-Iranian relationship 1941–1979', n.d. (~1980), p. 29. Top Secret/NODIS, *DNSA*. The copy is undated, presumably written by NSC in late 1980, for Reagan's transition team. National Security Archive.

30. Tehran (Sullivan), 9 September 1975, 'Security Assistance Requirements Report', *DNSA*.

31. MOC, Soviet First Secretary (Vlassov), American Officer (Escudero), Tehran, 28 April 1973. *DNSA*; J.C. Hurwitz, *The Persian Gulf*, pp. 36–7.

32. MOC: 'LMI seeks high level U.S. meeting', Bahram Bahramian, Mohammad Tavakoli LMI, John Stempel,

25. September 1978, US Embassy Tehran, *DNSA*; Tehran 9253 (Sullivan), 25 September 1978.

33. 'A Survey of U.S.-Iranian relationship, 1941–1979', *National Security Archive*, pp. 63–4.

34. The article describes the secret alliance between Khomeini and the US, and consequently with Israel, using sarcastic language: '*al-Shaytan al-akbar … Khalif akbar*' (The big Satan … is the big Ally). 'kyfa tajri al-umur –nizam Khomeini wal-wilayat al-muttahida', *Aafaq Arabiyya*, 3-4:1980, pp. 328–33; quotation of Saddam Hussein, K.M. Woods et al., *The Saddam Tapes: The Inner Workings of a Tyrant's Regime* (Cambridge and New York: Cambridge University Press, 2011), pp. 22–3: CRRC Records, SHTP-D-000-559.

35. T. Niblock, 'Iraqi policies', pp. 128–9.
36. CIA Memorandum, 'Prospects for US Access to World in the Next 15 Years or So', 28 August 1969, *FRUS* XXXVI # 8; London 2491 (Annenberg), 19 March 1971, *FRUS* E-4 #119.
37. Kuwait 2307, 2943 (Stoltzfus), 2 July, 15 August 1973; Baghdad 150 (Lowrie), 27 March 1973.
38. R.P. Cronin et al., 'The Indian Ocean, Arabian Peninsula and the Persian Gulf', *CRS Report* submitted to the Senate Committee on Foreign Relations, April 1979; J.C. Campbell, 'The Persian Gulf Region' in *Major U.S. Foreign and Defense Policy Issues*, CRS Compilation of papers prepared for the Commission on the Operation of the Senate, GPO 1977; Moscow 3437 (Dubs), 22 March 1973.
39. Sisco (State) & Noyes (DOD), House Committee of Foreign Affairs, Subcommittee on the Near East & South Asia, 'New Perspective on the Persian Gulf', 93rd Congress, First Session, 6 June 1973, *GPO* 1973.
40. Kuwait 5282, 3696 (Stolzfus), 9 December, 3 September 1974. Kuwaitis complained that Ba'thi activist, trained in Basra, agitated the oil workers to strike in September 1974.
41. Kuwait 618, 619 (Stoltzfus), 6 February 1975.
42. Kuwait 5779 (Maestrone), 14 December 1976.
43. CRRC Records, SHTP-A-000-835, 16 September 1980.
44. NSSM 66 (1969), 181(1973), 238(1976); Interagency Report: NSSM 199: 'Indian Ocean Strategy', 23 May 1974, *DNSA*; Bengio, 'Iraq', *MECS* I, p. 413, *MECS* II, p. 526; J.C. Campbell, 'The Persian Gulf Region'.
45. CIA Research Study, 'The Soviets in the Persian Gulf/Arabian Peninsula – Assets and Prospects', December 1976, *DNSA*.
46. House Committee on Foreign Relations, Subcommittee on the Near East: 'U.S. Interests and Policy towards the Persian Gulf', 2 February, 7 June 1972, *DDRS*; Marvin Howe, 'Trip around Persian Gulf shows Iran is a Chief Power', *NYT*, 25 January 1972.
47. Leslie Gelb interview, 17 July 2013.
48. Memorandum from Brzezinski for the President: Daily Report, 5 March 1979, *DNSA*.
49. CIA Memorandum: 'U.S. Relations with the Radical Arabs', 7 December 1979 (Secret), *Carter Presidential Library*, National Security Advisor Files, Brzezinski Material Country File.
50. CIA built the *Ilam* base using the code name IBEX. Four specially configured Iranian C-130 aircrafts collected Iraqi communication, and downloaded the intercepts to the ground station. George Cave in 'Toward an International History of the Iran-Iraq War: 1980–1988 A Critical Oral History Workshop', Woodrow Wilson Center , 19 July 2004, in D. Crist, *The Twilight War – The Secret History of America's Thirty-Year Conflict with Iran* (New York: Penguin Press, 2011), pp.81, 87.
51. State 244784 to US Mission NATO, 6 November 1974; US Mission NATO 5892, 'NATO Expert Group on the Situation in the Middle East and the Maghreb', 29 October 1975. US analysis of the Iraqi-Soviet Treaty, in Chapter II.
52. Tehran (Helms) to Washington Signal Center for General Scowcroft (Top Secret/ Eyes Only), 11 October 1973, http://www.foia.cia.gov/helms/pdf/73_1501621.pdf, last accessed February 2012.
\http://www.foia.cia.gov/document/message-brent-scowcroft-ambassador-helms-11-october-1973, last accessed February 2012.
53. ABSP, *Revolutionary Iraq 1968–1973 – The political report adopted by the Eighth Regional Congress of the Ba'ath Socialist Party-Iraq* (Baghdad, 1974), p. 207.

54. 'In case of strangulation of the West by the oil producers', President Ford, *U.S. News & World Report*, 25 November 1974; Secretary Kissinger in *Newsweek*, 18 December 1974, in *State Department Bulletin*, 20 January 1975, pp. 61–2.

55. CRS Report prepared for Senator Henry M. Jackson, S Res 45, 'A National Fuel & Energy Policy Study', *GPO* 1976; *NYT*, 10 January 1975; *Al-Jumhuriyyah*, 16 January 1975.

56. *Al-Jumhuriyya*, 4, 8, 23 January 1975.

57. *Alif Baa* (February–March 1973), p. 227.

58. *Al-Jumhuriyyah*, 13 January 1975, 'al-wisata al-Amrikiyya wa-diblomasiyyat al-madfa' (The American mediation and the diplomacy of the gun); *Baghdad Observer*, 25 January 1975 in Baghdad 77 (Lowrie), 26 January 1975; *Tariq al-Sha'b*, 18 February 1975, in Baghdad 071 (Killough), 19 February 1975.

59. Saddam Hussein, *harakat 'adam al-inkhiyaz, hakatha nafhamuha* (The Non-Alignment Movement – In our View) (Baghdad, 1979), pp. 25–6.

60. 'al-watan al-Arabi wal-sira' al-dawli fil muhit al-Hindi' (The Arab Land and the International Conflict over the Indian Ocean), *Al-Thawra al-Arabiyya* (March 1980), pp. 63–6.

61. CRRC SH-SHTP D-000-559, n.d. circa 4–20 November 1979, in K. Woods et al., *The Saddam Tapes*, pp. 22–3.

62. Sa'd al-Bazzaz, *harb talid ukhra – al-ta'rikh al-sirri liharb al-khalij* (The war that brings another war – The secret history of the Gulf War (Amman, Jordan: al-ahliyya lil-nashr wa al-tawzi', 1992), p. 8.

7

Harbingers of Iraq's Programs to Develop Weapons of Mass Destruction

Thorough research was conducted into the issue of Iraq's programs to develop weapons of mass destruction (WMD) – in particular in the decade following the Gulf War in 1991, led by a UN special commission and later by the UN Monitoring, Verification and Inspection Commission (UNMOVIC).[1] This chapter will focus on the early indications of the Ba'th intentions to develop nuclear, chemical and biological weapons – indications that should have prompted conclusions on the aggressive intentions of the Ba'th and of Saddam in particular.

The Ba'th initiated WMD programs in early 1970 and, by 1975, it had gained momentum with the active, personal involvement of Saddam. Developing WMD, particularly a nuclear program, was in line with Saddam's ambition to turn Iraq into a regional power that could tip the strategic balance against Israel.[2]

As a first step, Iraq intended to increase its existing, Soviet-made nuclear reactor from three to five megawatts. The Soviets conditioned the upgrade on strict monitoring, intended to secure compliance with safeguards of the International Atomic Energy Agency (IAEA) and ensure that the plant would not produce weapons-grade fissile material.[3] Saddam then approached France, a country friendly with Iraq. During his visit to Paris in March 1975, Saddam noted that France welcomed Iraq's procurement of its technology, including military equipment and weapons. Saddam's visit to Paris that September focused primarily on Iraq's nuclear project. He met with Andre Giraud, the head of France's Alternative Energies and Atomic Energy Commission (CEA), and visited the Cadarache research centre in southern France.[4] Iraq chose to build a research light water 40 MGW reactor, called by the French OSIRAK and his small pilot ISIS.[5]

The procurement contract, signed that November 1975, was worth 14.5 billion Francs – about $3 billion. The contract contained clauses that remained secret. The Paris-based investigative journalist Kenneth Timmerman exposed details of the agreement, such as French authorities concealing the deal from the US. France received 93 percent of the enriched uranium from the US at special rates, which was earmarked for French military facilities and plants – but it was bound to report any gram of spent fuel that could be converted to weapons-grade material. According to its secret agreement with Iraq, France was to provide nuclear fuel to Iraq from the American supply without reporting the transaction. When France's breach of its agreement with the US was leaked, it had to supply the Iraqis with more expensive, non-American fuel.[6]

Originally OSIRAK, and the highly enriched uranium (HEU) as a fuel, could produce a small amount of plutonium. Saddam wanted to have his own secret facility to produce weapons-grade material from his spent fuel as well. To complete the fuel cycle in 1979, Iraq purchased, from the Italian company Snia Techint, a radiochemical laboratory for research and reprocessing, along with a fuel-fabrication facility suitable for making natural uranium targets for secret irradiation in the French reactor. The French and Italian facilities would enable Iraq to produce fissile material, independently, between IAEA inspection periods.[7] In addition to the overt, presumably safeguarded plutonium-production project, which Iraq named Tamuz, Iraq was planning a parallel uranium-enrichment program that would be even more difficult to detect. Most of these programs were established following the Israeli bombing of the French-built Osirak plant in June 1981.The French agreed to supply nuclear fuel for the reactor up to the end of 1981 (about 80 kg of 93 percent enriched uranium).[8]

Iraqi Diplomacy

In the 1970s, Iraq enjoyed a good reputation with the IAEA. Iraq was one of the first nations to sign and ratify the Treaty on the Non-proliferation of Nuclear Weapons (NPT), and as early as February 1972, it agreed to allow inspection of its nuclear facilities.[9] As a result, Iraq was entitled to receive scientific assistance and purchase nuclear technology for peaceful purposes, including nuclear fuel to operate the nuclear facilities.[10] The Ba'th nurtured the image of Iraq as a law-abiding state that respected international charters and was active in such UN bodies as the Vienna-based IAEA. In this context, the deals with France and Italy were considered internationally to be legitimate. This was particularly so within the framework of the development momentum in Iraq and the country's optimistic forecast for further development due to its rich oil reserves. Iraq presented its nuclear-energy industry as consistent with its modernisation program.

To sustain this image, Iraq, in 1974, was elected to the IAEA Board of Governors.[11] From 7–11 April1975, Iraq hosted an international conference on the peaceful uses of atomic energy for scientific and economic development.[12] It also established a nuclear-engineering department at the University of Baghdad and promoted academic exchanges, procurement and scholarships. Iraq was active in election processes, for the IAEA institutions, and made financial contributions to the IAEA's Technical Assistance Committee. That had the authority to approve technical assistance for peaceful nuclear projects in States that signed the NPT. According to Khaidhir Hamza, a scientist who fled Iraq in 1994, his country's diplomatic activity at the IAEA served another practical purpose. An Iraqi physicist, Abd al-Wahid al-Saji, joined the IAEA's body of inspectors and consequently had access to inside information and methods that could assist Iraq in hiding a secret site[13].

Adding to Iraq's manipulations of the IAEA were Western states eager to sell their advanced technology – discussions that were not brought up with the US administration and thus failed to raise American suspicion, despite the US's leading role in the IAEA. The fact of Saddam's having a nuclear-weapons program became known only after the Gulf War.[14] Both the UK and the US intelligence reports on the Iraqi WMD program confirmed[15] that from the earliest stages, the purpose of the civilian nuclear program was to acquire technical knowledge and material under the auspices of the IAEA, then reach self-production capability to establish a parallel program for weapons production that would be unknown to international inspectors.[16]

After the US-led invasion of Iraq in 2003, and the criticism about the US's false intelligence on Iraq possessing WMDs, the multinational Iraq Survey Group (ISG) sent a fact-finding mission to Iraq. Both the US and the UK conducted intrusive inquiries into their intelligence services: the Robb-Silberman commission (US, 2005)[17] and the Chilcot Report (UK, 2016).[18] The investigations detected serious intelligence failures that led to the 2003 invasion. Yet the information used in this study, referring to the early period (1968–79) and collected by the UN special commission, seems to have been accurate, since it was based on a thorough, on-site investigation of experts, including interviews with employees of the WMD programs.

Another indication of the Ba'th intention to develop a secret nuclear program in the period researched in this book was the exploration of natural uranium suitable for the nuclear program. Such a site was detected and developed in Al-Qa'im, in western Iraq, from 1976. In addition, Iraq was legally purchasing stocks of natural uranium from Portugal, Italy, Niger and Brazil, and enriched uranium from France and Russia.[19] The enrichment technology required equipment and materials that were to be imported. Yet in February 1978, the IAEA issued an information circular (INFCIRC/254), containing guidelines for the Nuclear Suppliers Group (NSG) to control the transfer of nuclear material to any non-nuclear state. Annexes of the guidelines, later known as a 'trigger list', specified the items designed or prepared for nuclear use, as well as those usable for nuclear weapons, including enrichment technology. These guidelines referred to dual-use material and presented difficulties by causing some delays for the program that Saddam was determined to pursue.

The US was well aware of Iraq's ambition to acquire nuclear weapons. In September 1975, Saddam told the Beirut magazine *Al-Usbu' al-Arabi* that Iraq was searching for a peaceful nuclear reactor as part of 'the first Arab attempt at nuclear arming'. RCC member Na'im Haddad was quoted, in 1977, as saying that 'the Arabs must get an atomic bomb [and] should possess whatever is necessary to defend them'.[20] Reports on the negotiated deal reached the US Interest Section in Baghdad as early as April 1975. Lowrie reported that Iraq was determined to procure a nuclear reactor from the USSR, Canada or France.[21]

Even then, there were more indications of the non-peaceful intentions of Iraq's nuclear program:

The rejection of the Soviet proposal due to its insistence on tight safeguards, such as full Soviet control of nuclear fresh and spent fuel.

Iraq refused certain types of reactors and fuels that might have complicated its development of a secret military nuclear program. For example, Iraq turned down a Canadian offer to supply a reactor known as CANDU, and asked the French for a 500-megawatt, natural uranium, gas-cooled, graphite-moderated type – the preferred type for producing weapons-grade fissile material. The French offered the Osiris 70-MGW, light-water nuclear reactor, fueled by high-enriched uranium.[22] As the Iraqi-French nuclear project progressed, the subject was discussed openly in the US media, including the risk that the reactor might tip the fragile balance in the Middle East and ignite a nuclear arms race.[23] Yet, Iraq was not perceived as being capable of developing nuclear weapons, which required an advanced technological base and specific materials, far beyond the peaceful facility then operating.

US allies, including Israel, raised concerns about Iraq's buildup. They reiterated that the buildup and the procurement of nuclear facilities, allegedly 'for peaceful purposes', constituted a strategic threat for the region, especially Israel. The Israeli assessment of Iraqi intentions was considered exaggerated, anxiety-driven and biased.[24] The special relationship enjoyed by Helms and Israel's representative in Tehran served as an additional channel for presenting Israeli concerns. Helms, who considered his counterpart, Uri Lubrani, as the unofficial ambassador of Israel in Tehran, conveyed Israel's concerns about the Iraqi threat to Washington, along with information about the progress of the French-Iraqi nuclear deal and details of the Soviet supply to Iraq, which grew in volume and quality significantly after 1975 to include surface-to-surface (SSM) missiles and aircraft.[25]

Al-Jumhuriyya responded to the Israeli campaign against the nuclear deal by saying that Israel feared any Iraqi scientific and technological achievements, as well as the Arab ambition to join the nuclear age. The US, the UK and other imperialistic states that supported Israel, except France, preferred to keep the Arabs underdeveloped, deprived of science and technology, the newspaper stated.[26]

While there was no hard evidence in the 1970s regarding Iraqi intentions to develop nuclear weapons, the pessimistic assessment proved right after 1991, at least regarding Iraq's ambitions, though not necessarily Iraq's capabilities. The Iraqi nuclear scientist Khidhir Hamza escaped Iraq in 1994, and testified that Iraqi scientists, trained in the UK (like Ja'far Dhia Ja'far and Immad Khadduri) and in the US (like Hussein Shahrastani and Hadi al-Ubeidi) had joined the Iraqi Atomic Energy Commission (IAEC) in 1975. The Iraqi scientists were working under coercive and oppressing measures, constantly threatened by the regime. Shahrastani, a Shi'i scientist, expressed concerns regarding Saddam's intentions to develop a nuclear weapons program, and was detained and tortured for eleven years. According to one rumour, he supported the Shi'i Da'wa Party; another suggested that he was involved in sabotaging a shipment addressed to the IAEC and stored in La Seyne-sur-Mer, France, an action attributed to Israeli intelligence.[27] His colleague, Ja'far Dhia Ja'far, was detained and returned to the nuclear project following aggressive persuasive efforts.[28]

Thirty years later, in 2003, hard evidence of Saddam's intentions to develop a nuclear weapons program came out in cassette tapes seized by US invading forces. In a recording of a June 1978 speech to Iraqi army officers at the Al-Bakr University for Strategic Studies, Saddam said that the Arabs must acquire nuclear weapons to reach a strategic balance with Israel, and then fight Israel by conventional warfare.[29]

US Disarmament Diplomacy: Ignoring Iraqi WMD Programs

Under both Presidents Ford and Carter, American disarmament policy on nuclear and long-range missiles focused on NATO deployment to deter the Eastern bloc. Carter ceased to support uranium processing to reduce the production of fissile material for civilian purposes. He also endorsed two pieces of legislation in Congress: the Nuclear Nonproliferation Act, in 1978; and strengthening the Arms Export Control Act to include third parties in existing contracts.[30] The Carter administration also endorsed the Nuclear Suppliers Group (NSG) guidelines, published in 1978 by the IAEA, which controlled the transfer of nuclear-related technology and materials to non-nuclear states.[31]

The US Ambassador to France Kenneth Rush was not concerned. He reported from Paris that the Iraqi-French deal was consistent with President Valéry Giscard d'Estaing's plan to expand French technological exports to Arab states. Rush viewed the $3 billion procurement deal, following Saddam's 1975 visit to Paris, as a positive indication of Iraq's openness to the West.[32]

The deal was legal according to international law and, in February 1976, the purchase of the nuclear research plant was reported to the IAEA. The agency had no reservation about the deal, since Iraq was fully eligible to receive technical assistance for civilian nuclear programs and was a signatory to the Comprehensive Safeguard Agreement (CSA) that provided transparency in fissile-material production, including inspection by the IAEA.[33] The issue arose again when a US company, Westinghouse, intended to sign a deal to build and provide a nuclear plant in Egypt. The State Department reassured Paris that, in both cases, the spent nuclear fuel irradiated from the reactor, should be transferred out of the country for recycling, and that there was no reason for concern.[34]

In his election campaign in 1976, Carter stressed his commitment to containing the proliferation of nuclear weapons. He appointed Joseph Nye, a liberal from Harvard, as Deputy under Secretary of State for Science and Technology and chairman of the NSC Group on Nonproliferation of Nuclear Weapons.[35]

In November 1977, the US, together with Britain and other European countries, approached the French government regarding its nuclear deal with Iraq. The French Quai d'Orsay responded firmly by stating that France had 'no intention of consulting others regarding its exports', in particular since the Iraq deal was covered by safeguard agreements and followed the principles of the suppliers group.[36] Gaullist politicians criticised US intervention in French affairs; some considered the US approach to be driven by jealousy of French competitiveness. Others, like Iran, Saudi Arabia, Syria and the USSR, conveyed to France their concerns over the reactor deal.[37] After the US and UK applied diplomatic pressure, d'Estaing cancelled his country's agreement of technology transfer to Pakistan's Chashma facility.

However, France was adamant about carrying out the Iraqi nuclear agreement, anxious about refuting Gaullist allegations that France would submit to American pressure.[38] The US-UK initiative committed twelve industrial states to refrain from any nuclear-related export. It also became a pattern for diplomatic action.[39] As a result, France was compelled to rewrite the clauses that dealt with nuclear fuel for French reactors; since France was not allowed to re-export the highly enriched uranium (HEU) fuel supplied by the US. Iraq's outright rejection of the French proposal to use low-enriched uranium (LEU) fuel, also known as 'caramel', should have raised doubts about the supposed civilian purpose of the nuclear reactor. France had to follow the original agreement and supply French nuclear fuel to operate the reactor; this was four times more expensive to produce.[40]

France and Iraq had additional reasons to keep parts of the nuclear contract unpublished. The text of the agreement was published officially eight months later in *Le Journal Officiel*, including the clause prohibiting Jews from taking part in the project in Iraq and outside Iraq.[41] How did the deal with France materialise in the first place? There were a few indications, though no hard evidence, that Iraq was interested in a plant to produce plutonium (weapons-grade), and that it acquired a reprocessing facility in order to become independent in the fuel cycle. Iraq refused to change the Highly Enriched Uranium fuel for Low Enriched Uranium (LEU) fuel – known as caramel. France was eager to sell, the US perhaps trusted the IAEA safeguards, or rather assessed that Iraq lacked the technical capability to extract plutonium from spent fuel, let alone to develop nuclear weapons, which required advanced technological and scientific skills. Iraq also calculated the time it would take to reach production level, given its lack of expertise.[42] The CIA had alerted that Pakistan had a body of scientists who might offer a rich Arab state, such as Iraq, the technological assistance to develop nuclear weapons, but there was no follow-up or further discussion on Iraq.[43] The US embassy in Paris reported that, in 1978, thirty-eight Iraqi trainees arrived in Paris to join other Iraqi scientists and technicians training in French universities and institutes, as well as at a French reactor.[44] Some French scientists, speaking with *Washington Post* correspondent J.P. Smith, raised the concern that Iraq might use the French reactor to develop, in the future, a nuclear-military capability. Smith published a series of stories on the Iraqi military buildup.[45]

The UK, unlike the US, had closely followed the Iraqi nuclear research program since 1968, when the Soviet research reactor was installed, as well as Baghdad's diplomatic activity on the matter and the academic progress of Iraqi scientists. In April 1975, a scientist from the British Harwell University attended an international conference in Baghdad on nuclear research. He reported that the Iraqi organisers arranged an official visit to the Tawitha nuclear site for conference participants.

Following the conference, an Iraqi nuclear physicist arrived at Harwell for training. These academic exchanges, as well as Iraqi commercial contacts with British firms selling nuclear equipment (mostly for medical use), had to be reported and authorised by the British government's Foreign & Commonwealth Office (FCO).[46] The US did not take precautions regarding two students of nuclear physics: Immad Khadduri (University of Michigan, and PhD from the University of Birmingham, UK) and Khidhir Hamza (MIT and Florida State University) who, after graduation, were drafted into the Iraqi nuclear program. In 1975, two scientists from the IAEC, Hkidhir Hamza and his colleague Hadi al-Ubeidi, arrived at a conference in Santa Fe, New Mexico. They were interested in uranium enrichment by laser, known as atomic vapor laser isotope separation (AVLIS), a costly process then at the experimental stage. They visited the Los Alamos National Laboratory, and then visited the National Electrostatics Corporation, in Wisconsin, where they inquired about purchasing a Pelletron accelerator for $1.5 million.[47] Both Hamza and Khadduri noted how they made use of open source material. The IAEC (Iraqi Atomic Energy Commission) based in Baghdad library had a rich selection of updated publications on nuclear issues, mostly from the US. In the early 1970s, Iraqi scientists had used the full set of abstracts from the Manhattan Project which had been given by the US administration as a gift in 1956, within the 'Atom for Peace' Initiative drafted by President Eisenhower to encourage peaceful use of nuclear technology. Later, the IAEC purchased specific information and patents for its nuclear industry from the World Intellectual Property Organization (WIPO), and from the National Technical Information Service (NTIS) in the US.[48]

In 1979, following repeated Israeli requests, the US Director of Central Intelligence was instructed to check the status of the Iraqi nuclear project. The report it submitted to Carter in October 1979 concluded that Iraq was trying to develop nuclear capability – allegedly for peaceful purposes, but simultaneously to upgrade its military. The report recommended follow-up, yet it concluded that Iraq would not be able to develop a nuclear weapon before the late 1980s.[49] In July 1980, Brzezinski ordered a State Department status update on Iraq's attempted nuclear procurement from France and Italy, along with recommendations for nonproliferation measures.[50]

However, the issue was set aside, due to the assessment that Iraq did not pose a threat to US interests and that measures taken against the deal would harm US-European relations. America's confidence that her allies France and Italy would control the end use of the exported equipment coincided with its low esteem for Iraqi technical capabilities. That assessment continued for years. Furthermore, the US had no interest in harming relations with Saddam, in particular after the fall of the Shah. A senior official in the administration in the late1980s was quoted as saying: 'we knew about the bomb program, but Saddam was our ally, and anyway we did not realize how far along they really were. It was off the radar.'[51]

Not only did Iran and Israel raise their concerns over Iraq with the United States – they discussed the threat with each other. In a meeting in Tel Aviv, in July 1977, between Israeli Defense Minister Ezer Weizman and Iranian General Hasan Tufanian, the latter shared the American perception of Iraq's technological and scientific inferiority in designing its own nuclear weapons. However, he raised concerns over the Soviet-made long-range SSMs possessed by Iraq, which, in the future, would be able to carry nuclear warheads. At the meeting, Israel's Chief of General Staff Mordechai Gur told Tufanian that the French-built plant could enable Iraq to develop nuclear weapons within five to seven years.[52]

The US, in the 1970s, had no hard evidence to indicate that an Iraqi nuclear program would be used aggressively and for military purposes. It thus underplayed the concerns of its allies.-

Chemical and Biological Weapons Programs

Nuclear facilities require specific technologies and material, and are difficult to hide. By contrast, chemical and biological weapons programs, while banned by international charters, could have proceeded under cover of legitimate production of civilian substances. Raw materials for production of CW and BW were common in the chemical and pharmaceutical industries, and the production facilities and labs had no strict specifications.

The US did not suspect that scientific or medical cooperation with Iraq might lead to Iraq's developing chemical or biological weapons. Iraqi Lt. Gen. Nizar al-Attar led an intelligence unit which, from the 1960s, investigated the feasibility of developing chemical and biological weapons. He even visited the Fort McClellan National Guard base in Alabama. Under the Ba'th, he became the leader of the chemical and biological weapons programs. A British dossier on WMD found that Iraq's chemical weapons program had begun secretly in Rashad, north east of Baghdad, in 1971. In 1974, an institute named after the tenth century mythological scientist *Al-Hasan Ibn al-Haytham* was established for research and development.[53] By the late 1970s, a commercial-scale production plant, to be known as Al-Muthana, was planned in the desert, forty-two miles northwest of Baghdad. Officially, the site was a government-run plant that manufactured pesticides for agriculture. Actually, it produced tear gas, known as CS, for riot control, and mustard gas. Later, it produced nerve agents, such as Tabun, Sarin and VX, as well as organic phosphates, such as Malathion and Parathion, which were used for agriculture. The Ba'th used mustard gas and nerve agents in Iraq's war with Iran, and later against Iraqi Kurds in Halabja in 1988.[54]

Iraq's biological-weapons program was boosted in the mid-1970s, in the Salman Pak military facility near Baghdad, which was surrounded by three tributaries of the Euphrates River. The program made slow progress. In this early period in the 1970s, it developed known pathogenic agents, such as anthrax, botulinum and aflatoxin. In 1978, following reorganisation, the program was boosted by the addition of scientists and was moved to Al-Muthana, near where the chemical weapons project and other secret programs were being developed.[55] It is likely that the Soviets, who were known to produce chemical weapons, assisted Iraq at least in the early stages of those programs. In June 1974, a Kurdish delegation led by Sami Abd al-Rahman, met with members of the US mission to the United Nations and discussed the heavy bombing by Iraq of the Kurdish area. The Kurds, who were known to supply reliable intelligence on Iraqi military operations, insisted that the USSR provided Iraq with poison gas, which Baghdad was 'prepared to use' at any time.[56]

It is not clear to what extent the US was aware of the status of these programs. In that early period, there was no inspection mechanism to enforce the ban on the production of chemical and biological weapons. The US's misperception that Iraq would not dare to, or was not able to, develop such weapons – banned and delegitimised, as the weapons were, by the international community – was consistent with its complacency towards the Iraqi nuclear program, ignoring concerns raised by allies.

Retrospectively, one can find signs of Iraq's intention to develop biological weapons in 1971. Thousands of Iraqis in the northern periphery were accidently poisoned in 1971 by methyl mercury, as a result of eating mercury-treated grains imported from the US. Dr T.W. Clarkson, a specialist from the US's University of Rochester, was invited by Iraq to treat the victims. This medical cooperation with an Iraqi medical team formed the basis for the publication in the West of important articles on mercury in food, in particular in the tuna-fish industry. In September 1974, Baghdad hosted an international conference sponsored by the World Health Organization and the UN's Food and Agriculture Organization to present the findings of this joint research.[57] In 1975, when Iraq was developing its chemical weapons program, it approached Pfaudler, a firm based in Rochester NY, to construct a turn-key production plant for producing organic pesticides for agriculture. Negotiations stalled when Iraq insisted on skipping the stage of building a pilot plant and demanded the immediate construction of a factory capable of producing 1,200 tons of organic toxins annually. The procurement did not materialise, but Iraq benefitted from these negotiations, since it now had Pfaudler's blueprints for the pilot plant and could approach other Western firms. Eventually, Iraq built up its own industry, in particular for production of fertilisers and pesticides for farming that could be a legitimate cover for developing chemical weapons.[58]

Saddam was the driving force behind these ambitious programs. Yet, one can find circumstantial parallels between Saddam's decisions to go nuclear and peak humiliating events experienced by Iraq with its rival Iran. Two major events demonstrated the Shah's power over Iraq, which Saddam took to be most humiliating, personally and nationally. The first was Iran's takeover of the Shatt al-Arab in 1969 by unilaterally annulling the 1937 agreement with Iraq, followed by Iran's seizure, in 1972, of the Straits of Hurmuz islands belonging to the UAE. According to some sources, Saddam, in 1972, had decided to initiate a nuclear program as a consequence. The second event was the Algiers Agreement in March 1975, when Saddam had to give up Iraqi claims to the Shatt al-Arab and the province of Khuzistan in exchange for ending the Kurdish rebellion. Saddam then initiated the project to build, with French assistance, the Osirak nuclear reactor so he could independently produce weapons-grade fissile material immediately after the Algier's Agreement with Iran. Indeed he visited Paris on his way from Algiers in April 1975. The Iraqi determination to become nuclear was not tied to the Iranian threat alone, yet Saddam's feeling of dishonour, defeat and helplessness generated the incentive for his nuclear ambition.[59]

Notes

1. UNSCOM (United Nations Special Commission) was created in April 1991 upon Security Council Resolution 687 to oversee Iraqi compliance of destruction of WMD sites, succeeded in 1999 by UNMOVIC (United Nations Monitoring, Verification and Inspection Commission).
2. A. Baram, 'An Analysis of Iraqi WMD Strategy', *The Nonproliferation Review* (Summer 2001), pp. 25–39; K. Hamza, *Saddam's Bombmaker* (New York: Scribner, 2000), pp. 74–7.
3. The Soviet IRT-2000 research reactor, set in 1968, was a pool-type reactor, which originally used light water as a moderator and coolant, but could be upgraded to produce enriched uranium. The Soviet-Iraqi Agreement for Scientific and Technical Cooperation on nuclear energy was signed on 19 December 1971, INA, 19 December 1971.
4. K. Timmerman, *The Death Lobby – How the West Armed Iraq* (New York: Bantam Books, 1991), pp. 25, 29; Tehran 3509 (Helms), 13 April 1975; Tehran 3811 (Miklos), 24 April 1975. According to Timmerman, Giraud's close relations with Iraq helped his appointment as Minister of Industry in 1978.
5. I. Khadduri, *Iraq's Nuclear Mirage, Memoirs and Delusions* (Richmond Hill, Ontario: Springhead Publishers, 2003), p. 71
6. Memorandum (Brzezinski) to the President, 11 November 1977, NSC Weekly, *DDRS*; Timmerman, *The Death Lobby*, pp. 30–3.
7. C. Duelfer, 'A *Comprehensive Report of the Special Advisor to the DCI on Iraq*', WMD, 30 September 2004, http://www.cia.gov/cia/reports/iraq_wmd_2004; http://permanent.

access.gpo.gov/DuelferRpt/Volume_3.pdf., last accessed 7 July 2008; P. Malovany, *The Wars of Modern Babylon* (Tel Aviv: Maarachot, 2009) p. 906; Albright & Hamza, 'Iraq's Reconstitution of its Nuclear Weapons Program', *Arms Control Today* (October 1998), http://legacy.armscontrol.org/act/1998_10/daoc98, last accessed 7 July 2008.

8. K. Weissman & H. Krosney, *The Islamic Bomb* (New York: NYT Books, 1981), p. 97; Iraqi scientists worked on various methods to enrich uranium. Some were still experimental in Western publications and could produce very small quantities of fissile material, such as EMIS (electromagnetic Isotope separation), of AVLIS (atomic vapor laser Isotope separation). Albright & Hamza, 'Iraq's Reconstitution of its Nuclear Weapons Program'.

9. *IAEA* INFSIRC 172, 22 February 1973.

10. The Ba'th ratified the NPT, 29 October 1969, http://disarmament.un.org/treaties/s/iraq, last accessed 15 August 2017.

11. In 1975, Iraq pledged to contribute $25,000 voluntarily to the IAEA Technical Cooperation Program.
    US Mission IAEA Vienna 10165, 6 December 1974; Vienna 314, 15 January 1975.

12. *NUCLEAR NEWS*, March 1975, 18:4, p. 5; Tel Aviv 1185 (Toon), 18 February 1976.

13. Hamza, *Saddam's Bombmaker*, pp. 74–7; K. Hamza, 'Inside Saddam's Secret Nuclear Program', *Bulletin of the Atomic Scientists*, 54(5) (September/October 1998).

14. Hamza, *Saddam's Bombmaker*, pp. 67–84.

15. Joint Intelligence Committee (JIC), *Iraq's Weapons of Mass Destruction: The Assessment of the British Government*, 24 September 2002 ('The British Dossier'), www.archive2.officiqal-documents.co.uk/document/reps/iraqdossier.pdf; 'The British Dossier', released summary, February 2003, http://nsarchive.gwu.edu/NSAEBB/NSAEBB80/wmd11.pdf, last accessed June 2008; C. Duelfer, 'A Comprehensive Report of the Special Advisor to the DCI on Iraq'; Malovany, *The Wars of Modern Babylon*, pp. 902–8.

17. The Commission on the Intelligence Capabilities of the United States Regarding WMD was co-chaired by Senator Charles Robb (left) and Judge Laurence Silberman (right). The commission had no mandate to oversee political decision making processes, based on the false intelligence.

18. The Commission was formed in 2009, chaired by Sir John Chilcot and, unlike the US Inquiry, had a broad mandate. Report was submitted in July 2016.

19. Khadduri, *Iraq's Nuclear Mirage, Memoirs and Delusions*, p. 61.

20. Weissman & Krosney, *The Islamic Bomb*, p. 89.

21. The French Chargé d'Affairs in Baghdad told the Canadian ambassador about the sale of the French nuclear reactor to Iraq. The Canadians passed the information to Washington. Baghdad 1149, 11 November 1975. Baghdad 507, 661 (Lowrie), 10 May, 19 June 1975.

22. Weissman & Krosney, *The Islamic Bomb*, p. 92; http://fas.org/nuke/guide/iraq/facility/osiraq.htm, last accessed July 2008.

23. Jack Anderson, 'France to Push Iraqi Nuclear Deal', *WP*, 12 January 1978; William Branigan, 'Iraqi Buildup Stirs Concern', *WP*, 27 February 1978.

24. The quality of Israeli intelligence was appreciated, in spite of the interpretation and assessment regarding Iraqi intention being disregarded: for example, Meeting of Israeli FM Alon with Congressional delegation led by Senator Ribicoff, Tel Aviv 7616 (Toon), 9 November 1976; Briefing by Israeli MFA analyst Yael Vered to US ambassador Toon, Tel Aviv 5698 (Toon), 5 September 1975; Tel Aviv 1436 (Keating), 12 March 1974.

25. Tehran 11468, 11478 (Helms), 16 November 1976.

26. *Al-Jumhuriyya*, 21 July 1980. Egypt was the first to argue that the opposition in the West to the Arabs developing nuclear capabilities was due to Israeli interest in keeping the Arabs undeveloped.

27. E. Goldstein, Human Rights Watch, 'Profile of Dr. Hussein Shahristani', Huqoqalinasan.org. www.mafqud.org/en/partners/hio/goldstein.htm; S. Salama & C. Hunter, 'Leading Iraqi Nuclear Scientist, Once Imprisoned, Elected to Prominent Post', CNS at the Monterey Institute of International Studies, 7 June 2005, http://cns.miis.edu/stories/050615.htm; I. Khadduri, *Iraq's Nuclear Mirage, Memoirs and Delusions*, p. 71; the explosion (6 April 1979) in a French storage facility of components for the Iraqi reactor was attributed to Israel: Paris 11683 (Hartman), 11 April 1979, DNSA.

28. The torture of Shahrastani was published by Amnesty International which approached the Iraqi ambassador in Paris in July 1981. Weissman & Krosney, *The Islamic Bomb*, pp. 252–25; Hamza, *Saddam's Bombmaker*, p.126.

29. Saddam Hussein: 'If we were to have the atom, we would make the conventional armies fight without using the atom', *CRRC SH* PDWN-D-000-341, 3 June 1978.

30. A. Andrews, 'Nuclear fuel reprocessing: U.S. policy development', *CRS Report for Congress*, 27 March 2008; *Nuclear Regulatory Legislation*, NUREC 0980, Vol. 3, No. 9, January 2011, U.S. Nuclear Regulatory Commission, Washington DC, 1029–1061, http://www.nrc.gov/reading-rm/doc-collections/nuregs/staff/sr0980/v3/sr0980v3.pdf, last accessed January 2012.

31. INFCIRC/254, 'to apply to nuclear transfers for peaceful purposes to help ensure that such transfers would not be diverted to an unsafeguarded nuclear fuel cycle or nuclear explosive activities', http://fas.org/nuke/control/nsg/text/inf254.htm, last accessed January 2014.

32. Paris (Rush) 410, 430, 5534, 23731, 3, 4, 7 January, 15 September 1975.

33. IAEA Vienna 874 (Labowitz), 4 February 1976.

34. 'All of the reprocessing of the irradiated material as well as the storage and fabrication of the plutonium will occur outside of Iraq.' State 80410 to Paris, 3 April 1976.

35. J. Carter, *Keeping Faith: Memoirs of a President* (New York: Bantam Books, 1982), pp. 212–65; J.S. Nye, 'Nonproliferation: A Long-Term Strategy', *Foreign Affairs*, 56(3) (April 1978), pp. 601–23.

36. Paris 01144 (Hartman), 13 January 1978.

37. Weissman & Krosney *The Islamic Bomb*, pp. 233–7.

38. State 227260 to Paris, 7 September 1978; Vienna, 13 September 1978, 'The Nuclear Vault', *National Security Archive*, www.gwu.edu/~nsarchiv/nukevault/index.htm.

39. State 281962 (Vance), 4 November 1978.

40. Jack Anderson, 'France to push Iraqi Nuclear Deal', *WP*, 12 January 1978.

41. Eric Laurent, *La Figaro*, 3 September 1990, in Timmerman, *The Death Lobby*, p. 33, note 6.

42. Self-production of fissile material, plutonium or enriched uranium weapons-grade, was an ambitious challenge, required import of knowledge, and specific materials, that are under export controls.

43. NIO for Nuclear Proliferation (Despres) to the DCI NFAC 3871-79, 24 July 1979, 'The Nuclear Vault', *National Security Archive*, http://nsarchive.gwu.edu/nukevault/ebb333/doc41.PDF, last accessed June 2012.

44. Paris 11983 (Hartman), 11 April 1979, *DDRS*.

45. J.P. Smith, 'Iraq's Nuclear Arms Option', *WP*, 8 August 1978.
46. British Embassy Baghdad (Graham), 16 April 1975; UK Atomic Energy Authority (Phelps) to Energy Department and FCO, 23 July 1975, FCO 8/2565, *TNA*.
47. Hamza, *Saddam's Bombmaker*, pp. 97–100.
48. I. Khadduri, *Iraq's Nuclear Mirage, Memoirs and Delusions*, pp. 98–9.
49. DCI Stansfield Turner to the President, 22 October 1979, *Carter Presidential Library*, Brzezinski Material.
50. Memorandum from Brzezinski to Secretary of State, 'French and Italian Nuclear Cooperation with Iraq', secret/sensitive, 28 July 1980, *Carter Presidential Library*, Brzezinski Material.
51. Cockburn & Cockburn, *Out of the Ashes, The Resurrection of Saddam Hussein* (New York: Harper Collins, 1999), p. 90.
52. Israeli Minister of Defense Weizman and Iranian Deputy Minister of Defense General Tufanian, Tel Aviv, 18 July 1977, transcript transferred to the US, DNSA; General M. Gur statement to the Washington *WP*, 30 July 1977.
53. *Al-Hasan Ibn al-Haytham*, born in Basra 965, considered one of the founding fathers of mathematics and experimental science in the Golden Age of Muslim civilisation.
54. JIC, *Iraq's Weapons of Mass Destruction*; Albright & Hamza, *Arms Control Today* (October 1998).
55. JIC, *Iraq's Weapons of Mass Destruction*; Duelfer Report, 'A *Comprehensive Report of the Special Advisor to the DCI on Iraq*', Vol III.
56. USUN2213 (Schvafele), 19 June 1974.
57. Iraq hosted a WHO Conference on mercury poisoning in Baghdad, 9–13 September 1974. Most scientific literature published on this case had been based on the same group of patients treated in the Baghdad Hospital, with no reference to other areas in Iraq or unreported cases. For example, publication by Iraqi pediatricians: Rustum & T. Hamdi, 'Methyl Mercury Poisoning in Iraq: a Neurological Study', *Brain*, 47 (1974), pp. 499–510; Laman Amin Zaki et al., 'Methyl Mercury Poisoning in Iraqi Children: Clinical Observation over Two Years', *British Medical Journal*, 1(1978), pp. 613–16, http://www.bmj.com/cgi/reprint/1/6113/613, last accessed April 2011.
58. Timmerman, *The Death Lobby*, pp. 36–7; C. Coughlin, *Saddam: King of Terror* (New York: Harper Collins, 2002), pp. 129–31.
59. Khidhir Hamza in an interview to A. Baram (1999), 'An Analysis of Iraqi WMD Strategy', *The Nonproliferation Review* (Summer 2001), pp. 25–6.

8

Bilateral Relations: Courtship and Rebuff

Though formal diplomatic relations with the United States remained at a low level, the Iraqi regime welcomed visits by US administration officials, congressional delegations, journalists and business people. The flow of American visitors increased in the second half of the 1970s, when Iraq issued international tenders for infrastructure projects. American visitors received generous hospitality, guided tours and meetings with Ba'th officials. The regime apparently viewed them as valuable, too, for public-relations purposes without having to resume full diplomatic relations.

Iraq made a special effort at the peak of its fighting on the Iranian-Kurdish front and the Ba'th regime sent more signals, and moderated the aggressive rhetoric towards the US. Senator James Abourezk visited Baghdad in January 1974.[1] David Rockefeller, chairman of Chase Manhattan Bank and a prominent figure in the American corporate world with leverage in both The World Bank and the International Monetary Fund (IMF), came in January 1975 and was received by Saddam. That constituted a special Iraqi gesture, given that Saddam usually avoided meeting American dignitaries. Rockefeller was close to Kissinger, and reported upon his return that the Kurdish rebellion was stressful for Iraq. Rockefeller urged Kissinger to intervene with the Shah to cease his support of the Kurds. The general impression of the American visitors was that the Kurdish issue was the main obstacle for normalisation of relations with the US, and that Iraq was eager to expand trade with the US.[2]

The US Interest Section promoted trade with Iraq, sending such information as bids and tenders to Washington, since most major projects were initiated and run by the Iraqi government, offering contacts for promoting business. Visitors were advised to be aware of Iraqi sensitivities, for example, by calling the Persian Gulf the 'Arab Gulf' only, avoiding any mention of Israel and concealing any sign of affiliation with the Jewish faith or with the Free Masons.[3]

Iraq's attitude to Western Europe was distinctly different. Full relations were resumed with most countries in that region, and many European visitors were honoured with a meeting with Saddam, including the delegation of the Socialist International (SI), led by chairman Bent Carlsson (Sweden) and his deputy Bruno Kreisky (Austria), as mentioned earlier. Those meetings impressed the SI delegation deeply, despite SI's having a different policy towards the Middle East conflict, as shown by their support for the US-led Geneva conference for peace in the Middle East.[4]

On his second visit in April 1975, following the Algiers Agreement that ended the Kurdish rebellion, Rockefeller was not met by Saddam. Senators Kennedy (May 1975), Fulbright (June 1975) and Stevenson (February 1976) also had their request to meet Saddam rejected. Kennedy was persistent about having an open discussion with Saddam; he was kept waiting until the last minute, when his request was denied. Lowrie reported that officials of the Ministry of Foreign Affairs led Kennedy to believe that the meeting would take place. Lowrie later explained that the reason for Saddam's reluctance to meet Americans was to avoid criticism from some Ba'thi leaders who opposed close relations with the US, let alone set a date for resuming full relations.[5] The British ambassador, J.A.N. Graham, who met with Kennedy in Baghdad, offered a more sober analysis of the Iraqi policy of encouraging visits by congressional delegations: Baghdad had an interest in increasing the volume of trade, including food, with the US, while keeping a low profile in diplomatic relations so that it could carry on with an anti-American public policy. 'It suits their book to have the Americans as a foreign devil to abuse', Graham said.[6]

American expectations that the end of the Kurdish rebellion in 1975 would become a turning point in bilateral relations with Iraq proved to be a baseless illusion. Hostility to the US continued in the Iraqi media. Iraqis did not need US endorsement to end the Shah's aid to the Kurds, and the Ba'th could return to steadfastness (*sumud*) and rejection (*rafd*) of any political solution that would include Israel.

Growing US-Iraqi Trade: A Dubious Indication?

Iraq's persistent interest in expanding trade with the US raises a few questions. Firstly, to what extent did bilateral trade expand in absolute numbers and in relation to Iraq's overall foreign trade? Secondly, did these trade relations with the US serve the two countries' mutual interests? Most importantly, did the commercial relationship function as a channel for a possible political rapprochement?

US export of agricultural products to Iraq increased dramatically in less than a decade: from $4.9 million in 1971 to $142 million in 1979.[7] Expanding food exports had been an important American interest, mostly in rural states.

The governor of Mississippi, William Waller, visited Iraq in April 1975 and again in October. Senator Adlai Stevenson came in February 1976 on a trade mission that included representatives from such agricultural states such as Indiana, Illinois, North Carolina and Texas.[8] In 1974, Iraq became the fourth-large export destination in the Arab world for American food; it bought, primarily, poultry and rice.[9] This indicated a basic food shortage in Iraq, which made it an attractive client for American producers.

In spite of the growth of exports in the 1970s, the US's share of overall food exports to Iraq remained small relative to other Western exporters. This shortfall was discussed in a Senate hearing on US agricultural exports in June 1979. A Congressional Research Service report prepared for the Senate Subcommittee on International Trade estimated that, in spite of Iraq's wide investments in agricultural infrastructure, in particular irrigation, Iraq would be unable to produce sufficient food for its population, which was rapidly urbanising and would need such agricultural products as grain and rice. The report noted that the Ba'th's agrarian reform established cooperative farming to replace the private sector – reform that would lower productivity and increase the need to import food products.[10] The US supplied only 17 percent of all grain imports to Iraq, behind Australia and Canada. Senators called for increasing US food exports to OPEC states, and in particular to Iraq, to serve America's national and business interests.[11] The Iraqi regime was less bothered by those figures. It preferred to import grain from other suppliers. Its main interest in US products was technology, not food. However, even though the Ba'th kept contacts with the US low key, grain and other agricultural shipments reached Iraqi farmers and food distributers directly, carrying commercial logos of their country of origin, namely the US.

American technology and science had been highly admired by previous Iraqi regimes as well as by Saddam. Since US export controls were enforced on arms and military equipment, Iraqi procurement efforts were aimed at civilian technology, including full production lines ('turnkey' facilities).[12]

Iraq's import of agricultural machinery from the US grew from $649,000 in 1970 to $9.6 million in 1975 and $30.7 million in 1979. Still, that was only 3-7 percent of the total Iraqi procurement from the US. Iraq imported mostly heavy equipment, trucks, vehicles, spare parts, engines, machine tools, and such metal-treatment tools as milling and lathe machines to be able to produce their own machineries independently, which implied their intentions to develop clandestine programs. They avoided imports that would require long term contact with the exporter including maintenance and service. Imports from the US were restricted to spare parts and other items that could not be produced in Iraq or purchased outside the US.[13]

US exports to Iraq served Baghdad's interests without drawing suspicion back home regarding Iraqi intentions, aside from the export controls that had been tightened by Congress. Bilateral trade in this period generally increased in volume, but the growth rate of US exports did not catch up with the exponential growth of all international exports to Iraq. It remained much lower than other countries exporting to Iraq. US exports to Iraq increased from $3 million in 1970 to $440 million in 1979.[14]

Even this significant growth of US exports to Iraq was still small when considering that Iraq's imports in 1979 reached $10 billion. US food products made up only 10 percent of Iraq's total food imports. In the period of 1975–9, Iraq expanded trade with the West significantly to 80 percent of all of its imports and 60 percent of all its exports.[15] Iraqi-US trade remained relatively minor, compared to Iraq's trade with other Western states.[16] From 1972 to 1975, American imports to Iraq comprised less than 5 percent of the total imports to Iraq. In 1976, Iraq's US imports reached a peak of 9.8 percent, compared to 16 percent from Japan, 12 percent from France and 22 percent from West Germany. By 1979, American imports fell to 6 percent of the total, compared to 16 percent of Iraq's imports from West Germany and 22 percent from Japan.[17]

Neither Iraq nor the US fully pursued their trade interests. While the US wished to export mostly food and consumer goods, Iraq preferred to import these products from other Western states. Whereas Iraq wanted to procure advanced American technology, mostly for the military, US export controls restricted most transfers of this nature to countries with which the US did not have full diplomatic relations, or to countries involved in terrorism.

On its side, Iraq rejected all of the US's approaches to resume diplomatic relations. It used different arguments and excuses to postpone the process indefinitely, while continuously seeking to acquire more American technology. The Iraqi wish list included aircrafts (Boeing), tracks, other vehicles, agricultural and construction machinery, communication systems, and military items and much more. In short, trade relations did not pave the way for the rapprochement that the US was hoping for. The great expectations of both sides on either the technological (Iraq's) or the diplomatic level did not materialise.

Courtship and Rebuff

After the Algiers Agreement was signed in 1975, the US had high expectations for a breakthrough with Iraq. The long-awaited, high-level meeting between Kissinger and the Iraqi Foreign Minister Sa'dun Hammadi took place secretly on 17 December 1975, in Paris, as most diplomats and journalists were leaving New York for Christmas and the winter break. The Kissinger-Hammadi meeting, at the Iraqi ambassador's residence, lasted less than an hour. Kissinger, accompanied by Peter Rodman of the National Security Council, came to discuss three issues: resuming diplomatic relations, presenting the US position on the Arab-Israeli conflict and expressing the US's strong rejection of the Arab group's wish to expel Israel from the UN.

Kissinger's agenda would be too ambitious, as the only topic they discussed was the Arab-Israeli conflict, which proved to be a non-starter for Hammadi even though Kissinger did not refrain from harsh criticism of Israel.[18] From the US perspective, the meeting failed in that it did not establish a framework for a bilateral dialogue. To Iraq, the Kurdish issue was more important, with Hammadi requesting a clear assurance that the US would discontinue providing assistance to the Kurds.[19] While the US could not point to any progress following the meeting, Iraq could see the preservation of the status quo as an achievement in itself. It actually helped the expansion of trade without changing the low-level diplomatic relationship.[20]

Understanding that Iraq would not change its attitude towards the US, even after the Kurdish rebellion ended, Ford and Kissinger developed a realistic approach that marginalised Iraq in foreign policy discussions. A US intelligence report concluded that there was little likelihood of changing US-Iraqi relations, 'given the current regime's perception of US policies and given American support for its allies in the region – Saudi Arabia, Iran and Israel ... Iraq remains outside the periphery of American interests in the Middle East.'[21] The report concluded in this manner, which might explain the US marginalisation of Iraq:

> The prevailing Iraqi attitude towards the US – cool, slightly suspicious but not overtly hostile – is perhaps the best that can be expected, given the fundamental divergence of interests. So long as Iraq finds it advantageous to bar Soviet military use of its facilities and to cooperate in maintaining orderly relations among the several Gulf States, it contributes, albeit inadvertently, to overall US goals in the Middle East.[22]

Carter's foreign policy approach followed his optimistic worldview. It called for reconciliation and finding common ground with long-time rivals – Iraq, the USSR, China, Cuba and North Korea – 'based on mutual respect'.[23] Carter called for normalisation with such radical states in the Middle East and Africa as Iraq, Algeria and Somalia. [24] Consequently, the new administration sent indirect messages to Iraq via Middle Eastern leaders that it welcomed closer relations.[25] In May 1977, Under Secretary of State Philip C. Habib visited Baghdad, anticipating that Iraq would be more responsive to an American direct approach made by himself, a senior official of Lebanese-Christian descent.

But it did not happen. Hammadi told Habib that Iraq could not take the risk of resuming relations with the US, which he said would harm Iraq's image in the Arab world; moreover, Hammadi told Habib that his government believed that the US was involved in negotiating a collective security agreement for the Gulf, and warned that such an American-led pact would have generated further conflict. Habib denied any US involvement in such negotiations.[26] At the same time, Wiley, the head of the Interest Section, reported receiving 'positive', unofficial messages from Iraqi officials, and advised the administration to let Iraqi decision-makers advance at their own pace. He added that the US should not take Iraqi public statements too literally.[27] In late 1977, a Kuwaiti newspaper, *Al-Yaqza*, reported that Yugoslavia's president, Josip Broz Tito, would mediate discussions on the resumption of relations. In August 1977, Iraq's information minister denied rumours of secret negotiations, stating that, when the time was appropriate, Iraq would negotiate openly.[28]

In October 1977, Secretary of State Cyrus Vance met his counterpart, Hammadi, during the opening of the UN General Assembly in New York. The Iraqis insisted that the meeting be formal. Though his English was fluent, Hammadi spoke Arabic through an interpreter. According to a British report, Hammadi posed to Vance some nuisance questions on US involvement in a Gulf security pact, an obviously futile issue since months earlier, in May, Hammadi had posed the same question to Phillip Habib in Baghdad, and Habib had denied the claim on the spot.[29] The general impression of both the Americans and the British diplomats was that Hammadi avoided dealing with the main issue of bilateral relations.[30]

The Iraqis continued sending mixed messages. In early December, Saddam told Turkish Prime Minister Bülent Ecevit that the absence of Iraqi relations with the US was 'abnormal' and should be mended. He commended the US for not interfering in Iraqi affairs since 1975, and stated that relations would be resumed – but only when it would not look as if Iraq was surrendering to American pressure.[31] Vance did not give up. In December, he dispatched David Newsom, a veteran diplomat with wide experience in the Middle East, to meet with officials of the Iraqi Interest Section in Washington but it was to no avail.[32]

Most likely, the Iraqis themselves initiated the rumours of closer relations with the US, intending to encourage the American courtship, then rejecting the State Department's direct and indirect approaches in response. The tactics of sending ambiguous, positive messages served Saddam in several ways. Firstly, the signals encouraged the US State and Commerce departments to expand trade with Iraq and to issue waivers on technological exports. Secondly, it warned the US away from interfering in domestic Iraqi affairs (such as the Kurds resuming guerilla attacks in northern Iraq). Thirdly, and most importantly, this pattern of continuous courtship and rejection suited Saddam's ego, bolstering his image in the Middle East for defying the US.

Another example of America's goodwill approach failing involved Senator Kennedy in 1977. Fr Carney Gavin, curator of the Harvard Semitic Museum, visited Baghdad to bring back cuneiform Hittite clay tablets that were taken out of Iraq in the 1930s for a Harvard archeological exhibition and never returned. The hope was that the gesture would help to reestablish a wider US-Iraqi relationship. But there was no change of attitude as a result. Moreover, Iraqi media reported only about the return of the 'plundered' tablets.[33]

Medical Cooperation, 1977–8

Peter Bourne, a brilliant psychiatrist, and Carter's confidant, visited Iraq in early November 1976, soon after the US election, as a member of the president-elect's transition team. The official purpose of his visit was a Pan-Arab conference on drugs and alcohol addiction, which was Bourne's expertise. He was received by senior Ba'thi leaders like Health Minister Riad Ibrahim and Foreign Minister Sa'adun Hammadi; the latter was most curious about the incoming president, knowing that he was a nontraditional politician. In his report to Carter, Bourne wrote that Hammadi 'was particularly eager to discuss the large black vote that you received in the election, your interest in health and social programs, [and] the fact you were not a captive of big business, or any other special interest group'.[34]

Bourne and the State Department interpreted Hammadi's curiosity as a positive signal regarding Iraq's interest in turning a new page and establishing closer relations with the US.[35] It was far too optimistic and based on wishful thinking. It was natural for Hammadi, considered in the Ba'th to be an expert on US affairs, to follow US politics. Bourne would be appointed a special assistant to the president on health issues, responsible for health cooperation with Third World countries, including Cuba and Iraq.[36]

The administration, apparently, was not aware of previous medical cooperation projects with Ba'thi Iraq, such as the medical team led by Dr

Clarkson (from Rochester, NY), that visited Iraq to deal with mercury poisoning in 1971; and the discreet visit to Johns Hopkins Hospital in Baltimore made by Saddam's wife Sajida for medical treatment in May 1974. In April 1977, Wiley passed along the Ministry of Foreign Affairs' urgent request for a team of doctors to be sent secretly to treat 'a VIP at the Iraqi presidency'. It was Saddam, who was experiencing excruciating pain due to herniated vertebral discs.[37] Three specialists were assigned to Baghdad, led by neurosurgeon Henry Feffer. Upon arrival, they found out that similar medical teams from Great Britain, France, West Germany and Denmark had been invited, too, to provide diagnoses. Saddam was relieved to learn that the Western teams were unanimous in concluding that surgery was not needed, unlike Eastern bloc doctors, who had recommended surgery.[38] Each of the American doctors sent to Baghdad received a personal letter from Carter, thanking him for 'strengthening diplomatic relations with the Government in Iraq' and taking part in 'efforts in the cause of peace and security of the United States'.[39] In a letter to Bourne, Minister of Health Riad Ibrahim expressed thanks to the US team.[40]

The administration soon set up an interagency working group to define and initiate medical cooperation with Iraq. The detailed report, based on IMF reports (which had received the data from Iraq), focused on public health, medical education, and sanitation and on mapping health services in cities and in the periphery.[41] The report raised Iraqi sensitivity towards US contacts with Israel, and advised restraint and discretion while dealing with Iraqis, to avoid criticism by some Ba'thi senior officials opposed to close cooperation with the US. The report offered practical advice to minimise written correspondence and give preference to verbal interaction on international events. 'Ideally, because of Arab psychology, this should take place in a face-to-face gathering', it stated.[42] Vance urged Wiley to accelerate medical cooperation as an incentive for establishing diplomatic normalisation.[43] In the State Department, the medical channel was seen as a substitute for the lack of progress on the political-diplomatic level.

In October, Ibrahim arrived in Washington, and Bourne was invited to visit Baghdad to promote cooperation.[44] The Iraqis had no intention of promoting diplomatic relations, yet they had a vested interest in medical cooperation for the obvious benefit inherent in promoting medical standards by adopting modern medical practices and technologies. Saddam also appreciated American medicine, and had his own interest in employing medical experts to handle his personal care, with full discretion away from the public eye and the media. Moreover, there had been ongoing medical and health cooperation through various international organisations, such as the United Nations Development Program (UNDP), the WHO and the FAO.

The Ba'th considered that this cooperation demonstrated openness and a positive approach towards the new US administration, in a low profile manner, without publicity and without paying the political price of moderation (such as by resuming relations) that would raise harsh criticism against Iraq in the Arab world.

A possible, hidden benefit of scientific cooperation on public health and preventive medicine was access to substances that might be useful for an Iraqi biological-weapons program, such as that which had been established at the Salman Pak site, twenty kilometres south of Baghdad. The stockpiling and production of vaccines that did not require export licenses was one such step. Bourne had met Deputy Health Minister Dr A.D. Niyazi, who was Director of the Endemic Diseases Institute, Baghdad. In the 1980s, Iraq received, from the Atlanta-based Centers for Disease Control and Prevention, at least twenty samples of viruses and bacteria that cause diseases.[45] The comprehensive report and files of Bourne – dealing with the political, psychological and legal aspects of medical cooperation with Iraq – did not mention any suspicion that Iraq might have abused this cooperation to acquire scientific knowledge to produce biological weapons.[46]

In the summer of 1978, when Bourne and his delegation were about to leave for Baghdad, the State Department recommended slowing down the pace of contact with senior Iraqi officials. This was due to political sensitivity in Congress, so the visit was postponed. For example, Senator Abraham Ribicoff was then promoting economic sanctions against countries sponsoring international terrorism. The State Department's Bureau of Intelligence and Research (INR) intended to rebuff the legislation and present medical cooperation with Iraq as a strategic tool to dissuade Iraq from sponsoring terrorism. However, Deputy Assistant Secretary of State Morris Draper anticipated public objection in Congress to any form of cooperation with Iraq, which he believed would harm the sensitive nature of the bilateral medical cooperation.[47]

Bourne resigned from the White House in July 1978 following embarrassing reports on improper behavior.[48] A disappointed Bourne said that the cancellation of his visit and the delay in the bilateral cooperation opened the door for Cuba to arrange a program of medical cooperation with Iraq, although Iraq clearly preferred American medicine.[49] Iraqi officials who visited the United States in October 1977, attended the Annual Conference of Arab Postgraduates from American universities, held in Detroit. The Iraqi officials established contact with expatriates who had graduated from American universities, trying to attract them to return to Iraq and take part in the country's medical and scientific modernisation program. The cooperation continued because it was in Iraq's interest. The head of the Interest Section in Baghdad viewed the return of Iraqi-born doctors, graduates of American universities, and their placement in key positions, as improving the US's image in Iraq and strengthening bilateral relations.[50] On 16 October 1978, Health Minister Riad Ibrahim opened a conference in Baghdad of 130 Arab-American doctors, and presented them with career opportunities in medicine and science.[51]

Mutual Misperception

US Courtship vs. Iraqi Evasion

During the period under study, full diplomatic relations had not been resumed. A Belgian flag flew over US property in Baghdad, and an Indian flag represented Iraqi interests in Washington. The US was the only country with which Iraq had not resumed relations after ties had been cut in 1967. Iraq set a pattern: sending, through various channels, ambiguously positive signals to the US, insinuating readiness to improve relations. The US then responded by sending a clear message of its readiness to negotiate a resumption of relations, and Iraqi replied by stating that the situation remained premature and delaying the process indefinitely. At the same time, Iraq insisted on the US's representation not rising above that of the American Interest Section in Baghdad. The office operated during periods when Iraq might have wanted to shut it down, like during the 1973 war, when the US provided Israel with vital arms; or in 1975–6, when US assistance to the Kurds was exposed; or when the Israeli-Egyptian peace treaty was signed in 1979. Iraq was the side that dictated the level and pace of relations, utilising sometimes misleading and deceptive tactics to encourage continued US courtship and then rejecting US approaches to upgrade political relations.

Iraq's perception of US policy in the Middle East was generally correct. Ba'thi leaders understood America's eagerness for closer relations with Arab states, on the one hand, while, on the other hand, understanding that the US would not forsake Israel. But they had a simplistic, distorted perception of American capitalism, assuming that the business community and the administration were motivated only by greed and profit, and that they would not resist promising opportunities for trade with Iraq, even bypassing the need to resume relations. This misperception explains Iraq's anger regarding export controls that limited the American technology available to Iraq. For its part, the US held a misperception that trade relations would moderate Iraq and turn it away from the Soviets. The administration did not evaluate the depth of Iraq's rejectionist ideology in its emotional context and as an asset for a country presenting its leader, Saddam, as a heroic figure. Throughout this period, the administration was convinced that resuming relations was just a matter of time.

An Image Gap: Patronising and Mutual Ignorance

The administration did not pay much attention to Iraq; neither did the media and the public.[52]Archeologists, anthropologists, and Arabists – as well as travelers and missionary groups – held romantic views of Iraq as the Mesopotamia of old, the birthplace of ancient civilization. Many such individuals and groups were expelled by the Ba'th in 1968, including the American Christian missions that, beginning in 1932, established modern Iraqi educational institutions.[53] The US oil industry saw Iraq as an investment target, for which it competed with the Europeans. The administration generally considered Iraq to be an undeveloped country, ruled by a revolutionary, socialist regime affiliated with the USSR and hostile to the United States. Some diplomats who dealt with Iraq knew Arabic and had experience in the Middle East. However, unlike their British colleagues, at least in the period under study, they had little knowledge of or interest in Iraq's complex society, its tribal and clan loyalties or its multicultural nature. Moreover, American diplomats were not allowed to travel freely around the country, unless invited and guided by Iraqi officials, so they could not develop relations with common citizens or even in local and regional ruling and influential circles where, fearing the watchful eye of security services, individuals avoided any contact with Americans.

From 1974, Iraq's hosting of senior US delegations included tours of the Kurdish areas in the north and of Shi'i areas in the south, along with the requisite visits to archeological sites. The visitors met, of course, with ministers and senior officials; usually, the input of Interest Section diplomats into these visits was confined to technical arrangements, and usually they did not participate in most meetings between American dignitaries and senior Ba'th officials or ministers, and did not report home. David Rockefeller reported directly to Kissinger; others reported to the White House (Kennedy, Fulbright, Weller, Bourne), and to lawmakers in Congress.

By contrast, Iraqi leadership and media, as well as the educated public circles, intensely followed US global diplomatic activity and domestic developments. Opinion, editorial and analysis articles were critical and even hostile toward America, and thus sustained the Ba'thi rhetoric that the US was the Arabs' enemy. News reports from elsewhere – covering the Vietnam War and the protests in the US – amplified the negative perspectives. The US was portrayed, in the Iraqi press, as a capitalistic, predatory superpower that used its technological and military superiority to dominate the global economy and abused its veto power at the UN Security Council in favour of Israel.

The Ba'th, unsurprisingly, presented itself in the domestic media as standing for progressive socialism, and supporting Third World countries and the powerless. While magazines and newspapers covered American achievements in technology, medicine, culture, art and cinema, they had limited impact, read primarily by educated, middle-class Iraqis and those in Ba'th circles. Still, they pointed at Iraq's fascination with American culture. Iraqis who met US officials expressed their great appreciation of American technology, science and academic institutions, yet couldn't understand the US political system and the impact of the democratic system on scientific achievements and economic prosperity. For that reason, the American political system and its values were perceived as inferior to Ba'th ideology. This misperception produced conspiratorial interpretations and mistrust.

The Kurdish Rebellion: Crucial for One Side, a Side Show for the Other

The Kurdish issue forms a separate prism for evaluating mutual misperceptions, as well as a test case for US policy in the Persian Gulf. For the American administration, assisting the Kurdish rebellion was only one of many covert operations, limited in scope and budget, intended to weaken the Ba'th threat against Iran and Israel and prevent Barzani from joining the National Front under Soviet pressure. Barzani and his military forces represented a challenge to Ba'th authority. The more military assistance Iran, the US and Israel extended to the Kurds, the more the regime perceived them as an existential threat. The Ba'th saw it as foreign subversion on Iraqi soil. It fed into Saddam's assertion that the US targeted Iraq to undermine Ba'th rule.

Human Rights: American Principle vs. Iraqi Bewilderment

The Carter administration raised greater awareness of human rights concerns by connecting human rights to the execution of US foreign policy. During 1977 and 1978 the administration articulated the policy in various public statements, devised guidelines for its application, strengthened existing structures for managing human rights, and created new institutional arrangements for applying human rights considerations to economic and military aid. This policy was openly attacked by the Iraqi media.

Once the US made human rights a pillar of its foreign policy, the State Department instructed all US missions, including Baghdad, to report abuses in their accredited countries. The Washington cable specified inhuman punitive measures, torture, cruelty and extended detention without charge.[54]

Wiley responded in a cable to the State Department that he had no access to such information carried out by security services under secrecy. He added that Iraqi law allowed security and police services to take all measures for Iraq's national unity.[55] Carter did not relate to Iraqi security forces' abuses of individual citizens, and non-Ba'thi groups: Kurds, Shi'is and communists. Those included arbitrary arrests, torture and murder of opposition members in and outside Iraq. The administration continued to promote trade with Iraq, however.[56] Aside from the efforts the Nixon and Ford administrations extended to assist Iraqi Jews, and to some extent the Kurds, the US refrained from any involvement in Iraq's human-rights matters. A common explanation was their lack of full diplomatic relations. In fact, the State Department was reluctant to raise the issue in Baghdad, fearing that it would adversely affect bilateral trade, even while hoping that resuming relations was in the offing.

Events confirm Wiley's statement that the concept of individual human rights, as understood in the West, was alien to Iraq. Iraq had lived under violent rulers for many decades and centuries. In recent times, Iraq witnessed a mass killing of the Assyrians with the support the government in 1933.[57] The Violent conduct of Iraq continued under Qasim and beyond with zero tolerance of any expression of opposition. From the Ba'th perspective, it was natural that the regime would support all measures to suppress any opposition and keep citizens under the yoke of security forces. The regime considered these measures to be legitimate instruments of governing, while employing euphemisms like protecting national unity and combating treason and subversion. The fact that the USSR protested weakly when the Ba'th persecuted and executed Iraqi communists, and carried on cooperating with Iraq, indicated that the Ba'th felt confident in pursuing such conduct without significant criticism.

The US attitude to human rights was completely different, but it could not be appreciated by the Ba'th regime. Baghdad could not understand the American approach and was, therefore, disappointed that the Americans did not welcome its persecution of communists.

Israel, Iraqi Rejectionist Ideology and Conspiracies

The US did not realise how deeply rooted Iraq's animosity to Israel was, as well as the struggle of the Iraqi Ba'th with Syrian Ba'th for legitimacy as representing the authentic Ba'thi principle of Arab nationalism, i.e. the anti-Israeli motto. The Americans' somewhat naïve perception that a peace agreement between Israel and the Arabs, based on Israel's withdrawal from the Sinai, would bring Syria to the negotiating table, while keeping rejectionist radical Iraq out of the picture, proved to be wrong as well. The Iraqi Ba'th could not afford any change or moderation of its rejectionist position. As the regime became stronger and more stable, no doubt by force, the less Saddam was inclined to agree to any compromise, including upgrading diplomatic relations with the US.

Dealing with beliefs, ideologies, images and perceptions, one can easily detect conspiratorial thinking in Iraq – in particular by Saddam Hussein. The theory that Jews around the world and in Israel possessed supernatural powers and used them for evil purposes was not new in Arab countries, but in Saddam's Iraq this theory received additional meaning and intensity through linkage to the US. Saddam combined his ambition to turn Iraq into a regional power with his role as self-proclaimed leader of the struggle against Israel. To Saddam, the US and Israel stood on opposite ends against the Arabs. The special US-Israel relationship, as well as American intervention on behalf of Iraqi Jews, seemed irrational to Saddam, yet he realised that Washington's policy could not be changed. The US's increased supply of state-of-the-art military technologies to Israel, while Iraq's requests for US technology were rebuffed or delayed by Congress, contributed to Baghdad's notion that Israel and American Jews conspired not just against the Arabs in general but against Iraq in particular.

Two elements underlay this myth about Israel and the Jews, as well as the misperception of the US. Firstly, the Ba'th, particularly Saddam, did not understand the American political system, the checks and balances between the White House and Congress, and the legitimacy of lobbying legislators, even against the administration. Iraqis assumed that the administration and the president led the policy and decision-making exclusively, and that Congress generated unnecessary delays. Also, the political involvement and leverage of American Jews had increased since the late 1970s, and AIPAC gained more influence in generating support for Israel among both Republicans and Democrats. Pro-Israel legislators, whether Jews or non-Jews, confronted powerful interest groups, such as the agricultural lobby, the aerospace industry and energy corporations. The pro-Israeli lobby and the political power of American Jews fed the conspiracy theory that Jews had supernatural powers. The campaign on behalf of Iraqi Jews since 1969 amazed the Ba'th by its volume. The fact that Europeans joined to demarche the Iraqi government and follow the fate of the small Jewish community later on, coupled with successful Jewish activism for Jewish dissidents in the USSR astonished the Iraqi regime. The American system, combined with the growing influence of American Jews exerted in Washington, fed the prevailing anti-Semitic image amongst Iraq's leadership of Jews possessing mythical powers and evil purposes.

Saddam's own words in the 1990s, in a recorded discussion with his inner circle, instructed his people to research and study the Protocols of the Elders of Zion, in order to find out the source of Jewish power, and amplified his conspiratorial thinking, driven by irrationality and anxiety.[58]

Saddam Hussein's Personality: Mutual Misperception

Saddam had been known to both American and British intelligence services since the Ba'th coup in July 1968. Though second in command to Ahmad Hasan al-Bakr, he soon became recognised as the strongman of the regime, and gradually as the pivot point for crucial decision-making. The US became increasingly concerned with Saddam only after he formally assumed the presidency in July 1979, when he made belligerent statements against Iran, claiming that the Islamic Republic endangered the Gulf and its oil fields. As president, Saddam cultivated a personality cult and directed the spotlight of the Iraqi media, literature and culture upon himself. He commissioned statues, paintings and posters featuring his image to be placed in public spots all over Iraq. It could have attracted the attention of the analysts earlier.

Constructing psychological profiles of foreign leaders was a common analytical method to support intelligence assessments, decision-making and negotiations. In 1965, a psychological unit was established in the CIA, headed by the psychiatrist Jerold Post. It conducted analysis from a distance, based on both open and classified information that integrated various disciplines: psychology, anthropology, sociology and history, but focused on Saddam only in 1990.[59] As expected, the unit's main objects were the Kremlin's leadership, North Vietnam, Cuba, and the Begin-Sadat personalities at the Camp David talks. Iraq was not perceived as a threat to US interests. Administration reports portrayed Saddam as a self-confident strongman, the central figure in decision-making, someone who represented a pragmatic, relatively moderate faction of the Ba'th leadership. Because Saddam rarely travelled abroad, avoided meeting US officials, and did not speak English, US intelligence had little first-hand knowledge of his disposition and his personality remained unknown.

Similarly, Iraq's political culture and atmosphere were not researched thoroughly as such. There was no integrated study on Saddam's base of support, which was derived from traditional, social, and tribal loyalties, mainly from his hometown of Tikrit. Saddam's conduct with the various sectors in Iraq's diverse society, as a traditional leader, using tribal, clan and ethnic networks to establish loyalty, was not a cultural secret from Western and Arab scholars.[60]

British diplomats' reports from Baghdad reflected a wider angle and deeper knowledge of anthropological and cultural aspects of Iraqi society, including tribal and ethnic politics. Their analyses, in the 1970s, were more realistic, and they regularly shared them with their US counterparts. For example, they observed ahead of the Americans that the Ba'th became well established and strong enough to undermine any opposition. Another example was the insight of the British ambassador in Baghdad, Graham, that the Ba'th was playing games with the US and had no intention of giving up the opportunity to continue with anti-American slurs. Arab leaders such as Jordan's King Hussein, Gulf leaders and Syrian President Hafez Assad, were far more familiar with the political culture surrounding Saddam. They were well aware of his oppression of opponents and lack of trust towards others. Arab leaders tolerated and accepted his conduct, including his considering state funds as his own property. Even Arab leaders friendly to the US, did not speak much about the extreme conduct of Saddam towards his own people, yet they did raise their concerns about Iraq as a threat towards their own countries.[61]

Only in the late 1990s, following Iraq's invasion of Kuwait, was Saddam's personality finally analysed. Post did not find evidence that Saddam suffered from a psychotic disorder, but he did conclude that Saddam had personality disturbances he named 'malignant narcissism' with a 'strong paranoid orientation'.[62] Like Stalin, his role model, Saddam was convinced that he was surrounded by enemies, including in his own party, so he ruthlessly eliminated them in 1979. Saddam viewed himself as a great leader in world history who was given a messianic mission to make Iraq great, and had unlimited powers. He also identified himself completely with Iraq: 'Iraq is Saddam – Saddam is Iraq'.[63] Saddam saw himself as a successor to the ancient Babylonian emperor Nebuchadnezzar and on the level of twentieth century leaders who he believed changed history such as Nasser, Fidel Castro, Ho Chi Minh and Mao Zedong.

Saddam's personality and narcissism were manifest in his decision-making process. In the 1970s, he demonstrated rational pragmatic decisions that required persuasion and even courage in his own party. Most apparently, his concessions to the Iranian Shah in the Algiers Agreement, yet he made grave mistakes as a leader in later years such as attacking Iran (1980) and invading Kuwait (1989). Post defined him as 'a rational calculator who often miscalculates'.[64]

Post's analysis of Saddam concluded with the following: 'It is this political personality constellation – messianic ambition for unlimited power, absence of conscience, unconstrained aggression and a paranoid outlook – that makes Saddam Hussein so dangerous'.[65] Saddam's encouraging the US to court him, only to reject the advances, were his way of playing 'hard to get' – as a tactic and to please his own ego.

Whether in nationalising oil companies, signing a treaty of friendship with the USSR or loudly criticising US assistance for the Kurds, each action was taken with the anticipation of some US response. While examining his personality features, it seems that Saddam was hoping for a US statement that would demonstrate Iraq's worthiness as an opponent and would recognise Saddam as a strong leader. On the other hand, American indifference and lack of response to Iraqi so-called provocations generated continuous frustration.

Domestically, Saddam's paranoia, according to Post's analysis, caused mistrust. He relied on traditional loyalties and recruited confidants from his own clan and town for his security and intelligence services. Security services used ruthless measures against individuals and groups suspected of conspiring against the regime or voicing criticism of Saddam and his conduct. Ba'thi measures included punishing a defendant's family members, even children. His paranoia extended beyond Iraq. He was convinced that the US was targeting Iraq and felt encircled by US allies nearby: Iran, Saudi Arabia, Jordan and Israel. He distrusted US political intentions and suspected all American diplomatic activities of being CIA operations against Iraq. (Perhaps that was due to the CIA's assistance to the Ba'th in toppling Qasim.)[66] He was even certain that the US was behind toppling the Shah and establishing the Islamic Republic of Iran.[67]

Saddam's ability to alter his course dynamically enabled him to introduce any change he desired, abandoning existing orientation or ideology. Saddam never expressed regret or admitted mistakes. Any change of policy, and even political zig-zagging, involved Saddam's provision of ideological interpretations and justifications under the title of 'revolutionary pragmatism.'[68] He did this, for example, when deciding to retreat from Jordan in the Black September crisis in 1970, during negotiations with the Kurds and communists, or respecting Kuwaiti borders and making far-reaching concessions to Iran in 1975.

Saddam's pragmatism was perceived in the US as a positive indication of *realpolitik* reasoning that could lead to moderation regarding the Middle East peace process, while tilting towards the US. But these decisions were tactical measures to protect the regime in times of danger, or ways out of complex situations. Contrary to the American perception, Saddam inclined toward pragmatism in crises, especially, of course, when survival of the Ba'th was at stake. But when the regime was stable and confident, Saddam radicalised his positions, including his rejectionist attitude to the Middle East conflict, threatened Iraq's neighbours and avoided any sign of warming relations with the US.

Misreading Iraqi Proactive Foreign Policy

Unlike US policy towards the Qasim regime (1958–63), which considered the revolutionary regime as a viable pro-communist threat that should have been toppled – US policy in the 1970s recognised the legitimacy of the Ba'th revolution, though the main concern was still related to the Soviet Union and that Iraq would open the door to Soviet control of the oil fields and the Persian Gulf. The Ba'th alliance with the USSR was seen in Washington as a practical Iraqi preference, tied to the party's socialist ideology. Both the USSR and Iraq were joined by a bilateral treaty signed in 1972, which stated that the Soviets would not have a military presence in the Gulf. The Ba'th promoted territorial nationalism (known as *wataniyya*) and an independent foreign policy, and it opposed all foreign presence, including that of the USSR, in the Gulf.

Baghdad followed with concern and suspicion the détente negotiations between Washington and Moscow. It approached the West with a request for procurement of military equipment; the purpose was to diversify Iraq's military procurement in order not to depend solely on the Soviets. That also demonstrated Iraq's non-dependence on the USSR, even while expanding cooperation with it. Iraq showed a pragmatic and sophisticated approach, recognising America's sensitivity to any Soviet access to the Gulf and fearing a US presence as retaliation. For that reason, it adopted an independent foreign policy (known as *istiqlaliyya*). Subsequently, this policy facilitated having political and trade relations with both East and West, and continued courtship by all industrial countries. Iraq assumed correctly that the Soviets would carry on with military cooperation, even when Iraq purchased Western-made weapons. This was particularly based on the Egyptian example when the Soviet Union had continued to support Egypt throughout the 1973 war, even though Sadat had expelled all Soviet military presence in 1972.-

The Iraqi Communist Party, unlike under the Qasim regime, was not considered a threat since it joined the coalition with the Ba'th under the National Front. Communists, historically, were not trusted by the Ba'th and activists were persecuted and eventually the entire party was outlawed.[69]

For all these reasons and against the backdrop of US-Soviet improved communication during the Détente, Iraq was not perceived at risk of falling under the Soviet sphere of influence. Furthermore, the US was encouraged by Iraqi and Arab signals suggesting that Iraq intended to turn away from the Soviets and get closer to the US. These signals were most obvious in 1974, during the escalating fighting with the Kurds, conveyed by Arab leaders, and by Iraqi officials who told Americans that the Kurdish rebellion and the dependence on Soviet supplies were the main obstacles to closer relations with the US. The estimate that prevailed, particularly in the State Department, was clearly based on misperception of Ba'thi policy, or rather wishful thinking.

Iraq was active at the UN, within the NAM, initiating closer contacts with moderate Arab states and the Gulf, including with Iran after 1975. The diplomatic activism was initially meant to gain status and prestige internationally, and to glorify Saddam as a world leader. It was not, though, an indication of moderation and of a broad, universal view, or even the wish to seek a better understanding of the international system that could bring Iraq closer to the West, according to some American interpretations.

Marginalising Iraqi Military Buildup

By 1980, Iraq had doubled its military capacity to twelve divisions, from six in 1974. Half of those divisions were armoured divisions. Iraq accelerated its efforts and investments in building a technological and scientific infrastructure for the military industry, as well as a secret WMD program.[70] Saddam decided to launch an Iraqi nuclear program as early as 1972, with the intention of turning Iraq into a strong power regionally as well as internationally.

The US clung to the view that Iraq was not a serious threat to the Gulf States or to Israel. That can be explained by a low regard for Iraq's technological capabilities, on the one hand, and by the success of a sophisticated Iraqi PR campaign that was run by skilled professional diplomats who were educated in the West. Such people escorted American political and trade delegations visiting Iraq, conveying the message of Iraq as a stable, law-abiding state. This Ba'th PR campaign was so successful that, in most congressional hearings on export control for states sponsoring terrorism, applying Arab boycott or wishing to acquire highly sophisticated weapons, the administration always stressed that Iraq was very different from Qaddafi's lawless regime and, therefore, should not be sanctioned. Moreover, the views of the Arabists, including in the State Department, were based primarily on the Baghdad Interest Section's reports, but not on substantial information-gathering and research. That contributed to optimistic and unrealistic assessments.

Another source influencing the persisting American view could be found in Iraq's energy, industry and infrastructure sectors amongst US proponents who were eager to establish trade cooperation to catch up with the Europeans. The grain lobby overseas had vested interests in increasing exports to Iraq.

US business groups had an interest in Washington's restoring relations and expanding trade with Iraq. They were encouraged by the positions of the US Department of Commerce, USTR, and by the State Department, which had an interest in avoiding a focus on Iraq and in rendering US policy towards Iraq ambiguous, as long as the issue of export control was viable in Congress.[71] On the down side, references to Iraq – as being a major oil producer and active OPEC member (meaning an initiator and a beneficiary of the oil crisis), or Iraq's alliance with the USSR, with a significant army presenting a potential threat to Gulf States –were sporadic and not alarming enough to prompt an inter-agency study in the NSC or the relevant Departments: State, Defense, Commerce, Energy etc. on overall Ba'th intentions and its implications for US policy.

Misperceptions and their Consequences

Both the US and Iraq held mutual misperceptions throughout the period under study and in the ensuing decades. The US viewed Iraq as a marginal element of America's Middle Eastern policy; Iraq, aware of the might of a superpower, followed all aspects of American domestic and foreign policy closely, but failed to comprehend the American system and developed a distorted image of US politics. Yet Saddam did understand that he could benefit from low-key relations that would enable Iraq to maintain its radical positions and evince hostile anti-American rhetoric, even while obtaining American technology and promoting trade relations.

On the other hand, the US administration had no interest in dealing with Iraqi society, Ba'th ideology and Saddam's ambitions. The American interpretation of alleged Ba'th pragmatism proved wrong. It was based on the Western school of thought, according to which countries undergoing development and enjoying growing oil revenues with great potential of oil reserves and prospects for a prosperous future, would not risk their fortunes in war, and eventually would moderate their positions. The case of Ba'thi Iraq demonstrated the opposite: the Ba'th party, indeed, expressed moderation and even lowered its anti-American rhetoric during tough times, like at the peak of the Kurdish rebellion in 1974. But the prosperous times and periods of economic and infrastructure development did not prevent the continued radicalisation of the party's already hardline attitude.

In America's assessment, Iraq's growing trade relations with Western Europe, including diversification of the sources of its military equipment, indicated Baghdad's gradual retreat from the Soviet Union. However, in spite of occasional conflict with the Soviets, the Ba'th expanded relations with Moscow, just as its trade grew with Western Europe and Japan.

The US did not realise how deeply rooted was Iraq's hostility to Israel and how anxious the regime was about possible military attacks on Iraq by the US or Israel. Neither did Washington observe the duality in Ba'thi attitude towards the US: fascination and admiration on the one hand, and hostility and anxiety on the other.

Notes

1. The company that won the tender to construct a deep water terminal in Basra was Brown & Root of Texas. A deep water port would make the Basra oil terminal accessible to supertankers. Baghdad 3 (Lowrie), 6 January 1974.
2. Telcon: David Rockefeller to Kissinger, 19 April 1975, before his second visit to Iraq. Lowrie was invited only to the formal dinner, but not to Rockefeller's meeting with Iraqi officials. *DNSA*; Baghdad 99 (Lowrie), 31 January 1975.
3. Baghdad 854 (Killough), 15 August 1975.
4. See Chapter 5.
5. Baghdad 575 (Lowrie), 31 May 1975.
6. J.A.N. Graham, British Embassy, Baghdad, 29 May 1975, 21 July 1975, FCO 8/2544, *TNA*.
7. *International Trade by Commodities Statistics*, ITCS, SITC/CTCI, Rev. 2 1961–1990, CD; USA trade with the Middle East. US Bureau of the Census, Highlights of the US Export and Import Trade, *MEED* 20(37), 10 September 1976, p. 29. There is a slight difference between IMF data and MECS, perhaps because IMF received data from both Iraq and the US. And some barter deals had not been reported 'IMF Direction of Trade', in *MECS* II (1977–1978), p. 534; *MECS* III (1978–1989), p. 533.
8. Baghdad 1175 (Wiley), 15 November 1975; Governors William Hobby, Bill Waller, Baghdad 582 (Wiley), 4 May 1976.
9. Report by Senator Adlai E. Stevenson on his trip to the Middle East, 10–25 February 1976, Senate Committee on Banking, Housing & Urban Affairs, *GPO*, April 1976.
10. US Senate, 'International Grain Agreement Oversight', Hearing before the Subcommittee on Foreign Agricultural Policy of the Committee on Agriculture, Nutrition and Forestry, 14 June 1979, *GPO* 1979, pp. 88–9.
11. *Ibid.*
12. 'Investment Information for FY 1974 Fact Book', Baghdad 216 (Lowrie), 18 April 1973.
13. Trade by Commodities Statistics, *ITCS, SITC/CTCI* Rev. 2, 1961–1990, CD; USA trade with the Middle East.
14. Trade by Commodities Statistics, ITCS, *SITC/CTCI*, Rev. 2, 1961–1990, CD; U.S. Senate Subcommittee on Foreign Aid of the Senate Committee on Foreign Relations: *USA trade with the Middle East; 'International Terrorism'*, 95th Congress, 14 September 1977, *GPO* 1977.
15. Yizhak Gal in *MECS* IV (1979–1980); *MEED*, 15 February 1980.
16. General Union of Arab Chambers of Commerce, Industry and Agriculture, Arab Economic Report, in Sluglett & Sluglett, *Iraq since 1958: From Revolution to Dictatorship* (New York: Palgrave Macmillan, 1987), pp. 253–4.
17. *Quarterly Economic Review of Iraq*, The Economist Intelligence Unit, London, Annual Supplement, 1975, 1978, 1980, 1981.
18. Kissinger's criticism of Israel – Chapter 5.
19. Baghdad 29 (Wiley), 13 January 1976.
20. *Ibid.*

21. CIA Research PR 76-100701 Study, 'Iraq under Baath Rule, 1968–1976', November 1976, *FRUS XXVII* #317.
22. *Ibid.*
23. President Carter, Q & A with Department of State Employees, 24 February 1977, *APP.*
24. President Carter's Interview with the Magazine Publishers Association, 10 June 1977, *APP.*
25. Sadat Deputy Mubarak was asked to forward the American message to Saddam Hussein during their meeting in April 1977; the Shah of Iran was asked to deliver a similar message. Cairo 7312 (Eilts), quoted in White House Memorandum, 29 April 1977, *Carter Presidential Library*, President's Daily Report; NEA Background Paper for the Secretary's Meeting with the Shah of Iran, 13 May 1977, *DNSA.*
26. Memorandum for the Ad Hoc Working Group on US-Iraq Health Cooperation, Department of State n.d., *Carter Presidential Library*, Peter Bourne Files, 28 April, 1977–24 May 1978, Medical Intelligence Summaries.
27. Memorandum from Brzezinski to the President, 21 June1977, *Carter Presidential Library*, NSA-Brzezinski Material.
28. *Al-Yaqza*, 31 January 1977; British Embassy Baghdad (Shelton), 6 August 1977, FCO 8/3011, *TNA.*
29. Baghdad (Wiley), 18 May 1977, FRUS XVIII #132.
30. British Embassy Baghdad (Tait), 10 November 1977, FCO 8/3011, *TNA.*
31. Memorandum from State (Christopher) to the President, 12 December 1978, *DDRS.*
32. Memorandum from State (Vance) to the President, 19 December1978, *Carter Presidential Library*, Al Moses Files.
33. David L. Mack, Interview, 24 October 1995, *ADST*; Baghdad 1760 (Mack), 5 October, 1977.
34. Memorandum from Peter Bourne to President-elect Jimmy Carter, Carter-Mondale Transition Planning Group, 2, December 1976, *DDRS.*
35. Memorandum from Vance, 14 February 1977, *Carter Presidential Library*, Brzezinski Material.
36. MOC, Department of State, AID, 'Health Initiative in Iraq', 24 May 1977, *DDRS.*
37. Baghdad 691 (Wiley), 25 April 1977, *Carter Presidential Library*, WHCF Bourne Files.
38. Baghdad 712 (Wiley), 30 April 1977; Baghdad 742, 4 May 1977.
39. President Carter to Dr Sidney Aidinis, Assistance Professor of Anesthesiology, Alexandria VA, 24 May 1977, *Carter Presidential Library*, WHCF Bourne Files.
40. Dr Riad Ibrahim, Ministry of Health, Baghdad, to Dr Bourne, Washington DC, 12 June 1977; Terry Plane, 'Mystery mission to Iraq', *The Australian*, 22 March 2003.
41. The report reflects poor health conditions and health services in the periphery, for example that 4 million Iraqis had no access to running water, yet there is no mention of the Mercury poisoning of 1970–2, and the cooperation with the American medical team. Memorandum for the AD HOC Working Group on US-Iraq Health Cooperation, Department of State, n.d. (~1977-8), *Carter Presidential Library*, Bourne Files, Medical Intelligence Summaries.
42. Ad hoc Working Group, *Ibid.*
43. State (Vance) to Baghdad, 19 August 1977.
44. State to Baghdad, 2 November 1977.
45. 'A U.S. gift to Iraq: deadly viruses', *Business week News Analysis*, 20 September 2002.
46. Bourne discussed with Dr Niyazi, in Geneva, newly developed vaccines (malaria and chickenpox), stressing that President Carter considered disease control an important

humanitarian issue, unrelated to politics. Transcript, Peter Bourne, Dr Howard, Dr Niazi, Director of Endemic Diseases Institute, Baghdad, Geneva n.d. (~early 1977), *Carter Presidential Library*, Bourne Files.

47. Memorandum from Morris Draper to Gerald Fill, 24 May1978; State (Vance) to Baghdad, 18 November 1977, *Carter Presidential Library*, Peter Bourne Files.

48. Bourne resigned from his office in the White House in July 1978, following embarrassments. He supplied a prescription for sleeping pills to a White House employee, and rumours suggested that he took part in a cocaine party, *Time Magazine*, 7 July 1978.

49. Memorandum from Peter Bourne to State, 27 February 1978, *Carter Presidential Library*, Bourne Files.

50. Baghdad 1787 (Mack), 5 October 1977; Baghdad 1983, 1987 (Mack), 10, 12 November 1977, *Carter Presidential Library*, Peter Bourne Files.

51. Baghdad 2164 (Peck), 18 October 1978.

52. The US Army printed, in 1943, a manual entitled: *Instructions for American Servicemen in Iraq during World War II*. Lt. Col. John A. Nagl, who served as an operation officer in Iraq, 2003–4, wrote, in the forward to the reprint, that the same instructions were applicable in the 2000s, namely that it was a desert state, tribal society that foreigners must treat with respect and sensitivity for local customs. US Army, *Instructions for American Servicemen in Iraq during World War II* (Washington DC, 1943; Chicago, 2007).

53. Reeva S. Simon, *Iraq between the two World Wars* (New York: Columbia University Press, 1986), pp. 46–8. The Jesuits of New England founded The Baghdad College (1932) and *Al-Hikma* in 1956. Department of State, The Office of the Special Assistant of the Secretary for the Coordination of International Educational and Cultural relations, *International, Cultural and related activities for Iraq* (January 1961), pp. 16–17; E. Tejirian & R. Simon, *Conflict, Conquest and Conversion* (New York: Columbia University Press, 2012), p.194.

54. State 45319, 74981 (Kissinger), 25 February, 3 April 1975; State 231122 (Robinson), 17 September 1976.

55. Baghdad 1788 (Wiley), 3 December 1976.

56. David Newsom, under Secretary of State in the Carter administration, edited a book specifying cases and countries violating HR. Iraq was not even mentioned. D. Newsom, *The Diplomacy of Human Rights* (Lanham MD: Rowman & Littlefield, 1986).

57. The Assyrian Affair, 1933.

58. Saddam and his Inner Circle Discuss Zionism and 'The Protocols of the Elders of Zion', The Conflict Records Research Center (CRRC), SH- SHTP-A-001- 215 ~1990s, n. d.

59. J.M. Post, *Leaders and Their Followers in a Dangerous World* (Ithaca, NY: Cornell University Press, 2004), pp. XI–XVI.

60. Said K. Aburish, 'The Survival of Saddam: Secrets of his Life and Leadership', Interview for *Frontline*, *PBS*, 25 January 2000, http://www.pbs.org/wgbh/pages/frontline/shows/saddam/interviews/aburish.html. last accessed January 2010. Saddam admired Stalin as a role model. As a young Ba'thi, he told his party comrades that Ba'th rule in Iraq should follow the Stalinist pattern. Consequently, like Stalin, he did not trust the army and established his own security forces, which had been trained in East Germany. Yet he diligently adapted his authoritarian methods to the tribal structure of Iraqi society.

61. Fouad Ajami, *The Foreigners' Gift: The Americans, the Arabs and the Iraqis in Iraq* (New York: Simon & Schuster, 2006), pp. 65–7.

62. J. Post, *Leaders and their Followers*, p. 210.
63. J. Post & A. Baram, *Saddam is Iraq: Iraq is Saddam*, USAF Counterproliferation Papers, Future Warfare Series, No. 17, January 2002 (Maxwell Air Force Base, Alabama: Air University, 2002).
64. J. Post, *Leaders and their Followers*, p. 217.
65. *Ibid.*, pp. 217–19.
66. J. Prados, *Safe for Democracy, The Secret Wars of the CIA* (Chicago, IL: Ivan R. Dee, 2006), p.165.
67. 16 September, 1980, *CRRC Records*, SHTP-A-000-835.
68. J. Post, *Leaders and their Followers*, p. 215.
69. Saddam Hussein clarified Ba'thi attitude to the communists to the British Ambassador Balfour-Paul in 1969. British Embassy Baghdad, 'Saddam Hussein', 20 December1969, FCO 17/871, *DNSA*.
70. P. Malovany, *The Wars of Modern Babylon* (Hebrew) (Tel Aviv: Maarachot, 2009), p.55.
71. The Carter administration's officials admitted that Iraq had been marginalised, as a matter of priority, and not intentionally. If there was any neglect, then it was a 'Benign neglect', Interview with Stuart Eizenstat, 21 July 2013, Chevy Chase, MD.

Conclusion

The twenty-five-year US-Iraqi military confrontation that began in 1990 represented the peak of their mutual misperceptions over the preceding decades. It put an end to Saddam's Ba'thi Iraq, caused the country's political disintegration and generated a high cost in human lives and resources lost on both sides.

This book was conceived and researched over a decade, and was completed while the Middle East undergoes continued turmoil, with old borders dissolving and new, non-state entities assuming leading roles. Iraq has crumbled, and it is not certain to what extent it can reinvent itself following its long internal and external conflict. It is tempting to contend, as some writers do, that it is all America's fault, since the US trod with heavy boots all over Iraq, creating and leaving insoluble chaos that may have helped the creation of such jihadi organisations as ISIS and opened the gate for Iranian hegemony in the Middle East, beginning with Iraq.

In my view, that is a simplistic explanation, and it is premature to come to such conclusions. However, it is quite right to conclude that both Iraq and the US were drawn into an armed conflict that emerged from their mutual misconceptions. This was an unintentional process, based on ignorance and prejudice and lack of interest in the other side. It had strategic and political ramifications, culminating in the meeting between Saddam and American ambassador April Glaspie on 25 July 1990, on the eve of Iraq's invasion of Kuwait, which led to the US-led war. Saddam thought that he made it clear to Glaspie that the flow of Kuwaiti oil to the US and the West would not be interrupted, and was quite sure that this would placate the Americans after the invasion. Glaspie, on the other hand, was certain that she made it very clear to him that the US would not tolerate any infringement of Kuwaiti sovereignty. Both had misunderstood the other side's red lines.

Neither Iraq nor the United States could have expected that, twenty-five years after the period under discussion in this book, they would become so significant for each other. They have misperceived one another from the very beginning on almost every line of relations and communication. That crossing of wires may have led to the final mutual misunderstanding that paved the way for the 1991 Gulf War and the second US-led invasion of Iraq that crushed the Ba'th in 2003.

The mutual, prolonged failure of Iraq and the US to recognise each other's complexities and interests is best demonstrated when examined through a set of meeting points between the two sides. These meeting points should not be and were not analysed chronologically, but discussed as prisms through which perceptions and misperceptions could be illuminated and identified. These prisms are the Kurdish rebellion, the Arab-Israeli conflict and the Persian Gulf. However, two general perspectives are omnipresent throughout these prisms. The pattern of bilateral relations is one such perspective. Throughout the period under discussion, the US courted Iraq and assumed that, for Iraq's emerging economy, with a growing oil industry, the very idea of active trade and diplomatic relations with the US should be reward enough. Iraq, on the other hand, dodged the American pursuit, convinced that the US was interested only in the flow of oil through the Persian Gulf, and in making a profit. Iraq was oblivious to the values and practices that make up the United States. The US, too, failed to learn the complex tribal, political, social and party-affiliated structure of Iraq.

The second perspective is the Cold War. Although Iraq became closer to the USSR and was provided with Soviet-made arms, Baghdad never affiliated itself fully with Moscow. On the contrary, the persecution of Iraqi communists went on nearly unabated, as if to demonstrate the uneasy nature of Iraq's relations with the USSR. Iraq was, therefore, disappointed when the US did not approve of what could be presented as Iraq's anti-communist approach. All the while, the US seemed uninterested in the intricate party and coalition-building patchwork of the Ba'th and communist factions, seeming to care about them only as they related to the growing Soviet access to Gulf ports and oil fields.

The personality of Saddam was, perhaps, neither an omnipresent perspective nor a prism, but the US's ignoring it may have been another key misperception.

The first prism, chosen for examination of mutual perceptions, was that of the Kurdish revolt, which provides a powerful example of misperception. For Iraq, it was an existential issue, on which the Ba'th regime could never give up without endangering the credo that the integrity of Iraq lay in the wholesome ideal of Sunnis, Shi'ites, Christians and even non-Arabs like Kurds and others living together in an Arab-majority state. Kurdish secessionist aspirations could not be accepted, on the ideological and the emotional levels. Kurdish leadership, therefore, could not be trusted, even as it claimed fealty to the Iraqi state.

For the US, Kurdish national aspirations were a small, insignificant sideshow in a remote arena. A Kurdish homeland could be abandoned by the West, just like the abandonment of the short-lived Kurdish Republic of Mahabad, Iran, by the Soviet Union in 1946, despite the emotional inspirations this republic had stirred among Kurds. Likewise, the abandonment of the Kurdish revolt by Iran, Israel and the US took place in 1975 as easily as it was originally authorised and promoted.

The prism of the Arab-Israeli conflict provides another angle from which to consider the mutual misperception. Iraq jumped to the forefront of Arab rejectionist ideology as Egypt was busy making peace with Israel. There was a strong ideological aspect to Iraq's conduct that the US did not grasp. The Ba'th regime could not tolerate any moderation towards Israel or the United States without losing face internally and regionally. In the competition for Arab leadership, Iraq's rejectionist policy and its proclaimed hostility toward the US was an asset that Baghdad would not give up. Thus, only in the face of grave, existential threats, such as defeats on the Iranian front in 1982, did Baghdad allow itself to resume relations with Egypt, the country it termed 'perfidious' (*kha'in*). The US, on the other hand, viewed its effort to broker an Israeli-Egyptian peace as its most important thrust in the region, and brushed aside Iraq's rejectionist position as a mere nuisance.

Moreover, American commitment to Israel grew in all spheres during those years, to the chagrin and bewilderment of Arab states, including Iraq. That led Saddam and his government to this otherwise inexplicable and strange conclusion that the alliance between the US and Israel must have been a Jewish-led conspiracy.

A subsequent by-product was the fate of the Jewish community of Iraq. Though the US became more and more committed to the ideal of human rights (since 1976, the State Department has submitted to Congress an annual global report on the matter), the US did not interfere in atrocities and repression the Iraqi regime perpetrated against its civilians – except when it came to Iraq's Jews and, to a lesser extent, the Kurds. Iraq never understood why an internal issue like its own minorities should generate such interest.

The regime did not treat Jews any worse than it treated Assyrians, Kurds or Shi'ites, and it believed that it should not have been of interest to anyone outside Iraq, including the mighty US. Nevertheless, it did become a political issue in the US, recalling the struggle for the freedom of Soviet Jews, fitting in with the emerging issue of human rights and being promoted by a politically and organisationally empowered Jewish community. Iraq did not realise this at the time. It expected the administration to mind its own backyard and not cast its eyes elsewhere. It did not understand the role of

Congress, the media and the system of checks and balances in the American system of government.

The prism of the Gulf shows that the Persian Gulf not only became a strategic asset for both Iraq and US, but it bred misperception and generated disaster for both. Iraq viewed American interests as mostly relating to deterring the Soviet Union in the Gulf and ensuring the flow of oil to the West. Saddam could not see the US as ready to send troops to the Gulf and threaten Iraq to prove this point. The US failed to see Iraq as a real threat to the Gulf States, particularly to Kuwait. The US was beholden to the belief that countries with wealth, stability and international trade were not inclined to risk prosperity for military confrontation, so it disregarded Iraq's military buildup and nuclear program.

America was also negligent in taking into account Saddam's personality, and didn't account for its supreme role in Iraqi conduct. Only after his invasion of Kuwait did Washington begin to look into the complexities of Saddam.

In the period under review, Saddam continuously misled the US, pretending to be interested in re-establishing relations while constantly raising his asking price. He may have been right, at least up to a point, as the US preferred to look the other way when Iraq embarked upon a determined effort to obtain weapons of mass destruction, be they chemical or nuclear. Even when Iraqi forces had actually used chemical weapons against their own people, namely the Iraqi Kurds, the US continued to believe that once Iraq secured its geo-political goals and ambitions, it would turn onto a more moderate and constructive route and abandon its aggressive and offensive policies. These American convictions may have contributed to the US support of Iraq in its campaign against Iran (to be sure, Iran's venomous attitude towards the US, which culminated in the prolonged and humiliating hostage crisis, was a prominent factor), even though it was Iraq which started the war.

In historical research, it is generally difficult to assess the 'why' or 'to what extent' of recent history research. It may still be too early to quantify the relative weight of the many and various factors in the deterioration of relations between Iraq and the US over nearly a half a century or to ask – and answer – who was more at fault. The US, as the senior side in this unequal equation, bears responsibility, and, in any case, it is the one side that subjects itself to self-scrutiny and soul searching. The historian is left to identify the reasons for this shared failure and the process of its development.

This study shows that while Saddam entertained megalomaniac Babylonian aspirations for leadership, attempting to rub shoulders with the US, he in fact never rose to that role. He had never accepted his junior status vis-à-vis the US. Iraq never emerged from the situation into which it had cornered itself. A corner of internal sectarian strife, of local politics and of its adopted form of socialist and nationalist ideology embodied in the Ba'th. This Lebanese-originated, secular philosophy may have intended to encompass the overall Arab predicament from-ocean-to-ocean, but it failed, under Saddam, to provide a workable conduct manual for running a country without using despotic methods.

The US was unable, incapable and maybe even uninterested in delving into the depths of Iraqi complexities. Iraq was brushed aside, perhaps unwittingly, by a superpower that had not owned up to its tendencies and the ensuing need, or duty, to learn about smaller societies. In American eyes, Iraq was nothing more than an under-developed country. The US attitude towards Iraq was patronising and simplistic, disregarded the intensity of its ethnic, tribal and factional structures; its military aspirations and strong capabilities; the survivability of its regime; its secularism in an increasingly religious area; and even the personality of its ruler.

Iraq may have been too small and secluded to grasp the United States in a way that could have saved it from an un-winnable confrontation. The US, on the other hand, may have been too large and, through its super-power status, unable to correctly appreciate Iraq. This resulted in misperceptions that led to a conflict – a conflict that may have cast a lasting shadow over the Middle East as well as over American foreign policy and performance.

Appendix I

Chronological List of American and British Reports on the Kurdish Front

From 26 August 1974 to the Algiers Statement, 6 March 1975

1. 26 August 1974 – Kissinger updates Ford on the risk of collapse of the Kurdish uprising.[1]
2. 13 September 1974 – Helms reports from Tehran that the Soviets sent an indirect message to the Shah, which expressed concern about Iran's support for the Kurds and hinted that they could not continue to stand by. The Shah, responding to Brezhnev in Moscow in November 1974, expressed strong support for the Kurds and said he was not afraid of Soviet pressure.[2]
3. 27 November 1974 – Graham, the British ambassador in Baghdad, reported the Soviets were interested in ending the conflict between Iran and Iraq, as well as the Iraqis. He commented that the Soviets could apply sanctions on military supplies to Iraq.[3]
4. 23 December 1974 – Graham informed Head of the US Baghdad legation that Alam had told the UK that the Shah was determined to continue supporting Barzani in the lead-up to a spring offensive, but predicted large-scale fighting.[4]
5. 14 January 1975 – The Shah complained to the US ambassador to Tehran Helms about the heavy burden of having Kurdish refugees in Iran, with the cost of maintaining the camps already reaching $100 million.[5]
6. Late January 1975 – After visiting Baghdad, King Hussein reported to the British on Iraqi willingness to discuss the 1937 agreement on sovereignty over Shatt al-Arab.[6]
7. 4 February 1975 – Ibrahim al-Wali, director general of the Iraqi Foreign Ministry, informed Graham that the Iranians had offered the Iraqis a deal: they would cease supporting the Kurds in exchange for sovereignty over Shatt al-Arab. The Iraqis responded that they would consider it, but would not give up land.[7]

8. 6 February 1975 – Graham reported on a scheduled meeting between Saddam and the Shah at the OPEC conference in March.[8]
9. 6 February 1975 – The Shah visited Amman and Cairo. According to the Minister of the Royal Court Asadollah Alam the purpose of the Shah's visit was mostly to discuss the American peace initiative, yet it is reasonable to assume that the warfare between Iran and Iraq was high on the agenda for his meetings with King Hussein and President Sadat, respectively; both helped to mediate an end to the fighting.[9]
10. 19 February 1975 – Kissinger met with the Shah in Zurich and reported that the Shah was concerned with the weakening of the Kurds and a possible escalation of the war. Kissinger got the impression that the Shah was willing to reach an understanding with Iraq.[10] Kissinger warned the Shah that the collapse of the Kurdish uprising could destabilise the entire region and strengthen the Soviets.[11]
11. 22 February 1975 – Kissinger updated Israeli ambassador to Washington Dinitz about his conversation with the Shah, and the possibility that the Kurds may be abandoned.[12]
12. 2 March 1975 – The Shah met Ashraf Marwan, Sadat's envoy, who had come from Baghdad with a message of Saddam's willingness to withdraw from the Soviet sphere of influence if the Iranians removed the military pressure on the Kurdish front.[13]
13. 4–6 March 1975 – The Shah and Saddam Hussein met at the OPEC Convention in Algiers, and reached an agreement that generated an immediate collapse of the Kurdish uprising.

Notes

1. MOC, Ford, Kissinger, Scowcroft, 26 August 1974, *Ford Presidential Library*, Kissinger/Scowcroft West Wing Files, Box 19.
2. Tehran 7731 (Helms), 15 September 1974, *NARA* RG 57.
3. British Embassy Baghdad (Graham), 27 November 1974, FCO 8/2309/ TNA.
4. Baghdad 898 (Lowrie), 23 December 1974.
5. Tehran 344 (Helms), 14 January 1975.
6. King Hussein reported, in late January 1975, that Iraq was prepared for a compromise even on the Shatt al-Arab. It is likely that this information was passed to the US, yet it seems that the US as well as Britain did not attribute much importance or credibility to this report. Amman (Balfour-Paul), 31 January 1975, FCO 8/2547, TNA.
7. British Embassy Baghdad (Graham), 6 February 1975, FCO 8/2547 TNA.
8. *Ibid.*
9. A. Alam, *The Shah and I – The Confidential Diary of Iran's Royal Court* (London: I.B Tauris, 1991), p. 42; Alam notes that the Shah left for Jordan and Egypt on his way to Switzerland. My assumption is that the Iraqi-Kurdish issue was discussed with King Hussein and President Sadat as circumstantial since they were both involved in the

mediation efforts to end the fight. According to Alam, the CIA station in Tehran notified him, on 21 February 1975, that the Shah and Sadat had laid the foundations for a new peace initiative led by Kissinger. Further details on Ashraf Marwan's role and the possible link to Iraq are discussed later.

10. Memorandum from Scowcroft (passing message from Kissinger who had met the Shah in Zurich) to the President, 19 February 1975, *Ford Presidential Library*, Kissinger/Scowcroft West Wing Files, Box 19.

11. H. Kissinger, *Years of Renewal* (New York: Simon & Schuster, 2000), pp. 592–3.

12. *Ibid.*, p.593.

13. The Shah told Helms during the first audience the ambassador had following the Algiers Agreement. Helms confirmed that this fact was known to him from other sources as well. Tehran 2237 (Helms), 10 March 1975, 06:07.

Appendix II

Table 1 – US-Iraq International Trade, 1969–80

US Exports to Iraq	Iraqi Exports to the USA	Year
14.82	3.27	1969
22.23	3.03	1970
32.26	9.06	1971
22.89	9.48	1972
55.83	15.01	1973
284.65	0.89	1974
307.75	19.09	1975
380.82	110.04	1976
210.34	381.54	1977
316.24	265.23	1978
440.57	671.51	1979
719.60	369.29	1980

International Trade by Commodities Statistics (ITCS), SITC/CTCI, Rev. 22, 1961–90, Historical, CDRom, University of Chicago (Numbers refer to million dollars)

Bibliography

Archives

<u>USA</u>

US National Archives, College Park, MD
US National Archives, Washington DC
Nixon Presidential Library, College Park, MD
Ford Presidential Library, Ann Arbor, MI
Carter Presidential Library, Atlanta, GA
JDC (The American Jewish Joint Distribution Committee) Archives, New York
American Jewish Committee Archives, New York, FAD Collection
Central Intelligence Agency (CIA): http://www.foia.cia.gov
The National Security Archives at George Washington University, Washington, DC –unpublished collections include:
    Investigative Journalism – Scott Malone
    Transition Papers Collection 1980–1
    Human Rights, Kurds in Iraq
    Milton Moss 1973–90
    Digital National Security Archive (DNSA)
    US Department of Justice, Federal Bureau of Investigation, Baghdad Operation Center
Interview sessions with High Value detainee #1 conducted by George L. Piro, 1 January–21 March 2004: *Saddam Hussein Talks to the FBI*, www.gwu.edu/~nsarchiv/NSAEBB279/07.pdf
US Department of State – Office of the Historian:
    Foreign Relations Series, (FRUS) 1964-68, Johnson Administration
    Foreign Relations Series, (FRUS) 1969-72, Nixon Administration
    Foreign Relations Series, (FRUS) 1969-1976, Nixon-Ford Administration
Central Foreign Policy Files 1972–1978, NARA-AAD, http://aad.archives.gov/aad
US Department of State, INR: *World Strength of the Communist Party Organizations* 1973, GPO Washington DC
US Congress – Congressional Record

US Nuclear Regulatory Commission (NUREC), Washington DC
The Foreign Service Oral History Collection, *Frontline Diplomacy,* Manuscript Division, Library of Congress, Washington DC, http:// memory.loc.gov< (ADST)
National Defense University – Conflict Record Research Center (CRRC), 'Saddam Tapes'

United Kingdom

The National Archives of the United Kingdom, *TNA*

Austria

Bruno Kreisky Archives, Vienna, Bruno Kreisky Archives Foundation Collection, VII 4, Nahost, Box 25

Israel

The Israel State Archives (ISA), Jerusalem, MFA Files 1967–1973
The Central Zionist Archives, Jerusalem (CZA)

Newspapers, Magazines and Bulletins

English

Baghdad Observer
Business Week News Analysis
Chicago Tribune (CT)
Department of State Bulletin
Guardian
Jewish Telegraphic Agency (JTA)
The Los Angeles Times (LAT)
New York Magazine
New York Post
The New York Times (NYT)
The New Yorker
The Village Voice
Time Magazine
The Washington Post (WP)
The Wall Street Journal (WSJ)

Arabic

Aafaq 'Arabiyya
Al-Jumhuriyya

Alif Ba'
Al-Thawra
Al-Thawra al-'Arabiyya (*ABST Bulletin*)

<u>All Arab</u>

Sijl al-Aara'(Arab media excerpts service)

<u>Hebrew</u>

Haaretz

Books and Articles

Abdulghani, Jasim M., *Iraq and Iran: The Years of Crisis* (New York: Routledge, 1984).

ABSP, *The Central Report of the Ninth Regional Congress, June 1982* (English) (Baghdad, 1983).

ABSP, *About the 1973 October War: Report adopted by the Eighth Regional Congress (Iraq)*, January 1974 (Firenze, 1977).

ABSP, 'Al-Nidal al-Filastini, al-Wad' al-Rahin Wa Tariq al-Khilas al-Watani' (The Palestinian struggle, the current situation and the national salvation) in *Al-Thawara al-'Arabiyya*, March 1975, pp. 22–2.

ABSP, *Revolutionary Iraq 1968–1973 – The political report adopted by the Eighth Regional Congress of the Ba'ath Socialist Party-Iraq* (English) (Baghdad, 1974).

ABSP, *The 17th July Revolution in Two Years* (English) (Baghdad, 1970).

Aburish, Said K., *Saddam Hussein* (Hebrew, Tel Aviv: Matar Publishing, 2001).

Aburish, Said K., 'The Survival of Saddam: Secrets of his Life and Leadership': Interview for *Frontline, PBS*, 25 January 2000, transcript: http://www.pbs.org/wgbh/pages/frontline/shows/saddam/interviews/aburish.html.

Adams Schmidt, Dana, 'The Kurdish Insurgency', *Strategic Review*, 2(1974), pp. 51–8.

Adams Schmidt, Dana, *Journey among Brave Men* (Boston: Little Brown, 1964).

Aflak, Michel, *Choices of texts from the Ba'ath Party founder's thoughts* (Firenze: Cooperativa lavoratori, 1977).

Ajami, Fouad, *The Foreigners' Gift: The Americans, the Arabs and the Iraqis in Iraq* (New York: Simon & Schuster, 2006).

Alam, Asadollah, *The Shah and I – The Confidential Diary of Iran's Royal Court* (London: I.B. Tauris, 1991).

Albright, David and Hamza Khidhir, 'Iraq's Reconstitution of its Nuclear Weapons Program,' *Arms Control Today*, 28:7 (October 1998), pp. 9–15.

Amos, John W. II., *Palestinian Resistance Organization of a Nationalist Movement* (New York: Pergamon Policy Studies, 1980).

Andrews, Anthony, 'Nuclear fuel reprocessing: U.S. policy development', *CRS Report for Congress*, 27 March 2008.

Arab Ba'ath Socialist Party (ABSP), *How the Revolution Confronts the Imperialist and Counter Revolutionary Conspiracy, Political report approved by the Iraqi Regional Directorate of the Arab Ba'ath Socialist Party* (English) (Baghdad, November 1972).

Ashton, Nigel, *King Hussein of Jordan – A Political Life* (New Haven: Yale University Press, 2008).

Ashton, Nigel, 'A "Special Relationship" Sometimes In Spite of Ourselves: Britain and Jordan, 1957–73', *The Journal of Imperial and Commonwealth History*, 33:2 (May 2005), pp. 235–6.

Atlas, Yehuda, *'Ad 'Ammud Hatliyya: 'Alilot Hamahteret be Iraq* (To the gallows: The history of the Jewish underground in Iraq) (Tel Aviv: Maarachot, 1969).

Axelgard, Frederick W., *A New Iraq? The Gulf War and the Implications for U.S. Policy* (New York: Praeger, 1988).

Aziz, T.M., 'The Role of Muhammad Baqir al-Sadr in Shi'i Political Activism in Iraq from 1958 to 1980', *Journal of Middle East Studies*, 25 (1993), pp. 207–22.

Aziz, Tariq, *The Revolution of the New Way: Arab Ba'ath Socialist Party* (English) (Baghdad, 1974).

Al-Badri, Jamal Abd al-Razzaq, *Al-Thawra wal-Siyassa al-Dawliyya* (The Revolution and Foreign Policy) (Baghdad, 1980).

Al-Bakr, Ahmad Hasan, *Mithaq al-'Amal al-Watani allathi a'lanahu al-Ra'is al-Mmunadil Ahmad Hasan al-Bakr, 15 Tishrin al-Thani, 1971* (The National Charter as announced by President Ahmad Hasan al-Bakr, 15 November 1971).

Al-Baker and Saddam Hussein, *One Common Trench? Or Two opposite Ones?* Meeting of the Committees of the Progressive Patriotic and Nationalist Front (English) (Milano, August 1976).

Balfour Paul, Glencairn, *Bagpipes in Babylon – A Lifetime in the Arab World and Beyond* (London: I.B. Tauris, 2006).

Baram, A., *Saddam Husayn and Islam 1968–2003, Ba'thi Iraq from Secularism to Faith* (Washington DC: Woodrow Wilson Center, Johns Hopkins Press, 2014).

Baram, A., 'Deterence Lessons from Iraq – Rationality is not the only Key to Containment', *Foreign Affairs*, 91:4 (July/August 2012), pp. 76–90.

Baram, A., 'Saddam's power Structure: The Tikrities before, during and after the war' in Toby Dodge and Steven Simon (eds), *Iraq at the Crossroads: State and Society in the Shadow of Regime Change* (London: Routledge, 2003), pp. 93–113.

Baram, A., 'An Analysis of Iraqi WMD Strategy', *The Nonproliferation Review* (Summer 2001), pp. 25–39.

Baram, A., 'Saddam Husayn and Nasirism 1968–2000', *Orient*, 41:33(2000), pp. 461–71.

Baram, A., 'Baathi Iraq and Hashimite Jordan: From Hostility to Alignment', *Middle East Journal*, 45:1 (Winter 1991), pp. 51–70.

Baram, A., *Culture, History and Ideology in the Formation of Ba'athist Iraq 1968–1989* (New York: Palgrave Macmillan, 1991).

Baram, A., 'The Radical Shi'ite Opposition Movement in Iraq' in Sivan, Emmanuel and Friedman, Menachem (eds) *Religious Radicalism and Politics in the Middle East* (New York: SUNY University Press, 1990), Chapter IV.

Baram, A., *Syria* (unpublished, 1990).

Baram, A., 'The ruling political elite in Ba'thi Iraq 1968–1986: The changing features of a collective profile', *International Journal of Middle East Studies*, 21:4 (1989), pp. 447–93.

Baram, Amatzia, *National Integration and Exclusiveness in Political Thought and Practice in Iraq under the Ba'th, 1968–1982*, Ph.D dissertation, submitted to the Hebrew University, Jerusalem (Hebrew), 1986.

Baram, A., 'Qawmiyya and Wataniyya in Ba'athi Iraq: The Search for a New Balance', *Middle Eastern Studies*, 19:2 (April 1983), pp. 188–200.

Baram, A., 'Saddam Hussein: A Political Profile', *The Jerusalem Quarterly*, 17 (Fall 1980), pp. 115–44.

Bar-Joseph, Uri, *The Angel: Ashraf Marwan, the Mossad and the surprise of the Yom Kippur war* (Hebrew) (Or Yehuda: Kinneret Zmora-Bitan Publishers, 2011).

Bar-Joseph, Uri, 'Last chance to avoid war: Sadat's peace initiative of February 1973 and its failure', *Journal of Contemporary History*, 41(2006), pp. 545–56.

Bar Kokhva (Brill), Moshe, Maj. General, 'The armored corps campaign against the Iraqis in the Yom Kippur War' (Hebrew) Ma'arachot (IDF Bulletin), October–November 1977, pp. 2–6.

Bar Moshe Ishaq, *Al-Khuruj min al-'Iraq- Dhikrayat 1945–1950* (The exodus from Iraq-Memoirs 1945–1950) (Hebrew), edition published by The Sephardic Community Council, Jerusalem, 1975.

Al-Barrak, Fadil, *Al- Madaris al-Yahudiyya wal-Iraniyya* (The Jewish and Iranian Schools) (Baghdad, 1985).

Barzani, Massoud, *Al- Barzani wal-Haraka al-Tahririyya al-Kurdiyya* (Barzani and the Kurdish Liberation Movement) 2002, www. koord.com/webbook/aras/aras1/Book/sbarzani.

Basri, Carole, 'The Jews of Iraq: A Forgotten Case of Ethnic Cleansing', Policy Study No. 26, World Jewish Congress, 2003; Hebrew version: *Gesher*, 148:49 (2004), pp. 60–86.

Basri, Meir, *Rihlat al-Amer* (Memoires-Arabic) (Jerusalem, 1991).

Batatu, Hanna, 'Shi'i organizations in Iraq: Al-Da'wa al-Islamiyyah and al- Mujahidin', in Cole, Juan R.I. & Nikki R. Keddie (eds), *Shi'ism and Social Protest* (New Haven: Yale University Press, 1986), Chapter VII, pp.179–200.

Batatu, H., *The Old Social Classes and the Revolutionary Movements of Iraq* (Princeton: Princeton University Press, 1978).

Al-Bazzaz, Sa'd, *Harb Talid Ukhra – Al-Ta'rikh al-Sirri Liharb al-Khalij* (The war that brings another war – The secret history of the Gulf War) (Amman, Al-Ahliyya lil Nashr wa al-Tawzi', 1992).

Beeri, Eliezer, *The Officer Class in Politics and Society of the Arab East* (Hebrew) (Tel Aviv: Sifriyat Po'alim, 1966).

Bengio, O., 'Iraq Stepdaughter in the Gulf?' (Hebrew) in J. Kostiner (ed.), *Gulf States: Politics, Society, Economics* (Tel Aviv: Dayan Center, 2000), pp. 89–94.

Bengio, O., 'Crossing the Rubicon: Iraq and the Arab Israeli Peace Process', *Middle East Review of International Affairs*, 2(1) (March 1998), pp. 32–41.

Bengio, O., *The Kurdish Rebellion in Iraq* (Tel Aviv: Dayan Center, Tel Aviv University, 1989).

Bengio, O., 'Shi'is Politics in Ba'athi Iraq', *Middle Eastern Studies*, 21:1 (January 1985), pp. 1–14.

Bengio, O., 'The Kurds', in D. Dishon (ed.), *Middle East Record 1969–1970* (Jerusalem, 1977), pp. 730–40.

Bengio, O., 'Iraq', *Middle East Contemporary Survey*, 1(1976–7), pp. 403–16.

Bengio, Ofra and Uriel Dann, 'Iraq', *Middle East Contemporary Survey*, 3 (1978–9), pp. 513–35.

Ben-Zvi, A., *From Truman to Obama – The Rise and the Early Decline of American-Israeli Relations* (Hebrew) (Tel Aviv: Yedi'ot Ahronoth Publishers, 2011).

Ben-Zvi, Abraham, *The United States and Israel* (New York: Columbia University Press, 1993).

Bezalel, Yitzhak, *Alone in the Final Stronghold: The Disappearance of Iraqi Jewry* (Hebrew) (Tel Aviv: Maariv Publishers, 1976).

Bill, James A., *The Eagle and the Lion: The Tragedy of American-Iranian Relations* (New Haven: Yale University Press, 1989).

Binah, Shulamit, *The anti-Jewish Farhud in Baghdad, 1941–Jewish and Arab perspectives* (unpublished master's thesis, CUNY, New York, 1989).

Blight, James G. et al., *Becoming Enemies, U.S-Iran Relations and the Iran-Iraq War 1979–1988* (Plymouth, UK: *Rowman & Littlefield,* 2014).

Brown, Michael E., 'The nationalization of the IPC', *International Journal of Middle East Studies,* 10:1(1979), pp. 107–24.

Brzezinski, Zbigniew, *Power and Principle – Memoirs of the National Security Adviser 1977–1981* (New York: Farrar Straus & Giroux, 1983).

Buheiry, Marwan R., 'The Saunders Document', *Journal of Palestine Studies,* 8:1 (Autumn 1978), pp. 28–40.

CADRI (Committee against Repression and for Democratic Rights in Iraq), *Saddam's Iraq: Revolution or Reaction?* (London: Zed Books, 1986).

Campbell, John C., 'The Persian Gulf Region' in *Major U.S. Foreign and Defense Policy Issues,* CRS Compilation of papers prepared for the Commission on the Operation of the U.S. Senate, *GPO,* 1977.

Carter, Jimmy, *Keeping Faith – Memoirs of a President* (New York: Bantam Books, 1982).

Center for Strategic and International Studies, *The Gulf: Implications of British Withdrawal,* Special Report Series No. 8, Washington DC, February 1969.

Chaliand, Gerard, *The Kurdish Tragedy* (London: Zed Books, 1994).

Cobban, Helena, *The Palestinian Liberation Organization – People, Power and Politics* (New York: Cambridge University Press, 1984).

Cockburn, Andrew and Cockburn Patrick, *Out of the Ashes – The Resurrection of Saddam Hussein* (New York: Harper Collins, 1999).

Copland, Miles, *The Game of Nations – The Amorality of Power Politics* (New York: Simon and Schuster, 1970).

Coughlin, Con, *Saddam: King of Terror* (New York: Harper Collins, 2002).

Crist, David, *The Twilight War – The Secret History of America's Thirty-Year Conflict with Iran* (New York: Penguin Press, 2011).

Cronin, Richard P. et al., 'The Indian Ocean, Arabian Peninsula and the Persian Gulf', *CRS Report* submitted to the Senate Committee on Foreign Relations, April 1979.

Dallek, Robert, *Nixon and Kissinger – Partners in Power* (New York: Harper Collins, 2007).

Daoudi M.S. & Dajani, M.S., *Economic Diplomacy – Embargo Leverage and World Politics,* Westview Special Studies in International Relations (Boulder CO: Westview, 1985).

Davis, Eric, *Memories of State: Politics, History, and Collective Identity in Modern Iraq* (Berkley: University of California Press, 2005).

Dawisha, Adeed, *Iraq – A Political History* (Princeton: Princeton University Press, 2006).

Dawr Al-Jaysh Al-Iraqi fi Harb Tishreen 1973 (The role of the Iraqi army in the 1973 October war) (Beirut, 1975, unknown writer).

Department of State, The Office of the Special Assistant of the Secretary for the Coordination of International Educational and Cultural relations, *International, Cultural and related activities for Iraq* (Washington DC, January 1961).

Dowty, Alan, *Middle East Crisis: U.S. Decision-Making in 1958, 1970, 1973* (Berkley: University of California Press, 1984).

Duelfer, Charles A., *Comprehensive Report of the Special Advisor to the DCI on Iraq*, WMD, 30 September 2004, http://www.cia.gov/cia/reports/iraq_wmd_2004.

Eagleton, William L., 'Evaluation of the U.S. interest sections in Algiers and Baghdad', in David D. Newsom (ed.) *Diplomacy under Foreign Flag:* When Nations Break Relations (Washington DC: Georgetown University Press, 1990), pp. 90–8.

Embassy of the Republic of Iraq, Office of the Press Attaché London, *Iraq: Official Statements of Policy on Internal, Arab, and Foreign Affairs*, Bulletin of the Republic of Iraq for the months November–December 1965.

Entessar, Nader, *Kurdish Ethnonationalism* (Boulder CO: Lynne Rienner, 1992).

Eppel, Michael, 'The Elite, the Effendiyya, and the Growth of Nationalism and Pan-Arabism in Hashemite Iraq, 1921–1958', *International Journal of Middle East Studies*, 30:2 (1998), pp. 227–50.

Fukuyama, Francis, *The Soviet Union and Iraq since 1968* (Santa Monica: The Rand Corporation, 1980), http://www.rand.org/pubs/notes/N1524.html.

Gantner, Serge, 'Le Mouvement National Kurde: Ses Origines son Développement Historique et ses Perspectives', *Orient*, (Paris) 9:32–3 (1964–1965), pp. 28–120 (Hebrew edition: Tel Aviv: 'Am Hassefer Publishers, 1968).

Ghali, Boutrus Boutrus, *Egypt's Road to Jerusalem: A diplomat's story of the struggle for Peace in the Middle East* (New York: Random House, 1997) (Hebrew edition: Tel Aviv: Yedioth Ahronoth, 1998).

Ghareeb, Edmund, *The Kurdish Question in Iraq* (Syracuse NY: Syracuse University Press, 1981).

Gilboa, Eitan, *American Public Opinion toward Israel and the Arab-Israeli Conflict* (Tel Aviv: MOD Publishers, 1993).

Goldstein, Eric, 'Profile of Dr. Hussein Shahristani', Huqoqalinasan.org., www.mafqud.org/en/partners/hio/goldstein.htm.

Goldstein, Lyle J. and Zhukov, Yuri M., 'Tales of Two Fleets, A Russian Perception on the U.S. Naval Standoff in the Mediterranean', *U.S. Naval War College Review*, 7:2 (Spring 2004), pp. 27–63.

Gunter, Michael, *The Kurds of Iraq: Tragedy and Hope* (New York: Palgrave Macmillan, 1992).

Hamza, Khidhir, *Saddam's Bombmaker* (New York: Scribner, 2000).

Hamza, Khidhir, 'Inside Saddam's secret nuclear program', *Bulletin of the Atomic Scientist*, 54:5(September/October 1998), pp.26–33.

Harakabi, Y., 'La'antishemiyut ha'arvit Mehadash' (The renewed Antisemitism) in *Anti-Semitism Through the Ages*, S. Almog (ed.) (Jerusalem: The Shazar Center, 1980), pp. 247–59.

Heikal, Mohamed, *Illusions of Triumph – An Arab View of the Gulf War* (London: Harper Collins Publishers, 1992).

Heikal, M., *Iran: The Untold Story* (New York: Pantheon Books, 1982).

Helms, Richard with William Hood, *A Look over My Shoulder – A Life in the CIA* (New York: Random House, 2003).

Hersh, Seymour M., *The Price of Power –Kissinger in the Nixon White House* (New York: Summit Books, 1983).

Hightower, Jane M., MD, *Diagnosis: Money, Politics and Poison* (Washington DC: Island Press, 2009).

Hurwitz, J.C., *The Persian Gulf* after Iran's Revolution, Headline Series 244 (New York: Foreign Policy Association, 1979).

Hussein, S., *Iraqi Policies in Perspective*, Press Conference, 20 July 1980 (Baghdad, 1981).

Hussein, S., *On Zionist Aggression against Iraqi Nuclear Installations* (Baghdad, 1981).

Hussein, S., Interview with the Egyptian Journalist Sakina al-Sadat, 19 January 1977, in S. Hussein, *Social and Foreign Affairs in Iraq* (London: Croom and Helm, 1979), pp. 85– 110.

Hussein, S., *Harakat 'Adam al-Inkhiyaz, Hakatha Nafhamuha* (The Non-Alignment Movement – In our View) (Baghdad, 1979).

Hussein, S., 'Ma'rakat al-Istiqlaliyya wal-Siyyasa al-Dawliyya', (Our struggle for independence and foreign policy, Press Conference ,18 July 1978), *Al-Mukhtarat*, Vol. 5, pp. 153–248.

Hussein, Saddam, *Al-Tahaddi al-Imberyali wa Dawr al-Jabha al Wataniyya* (The Imperialistic Challenge and the Role of the National Front) (Beirut, 1975).

Hussein, S., 'Nidaluna wal-Siyyasa al-Dawliyya' (Our struggle and foreign policy), 12 June 1975. Saddam Hussein, *Al-Mukhtarat*, Vol 5:1, pp. 9–22.

Hussein S., 'The National and International Politics', Statement to the Iraqi ambassadors in Western Europe and Japan, 12 June 1975 (English version by Khalid Kishtainy) in S. Hussein, *Social and Foreign Affairs in Iraq* (London: Croom Helm Ltd., 1977), pp. 63–84.

Hussein, S., *On Current Events in Iraq: Q & A session with journalists*, 8 April 1974, Baghdad.

Iskandar, Amir, *Saddam Hussein the Fighter, the Thinker and the Man*, translated by Hasan Salim (Paris: Hachette Book Group, 1980).

Ismael, Tareq Y., *The Rise and Fall of the Communist Party of Iraq* (New York: Cambridge University Press, 2008).

Isaacson, Walter, *Kissinger –A Biography* (New York: Simon and Schuster, 2005).

Jaber, Fuad, 'The Arab Regimes and the Palestinian Revolution 1967–1971', *Journal of Palestine Studies*, 2:2 (Winter 1973), pp. 79–101.

Jawad, Sa'ad, 'Recent Developments in the Kurdish issue' in Tim Niblock (ed.) *Iraq: The Contemporary State* (London: Croom Helm, 1982), pp. 50–1.

Jawad, S., *Iraq and the Kurdish Question 1958–1970* (London: Ithaca Press, 1981).

Jervis, R., 'The Compulsive Empire', *Foreign Policy*, 127 (July–August 2003), pp.82–7.

Jervis, R., 'War and Misperception', *Journal of Interdisciplinary History*, 18:4 (1988), pp. 675–700.

Jervis, Robert, *Perception and Misperception in International Politics* (Princeton NJ: Princeton University Press, 1976).

Johnson, Lock K., 'Covert Action and Accountability: Decision Making for America's Secret Foreign Policy', *International Studies Quarterly*, 33:1(March 1989), pp. 81–109.

Joyce, Miriam, *Kuwait 1945–1996: An Anglo-American Perspective* (London: Frank Cass, 1998).

Kaplan, Robert D., *The Arabists – The Romance of an American Elite* (New York: Free Press, 1993).

Karsh, Efraim and Rautsi, Inari, *Saddam Hussein – A Political Biography* (Tel Aviv: Maarachot, 1991).

Kennedy, Edward M., 'The Persian Gulf: Arms Race of Arms Control?' *Foreign Affairs*, 54:1 (1975), pp. 14–35.

Khadduri, Imad, *Iraq's Nuclear Mirage, Memoirs and Delusions* (Richmond Hill Ontario: Springhead Publishers, 2003).

Khadduri, Majid, *Socialist Iraq – A Study in Iraqi Politics since 1969* (Washington DC: Middle East Institute, 1978).

Khadduri, Sassoun Shaul, *Ra'i wa Ri'aya – Sirat Khayat al-Hakham Sassoun Khadduri* (The Biography of the Rabbi Sassoun Khadduri) (Jerusalem, 1999).

Al-Khalil, Samir (Kanan Makiya), *Republic of Fear – The Politics of Modern Iraq* (Berkeley and London: University of California Press, 1989).

Al-Khorsan, Sallah, Al-Tayyarat al-Siyyasiya fi Kurdistan al-Iraq: Qira'a fi Mulaffat al-Harakat wal Ahzab al-Kurdiyya fil 'Iraq 1946–2001 (The Political Movements in Iraqi Kurdistan) (Beirut: Mu'asasat al-Ballagh, 2001).

Khoury Rizk, Dina, *Iraq in Wartime: Soldiering, Martyrdom, and Remembrance* (Cambridge and New York: Cambridge University Press, 2013).

Kiely, Patrick, 'Through distorted lenses – Iraq and balance of power politics 1969–1979', in Ryan, David and Kiely, Patrick (eds) *America and Iraq: Policy-Making Intervention and Regional Politics since 1958* (New York: Routledge, 2008), pp.44–5.

Kienle, Eberhard, *Ba'ath v. Ba'ath – The Conflict between Syria and Iraq 1968–1989* (London: I.B. Tauris, 1991).

Kimche, David, *The Last Option – After Nasser, Arafat, and Saddam Hussein – The Quest for Peace in the Middle East* (New York: Scribner, 1991).

Kipnis, Yigal, *1973, The Way to War* (Hebrew, Tel Aviv: Kinneret, Zmora-Bitan- Dvir, 2012).

Kissinger, H., *Crisis – The Anatomy of Two Major Foreign Policy Crises* (New York: Simon and Schuster, 2003) (Hebrew edition: Jerusalem, Shalem Center, 2004).

Kissinger, H., *Years of Renewal* (New York: Simon and Schuster, 2000).

Kissinger, H., *Years of Upheaval* (Boston: Little Brown & Company, 1982).

Kissinger, Henry A., *White House Years* (Boston: Little Brown & Co., 1979).

Korn, David A., 'The last years of Mustafa Barzani', *The Middle East Quarterly*, 1:2 (June 1994), http://www.meforum.org/220/the-last-years-of-mustafa-barzani.

Latham, Aaron, 'What Kissinger was afraid of in the Pike Report', *New York Magazine* (4 October 1976), pp. 50–68.

Latham, A., 'The CIA Report the President doesn't want you to read – The Pike Papers: An introduction', *The Village Voice* (16 February 1976), pp. 72–85.

Levey, Zach, 'Anatomy of an airlift: United States military assistance to Israel during the 1973 war', *Cold War History*, 8:4 (April 2008), pp. 481–501.

Levin, Itamar, *Locked Doors – The Seizures of Jewish Property in Arab Countries* (Hebrew, Tel Aviv: Maarachot, 2001).

Little, Douglas, 'The United States and the Kurds, A Cold War Story', *Journal of the Cold War Studies*, 12:4(Fall 2010), pp. 63–97.

Longrigg, Stephen H., *Iraq, 1900 to 1950 – A political, social and economic history* (London: Oxford University Press, 1953).

Macris, Jeffrey R., *The Politics and Security of the Gulf: Anglo-American hegemony and the shaping of a region* (London: Routledge, 2010).

Mallat, C., 'Shiism and Sunnism in Iraq: Revising the Codes', *Arab Law Quarterly*, 8:2(1993), pp. 141–59.

Mallat, Chibli, 'Religious militancy in contemporary Iraq: Muhammad Baqer as-Sadr and the Sunni-Shia paradigm', *Third World Quarterly*, 1:2 (1988), pp. 699–729.

Malovany, Pessach, *The Wars of Modern Babylon* (Hebrew) (Tel Aviv: Maarachot, 2009).

Mansfield, Peter, 'Saddam Husain's Political Thinking: The Comparison with Nasser' in Tim Niblock (ed.), *Iraq: The Contemporary State* (London: Croom Helm, 1982), pp. 62–73.

Marr, Phebe, *The Modern History of Iraq* (Boulder CO: Westview Press, 1985).

Matar, Fuad, *Saddam Hussein – The Man, the Cause and the Future* (London: Third World Center, 1981).

McDowall, David, *A Modern History of the Kurds* (London: I.B. Tauris, 2004).

Melman, Yossi, *The Master Terrorist: The true story of Abu-Nidal* (New York: Adama Books, 1986).

Melman Y.and Raviv, Dan, *Friends In Deed: Inside the U.S.-Israel Alliance* (Hebrew) (Tel Aviv: Sifriyat Maariv, 1994).

Melman Y. and Raviv, Dan, *Imperfect Spies* (Hebrew) (Tel Aviv: Sifriyat Maariv, 1990).

Merari, Ariel and Elad, Shlomi, *The Interational Dimension of Palestinian Terrorism* (Hebrew) (Hakibbutz Hameuchad, 1986) (English edition: Boulder: Westview Press, 1987).

Milbank, David L., 'International and Transnational Terrorism: Diagnosis and Prognosis', *Research Study prepared for the CIA*, PR 76 10030, April 1976, http://www.higginsctc.org/patternsofglobalterrorism/1976PoGT-Research-Study.pdf.

Mobley, Richard, 'U.S. Joint Military Contribution to Countering Syria's Invasion of Jordan', *Joint Force Quarterly*, 55:4(2009), pp.160–7.

Moss-Helms, Christine, *Iraq: The Eastern Flank of the Arab World* (Washington: Brookings Institution Press, 1984).

Mufti, Malik, *Sovereign Creations: Pan-Arabism and Political Order in Syria and Iraq* (Ithaca NY: Cornell University Press, 1996).

Murphy, John F. and Downey, Arthur T., 'National Security, Foreign Policy and Individual Rights: The Quandary of U.S. Export Controls', *The International and Comparative Law quarterly*, 30:4(October 1981), pp. 779– 834.

Nakash, Yitzhak, *The Shi'is of Iraq* (Princeton NJ: Princeton University Press, 1994).

Nakdimon, S., A Hopeless Hope: The Rise and fall of the Israeli-Kurdish Alliance 1963–1975 (Hebrew, Tel Aviv: Yedioth Ahronoth-Chemed, 1996).

Nasr Kameel, B., *Arab and Israeli Terrorism: The causes and effects of political violence 1936–1993* (Jefferson NC: McFarland, 2007).

Neff, Donald, 'The U.S., Iraq, Israel and Iran: Backdrop to War', *Journal of Palestinian Studies*, 20:4(Summer 1991), pp. 23–41.

Newsom David D., *The Diplomacy of Human Rights* (Lanham MD: Rowman & Littlefield, 1986).

Niblock, Tim, 'Iraqi policies towards the Arab states in the Gulf, 1958–1981', in Niblock T. (ed.), *Iraq: The Contemporary State* (London: Croom Helm, 1982).

Nuri, Jammal al-Din, *Mudhakirat Baha'al-Din Nuri* (Memoires of Baha' A-Din Nuri) (London: Dar al-Hikma, 2001).

NUREC 0980, Vol. 3:9 (January 2011), U.S. Nuclear Regulatory Commission, Washington DC, pp. 1029–61.

Nye, Joseph S., 'Nonproliferation: A Long-Term Strategy', *Foreign Affairs*, 56:3(April 1978), pp. 601–23.

Nyrop, Richard F., *Area Handbook for the Persian Gulf States* (Washington DC: GPO, 1977).

O'Ballance, Edgar, *The Kurdish Struggle 1920–1994* (New York: Palgrave-Macmillan, 1996).

Oren, Elchanan, 'IDF confrontation with the Iraqi Expedition Force in the Syrian Front at the Yom Kippur War', in S. Shay (ed.), *The Iraqi-Israeli Conflict –1948–2000* (Hebrew) (Tel Aviv: Maarachot, 2002), pp. 74–87.

Penrose, Edith and Penrose, E. F., *Iraq: International Relations and National Development* (Boulder CO: Westview Press, 1978).

Phillips, Charlotte A., 'The Arab Boycott of Israel – Possibilities for European Cooperation with U.S. Anti-Boycott Legislation', *CRS* 215F, May 1979.

Post, J., *Leaders and Their Followers in a Dangerous World* (Ithaca NY: Cornell University Press, 2004).

Post, J., 'Explaining Saddam Hussein: A psychological Profile', Testimony presented to the House Armed Services Committee, December 1990, http://www.au.af.mil/au/awc/awcgate/iraq/saddam_post.htm.

Post, Jerrold and Baram, A., Saddam is Iraq: Iraq is Saddam, USAF Counter-proliferation Papers, Future Warfare Series, No. 17, January 2002 (Maxwell Air Force Base, Alabama: Air University, 2002).

Powers, Thomas, *The Man Who Kept Secrets, Richard Helms and the CIA* (New York: Knopf Book Club Edition, 1979).

Powers, T., Interview: 'In Memoriam Richard Helms', *PBS News Hour*, 23 October 2002.

Prados, John, *Safe for Democracy: The Secret War of the CIA* (Chicago: Ivan R. Dee, 2006).

Qazzaz, Nissim, *Sofa Shel Gola, Hayehudim be – Iraq 1951–2000* (The End of the Iraqi Jewish Diaspora 1951–2000) (Or Yehuda: Babylonian Jewish Heritage Center, 2011).

Quandt, William B. (ed.), *The Middle East: Ten Years after Camp David* (Washington DC: The Brookings Institution, 1988).

Quandt, William B., 'The Middle East conflict in U.S. strategy 1970–1971', *Journal of Palestine Studies*, 1:1(1971), pp. 39–52.

Rabin, Yitshak & Shlomo Goldstein, *Pinkas Sherut* (Hebrew) (Tel Aviv: Sifriyyat Maariv, 1997).

Ramazani, Rouhollah K., 'The Persian Gulf and the Straits of Hormuz', in *International Straits of the World*, vol. III (Alphen on the Rhine, Netherland: Sijthoff & Noordhoff, 1979).

Randal, Jonathan C., *After Such Knowledge What Forgiveness?* (Boulder CO: Westview Press, 1998).

Reich, Bernard, *Quest for Peace – United States-Israel Relations and the Arab-Israeli Conflict* (Piscataway NJ: Transaction Books, 1977).

Rohde, Achim, *State-Society Relations in Ba'athist Iraq* (London and New York: Routledge, 2010).

Rubin, Avshalom, H., 'Abd al-Karim Qasim and the Kurds of Iraq: Centralization, Resistance and Revolt 1958–1963', *Middle Eastern Studies*, 43:3(2007), pp. 353–82.

Rustum H. and Hamdi, T., 'Methyl Mercury Poisoning in Iraq: a Neurological Study', *Brain*, 97 (1974), pp. 499–510.

Ryan, David and Kiely, Patrick, *America and Iraq: Policy-Making, Intervention and Regional Politics since 1958* (London and New York: Routledge, 2008).

Safi Naz Kazem, *Yawmiyyat: Baghdad 1975–1980* (The Baghdad Diary 1975–1980) (London: Open Press, 1984).

Al-Sadat, Sakina, 'Détente and the Arab-Zionist conflict', 19 January 1977 in Saddam Hussein, *Social and Foreign Affairs in Iraq* (London, 1979).

Safran, Nadav, *Israel the Embattled Ally* (Cambridge MA: Harvard University Press, 1981).

Sakr, Naomi, 'Economic relations between Iraq and other Arab Gulf States', in Niblock T. (ed.), *Iraq: The Contemporary State* (London: Croom Helm, 1982), pp. 150–67.

Salama, Sammy and Hunter, Cameron, 'Leading Iraqi Nuclear Scientist, Once Imprisoned, Elected to Prominent Post', *Center for Nonproliferation Studies*, 7 June 2005.

Sale, Richard, 'Saddam Key in Early CIA Plot', *UPI* International Desk, 10 April 2003.

Al-Samra'i, Mahmud Salim, *Istiqlaliyyat al-Siyyasa al-Kharijiyya al-Iraqiyya* (Iraqi Independent Foreign Policy, Baghdad, 1985).

Sassoon, Joseph, *Saddam Hussein's Ba'ath Party: Inside an Authoritarian Regime* (Cambridge and New York: Cambridge University Press, 2012).

Sawadayee, Max, *All Waiting to be Hanged: Iraq Post-Six-day War Diary* (Hebrew) (Tel Aviv: Naharayim, 1994).

Schiff, Zeev and Yaari, Ehud, *War of Deception* (Hebrew) (Tel Aviv: Shocken Books, 1984).

Seale, Patrick, *Abu Nidal: A Gun for Hire* (New York: Random House, 1992).

Seale, P., *Asad of Syria, The Struggle for the Middle East* (Berkley: University of California Press, 1990).

Shay, Shaul (ed.), *The Iraqi-Israeli Conflict – 1948–2000* (Hebrew) (Tel Aviv: Maarachot, 2002).

Shemesh, Haim, *Soviet Iraqi Relations 1968–1988: In the Shadow of Iraq-Iran Conflict* (Boulder CO: Lynne Rienner, 1992).

Sluglett Farouk, Marion and Sluglett Peter, *Iraq since 1958: From Revolution to Dictatorship* (New York: Palgrave Macmillan, 1987).

Smolansky, Oles M. and Smolansky Bettie, *The USSR and Iraq – The Soviet Quest for Influence* (Durham NC: Duke University Press, 1991).

Sousa, Aliya, 'The Eradication of Illiteracy in Iraq', in Niblock Tim (ed.), *Iraq: The Contemporary State* (London: Croom Helm, 1982), pp. 100–8.

Spector Simon, Reeva, *Iraq between the Two World Wars – The Militarist Origin of Tyranny* (New York: Columbia University Press, 2003).

Stein, Kenneth W., 'Henry Kissinger to Iraq in 1975: "We can reduce Israel's size"', *Middle East Quarterly* (Fall 2006), pp. 71–8.

Stein, K., *Heroic Diplomacy: Sadat, Kissinger, Carter, Begin and the quest for Arab-Israeli peace* (New York, 1999) (Tel Aviv: Maarachot, 2003).

Stevens, Paul, 'Iraqi Oil Policy: 1961–1976', in Niblock Tim (ed.), *Iraq: The Contemporary State* (London: Croom Helm, 1982).

Al-Takriti K. & Al-Mufti A., 'An Outbreak of Organomercury Poisoning among Iraqi Farmers', *WHO Bulletin*, 53(1976), suppl., pp.15–21.

Tawelba, Hassan, *The Ba'ath and Palestine* (Baghdad, 1982).

Tejirian, Eleanor H. & Spector Simon, Reeva, *Conflict, Conquest and Conversion* (New York: Columbia University Press, 2012).

Al-Tikrītī, Ḥardān Abd al-Ghafar, *Kunna ʻiṣabah min al-luṣūṣ wa-al-qatalah khalfa milīshiyat Ṣaddām lil-iʻdām! : mudhakkirat siyāsī ʻIrāqī* / bi-qalam; dirāsat Aḥmad Raʼif (We were a gang of thieves and murderers behind Saddam's militia of executioners – Memoirs of an Iraqi politician – Ahmad Raif Study) (Cairo: Al-Zahra, 1990).

Timmerman, Kenneth R., *The Death Lobby – How the West armed Iraq* (New York: Bantam Books, 1991).

Tripp, Charles, *A History of Iraq* (Cambridge UK: Cambridge University Press, 2001).

Tsafrir, Eliezer (Geizi), *Ana Kurdi* (Hebrew) (Or-Yehuda: Hed Artzi, 1999).

Tucker, David, *Skirmishes at the Edge of Empire* (Westport CT: Praeger, 1977).

Turner, Louis, 'The Politics of Energy Crisis', *Royal Institute of International Affairs*, 50:3 (July 1974), pp. 404–15.

United States Army, *Instructions for American Servicemen in Iraq during World War II*: 'pocket guide' prepared by the Special Service Division of the Army Service Forces, 1943 (reprinted Chicago IL: University of Chicago Press, 2007).

Vance, Cyrus Roberts., *Hard Choices: Four Critical Years in Managing America's Foreign Policy* (New York: Simon and Schuster, 1983).

Vanly, Ismet Sheriff, 'Kurdistan in Iraq', in Chaliand, Gerard (ed.), *People Without A Country* (London, Zed Books, 1993), pp. 153–204.

Warwick, Donald P. et al., *A theory of Public Bureaucracy: Politics, Personality and Organization in the State Department* (Cambridge MA: Harvard University Press, 1975).

Weiss, Martin A., 'Arab League Boycott of Israel', *CRS Report to Congress*, updated 27 August 2008.

Weissman Steve & Herbert Krosney, *The Islamic Bomb* (New York Times Books, 1981).

Williams, Julie L., 'U.S. Regulation of Arab Boycott practices', *Law and Policy in International Business* (1978), pp. 815–26.

Winkler, David F., *Amirs, Admirals and Desert Sailors: Bahrain, the United States Navy and the Arabian Gulf* (Annapolis MD: Naval Institute Press, 2007).

Woods, Kevin M., *The Mother of All Battles: Saddam Hussein's Strategic Plan for the First Gulf War* (Annapolis MD: Naval Institute Press, 2008).

Woods, K.M., Palkki David D. and Stout, Mark E. (eds), *The Saddam Tapes: The Inner Workings of a Tyrant's Regime* (Cambridge and New York: Cambridge University Press, 2011).

Woods, K.M. and Stout, Mark E., 'Saddam's Perceptions and Misperceptions: The Case of "Desert Storm"', *Journal of Strategic Studies*, 33:1(2010), pp. 5–41.

Yaniv, Avner, 'Israel faces Iraq: The politics of confrontation', in A. Baram and Rubin B. (eds), *Iraq's Road to War* (London: Macmillan, 1994), pp. 234–51.

Zaher, U., 'The Opposition', in *Saddam's Iraq: Revolution or Reaction?* CADRI (Committee Against Repression and For Democratic Rights In Iraq) (London, 1989).

Zaki, Laman Amin et al., 'Methyl Mercury Poisoning in Iraqi Children: Clinical Observation over Two Years', *British Medical Journal*, 1(1978), 613–16

Internet Sites

American Jewish Committee, 'The Impact of Arab-Boycott Laws on U.S. Mideast Trade', May 1979, http://www.ajcarchives.org/AJC_DATA/Files/778.PDF.

Anti-Hijacking Act of 1974, 'Implementing the Convention for the Suppression of Unlawful Seizure of Aircraft', The Hague 1970, https://www.ncjrs.gov/App/publications/Abstract.aspx?id=77549.

CIA National Foreign Assessment Center, www.foia.cia.gov.

Corrosion Doctors, http://corrosion-doctors.org/Elements-Toxic/Mercury-Iraq-1.htm.

Farah, Joseph, 'Is U.S. hiding Arafat murders?' 17 January 2001; 'Ex-NSA op asks Congress to probe Arafat murders', 17 April 2001, *WND*, http://www.wnd.com/news/article.asp?ARTICLE_ID=21365.

Iran Chamber Society, http://www.iranchamber.com/history/rkhomeini/ayatollah_khomeini.php.

NARA AAD, http://aad.archives.gov/aad.

PBS, http://www.pbs.org.

President Ford Remarks on the Assassination of US Officials in Lebanon, 16 June 1976, www.arlingtoncemetery.net/rowaring.htm.

Project Syndicate, www.project-syndicate.org/commentary/jernelov3/English.

Sardar Aziz official blog, http://namoy.blogspot.com.

Saunders, Harold H., Statement before the House Foreign Affairs Subcommittee on the Middle East, 12 November 1975, http://www.mideastweb.org/saunders.htm.

The American Presidency Project, http://www.presidency.ucsb.edu.

The Center for Public Integrity, http://projects.publicintegrity.org/wow/bio.aspx?act=pro&ddlC=6.

Terrorism Analysis in the CIA: The Gradual Awakening 1972–1980, n.d. (partially sanitised), Studies in Intelligence, National Security Archive Electronic Briefing Book No. 431, 4 June 2013, www.gwu.edu/~nsarchiv/NSABB/NSAEBB431.

US Trade, http://www.ustr.gov.

http://www.bis.doc.gov/complianceandenforcement/antiboycottcompliance. htm.

Additional Sources:

International Trade by Commodities Statistics (ITCS), SITC/CTCI Rev. 22, 1961–1990,

Historical, University of Chicago; Organization for Economic Cooperation and Development (OECD), Paris 1997, CD Rom.

Israel MFA Foreign Relations III (1974–7).

Joint Intelligence Committee (JIC), *Iraq's Weapons of Mass Destruction, The Assessmentof the British Government*, 24 September 2002, www.archive2.officiqal-documents.co.uk/document/reps/iraqdossier.pdf.

Middle East Contemporary Survey, Shiloah Center, Tel Aviv.

Middle East Economic Digest (MEED), London, UK.

Middle East Economic Survey (MEES), Nicosia, Cyprus.

Nuclear Regulatory Legislation, NUREC 0980 Vol. 3, No. 9 January 2011, U.S. Nuclear Regulatory Commission, Washington DC, 1029–1061, http://www.nrc.gov/reading-rm/doc-collections/nuregs/staff/sr0980/v3/ sr0980v3.pdf.

Quarterly Economic Review of Iraq, The Economist Intelligence Unit, London, Annual Supplement, 1975, 1978, 1980, 1981.

UN disarmament treaty, http://disarmament.un.org/treatystatus.nsf/ e03053a22d4bf8478525688f00693182/519faffde27b04828525688f006d2 662?OpenDocument .

'U.S. Trade with the Middle East', *Middle East Economic Digest* (MEED), 20(37), 10 September 1976.

Interviews

Eliezer (Geizi) Tsafrir, Liaison Officer to the Kurds, Ramat Hasharon, November 2010.

Sir Harold B. Walker KCMG, British Ambassador to Baghdad 1990–1, 26 February 2008, London.

Leslie H. Gelb, Assistant Secretary of State, Bureau for Political Military Affairs 1977–81, New York, 17 July 2013.

Maurice Shohet, Jewish-Iraqi activists, left Iraq in 1970, June–July 2013, Washington DC.

Ralph Goldman, Joint Distribution Committee veteran leader, 28 August 2008, JDC, Jerusalem.

Stuart E. Eizenstat, Domestic Policy Adviser, and Executive Director of the
    White House Domestic Policy Staff, 1977–81, 21 July 2013, Chevy Chase,
    MD.
Yosef Ben Ahron, Political Counsellor in the embassy of Israel, Washington,
    24 August 2011, Jerusalem.

Index